Natural and Cosmic Theodicy

Natural and Cosmic Theodicy

A Trinitarian Panentheistic Vision

Jongseock James Shin

Foreword by Veli-Matti Kärkkäinen

☙PICKWICK *Publications* · Eugene, Oregon

NATURAL AND COSMIC THEODICY
A Trinitarian Panentheistic Vision

Copyright © 2022 Jongseock James Shin. All rights reserved. Except for brief quotations in critical publications or reviews, no part of this book may be reproduced in any manner without prior written permission from the publisher. Write: Permissions, Wipf and Stock Publishers, 199 W. 8th Ave., Suite 3, Eugene, OR 97401.

Pickwick Publications
An Imprint of Wipf and Stock Publishers
199 W. 8th Ave., Suite 3
Eugene, OR 97401

www.wipfandstock.com

PAPERBACK ISBN: 978-1-6667-3492-8
HARDCOVER ISBN: 978-1-6667-9144-0
EBOOK ISBN: 978-1-6667-9145-7

Cataloging-in-Publication data:

Names: Shin, Jongseock James, author.

Title: Natural and cosmic theodicy : a trinitarian panentheistic vision / by Jongseock James Shin.

Description: Eugene, OR : Pickwick Publications, 2022 | Includes bibliographical references and indexes.

Identifiers: ISBN 978-1-6667-3492-8 (paperback) | ISBN 978-1-6667-9144-0 (hardcover) | ISBN 978-1-6667-9145-7 (ebook)

Subjects: LCSH: Theodicy. | Trinity—History of doctrines. | Panentheism—History of doctrines. | Creation. | Religion and science.

Classification: LCC BT160 S556 2022 (print) | LCC BT160 (ebook)

10/18/22

Scripture quotations marked (NIV) are taken from the Holy Bible, New International Version®, NIV®. Copyright © 1973, 1978, 1984, 2011 by Biblica, Inc.™ Used by permission of Zondervan. All rights reserved worldwide. www.zondervan.comThe "NIV" and "New International Version" are trademarks registered in the United States Patent and Trademark Office by Biblica, Inc.™

Contents

Foreword by Veli-Matti Kärkkäinen | vii

1 Introduction | 1
2 The Significance of Natural and Cosmic Theodicy in a Robust Trinitarian Panentheistic Vision of Creation | 29
3 Natural and Cosmic Theodicy of Peackocke and Keller | 74
4 Natural and Cosmic Theodicy of Pannenberg and Russell | 135
5 Envisioning a Kenotic-Eschatological Panentheistic Framework of the Trinitarian Creation | 222
6 Conclusion | 256

Bibliography | 263
Index | 279

Foreword

AMONG A NUMBER OF fast developing fields of inquiry in contemporary international theological scholarship, only a few are more exciting and revolutionary than science-religion/theology engagement—what the late Cambridge physicist-priest John Polkinghorne aptly named a new form of "contextual theology." In light of the vast influence of natural sciences on culture, religion, and civil life of the contemporary global world, it is only fitting that those interested in what God is doing in the world, seek to penetrate deeply into the implications of science to faith.

Dr. Jongseock (James) Shin's innovative and constructive study taps into the stream of publications in this genre, in its attempt to investigate the problem of natural and cosmic theodicy through a careful comparative engagement of four leading theology-science-experts, namely Catherine Keller, Arthur Peacocke, Wolfhart Pannenberg, and Robert Russell. This book puts these four theologians' proposals concerning the evil and its overcoming in the context of their engagement with modern physics, cosmology, and evolutionary biology. Throughout the book, a trinitarian pneumatological framework serves as framework to the conversation. While dialoguing with his interlocutors, the author also develops his own constructive proposal.

Placing the philosophical, cultural, and religious problem of natural theodicy—God's capacity to maintain divine "innocence" and love against the rampant existence of evil and suffering not only in human life but also in the life of cosmos created by the same allegedely good

God—in the context of trinitarian and pneumatological theology is a major contribution of this study. Not only that but the fact that Dr. Shin approaches this ancient dilemma from the perspective of the "end" of the world, i.e., eschatology, distinguishes this inquiry. As is well known, the question of the "origins" have stood at the center of theology-science engagement at large and theodicy studies in particular; hence, to study the suffering of nature in light of the promised consummation in the coming of God's kingdom breaks new grounds.

Throughout the study there is the healthy and dynamic combination between the "controls" and guidance of (classical) trinitarian theology, on the one hand, and the emphasis on the openness of God's creative and loving work in God's creation. One could easily err on either side but this study does not.

While, of course, the problem of evil and suffering cannot be "resolved," it makes a difference to faith and theology to provide thoughtful and reasonable insights and reflections on the topic that has always haunted particularly the representatives of Abrahamic faiths. The wide and deep engagement of current literature alone—both theological and that related to various scientific disciplines—makes this study a rich reservoir of insights. And the fact that the author is able to navigate the development of the argument seamlessly between various kinds of materials, is in itself a remarkable achievement.

This book belongs to the growing list of "must" readings for all scholars, instructors, and students interested in the question of how to to even begin to understand the meaning and overcoming of evil and suffering in God's good creation—in anticipation of the bringing about the new heavens and new earth by the same loving and powerful God.

Veli-Matti Kärkkäinen
Professor of Systematic Theology at Fuller Theological Seminary

---

1

Introduction

IN THIS BOOK, I engage with the problem of natural and cosmic theodicy through a careful comparative evaluation of the theodical arguments advanced by Catherine Keller, Arthur Peacocke, Wolfhart Pannenberg, and Robert Russell in the context of their dialogue with modern physics, cosmology, and evolutionary biology. I critically investigate how to understand the problems of natural and cosmic evil by engaging with the main interlocutors' understandings of these problems in God's good creation. In so doing, I propose that *creatio ex nihilo* is a trinitarian panentheistic project that is both kenotic and eschatological. This book further develops my PhD dissertation (Fuller Theological Seminary, Passed with Distinction, 2020) by adding more clarity to my arguments and providing more supporting resources.

Creatio ex nihilo means that "God, in creating the universe, was not constrained by the limitations of the already existing stuff from which the universe was to be fashioned, but was free to bring into existence a universe in which the divine will was recognizably embodied and enacted."[1] First, scientific cosmology keeps changing as has already happened with the introduction of quantum cosmologies; thus, it is impossible to pinpoint a sharp t = 0 singularity as an absolute beginning of the universe considering its infinite state in terms of size and time. Second, theologically, "[t]he identification of *ex nihilo* with t = 0 would seem too

---

1. McGrath, *Scientific Theology*, 1:166.

narrow."² If the being and becoming of the entire creation are dependent on God's Creatorship, God's creation of all things does not have to be a one-time event.

Thus, rather than limiting *creatio ex nihilo* to the beginning of the universe and the biosphere, many contemporary theologians learn from the tradition of *creatio continua*. According to this concept within the Christian doctrine of creation, specifically within the Eastern Orthodox tradition, God's continuing creativity is the source of genuine novelty that emerges and evolves within creation.³

Jürgen Moltmann points out that for a long time the traditional doctrine of creation tended to limit God's creative work to God's bringing the world into existence in the beginning. God's creative activity in history was regarded as God's providence or "[God's] preserving and accompanying work."⁴ However, the preservation of the created order of nature tended to mean that "God unceasingly repeats what God has set in the beginning." Likewise, as concurrence or God's continuing work in and through creatures was connected to preservation, it transpired that God's work in nature was not taken as having open potentialities but as unfolding the predetermined course of development. In a similar vein, divine governance in nature was understood as God's providence primarily through eschatological redemption rather than through constantly bringing new things into emergence.⁵

When God's creation of all things is limited to the original creation (*creatio originalis*), the discussed components of divine providence rarely befit the scriptural idea that God does unexpected new thing of liberation and salvation throughout history (Isa 43:18). God's creative activity in nature reflects God's saving work in history (Ps 104:30). Ultimately, the new creation is the ontological basis of the new things God does in nature.

If so, by "interpreting anew" the traditional doctrine of providence, one needs to regard preservation not only as God's *sustaining* what God created in the past, but also as God's act of new things in *preparing* creation for the eschatological redemption.⁶ Likewise, as the eschaton is the purpose of creation, concurrence involves God's "constant" act of doing

---

2. Russell, *Cosmology*, 84–85 (cited from 85).
3. Peters, "On Creating the Cosmos," 284–91.
4. Moltmann, *God in Creation*, 208.
5. Moltmann, *God in Creation*, 209.
6. Moltmann, *God in Creation*, 208–9.

new things in redemptive ways.[7] Here, divine governance is at work in concurrence as the trinitarian dynamic life constitutes the ontological ground of the new creation which opens the new possibilities for creatures to actualize in *creatio continua*.

Through the dialogue with the four interlocutors of this study, I contend that in *creatio continua* God co-suffers with creatures amidst natural and cosmic evil. However, based on the credibility of the bodily resurrection of Jesus Christ, we can have a well-motivated belief of God's eschatological fulfillment of the purpose of God's creation in the eschatological new creation. Importantly, the eschaton is not the endpoint of creation, but the ontological ground of *creatio ex nihilo*. The eschatological fulfillment of creation is not only the goal but also the ontological basis of creation. With the eschatological *telos*, God begins *creatio continua* through the development of the universe and biological evolution in both general and special providence.

The eschatological future of creation does not fully determine the course of *creatio continua*. Rather, *creatio continua* is God's mutual and dynamic interaction with creatures, since God grants them their genuine *contingency* without which God cannot eschatologically fulfill the loving communion among creatures in the new creation. Ultimately, the creaturely contingency is ontologically grounded in the otherness-in-unity of the trinitarian life of the Creator.

Through engaging with the four interlocutors of this study comparatively, I constructively propose how the triune Creator patiently and non-coercively brings forth sentient living creatures, consciousness, and self-consciousness with the ability to personally relate to God in voluntary self-transcendence in the midst of universal, contingent, but inevitable evil. I contend that God carries out this creative project through both *general* and *special* divine creative action in cooperation with the established order of nature that is genuine openness to the emergence of novelty.

The four interlocutors claim a mutual dialogue between theology and science without dissolving one into the other in the framework of "epistemic holism."[8] Hence, they diverge from "scientism," or "metaphysical

---

7. Pannenberg, *Systematic Theology*, 2:58–59. Henceforth, *ST* II. I discuss Pannenberg's understanding of providence in the matrix of his eschatological ontology of creation in chapter 4. Also, for a similar account, see Moltmann, *God in Creation*, 211–12.

8. As a critical realistic approach, epistemic holism is also known as "epistemic antireductionism" and "affirms emergence, and puts top-down and bottom-up explanations in a mutually conditioned relationship." Kärkkäinen, *Creation and Humanity*, 28.

naturalism,"[9] "scientific imperialism,"[10] "ecclesiastical authoritarianism,"[11] "creation science,"[12] and "the two-language approach."[13] For these theologians, science and religion can find consonance while not being dissolved into each other in the context of the contemporary scientific view of the universe as an open and ontologically indeterminate web of chance and law-like regularities. This open-ended cosmology centers upon six crucial areas: (a) contemporary big bang and quantum cosmology, (b) quantum physics, (c) the second law of thermodynamics, (d) chaos theory, (e) neo-Darwinian evolution and the epigenetic theories of contemporary developmental biology, and (f) non-reducible emergent monism.[14] These

---

9. This scheme is well reflected in the British philosopher and atheist Bertrand Russell's interview with the BBC earlier in the twentieth century: "What science cannot tell us, mankind cannot know" Cited in Peters, "Science and Theology: Toward Consonance," 13. Also, according to Fred Hoyle, the Jewish and Christian religions have become outmoded by modern science. Peters, "Science and Theology: Toward Consonance," 13.

10. This approach "affirms the existence of something divine but claims knowledge of the divine comes from scientific research rather than religious revelation." Cited in Peters, "Science and Theology: Toward Consonance," 14. For example, Frank Tipler believed that the Big Bang theory, coupled with quantum theory, can explain the future resurrection of the dead. Furthermore, E. O. Wilson and Michael Ruse aver that every part of the universe is obedient to physical laws without requiring any external control. Peters, "Science and Theology: Toward Consonance," 14.

11. This stance represents the fundamentalist "[a]ppeal to the authority of the church's revelation" followed by "some in the Roman Catholic tradition who perceive science and scientism as a threat." Peters, "Science and Theology: Toward Consonance," 15.

12. This model takes root in fundamentalist Biblicism. When there is a conflict between theology and science, they find scientific theories subject to revision by virtue of counterevidence within the biblical accounts, which is, in numerous cases, not seen as scientific by mainline scientists. For example, the creationists argue that the book of Genesis is itself a theory that tells us the fact of how the world was physically created. Namely, "God fixed the distinct kinds of organisms at the point of original creation. They did not evolve. Geological and biological facts attest to biblical turret, they argue." Peters, "Science and Theology: Toward Consonance," 16.

13. This position is mainly advanced by neo-orthodox and liberal theologians such as Langdon Gilkey. He claims that science asks "how" and the religion asks "why." Science and theology do not confront each other since they simply speak of their subject matters on qualitatively discrete domains. Peters, "Science and Theology: Toward Consonance," 17.

14. By understanding reality as causally irreducible emergent levels that have novel properties and their causal efficacy, Nancey Murphy advances "nonreducible physicalism." Murphy, *Bodies and Souls*. In a similar vein, Philip Clayton proposes "ontological pluralism." Clayton, *Mind and Emergence*. They commonly acknowledge

elements of the contemporary natural scientific cosmology provide a point of contact with the theological concept of the trinitarian grammar of creation, which is seen in the biblical concept of the triune God's universal immanence in the cosmos through *creatio continua*.[15]

However, based on their different ways of integrating science and theology, they present diverging sorts of *methodological naturalism* (as opposed to metaphysical naturalism) in their interdisciplinary enterprise.[16] These divergences consist of their understandings of the resurrection of Jesus, the divine act in the event, and its implications for the eschatological new creation and the scientifically plausible view of non-interventionist special divine action in this *aeon*.[17] These elements of God's creative act in nature bear high significance in a theodical argument, since they relate to God's involvement with the world ridden with natural and cosmic evil universal in God's creation.

Defining Natural and Cosmic Evil

In this book I discuss natural and cosmic theodicy and its significance for the Christian belief in creation as a trinitarian project of *creatio ex nihilo*. Hence, it is proper to define the terms before developing the main arguments. The current landscape of the biosphere on the Earth is the product of the continuous evolution of life through the indeterminate variation of species and natural selection. The evolution of life on our planet is placed in the broader context of the universe that is constrained by the principle of entropy.

In this book, I focus on God's faithfulness to the pain, suffering, and death of non-human lives in the course of Darwinian evolution. Yet as

---

causally irreducible properties emergent in evolution while subtly differing in understanding the ontological status of the emergent levels. In an eschatological ontology of creation, I think divine agency must be involved not only in whole-part and top-down causations but also in bottom-up causation to make the former actualized from the fundamental level of physics.

15. Kärkkäinen, *Creation and Humanity*, 51–69.

16. In chapter 2, I discuss different types of naturalism, and then, in the following chapters, I compare how the interlocutors differ in the understanding of methodological naturalism through my comparative analysis and assessment.

17. In this book, I maintain that if the increases of entropy are both contingent and inevitable, it is imperative to call for God's spontaneous and gracious standing in solidarity with suffering creatures by the redemptive divine lure, while being faithful to the order of nature that God establishes.

Russell contends, I find it helpful to place "evolutionary evil" under the category of "natural evil" with physical natural evil such as "geological phenomena (i.e., hurricanes), oceanographic phenomena (i.e., tsunamis), astrophysical phenomena (i.e., the impact of asteroids), radioactive phenomena (i.e., radioactive decay)."[18] In biological evolution, the pain, suffering, disease, and death are inextricably intertwined with the physical natural phenomena.

Ultimately, the contingent increase of entropy serves the fundamental context of both of those physical and evolutionary evils.[19] In that sense, the problem of pain, suffering, and death is contingent but inherent in the fabric of the universe because the second law of thermodynamics is universal. In that vein, according to Russell, "[u]niversally all forms of life that we know are open systems, and hence all are subject to these kinds of thermodynamic contingencies."[20] Thus, what I mean by natural evil is the death, suffering, and pain that living creatures undergo in violent predations, diseases, parasitism, and natural disasters throughout evolutionary history in the presence of the inevitable but contingent increases of entropy. The same life-giving presence of entropy will cause our universe including the Earth and all life to end in demise in the far future according to contemporary Big Bang cosmology. Accordingly, without cosmic theodicy, one cannot speak of natural theodicy.

Entropy makes possible the expansion of our universe from the Big Bang event. In this universe, entropy produces pain, death, and decay that are "inevitably" essential for the birth of individual living creatures. Ironically, without it, there could be no diversification of their species and interdependence among creatures. Furthermore, without it, genuine loving communion among creatures cannot emerge in the message and the life of Jesus Christ. Such an emergent reality cannot continue to be embodied in God's creation with the eschatological *telos*.[21]

---

18. Russell, "Physics, Cosmology, and the Challenge to Consequentialist Natural Theodicy," 109n3. Here, evolutionary evil can be dubbed as "biological natural evil."

19. I further explain the contingent nature of the increase of entropy in chapter 2.

20. Russell, *Cosmology*, 245.

21. Peters, "Evolution of Evil," 19–52. Peters maintains that moral sin is an emergent property, rather than a genetically determinant one. Moral good is cultivatable and cannot be reduced to the selfishness of genes. Furthermore, genes cannot be determined to be selfish as their phenotypic expressions are contingent. Particularly, in the human level, moral behaviors cannot be proven to be directed by the selfish meme of their genes.

Introduction

All in all, considering the inherent interrelatedness among the physical, biological, and cosmic dimensions of our universe, I constructively develop a natural theodicy by exploring the theological implications of evolutionary history in the matrix of the anthropic (or biopic) and thermodynamic universe. For this reason, I think, in constructing a robust trinitarian doctrine of creation in an age of science, it is imperative to construct a robust natural and cosmic theodical argument and an account of divine creative and redemptive action developed through a mutual dialogue with the natural sciences. The prevalence of pain and suffering in the biosphere and the demise of the universe raise a theological question concerning the perfection and the goodness of God's creation when God is posited as all-loving and all-powerful as the Christian tradition confesses.[22]

The Lacuna of the Traditional Doctrine of Creation: Creation Subsumed Under Redemption

According to Veli-Matti Kärkkäinen, a lacuna in Christian theology is the forgetfulness of the cosmic dimensions.[23] That is, "In the biblical and patristic traditions, 'cosmic' Christologies and pneumatologies are present," and the retrieval of tradition is "important both for the sake of interfaith hospitality and improving Christianity's self-understanding" in interdisciplinary dialogue.[24] Kärkkäinen points out that the cosmic Christology of the NT (John 1:1-14; Col 1:15-19; Heb 1:2-4) points to "the integral link between Christ's role in creation and in reconciliation."[25]

Yet I notice that there is an anthropocentric tendency in the Christian tradition. Creation tends to be subsumed under reconciliation because creation is not seen in the light of the trinitarian economy of

---

22. Here, I agree with Daniel Migliore that God's omnipotence does not have to suppress the freedom and contingency of creatures. Rather, God works providentially through preserving the order of nature and cooperating with it thanks to its genuine openness to the future. Moreover, if the eschaton is the ground of *creatio continua*, God is regarded as governing creation in accordance with the divine purpose. Migliore, *Faith Seeking Understanding*, 129-32.

23. Kärkkäinen, *Creation and Humanity*, 9.

24. Kärkkäinen, *Creation and Humanity*, 9.

25. Kärkkäinen, *Creation and Humanity*, 58. In the next chapter, I discuss in detail the theological problems of *subsuming* creation under redemption in a trinitarian framework of creation.

salvation. In separating the economic Trinity from God's creation, one runs the risk of making "a duality within the economy of salvation."[26] In that vein, Colin Gunton laments the Western inclination "to subordinate creation to redemption" because it transpires that "the status of the material world as a whole is endangered." [27]

Along the same lines, I also sympathize with Kärkkäinen's call for "Biopic Principle," recognizing that "the idea of 'fine-tuning' of our universe should not be limited to one species of creatures—to us."[28] As Paul Brett rightly brings up, we are to know with the head and feel with the heart that humans are made with the same stuff as animals, and we are to have an ecologically compassionate mindset for God's creation.[29] Evolutionary biology helps us avoid a dualistic view of the human person that separates the soul or mind from the body and tends to "isolate the human race from the remainder of the creation."[30] Likewise, Moltmann also argues that humanity is not only the *imago Dei*, but also the "*imago Mundi*"[31] in that the whole of the ecosystem is the "symbiosis of all systems of life and matter" just because they are part of the evolutionary history of the planet and the universe in inextricable unity.[32] The Spirit of Christ is immanent in creation as a whole in a *pathetic* but *redemptive* mode toward the fulfillment of the new creation.

Hence, I believe that while humans remain a special kind called to live up to the moral command of the Creator for their society and other creatures, they are not to be regarded as the only species purposefully created by the loving God who declared the whole of creation as good. The whole of creation is placed in the triune Creator's redemptive plan. With this eschatological hope, I disagree with Ruth Page's claim that pain and suffering do not serve a long-range *telos* but are instrumental for fulfilling one's own purpose. God created the world to unfold freely with God-given potentialities. Thus, pain and suffering are just an inherent

---

26. McGrath, *Fine-Tuned Universe*, 64.
27. Gunton, *Triune Creator*, 165.
28. Kärkkäinen, *Creation and Humanity*, 158.
29. Brett, "Compassion or Justice?," 235.
30. Gunton, *Triune Creator*, 186–87. Citing Zizioulas, "Preserving God's Creation," 1–5 [4].
31. Moltmann, *God in Creation*, 190.
32. Moltmann, *God in Creation*, 205.

Introduction

aspect of such a contingent world.³³ In this process, God companions with creation as the potentialities are freely actualized.

I think Page's proposal is inadequate. I wonder if her idea abnegates the "long-range" *telos* that can be found in evolution. As we look at the actual history of evolution, it does not make sense that each individual being fully receives "reimbursement" in its lifetime. There are sacrifices of certain species for the emergence of others.³⁴ For instance, the appearance of *Homo sapiens* in evolutionary history contradicts the continued flourishing of the myriads of species and individuals. Thus, predation and resultant extinction in the animal world cannot be deemed to be the fulfillment of their purpose, and the means-end problem cannot be avoided. Second, from the vantage point of individual preys, there are many prematurely killed lives that suffer excessive pain and cannot live up to their full potential. For example, when the "insurance chicks" of the White Pelican are sacrificed for the survival of their siblings, God does not take for granted their sacrifice.³⁵

Furthermore, I also find inadequate those positions that make natural theodicy marginally irrelevant by resorting to the inevitable existence of death and extinction constitutive of the developmental free processes of nature. Thereby, some theologians tend to identify the regeneration of life with God's soteriological presence as working against the power of death. Michael Ruse argues that God had no other choice but to use Darwinian evolution to create the diversity, beauty, and morality of life by bringing forth different levels of complexity.³⁶ Nonetheless, it is not proper to "expect that even the most sacrificial sharing of resources and work for the liberation of all would stop the cycle of entropy."³⁷ Darwinian evolution through random mutations and natural selection may involve emergent processes and downward causation that reduces the pain and suffering of other animals in the preconditions of morality (or proto-morality).³⁸

---

33. Page, *God and the Web of Creation*, 104.
34. Kärkkäinen, *Creation and Humanity*, 201–2.
35. Rolston, *Science and Religion*, 137–40.
36. Ruse, "Darwinism and Christianity," 86–98.
37. Kärkkäinen, *Creation and Humanity*, 206. In the same vein, Ted Peters contends that the continuous regeneration of life alone cannot fulfill the purpose of God's good creation due to the contingent nature of the increase of entropy as well as the inevitable waste of too many species in evolutionary history. Peters, "Evolution, Evil, and the Theology of the Cross," 98–120.
38. For example, see Barbour, "Five Models of God and Evolution," 419–30.

Yet it is undeniable that the second law of thermodynamics governs the cycle of entropy in the birth of a new life and the emergence of a higher level of complexity. If so, from the vantage point of each creature and species sacrificed in evolutionary history, without their redemption, God cannot be a faithful Creator.[39] I believe that as the genuine embodiment of the peaceable *basileia* of God, in which every creature and species is valued by a faithful God, is not fully completed in the present creation, it is anticipated only in an eschatological hope like in Isaiah 11 and 65.

The Four Interlocutors' Contributions and the Thesis of This Study

Russell, Pannenberg, and Peacocke maintain that the existence of natural and cosmic evil, which is represented by the increase of entropy, is both contingent and inevitable for the emergence of organisms of higher complexity and eventually the emergence of human beings. Here the increase of entropy has two definitions: the reduction of the availability of energy and the increase of disorder.[40]

That is, the *instability* and *disorder* of entropy can be likened to evil, since evil is regarded as a state of death, disorder, and decay, and thus it is an "affront to hope and peace."[41] At the same time, entropy can also signify the creative role in evolution and civilization, while in the Augustinian perspective, entropy is likened to "the brokenness of existence as our modes of interdependence."[42] Thus, the existence of natural evil is part of God's act of continuous creation that is ultimately good. Likewise, for Keller, never-dissipated chaos, which is generic to the fabric of the

---

According to contemporary developmental systems theory, organisms have the power to transform their own environment and affect the paths of the evolution of their descendants. I further discuss this epigenetic dimension of evolution in chapters 4 and 5. In the same vein, Joshua Moritz contends that even though eating and being eaten is inevitable, "self-interest, such as 'killing for gastronomic pleasure' introduces discord into the harmony of creation." Moritz, "Evolutionary Evil and Darwin's Black Box," 186.

39. God is faithful to every creature according to their species in the Genesis creation accounts. I agree with Southgate that a regenerative process through cooperation does not fulfill the God-granted *telos* for each creature and species when they cannot fully live out their God-given creaturely natures. Southgate, *Groaning of Creation*, 6.

40. Russell, *Cosmology*, 228–29.

41. Russell, *Cosmology*, 233.

42. Russell, *Cosmology*, 235.

entire creation and God, is not only evil but also good, since, without the existence of chaos in the universe, living organisms with higher complexity cannot emerge in the history of nature.

However, depending on their differing appreciation of the *autonomy* of theology within the framework of epistemological holism, the interlocutors present different theodical schemes. In other words, while differing in their particular positions, Russell, Pannenberg, and Peacocke commonly believe that God is responsible for the existence of evil that functions as an inevitable but unnecessary developmental hindrance in creation's growth in God's goodness. "God is 'ultimately ordaining sin and suffering' and hence, bears the ultimate responsibility."[43] On the other hand, for Keller, God is not ultimately responsible for the entry of evil into the creation. Rather, both God and creatures are metaphysically in the process of becoming in the face of the incessant crashes of the waves of chaos.

Depending on the diverging degrees of the autonomy of theology that the interlocutors recognize, they differ in their perspectives of the mode of divine action in continuous creation as well as the anticipation of the eschatological new creation, especially in view of the scientifically predicted cosmic death, namely *Freeze or Fry*.[44]

To be more specific, Peacocke understands the kenotic presence of creation as self-limitation in *creatio continua*. God's self-limitation means God's passive participation in the finely-tuned universe that creates life and consciousness after God's freely having created it *ex nihilo*. God actively continues to be creative only through sustaining the order of nature via the whole-part constraint. While Peacocke explicitly opposes deism, he also rejects the Whiteheadian notion of a "special lure" in creation because such a notion would imply God's going beyond a general providential ordering.[45]

In contrast, Keller claims that if God is the infinite *eros* (desire) or creative lure for novelty and higher complexity to emerge in creation, one can regard God as a responsive lure for each creature in the process. God can spontaneously persuade creatures to participate in the initial lure of the loving God. The lure of God calls forth the creaturely embodiment of

---

43. Kärkkäinen, *Creation and Humanity*, 169. Paraphrasing Hick, *Evil and the God of Love*, 228.

44. In chapter 2, I discuss this astrophysical theory of the thermodynamic equilibrium of our universe predicted in the far future.

45. Peacocke, "Cost of New Life," 33.

Christ-like expressions that befit the peaceable *basileia* of God. However, in contrast with Peacocke, Keller does not see creation as fundamentally constrained by God who is the ontological ground of the being and becoming of creation. Rather, Keller regards God's co-suffering with creatures as a loving God's necessitated choice to make within the dipolar reality where both creation and God are placed.

In Keller's process panentheism, *creatio continua* is brought into being by both the responsive lure of God and the subjective response of creatures in a non-binary fashion. Therefore, I wonder if Keller's process panentheism is strong enough to find the compatibility between the finely-tuned universe and the theological notion of teleology inherent in God's creation.[46] For Keller, God does not have lordship over the beginning and the end of creation.

In that sense, I think Keller and Peacocke contribute to each other in conceiving of creation as the work of the eschatological Redeemer who gives existence to the order of nature and works with and through it in *creatio continua*. That is, if the fundamental contingency of *creatio ex nihilo* is the ground of creation's openness to the emergence of novelty, the general ordering of the universe is not exclusive to special divine action. Furthermore, as I discuss in the following chapters, in the NT tradition, the eschatological Redeemership of the triune Creator is inseparable from the trinitarian Creatorship.

If so, *creatio continua* is the stage where the saving act of God takes place. In the emergence of higher levels of complexity,[47] God can be seen as working creatively through preserving the order of nature inherently open to the future. Furthermore, such a creative presence of God is essentially redemptive because the eschaton is the basis and the goal of *creatio continua*.

In this book, I contend that the eschaton is in both continuity and discontinuity with the present creation since it is a faithful Creator's fulfillment and redemption of creation, as proleptically experienced in the bodily resurrection of Jesus. Therefore, God's eschatological redemption is

---

46. I discuss in further detail the fine-tuning of the universe and the fundamental contingency of the universe in the following chapters. The four interlocutors appropriate the fine-tuning of the universe in diverging philosophical interpretations that are coherent with their natural and cosmic theodicy.

47. The four interlocutors adopt a strong version of emergence with subtle differences. I include my comparative analysis of their understandings of emergence in the following chapters in relation to their idea of the eschatological Redeemership of the triune Creator.

the point of departure of the single divine action of *creatio ex nihilo*. In that sense, Pannenberg's and Russell's contributions are significant since they respect the integrity of the contingent order of nature as the expression of God's faithfulness and rational intelligibility. At the same time, they regard the trinitarian Creatorship as inherently redemptive.[48] In that vein, I think Pannenberg's and Russell's trinitarian scheme of creation better suits the cosmic dimensions of Christ and the Spirit according to Scripture.[49]

Yet, at the same time, I believe that a "qualified notion of divine self-limitation"[50] can befit Pannenberg's and Russell's idea of the *non-zero-sum* relationship between the created and divine causalities in their ontological grounding of the present and the past in the eschaton. In their eschatological ontology of time and space, special providence can remain objectively particular within God's general ordering of creation. The eschatological redemption is not the replacement of the present creation but rather *creatio ex vetere* or the transformation of the old.

Yet, considering the cross of Jesus the Son as God's participating in the history of creation ridden by the contingent but inevitable power of death and evil, the "causal efficacy of the future" is a holistic causality rather than a determinative efficient causality in creation open to genuine novelty. Then, in my view, Keller's *creatio ex profundis* and Peacocke's whole-part constraint can provide Pannenberg and Russell with metaphors that enrich their understanding of creation through the mediation of the diverse causalities of nature.

Likewise, I think that the trinitarian solidarity with suffering creatures, for Russell and Pannenberg, can be further nuanced by God's redemptive co-suffering as *co-protesting*.[51] In his theology of the cross and

48. Pannenberg's trinitarian idea of creation is corrective to the traditional path of theology that "speaks of creation more narrowly in distinction from reconciliation and consummation." Pannenberg, ST II, 8.

49. I discuss in detail the biblical and historical support of the cosmic dimensions of Christ and the Spirit in chapter 2. In the following chapters, I discuss how the interlocutors differently present cosmic Christology and pneumatology in their natural and cosmic theodicy.

50. I discuss this notion in chapter 5, the most constructive chapter of this work.

51. While Keller regards divine *kenosis* as metaphysically necessitated by her dipolar panentheism, Peacocke affirms that *kenosis* is God's free choice in his doctrine of *ex nihilo*. For both of them, *kenosis* entails the limitations in God's knowledge of the future and God's ability to fulfill the eschatological new creation as *creatio ex vetere*. For Pannenberg and Russell, the *kenotic* presence of God in creation means self-giving and self-sacrificing but not self-limiting in omniscience according to their eschatological ontology of creation. The different nuances of God's *kenosis* are discussed in the

the resurrection, Russell claims God's *theopaschitic* participation in time through co-suffering to overcome natural and cosmic evil. Yet Russell rejects the notion of divine self-limitation in terms of God's limiting of divine omniscience.

Russell honors the genuine contingency of creatures through adopting the indeterminate interpretation of quantum mechanics within the matrix of his eschatological ontology of creation.[52] Thus, the omniscience of the eschatological Redeemer cannot be compromised. Yet, in my view, divine self-limitation can be accepted without compromising divine omniscience and God's eschatological Redeemership when it is in a qualified sense.[53] By appropriating this idea, I think that one should seriously consider the significance of the cross as God's *co-protesting* or *co-resisting* against the contingent but inevitable presence of death and evil in the light of the resurrection of Jesus.

Whereas Russell accepts the *theopaschitic* understanding of the cross of Jesus, Pannenberg is more interested in rendering the cross of Jesus Christ as the locus of his self-distinction from the Father as the principle of creaturely independence. Pannenberg does not regard the cross in a *theopaschitic* sense. In the same vein, Pannenberg understands the Father as compassionate or in sympathy with the Son in his suffering and death, yet he distinguishes the death of the Son in his human nature from his divine nature to which the death on the cross is not attributed.[54]

Likewise, for Pannenberg, the Spirit is a creative field of the eschatological power in which the triune God continues to bring into existence independent creatures through the Son as the principle of creation. Yet the Spirit rarely co-suffers in solidarity with creatures in the face of natural and cosmic evil in *creatio continua*. In my view, by appropriating the suggested notion of divine self-limitation in a qualified sense, the notion of the transcendent immanence of God in these scholars' schemes can be further nuanced by the "vulnerable yet unconquerable"[55] Redeemership of the triune Creator.

---

following chapters in relation to God's soteriological presence in creation.

52. Russell agrees with Pannenberg that the differentiated unity of the eschaton grounds the fundamental contingency of *creatio continua*.

53. I discuss this notion in detail in chapter 5.

54. I discuss my critical assessment of Pannenberg's and Russell's kenotic understanding of creation in chapters 4 and 5.

55. Migliore, *Faith Seeking Understanding*, 88–90 [88].

If creating genuine independence-in-unity takes a Darwinian way of evolution through random genetic mutations and natural selection, it is inevitable for God to co-suffer with creatures toward fulfilling the eschatological purpose of creation.[56] As Jürgen Moltmann says, in light of the resurrection, the cross becomes "an eschatological saving event" and reveals God's solidarity with the suffering of the world for its *liberation* from all the powers of sin and evil.[57] On the cross, not only the Son, but also the Father and the Spirit suffered with creation and protested against the powers of sin, death, and violence.[58]

In this interdisciplinary and comparative study, I aim to present a theologically plausible understanding of God's creative and redemptive act within creation amidst the evil that is prevalent in the cosmic level. In this critical evaluation, four theological tenets are adopted: "(a) evil exists; (b) God is good; (c) God is omnipotent; (d) a good being will always eliminate evil as far as it is able."[59] While exploring the origin of evil in nature, I focus more on divine action in the creation ridden with natural/cosmic evil and, accordingly, a "defense" investigation in central to this study.[60]

In so doing, I argue that, in God's absolutely free act of *creatio ex nihilo*, evil is not willed by God but universally, contingently, and inevitably caused in *creatio continua* through emergent evolution, and that even so the cross and the resurrection of Jesus give us the credible hope that

---

56. Sallie McFague interprets the *agapic* love shown in the life and the cross of Jesus Christ as the representation of the goal to embody in creation through kenotic divine immanence: namely, the direction "toward inclusive love for all, especially the oppressed, the outcasts, the vulnerable." This cannot be read from biological evolution (especially, in the Darwinian natural selection) per se, but is a theological interpretation in the light of the life and the cross of Jesus Christ. McFague, *Body of God*, 160. However, I believe that the genuine embodiment of the peaceable *basileia* of God is not fully completed in the present creation and that it is anticipated only in an eschatological hope.

57. Moltmann, *Crucified God*, 182.

58. I further discuss the historical credibility and the significance of the bodily resurrection of Jesus in chapter 3.

59. Southgate and Robinson, "Varieties of Theodicy," 68. In this book, considering the contingent nature of natural evil, I hold that God is redemptive not only in the new creation but in *creatio continua*.

60. "Theodicy tries to account for suffering, giving the true explanations for why creatures suffer. A defense gives a possible explanation for the existence of suffering, showing the argument that God and suffering are incompatible is unsuccessful." Edwards, *C.S. Lewis*, 14.

the triune God unfailingly continues to redeem the creation from evil in both pathetic and eschatological immanence.

Earlier Research and Contributions of This Work

The problem of pain and suffering has been investigated in other works too. However, I believe that my work makes contributions in distinction from previous research. To be more precise, in his PhD dissertation, *Evil as God's own Problem*, Lloyd Philip Dunaway (Baylor University, 1979) performed his comparative study between Barth's top-down approach to theodicy and Dunaway's philosophical bottom-up approach to theodicy. In so doing, he drew upon the insights of process theologians, such as Whitehead and Hartshorne. Here the author seeks to find the way to plausibly explain the presence of evil in the world by putting in dialogue Barth's theology from above and the theology from below of process thinkers and Dunaway. Dunway's dissertation provides a balanced presentation of the kenotic yet redemptive presence of God amidst evil.

Nonetheless, Dunway's work certainly lacks in consideration of natural evil prevalent in the universe according to the second law of thermodynamics and the cosmic death that is predicted by contemporary astrophysics. In that manner, he does not find the inseparable linkage between moral theodicy and natural theodicy while not presenting a panentheistic model that is both theologically and scientifically plausible.

The core concepts of the trinitarian panentheism which I discussed above are well taken into consideration in the recent PhD dissertation authored by Hillegonda Koster at the University of Chicago, titled "For the Future of the Earth: Creation and Salvation in the theologies of Moltmann, Keller, and Tanner" (2011). Kostar's dissertation discusses the relationship between the doctrines of creation and salvation in the theologies of Jürgen Moltmann, Catherine Keller and Kathryn Tanner within the context of the ecological crisis. Thereby, the author focuses on the immanence of God in creation and natural evil indirectly caused by human abuse of nature. I find this work helpful in that Koster acutely presents the significance of the cosmic Christology and pneumatology for nature as creation. However, I find it lacking in consideration of theology-science dialogue in the author's engagement with the problem of evil within nature. Furthermore, she does not deal with the cosmic resurrection that is proleptically revealed in the bodily resurrection of Christ as a historical event.

Further, I find helpful the recent PhD dissertation written by Dongsik: "The God-World Relationship between Joseph Bracken, Philip Clayton, and the Open Theism" (Claremont School of Theology, 2009). In his work, Dongsik investigates the God-world relationship among Joseph Bracken as a process theologian, Philip Clayton as a panentheist, and the open theism. For the author, they have affinities and differences as conversational partners in their multilayered relations. He seeks to frame a new constructive theology whose primary aspect must synthesize both classical theism and process theology.

While Park's work sheds an illuminative light on the manners in which classical theism can be reconciled to panentheism and open theism, it does not develop a solid argument of natural and cosmic theodicy. Moreover, he does not discuss an eschatological vision of the new creation in the context of theology-science dialogue. A hypothetic consonance between theology and science is imperative in contemporary theology, since as McGrath affirms that "[t]he natural sciences today offer to Christian theology . . . precisely the role that Platonism offered our patristic, and Aristotelianism our medieval forebears."[61]

In his PhD dissertation, "Cosmic Hope in a Scientific Age: Christian Eschatology in Dialogue with Scientific Cosmology," Junghyung Kim (Graduate Theological Union, 2011) presents a well-rounded cosmic eschatology. He critically investigates diverse theologians' eschatology with the scientific premise of the predicted end of the Earth and the demise of our universe. In so doing, Kim attempts to re-configure the mutual interaction between scientific cosmology and eschatology. Yet the author rarely deals in depth with the theme of special divine action in *creatio continua* while regarding the history of our universe as the proleptical immanence of the eschaton promised in the bodily resurrection of Jesus.

Furthermore, while Kim discusses the significance of eschatological panentheism, in which God is believed to be "all in all" for creation only in the eschaton, he does not coherently integrate his arguments as to *creatio continua* within the matrix of the *pathetic-yet-redemptive* trinitarian panentheism. I agree that only in the eschatological new creation, God and the world will be in a *perichoretic* fellowship without the stings of death and evil. Yet I believe that in order for a trinitarian panentheism to be more theologically robust, it should not leave out the pathetic immanence of God as *divine co-resistance* against evil with the promise of the new creation in the eschatological horizons.

61. McGrath, *Scientific Theology*, 1:7.

In her dissertation, "Unto the Least of These: Animal Suffering and the Problem of Evil," Beth Seacord (The University of Colorado at Boulder, 2013) argues that classical theism is incompatible with the contemporary scientific knowledge of animals' pain and suffering in evolution. She engages with David Hume's abductive approach to the problem of evil by comparing it to Michael Murray's neo-Cartesian defense and Richard Swinburn's animal virtue theodicy. However, she does not deeply engage with the biblical and theological traditions as well as the eschatological ontology of creation, focusing instead on the cosmic implication of the cross and bodily resurrection of the Logos. Furthermore, she rarely deals with the problem of divine action in the matrix of natural and cosmic theodicy.

Among published books I find my work distinct and contributive. For example, in *Satan and the Problem of Evil*, Gregory Boyd engages with the problem of evil from a perspective of open theology. Boyd supports the idea of God's self-limitation of the knowledge of future events in his theodical argument. The God of love limits God's power and knowledge in interacting with creatures. In contrast to Boyd, while I agree that God embraces the creaturely potentialities in the trinitarian life of God, I contend that all the potentials of creation are known to God. Furthermore, while God grants contingency and freedom to creatures out of God's interpersonal love, that act does not mean that God's withdrawal from creaturely agencies, but rather that the triune God works through them within the creative and redemptive field of the Spirit. God is immanent in creation without giving up God's transcendence as the eschatological Redeemer.

More recently, *God, Evolution, and Animal Suffering*, Bethany Sollereder investigates the pain and suffering of animals in God's good creation. Sollereder rejects the natural theodicy according to which animals' suffering resulted from the fall of human beings and the angelic beings. She also rejects the view that the presence of suffering in creation is intended by God for their good. Rather, she contends that the wasteful and messy history of evolution shows the loving God who extravagantly gives freedom to creatures for their growth and development while compassionately accompanying the suffering animals, drawing them to eschatological "healing and fulfillment" in the unfolding drama of God's good creation. My work is distinguished from her book in that my research investigates the problem of evolutionary evil in the larger context of cosmic evil. Furthermore, I approach the problem of cosmic/natural evil from a perspective of trinitarian and soteriological-panentheistic framework of creation.

Lastly, *Suffering Life's Pain*, David Gooding and John Lennox present diverse approaches to the problem of natural evil from scientific, philosophical and theological perspectives. However, they rarely engage with the theological implications of the cosmologically predicted end of our universe, the life-birthing construct for all creatures within. Furthermore, they do not develop a robust trinitarian framework of *creatio ex nihilo* and *continua*, based on diverse biblical and theological traditions, which is the main focus of my work.

Based on the earlier writings listed above, I believe that my attempt to develop an *eschatological-kenotic* panentheistic framework of the trinitarian creation bears significance since it seeks to present a constructive and well-nuanced vision of creation in the face of natural and cosmic evil. To that end, this study performs mutual and open-ended dialogue among scientific, philosophical, and theological perspectives on the problem of natural and cosmic evil in pursuit of a fuller understanding of the triune God's creation.

Methodology: Reaching a Deeper Level of Consonance through Open-Ended Interaction

Despite the popular image of unwavering warfare between science and religion, as we take a closer look at their relationship, it reveals a more peaceful yet dynamic harmony of interests. In my understanding, natural sciences and theology can mutually interact with each other in hypothetical consonance.[62] "Consonance" means coherence between the understanding of the universe according to natural sciences and the understanding of the universe as God's creation according to Christian faith.[63] This coherence remains "hypothetical" because of the open-ended character of natural sciences and theology.[64] The subject matters of both dialogue partners are explored *a posteriori*, rather than *a priori*. Thus, natural sciences and theology can interact in mutual hospitality as they engage with different subject matters that are yet interrelated within

---

62. I glean this insight from Peters, "Science and Theology," 11–42.
63. Peters, "Introduction," 1.
64. Peters, "Introduction," 10.

epistemic hierarchy. Thus, both theology and natural sciences engage with "tradition-mediated" data in a critical realist approach.[65]

In a scientific model, while a set of observations may contribute to constructing a hypothesis, the hypothesis is *suggested* rather than unchangeably established by those observations. First, the reality of the observed world is not deterministic. The observation of an entity is inherently spatiotemporally relative, and indeterminacy is universally inherent in nature according to contemporary natural sciences.[66] Second, the design of a hypothetical model is inherently theory-laden and paradigm-laden, in that existing theories and paradigms influence a scientist's observation and interpretation.[67]

With this in mind, Nancey Murphy and George Ellis hold that a scientific research program works in the midst of the problems of circularity and relativism that arise in the coherence-oriented research programs via coherently integrating novel facts in their relation to higher levels of knowledge.[68] A good paradigm or a progressive research program is positive and heuristic by occasionally predicting novel facts and successfully addressing those novel facts through integrating more coherent auxiliary hypotheses under a hardcore theory. Likewise, theological data are not only affective and ethical, but also cognitive, laden with truth claims based on reliable information that is communally discerned and transmitted by traditions. This information is gleaned from God's trinitarian self-revelation in history that is communally discerned and received by the church through the illuminating wisdom of the Spirit.[69]

Likewise, for McGrath, the book of nature cannot show us the creation of God when seen through our naked eyes, if God is posited as the Infinite that is immanent in nature yet goes beyond it in transcendence. However, the book of nature can serve to support and verify the Scripture's portrayal of nature as God's creation through the "empirical fit" between scientific theories and a theology of nature.[70] In the unfolding

---

65. McGrath, *Scientific Theology*, 3:138. I discuss the possibilities of mutual interaction between theology and sciences as traditions in further detail in chapter 4.

66. Barbour, *Myths, Models, and Paradigms*, 1–3.

67. Barbour, *Myths, Models, and Paradigms*, 36.

68. Murphy and Ellis, *On the Moral Nature of the Universe*, 10–13.

69. Polkinghorne, *Science and Religion in Quest of Truth*, 127–30.

70. McGrath, *Fine-Tuned Universe*, 57–59. Similarly, Clayton discusses the importance of "intersubjective" efforts to find consonance to the point where the "maximum traction" between sciences and theology can be achieved. Clayton, *Adventures in the Spirit*, 52–57.

history of the universe both natural sciences and theology can more fully understand the reality of the universe in mutual dialogue in pursuing "inference to the best explanation," while respecting each discipline's proper research method for its subject matters.[71]

Therefore, McGrath seeks not only "intra-systemic coherence" of theological doctrines but also their "extra-systemic correspondence" to the statements of nature according to natural sciences.[72] Christians are called to humbly ask God for wisdom in seeking *coherence* between the book of nature and the book of Scripture, if the God who saves is the One who creates the cosmos. Yet, by doing this, they are to acknowledge the difference in the logic and methodology of research that theology and natural sciences employ.

If our universe is to be put in a "stratified view of reality" with diverse emergent levels of complexity,[73] a trinitarian theology of nature as a tradition can make our understanding of reality intellectually more complete by giving it meaning and purpose. Both natural sciences and the theological interpretation of nature as creation should be in mutual interaction in open-ended dialogue. By the same token, as Pannenberg rightly claims, if the universe is the creation of God, the universe cannot be fully understood by natural sciences without God. In other words, if the universe can be perfectly understood without God, how could God be the One who creates it *ex nihilo*?[74] In that sense, theology (in particular, a Christian theology of nature) embraces and explains "overall patterns of ordering that are discerned in the universe" under the theme of the triune God while natural sciences provide a detailed explanation of their subject matters.[75]

In this manner, they constitute different levels of an emergent hierarchy of reality, and accordingly, there can be consonance between theology and natural sciences when it comes to interpreting the universe as the triune God's creation. The development of the universe is still unfinished, as God's creation is not finished until the new creation.

---

71. McGrath, *Fine-Tuned Universe*, 48.

72. McGrath, *Scientific Theology*, 2:39–54.

73. McGrath, *Scientific Theology*, 2:219–24. Drawing upon Roy Bhaskar's "stratified view of reality," McGrath affirms that the universe is composed of diverse epistemic levels that cannot not be reduced into each other in inseparable relations and unity.

74. Pannenberg, *Toward a Theology of Nature*, 16.

75. McGrath, *Scientific Theology*, 3:195.

Dissonance may consistently appear, but through it, we can reach a deeper level of consonance.

In my view, both Peacocke and Keller share an *assimilationist* tendency in theology-science dialogue,[76] in that, for both theologians, the new potentialities for the future of creation, though ultimately grounded in God, do not theologically imply the eschatological new creation, based on the bodily resurrection of Jesus Christ. In his "Emergentist-Naturalist-Panentheistic" research program, Peacocke does not reduce the eschatological new creation to an existential metaphor, as Keller does. However, for Peacocke, the new creation as a radically new event still remains merely part of the way God created the world in the beginning, since Peacocke tries to "wrestle more thoroughly with the actual scientific ideas and seek a fuller integration with theological ideas."[77] In the same context, while endorsing the indeterminate interpretation of quantum mechanics in his whole-part approach to God's creative act in nature, Peacocke affirms that there is no room in the established order of nature for divine bottom-up causation through special divine action.

In her *Tehomic* perspective of creation, Keller rightly regards the infinite *eros* (or desire) of God as working in *creatio continua* through continuously luring every creature into embodying the love of God as we see in the life of Jesus. However, the expression of special divine action in the macroscopic level metaphysically cannot take place through direct divine action because every occasion is a creaturely subjective response to divine lure.

Both Pannenberg and Russell place confidence in the fact that "the Christian faith exhibits an honest pursuit of truth accompanied by confidence in its rational motivation when it is subjected to the same

---

76. As opposed to the models of conflict, independence, and dialogue, Barbour places Peacocke's approach in the category of integrating theology and science. Peacocke's "theology of nature" locates its main sources in theological discourses but is open to doctrinal deconstruction and reconstruction in the light of scientific theories. Barbour, *When Science Meets Religion*, 31–34. However, in so doing, Peacocke does not endorse the objective status of special divine action in God's kenotic creation. Similarly, Barbour places process theology in "systematic synthesis" that incorporates both science and religion under a common metaphysics. Barbour, *When Science Meets Religion*, 34–38. Yet, while both schemes seek dialogue between theology and sciences in different degrees of mutuality, Polkinghorne understands Peacocke's idea is closer to consonance than Barbour's while the latter is closer to assimilation than Peacocke's. Polkinghorne, *Scientists as Theologians*, 6–7, 83–84.

77. Peters, "Science and Theology," 31.

rational scrutiny that science exacts upon its data and theories."[78] Russell and Pannenberg seek more mutual interaction between theology and science than Peacocke and Keller. Russell does so by advancing *Creative Mutual Interaction*, and Pannenberg by putting forth his *Sub Ratione Dei* approach in his theology-science dialogue.[79]

If coherence is to be pursued continuously, I think, as Pannenberg and Russell argue, the interaction between theology and science is to be reciprocal rather than one-way. This means that one can state the challenge from theology to science as well as from science to theology. "The challenge from science is this: if the predictions of science for the far future of the universe come to pass—the standard Big Bang / the *Freeze or Fry* scenarios—this undermines the intelligibility of a coming General Resurrection of the dead and a new creation of heaven and earth."[80] In that vein, Russell contributes to Pannenberg's natural and cosmic theodicy by more thoroughly considering the theories of special relativity, quantum mechanics, and quantum cosmology. I appreciate Russell's contributions because the mutual interaction in seeking deeper consonance must be open to revision in the contingency of nature and God's act of creation open to the future.

A Call for a Well-Nuanced Panentheistic Vision of Creation

In the same vein, I present a trinitarian panentheistic view of God's immanence as a revision of classical theism,[81] which is theologically more plausible, as we consider the contemporary scientific cosmology as well as the theodical dilemma looming in classical theism. In classical theism, God's eternity tends to be counted as *timeless*. As Keith Ward rightly

---

78. Peters, "Science and Theology," 31. According to Peters, this approach is taken in Polkinghorne's *Bottom-Up Systematics*. For Polkinghorne, both science and theology are to cooperate mutually in seeking the truths in an *a posteriori* communally discerned manner. Both Pannenberg and Russell share this position. Peters, "Science and Theology," 25–26, 29–32.

79. I comparatively engage with their methodology in chapter 4 of this book.

80. Robert Russell, *Cosmology, Evolution, and Resurrection Hope*, 45–46.

81. It is "customary to speak of 'classical theism' as a generic term designating the approaches of traditional postbiblical developments of early Christian theology that sought to express its faith in the biblical God with the help of Greco-Roman philosophical categories and later found its highest sophistication in medieval scholasticism." Kärkkäinen, *Trinity and Revelation*, 228.

points out, because of the emphasis of divine omnipresence, in classical theism "no part of the physical universe is ever absent from God."[82] Simultaneously, however, God as the unchangeable and immortal first cause is not affected by the ups and downs of history and nature.[83] Catherine Keller claims that in Calvinism this juxtaposition of eternity and time finally led to the view of God as all-controlling power without giving genuine freedom to creation.[84]

I affirm that this view of divine providence is problematic (a) in the contemporary natural sciences that regard the universe as self-organizing through the interplay of chance and regularities. Also, as we consider (b) the prevalence of evil in the cosmos, the classical theism's view of an all-controlling Creator based on its eternity-time relationship demands a critical revision. That is, the awareness of evil universal not only in human society, but also in the physical and biological levels, and the scientifically predicted demise of the universe through a thermodynamic equilibrium (*Freeze or Fry*), is raised among scientists and theologians who participate in theology-science dialogue.

In avoiding atheism and deism in a scientific age, a panentheistic view of creation provides a way to theologically posit the "transcendent immanence" of God the Creator in the universe without violating the order of nature.[85] Bearing this in mind, Niels Henrik Gregersen presents three varieties of panentheism as alternative ideas of divine action in creation: "expressivist panentheism in the context of German Idealism," "soteriological panentheism in the context of trinitarian thought," and "dipolar panentheism." Gregersen points out that generic panentheism has its origin in the romantic expressivism of German Idealism.[86] According to this view, first, God contains the world, yet is more than the

---

82. Ward, "Personhood, Spirit, and the Supernatural," 153–55. Also, see Kärkkäinen, *Trinity and Revelation*, 228–49.

83. Augustine, "On the Trinity," 1.1.2.

84. Keller, *On the Mystery*, 80–81. For the important accounts of panentheistic turns in the Christian doctrine of creation in a scientific age, see Griffin, "Panentheism," 36–47. Knight, "Theistic Naturalism and the World Made Flesh," 48–61. Clayton, "Panentheism in Metaphysical and Scientific Perspective," 73–94.

85. In the same vein, Philip Clayton claims that divine transcendence should not be trumped in a panentheistic vision when God is portrayed as immanent in the history of nature. For example, in Samuel Alexander's idea, God is presented as the One who ends up as emerging in the evolution of nature as an emergent whole. Clayton, "Panentheism in Metaphysical and Scientific Perspective," 89–91.

86. Gregersen, "Three Varieties of Panentheism," 22–23, 27–31.

world. Accordingly, the world is (in some sense) *in God*. Second, "[a]s contained 'in God,' the world not only derives its existence from God but also returns to God while preserving the characteristics of being a creature. Accordingly, the relations between God and the world are (in some sense) bilateral."[87] In these tenets, the phrase "in some sense" may place a panentheistic vision of creation in a different position within a wide-ranging spectrum as a research program that seeks the best inference to explanation through interdisciplinary dialogue from philosophical, theological, and scientific perspectives.

For instance, in Georg Hegel's panentheistic idea of the God-world relationship, creation tends to be necessitated by his metaphysics, whereas Schelling finds genuine freedom in God's decision to create the world.[88] Gregersen points out that Hegel disagrees with Leibniz's idea of the perfection of the world in his theodicy and his understanding of the ontological status of the world's temporal development. However, Pannenberg points out that Hegel stops short of aligning their logical analyses in historical occurrences in religion. In other words, while Hegel finds an analogy between the biblical God as the Spirit and his idea of the Absolute as the Spirit, Hegel's view of the Trinity remains ideological without being grounded in the historical revelation of God in which the trinitarian persons are personal and active rather than merely intellectual.[89]

Furthermore, whereas Hegel's panentheism is a near-pantheism in his view of the world's consummation in God,[90] for Schelling, the Godself is in structured or stratified unity as the ontological ground of creaturely diversity.[91] Like Hegel, Whitehead and Hartshorne also regard God's existence as inseparable from generating a world. However, unlike Hegel, the process thinkers posit that there is "a metaphysical necessity that God and world coexist and co-determine one another."[92]

As opposed to these two types of panentheism, Gregersen proposes "soteriological panentheism in the context of trinitarian thought."

87. Gregersen, "Three Varieties of Panentheism," 22.

88. Clayton, *Adventures in the Spirit*, 164–70.

89. Pannenberg, *Metaphysics and the Idea of God*, 40–43.

90. Gunton, *Triune Creator*, 156. Gunton points out that Hegel's understanding of the relationship between creation and God tends to be modalistic since Hegel excludes the mediating roles of the Son and the Spirit in the economy of salvation. For Hegel, the world is "the outcome of God's self-externalisation in time."

91. Clayton, *Adventures in the Spirit*, 165.

92. Gregersen, "Three Varieties of Panentheism," 23, 31–34.

According to this view, whereas God can freely create the world, it is God's freedom to invite creatures to participate in divine life through co-determining interaction between God and the world. However, this self-limiting act of God is not God's withdrawal from creation, but God's providence that involves general and special divine action. In this view, general providence is not exclusive to special divine action, but the latter fulfills the former.[93] In the same vein, the economic Trinity as God's soteriological immanence in creation finds its fulfillment in the eschaton, yet the independence of creaturely existence is not dissolved but thrives.

I find the last type of panentheism coherent with the scriptural portrayal of God's involvement in the world. According to Colin Gunton, Irenaeus of Lyons affirmed that creation is a narrative of God's unfolding creative act in which contingent creatures participate in the process of God's perfecting toward the new creation.[94] Irenaeus does not make the cross of Christ and his resurrection redundant like in the Hegelian and Darwinian dialectical ideas of history.[95] Rather, he understands *creatio continua* as developmental, but only in the light of the transformative process of the new creation that is "a radical redirection from the movement it takes backwards whenever sin and evil shape its direction."[96]

In the OT, God is the one who mightily brought Israel out of Egypt when they were left with the threat of death without any hope for the future. However, it is also notable that God established the covenant with Israel, so they were to learn to respond to the promise of God in freedom. Likewise, in the NT, the same God is the one who raised Jesus from the dead and is the one who fulfills the reality of Jesus' resurrection in our own reality. In these saving acts of God, God is not bound to the past, but overcomes the past, and fulfills Jesus' triumph over death in history. In that sense, Robert Jenson writes that in Scripture God is portrayed as "the power of the future."[97] God is the one who leads history to a concrete end that is the triumph of Jesus over the power of death and evil.[98]

However, the redemptive meaning of Easter can be seen only in the light of Jesus' free act of obedience to the Father in his self-distinction

---

93. Gregersen, "Three Varieties of Panentheism," 23–27. I discuss the significance of this type of panentheism further in detail in chapter 2 of this book.

94. Gunton, *Triune Creator*, 11–12.

95. Gunton, *Triune Creator*, 11–12.

96. Gunton, *Triune Creator*, 12.

97. Jenson, *Triune Identity*, 23.

98. Jenson, *Triune Identity*, 23–25.

from the Father on the cross.⁹⁹ In the light of the cosmic Christology and pneumatology of the NT, the inherent unpredictability in nature implies the presence of God who performs particular things in particular circumstances while honoring and being faithful to what God creates. Likewise, in fulfilling the eschatological new creation, God does not violate natural laws but by ultimately fulfilling God's purpose of creating the order of nature.¹⁰⁰ Likewise, in *creatio continua*, God can do "unprecedented things in unprecedented circumstances." ¹⁰¹

In this vein, I develop a trinitarian panentheism, according to which creation, reconciliation, and consummation of the world comprise the history of the trinitarian God that culminates in God's kingdom. In other words, God's creation is "the fruit of the loving God's longing for the other and for that other's free response to the divine love."¹⁰² This work is in pursuit of a panentheistic vision of the God-world relationship that is coherent with the corresponding theories of natural sciences, but also with the biblical witnesses to the indirect revelation of the triune God in history. To that end, I perform a comparative and reconstructive study of the panentheistic ideas of divine action in the context of natural and cosmic theodicy advanced by Peacocke, Keller, Pannenberg, and Russell.

In so doing, I comparatively engage with the different nuances and implications of God's *kenotic* creation of the world by investigating how these theologians understand the meanings of the cross and the resurrection of Christ for creation. The different nuances of God's *kenosis* are inextricably related to the four's differing understandings of creation's contingency, which determines the way that God interacts with the world in *creatio continua* and the eschatological new creation that is *creatio ex vetere* (or the transformation of the old), rather than the second *creatio ex nihilo*.

The Layout of this Work

In chapter 2, I discuss the significance of natural and cosmic theodicy, exploring the problem of the subjugation of creation under the redemption

---

99. Pannenberg, *ST* II, 374–75.

100. Polkinghorne, *Science and Religion in Quest of Truth*, 102.

101. Polkinghorne, *Science and Religion in Quest of Truth*, 96. I discuss in detail the cosmic dimensions of Christ and the Spirit in a trinitarian framework of creation in chapter 2.

102. Kärkkäinen, *Trinity and Revelation*, 236.

of human beings in the Christian tradition. This is problematic considering the theodical problems of pain and suffering prevalent in evolutionary history. Therefore, I set the stage for the following chapters by interpreting the self-organizing universe and the evolution of life as a purposeful creation of the triune Creator. In that process, I find helpful soteriological panentheism as consonant with the kenotic-eschatological panentheistic vision of creation that I construct in this work.

In chapter 3, I engage with a comparative investigation of Peacocke's and Keller's natural and cosmic theodicy and discuss how they can mutually contribute to each other's understanding of God's creative and redemptive panentheistic immanence in creation amidst the inevitable and contingent natural evil. In this dialogue, I propose a non-coercive and kenotic presence of God while affirming the significance of special divine action as God's co-protesting against the contingent and inevitable natural evil.

In chapter 4, considering the problem of the means-end interpretation of Darwinian evolution, the existence of excessive pain and suffering in nature, and the scientifically predicted cosmic demise, I discuss the significance of an eschatological ontology of creation based on the bodily resurrection of Christ that has cosmic implication by putting Pannenberg's and Russell's perspectives in dialogue. While Russell gleans his framework of the trinitarian *creatio continua* from Pannenberg, Russell contributes to Pannenberg's scheme by thoroughly engaging with physical and cosmological theories.

In chapter 5, drawing upon the argument developed through the previous chapters, I construct a holistic kenotic-eschatological vision of the trinitarian creation. In this way, I appropriate a qualified concept of divine self-limitation, so Russell's and Pannenberg's *non-zero-sum* approach to divine action can be more nuanced with God's genuine honoring of creaturely contingency and God's redemptive co-suffering as co-resisting in solidarity with creatures. By doing this, in my view, Keller's dipolar metaphysics and Peacocke's whole-part approach can help Pannenberg's and Russell's eschatological ontology of the trinitarian creation by further nuancing Pannenberg's and Russell's kenotic ideas of creation. Thereby, I propose a well-nuanced kenotic-eschatological panentheistic vision of the trinitarian creation.

2

The Significance of Natural and Cosmic Theodicy in a Robust Trinitarian Panentheistic Vision of Creation

IN THIS CHAPTER, I discuss the significance of natural and cosmic theodicy for the Christian belief in creation as a trinitarian project. In this regard, I set the stage for the following chapters where I perform a comparative and constructive study on the problem of pain, suffering, death, and decay throughout biological evolution on the Earth and in the universe as a whole and God's trinitarian creative and redemptive immanence therein.

As discussed in chapter 1, the natural evil of our planet is placed in the matrix of our universe constrained by the same principle of entropy. Accordingly, without cosmic theodicy, one cannot speak of natural theodicy. I think, in constructing a robust trinitarian doctrine of creation in an age of science, it is imperative to construct a robust natural and cosmic theodical argument and an account of divine creative and redemptive action developed through mutual dialogue with the natural sciences. The prevalence of pain and suffering in the biosphere and the demise of the universe raise a theological question concerning the perfection and the goodness of God's creation when God is posited as all-loving and all-powerful as the Christian tradition confesses.[1]

In paving the way for the development of this theodical discourse through a comparative study of the four interlocutors' understandings of the universe and biological evolution as the locus of God's creation, in my argument, I follow the order of the sections as follows. In the first section, I discuss the prevalence of natural evil across all levels of the universe, including the scientifically predicted demise of our universe and all the living creatures in it.

In the following section, I move onto the *eclipse* of natural evil in the traditional doctrine of theodicy and analyze the reasons why it is so. This tendency contrasts with the cosmic dimensions of Christology and pneumatology according to scriptural accounts as well as patristic traditions. Hence, in the section thereafter, I discuss how the cosmic aspects of Christ and the Spirit make possible conceptualizing the trinitarian panentheistic vision. Since in the following chapters, I will present a trinitarian panentheistic vision via the comparative study of the four interlocutors' theodicies, I bring up the theological and scientific plausibility of the trinitarian panentheistic vision of creation through the mediation of cosmic Christ and the cosmic Spirit in the original, continuous, and new creation in unity as *creatio ex nihilo*. Here, the concept of the fundamental contingency of creation is important in the matrix of creation–the work of the Son and the Spirit as the two hands of the Father.

In the subsequent sections, I present from a holistic perspective of reality how the universe is seen as the locus of the triune Creator's *kenotic* and *redemptive* panentheistic immanence through *creatio continua* toward the new creation. This interpretation enables the reader to find compatibility between God's creative act and the self-organizing universe that proceeds from the hot Big Bang through the accelerating expansion toward the cosmic death, *Freeze or Fry*.

This prevenient discourse sets the crucial stage for the remaining chapters where I perform a comparative study of the four interlocutors' schemes as to natural and cosmic theodicy and explore a trinitarian panentheistic vision of creation focusing on the diverse modes of divine creative and redemptive action as a response to natural and cosmic evil.

1. As I will discuss in chapter 3, the omnipotence of God does not have to be in a zero-sum relationship with creaturely freedom like Peacocke contends. Rather, I find Russell's non-zero-sum interpretation of the God-World relationship helpful as I will discuss in chapters 4 and 5.

Natural Evil Prevalent in All Dimensions of the Universe and in Biological Evolution

The problem of pain and suffering is not limited to human society. The problem of pain and suffering reaches to non-human creatures and has its origin in the physical level. The problem of evil is universal within creation.[2] To be more specific, in the physical level, the increase of entropy, according to the second law of thermodynamics, is analogous to the notion of evil in the physical level.[3] That is, open (or dissipative) systems within a closed system return to a state of equilibrium through taking energy from its environment. In this process, the entropy of the open systems decreases as they imbibe energy from their environment with limited resources. In contrast, the entropy of the environment increases. Thus, the increase of entropy means, on the one hand, the decrease in the availability of energy, and on the other hand, the increase of disorder.[4] The *instability* and *disorder* of entropy can be likened to evil, since evil is regarded as a state of death, disorder, and decay, and thus it is an "affront to hope and peace."[5]

The continuous increase of entropy within the universe is the fundamental cause for decease and decay. For that reason, entropy also constitutes the ultimate cause of the pain and suffering that results from the process of dying.[6] To be more specific, according to J. D. Hardy, "Pain results from noxious stimulation which indicates the beginning of damage to the pain fiber ending."[7] That is, individual living organisms with central nerve systems experience pain. They have sentience in different

---

2. Kärkkäinen, *Creation and Humanity*, 200-201.

3. Russell, *Cosmology*, 228.

4. Russell, *Cosmology*, 228-29.

5. Russell, *Cosmology*, 234-35. According to Robert Russell, the presence of entropy is inevitable and inherently prevalent in all open systems. Since this takes place to all open systems in the physical and biological levels, "universally all forms of life that we know are open systems." This demonstrates that the presence of suffering, death, and decay is not limited to the level of human life, but also covers the whole of the physical and biological levels of the cosmos. For my pneumatological approach to God's creative and saving presence in nature, refer to Shin, "Cosmic Spirit's Creatorship and Redeemership in the Context of Natural Theodicy."

6. I also discuss a similar account in my article, "Non-Anthropocentric Understanding of the Trinitarian Creatorship and Redeemership," 12-13. Here, I further develop the discussion by reinforcing supporting arguments and research results.

7. Hick, *Evil and the God of Love*, 297. Citing Hardy, "Pain Threshold and the Nature of Pain Sensation," 195.

degrees when they undergo parasitism, diseases, predation.[8] Their pain experience might not be directly connected with their pain sensation. However, the pain that is felt at the receptors does have biological values.[9]

For example, a cat feels pain when getting burned by fire as it mistakenly walks too closely to the source of the fire. This is evidenced by the cat avoiding fire next time due to the past painful experience. On the contrary, crabs might not feel pain when cutting off their claws to run away from their predators.[10] However, at other times, they are known to have sentience to experience physical pain due to damages to their bodies. In biology, the study of the pain felt by insects is highly complicated and ongoing. The topic is gaining more awareness of biologists in their research. For example, injured fruit flies undergo a continuing pain that is acute and chronic. Roughly fifteen years ago, biologists found that insects experience acute pain in response to extreme heat, cold, and physically damaging stimuli. According to a new study by Thang M. Khuong and his colleagues recently, fruit flies can experience chronic pain that lingers even after healing.[11]

On the other hand, according to a study by Julia Groening and her colleagues, amputation of honeybees' legs may lead to their suffering due to the deficiency of water and nourishment, while their experience of nerve pain is not apparent according to their experiment.[12] Yet, other research outcomes also report that injured honeybees tend to become more cautious in their navigation for food sources, and stop other bees when they approach the locations of predators.[13] That said, it is undeniable that the problem of physical pain is not significant only to humans

---

8. Southgate, "God and Evolutionary Evil," 804 [803–24].

9. A prefrontal lobotomy can influence an animal's pain sensations and different emotional responses to them. In so doing, a stimulus causes chemical excitement near the pain receptors but may lead to diversified experiences of suffering in kinds and degrees. Grantham, "Frontal Lobotomy for the Relief of Intractable Pain," 181–90.

10. For a recent biological account of crabs' pain and stresses, see https://www.sciencemag.org/news/2015/11/crabs-feel-pain.

11. According to Khuong et al., "Nerve Injury Drives a Heightened State of Vigilance and Neuropathic Sensitization in Drosophila," after the flies healed from their legs' injury due to extreme heat, they were observed to avoid an environment in a lower temperature even after healing. They were hypersensitive in their response to similar painful stimuli and tried to protect themselves.

12. Groening et al., "In Search of Evidence for the Experience of Pain in Honeybees."

13. Jack-McCollough and Nieh, "Honeybees Tune Excitatory and Inhibitory Recruitment Signaling to Resource Value and Predation Risk, 9–17.

and other vertebrate animals, but also to the other species of lower complexity like insects.

Furthermore, non-human animals are known to undergo psychological suffering even in their limited consciousness. Interestingly, lobsters are known to experience a sort of psychological stress when they are exposed to threats to life in their habitat.[14] The lobsters in a stress-level-measuring experiment showed different volumes of urine output and different compositions of their urine when they undergo stresses when they are isolated, threatened by predators, and experience drastic changes in the environment.

Not only these ordinarily experienced pain as the threat of death, but there is also mass extinction of species as part of natural selection in the process of evolution. There are "so many millions of species, each of which was an attempt on the part of the evolutionary process to establish a particular niche and many of which (like the dinosaurs) *had* to die for mammals to flourish."[15] The history of evolution is certainly "red in tooth and claw," as the title of Michael Murray's book says.[16] What is paradoxical is that the existence of death, pain, and suffering constitutes a launching pad for the birth and the conservation of new lives in our thermodynamic universe. In accordance with the second law of thermodynamics, it is impossible for anyone to flourish without some others' sacrifice. Without the death of the forerunners in the history of evolution, there is no emergence of new and more complex forms of life. In that sense, the physicist Richard Carlson writes:

> Starting with the products of the Big Bang, time, and the development of more and more complex entities, previously developed material in concert with the laws of the universe eventually resulted in the highest level of evolution. On Earth, given its finite size and resources and the need for millions of years to achieve this level, creaturely death is required as part of the process. In fact, it can be said that new life has always depended on the death of the now living.[17]

---

14. Bretihaupt et al., "Urine Release in Freely Moving Catheterized Lobsters with Reference to Feeding and Social Activities," 840–43.
15. Southgate, "God and Evolutionary Evil," 806.
16. Murray, *Nature Red in Tooth and Claw*.
17. Kärkkäinen, *Creation and Humanity*, 201. Citing his private email with Carlson (9/7/2013). Also see Kropf, *Evil and Evolution*, 100–128.

One may find hope in the good that the natural evil or evolutionary evil can bear. However, knowing what the final destiny of our entire universe and our planet Earth is, there may remain no hope for the future at all. That is, while the second law of thermodynamics is applied universally, according to the contemporary astrophysics, there are three basic options that are counted as valid based on Einstein's relativity theories. Namely, first, if we are in an open universe, the process of expanding leads to "freeze." Second, if the universe is "closed," then the expansion will reach the culmination point, and it will eventually contract until it results in "fry" in the Big Crunch. Lastly, if it is a "flat" curvature, it will expand forever and finally, reach the point of "freeze" in final heat death. In recent years, most scientists have become convinced that the open universe is a correct choice.[18]

Not only the far future of the universe as a whole, but our planet Earth is also predicted to face a catastrophic end at a certain point in the future. Specifically, modern sciences discovered numerous pieces of evidence that support the accounts of certain eventual life-ending and Earth-ending catastrophes. According to modern astrophysics, within the next five billion years, the Sun will witness its demise by becoming a red giant star and it will immerse the Earth, Mercury, and Venus, the three inner planets of the Sun in its red giant solar atmosphere.[19]

The Eclipse of Natural and Cosmic Theodicy in the Christian Tradition

Even though the prevalence of evil in the world raises a question concerning the goodness of a god in any religion, "The problem is particularly pressing for Abrahamic faiths that insist on God's fairness, love, and goodness."[20] In that sense, Kärkkäinen writes, "Rampant suffering and acts of evil in the world, both in relation to humanity (moral evil) and to nature (natural evil), constitute a major atheistic challenge concerning the existence of God."[21] I affirm, for this reason, that the problem of pain,

---

18. Russell, *Time in Eternity*, 57–61.

19. Stoeger, "Scientific Accounts of Ultimate Catastrophes in Our Life-Bearing Universe," 25. Also, see Russell, *Time in Eternity*, 60.

20. Kärkkäinen, *Creation and Humanity*, 194. Citing Andrew Linzey, *Christianity and the Rights of Animals*, 59.

21. Kärkkäinen, *Creation and Humanity*, 221.

suffering, death, and decay prevalent in the whole of the universe is to be taken into serious consideration, lest the Christian belief in the all-loving and all-powerful God should lose its persuasive force.[22]

However, in the Christian tradition, especially in the Western tradition, suffering, pain, and evil in nature have been given considerably little thought in the loss of cosmic Christology and pneumatology in the Christian tradition. The negligence of the cosmic dimensions of Christ and the Spirit are primarily due to the anthropocentric soteriology focused on the relationship among (a) God and the human soul, (b) the institutionalization of the saving grace of God,[23] and (c) the Cartesian mind-body dualism as well as the modern scientific naturalism and materialism.

The Humanocentric-Logocentric *Imago Dei*

First, the notion of *imago Dei* as human rationality is central to the anthropocentric understanding of God's redemptive work. Even though the patristic fathers did not neglect the significance of the body in the economy of salvation, they converged on the belief that the rationality of humanity is the image of God while the likeness of God is to be gained in perfection as the new creation comes to pass.[24] According to Athanasius,[25] John of Damascus,[26] Augustine,[27] and Aquinas,[28] human beings are the only rational animals as the image of God, who are endowed with the rational ability to envision the divine perfection and be brought into identity with the Logos.[29]

Likewise, Luther affirmed that Adam and Eve, the first humans enjoyed the ideal relationship with God without the fear of any harm or death before the loss of the image of God at the fall.[30] The fall of humans led to that of all other creatures. Here, the fate of non-human creatures

22. Also, see "Almighty Goodness" (chapter 2) of Kropf, *Evil and Evolution*, 29–36.

23. For a briefer account of the loss of the cosmic dimensions in pneumatology, see Shin, "Cosmic Spirit's Creatorship," 5–6.

24. Kärkkäinen, *Creation and Humanity*, 314.

25. Athanasius, *On the Incarnation of the Word*, #11–18. https://ccel.org/ccel/athanasius/incarnation/incarnation.iv.html.

26. John of Damascus, "Exposition of the Orthodox Faith," 2.12.

27. Augustine, *City of God*, 12.23.

28. Thomas Aquinas, *Summa Theologiae*, 1.93.7.

29. Grenz, *Social God and Relational Self*, 141–60.

30. Luther, *Luther's Works*, 1:61–63.

tends to be dependent on human beings. Calvin focused on the intelligence of human beings as a major faculty of the soul that marks them as the *imago Dei*, separating them from other creatures.[31] John Cobb points out that Calvin's claim that true and sound wisdom consists of two parts, "the knowledge of God and of ourselves,"[32] refers to "the human soul" rather than the whole of a human person embodied in the matrix of the material world in which all other creatures, including animals, are interrelated.[33]

These logocentric and humano-centric understandings of *imago Dei* render the saving economy of God anthropocentric. Even though the Reformers propose a doctrine of divine providence in nature, they rarely provide a robust discussion of the saving act of the Son and the Spirit for the sub-human creatures in their pain and suffering. Creation tends to be subsumed under the redemption of the human self.

The Institutionalization of the Spirit

According to José Comblin, especially in the Western tradition, the logocentric understanding of *imago Dei* is ultimately inseparable from the subordination of the Spirit under the Son in the Christian tradition in which the two divine Persons' mutual relationship is not properly respected due to Logos Christology's disjunction from Wisdom Christology.[34] To be more precise, whereas Logos Christology is originally Wisdom Christology and is as such a *cosmic* Christology,[35] traditionally, Logos Christology did not tend to be placed in proper conjunction with Wisdom Christology. The separation from Logos Christology from Wisdom Christology constituted a christological ground for the anthropocentric tendencies that have been prevalent in the Christian tradition.[36]

---

31. Calvin, *Institutes of the Christian Religion*, I.15.iii, 188–89.
32. Calvin, *Institutes of the Christian Religion*, I.1.i, 35.
33. Cobb, "All Things in Christ?," 173.
34. Comblin, *Holy Spirit and Liberation*, 13–15. Contra this tendency of the Western Church, a contemporary Eastern Orthodox theologian, Vladimir Lossky understands the work of Christ and the Spirit as the two dimensions of one divine economy as Irenaeus did. Rather than subordinating the Spirit under the Son, the two divine Persons are in mutual service. Lossy, *Mystical Theology of the Eastern Church*, 99–101.
35. Moltmann, *Way of Jesus Christ*, 282.
36. For this reason, traditional Christology attached no value to the presence of the Spirit in Jesus. It does violence to the fact that the ministry, passion, and resurrection

In contrast, there is "a link between the NT idea of Christ as the *Logos* and the [universally] creative power of the *dabar* of Yahweh."[37] Likewise, according to John 14:6, God reveals Godself to us in and through the Son or the Logos. God's creation through the Logos or the principle of creation includes all things that came into existence (John 1:4).

Yet, herein, we witness the contextualization of the early church in the formation of its theology since "theological tradition not only looked into the OT background but—as constructive theology has always done—also into the surrounding pagan resources."[38] Theological tradition appropriated the Middle-Platonic idea of *logos* according to which things were created in correspondence to the Ideas or divine *nous*. In this process, the OT idea of the word of God (*Dabar* of Yahweh) was regarded as "the divine intellect, which from all eternity contains within itself the images of things, the ideas" rather than all-enlivening dynamic breath of life.[39] Furthermore, due to the substance ontology adopted in the understanding of the relationships among the divine persons of the Trinity, the Spirit tended to be subsumed under the Son as the deity of the Spirit was understood as proceeding from the Son, rather than the dynamic mutuality between the Son and the Spirit was celebrated.

As Comblin appositely claims, the disconnection between the Spirit Christology and the Logos Christology eventually led to the ignorance of the cosmic role of the Spirit and the institutionalization of the Spirit for the sake of the salvation of a person's soul. [40] The Spirit was regarded as engaging with the inner piety of a believer through the celebration of the sacraments and the hearing of the word of God rather than understanding of the role of the Spirit as liberating the material world as a whole that is divorced from God.[41]

---

of Jesus are the work of the Spirit according to Scripture. Comblin, *Holy Spirit and Liberation*, 15.

37. Kärkkäinen, *Creation and Humanity*, 57.

38. Kärkkäinen, *Creation and Humanity*, 57.

39. Pannenberg, *Systematic Theology*, 2:25. Henceforth, *ST* II.

40. For the in-depth explanation of these two kinds of Christology and their relationship, refer to the next section on the cosmic dimensions of Christ and the Spirit.

41. Comblin, *Holy Spirit and Liberation*, 15. It was not until Vatican II that the Western churches began to rediscover the Creatorship of the Christ and the Spirit. On the contrary, in *Gaudium et Spes*, #37–#39, it is stated that not only humanity but also the earth is redeemed by Christ and renewed by the Spirit. This coheres with the Pauline literature that posits the new creation as a redeemed creation in unity, as can be seen in Romans 8. http://www.vatican.va/archive/hist_councils/ii_vatican_council/

The Cartesian Dualism and the Post-Enlightenment Materialism

The anthropocentric bent characteristic of the Christian tradition's development in the West certainly was influential to Descartes who understood the vitality of all living creatures as solely dependent on natural causes while also regarding the human body as a mechanism like a clock. However, what differentiated a human being from animals was his/her soul or "subject of consciousness."[42]

Thus, for Descartes, animals were merely insufferable automata, and the suffering of non-human creatures had to be removed from the theological discourse.[43] Also, after the Enlightenment, the cosmic dimension of Christian theology was even further eclipsed by the time of modern Classical Liberalism and the following Liberal Protestantism according to which Jesus was reduced to merely "a 'spiritual' teacher of personal piety."[44]

The "Cosmic" Dimensions of Christ and the Spirit in the Doctrine of *Creatio ex Nihilo*

In contrast with this anthropocentric bent developed later in the Christian tradition, biblical and patristic traditions are not foreign to the cosmic Christology and pneumatology. The retrieval of the universal Creatorship and Redeemership of Christ and the Spirit is "important both for the sake of interfaith hospitality and improving Christianity's self-understanding" in interdisciplinary dialogue, as the cosmic Christology and pneumatology constitute the basis of the doctrine of *creatio ex nihilo*.[45] Comparably, as Christology and pneumatology are placed in the cosmic dimension, the natural evil prevalent throughout the cosmos are taken into serious account as the creative and redemptive work of the Trinity certainly demands some theodical responses.

Based on the doctrine of *creatio ex nihilo*, since creation is ontologically dependent on God, God's creating act is not limited to the absolute beginning of all that is, but continues in divine providence towards the new creation. Even though the doctrine of *creatio ex nihilo* does not

---

documents/vat-ii_const_19651207_gaudium-et-spes_en.html.
  42. Badham, "Do Animals Have Immortal Souls?," 182.
  43. Badham, "Do Animals Have Immortal Souls?," 182–84.
  44. Kärkkäinen, *Creation and Humanity*, 58.
  45. Kärkkäinen, *Creation and Humanity*, 58.

consist in Scripture as a creedal form, it is biblically supported by both the OT and the NT. "While the first Genesis creation account could indeed depict creation as being a completed process, this must be set against the biblical affirmation of the continuing work of God (John 5:17) and the future hope of a new heaven and earth (Isa 65:17–19)."[46]

In Scripture, this continuing act of creation is grounded in the saving economy of God experienced in the history of Israel and the message, the ministry, the cross, and the resurrection of Jesus Christ. That is, the economic Trinity constitutes the ground of the Christian confession of *ex nihilo*. Thus, *creatio ex nihilo*, thus, is inherently trinitarian and has both creative and soteriological dimensions. As Irenaeus of Lyon affirms, "the original, continuous, and new creation constitute a panoramic drama of the Father, the Son, and the Spirit within one economy of salvation."[47] In that sense, Irenaeus employs a trinitarian approach to creation, rendering the Son and the Spirit "the two hands of God" in this process.[48]

In the same vein, Jürgen Moltmann understands the doctrine of *creatio ex nihilo* in a trinitarian grammar. In his trinitarian view of creation, Moltmann reclaims a cosmic Christology and a cosmic pneumatology. He contends that in consummating the new creation, God's continuously creative presence in the universe is an *ongoing* "messianic" liberation of the universe from the powers of death, violence, and cruelty, rather than merely preserving what God has created. In this regard, God continuously creates and redeems the universe and living creatures through the mediation of Christ and the Spirit that constitutes the ground of the contingency of creation.[49]

Supporting this idea, Alister McGrath claims that the doctrine of creation in the NT has a christological dimension and that it is instrumental to the development of the doctrine of *ex nihilo*. That is, the language of the OT creation narratives is jumbled up with the languages of "ordering" and "making." In the OT we see the interchangeable uses of "bringing into being" "imposing forms," and "assembling a structure."[50] The diversified terminology does not mean that the God of Israel competes with other deities and the intractable power of chaos. In contrast to the polytheistic

---

46. McGrath, *A Scientific Theology*, 1:184.

47. Shin, "Non-Anthropocentric Understanding of the Trinitarian Creatorship," 5.

48. Irenaeus, *Demonstration of the Apostolic Preaching*, 5–7. https://www.ccel.org/ccel/irenaeus/demonstr.iv.html. Also, see Gunton, *Triune Creator*, 166–71.

49. Moltmann, *God in Creation*, 94–98.

50. McGrath, *Scientific Theology*, 1:142.

creation myths, in the OT, especially in the prophetic tradition, chaos is put under control of the God of Israel in God's creation of order.[51]

According to the first Genesis creation narrative (1:1—2:4), the Creator is not dependent on pre-existing formless matter, but creation is contingent on God. Creation reflects the order of the all-powerful and all-loving Creator.[52] This creative power reflects Israel's experience of God's saving acts in cooperation with the contingent obedience of Israel and in accordance with God's covenant with Israel. This does not mean that creation is to be subsumed under the redemption of the people of God.

Rather, God's saving presence experienced in history reaches all the corners of creation. Similarly, while the redemptive act in history and the creative presence in nature are not subsumed under each other, they together represent the saving economy in God's creation.[53] The saving economy of salvation in the history of Israel is inseparable from God's ordering power in nature; nature as creation has its own rights apart from human beings, as can be seen especially in the Wisdom literature. This theology of nature is not to be reduced to merely the backdrop for God's saving of Israel.[54] According to Claus Westermann, in the OT, creation is not to be entirely subdued under soteriology.[55] Especially, the Wisdom literature tells us about God's continuous providential care of nature "rather than mythical origins, whereas the canonical creation theologies (Genesis, Isaiah, and some NT passages) subordinate creation under redemption."[56]

According to Walter Brueggermann, a new approach, namely, an eschatological or new-creation-centered paradigm in interpreting creation accounts of the OT, is taking place in the recent OT scholarship, challenging the old stance that creation is set only in the context of salvation history.[57] Herein, creation is regarded as God's continuous project rather than a means to the salvation of God's people.

Like in the OT, the vision of creation in the NT is also based on the saving act of God, but creation is not necessarily subsumed under

51. McGrath, *A Scientific Theology*, 1:148–49.

52. Küng, *Beginning of All Things*, 121–23.

53. Clifford, "Hebrew Scriptures and the Theology of Creation," 517–18.

54. Shin, "Non-Anthropocentric Understanding of the Trinitarian Creatorship," 4.

55. Westermann, *Creation*, 175.

56. Kärkkäinen, *Creation and Humanity*, 270.

57. Brueggermann, "Loss and Recovery of Creation in the Old Testament Theology," 177–90.

soteriology because of the cosmic dimensions of Christology and pneumatology in the NT. McGrath argues that in the Pauline literature and the gospels there is a christological dimension to the doctrine of creation which differentiates it from the OT's vision of creation. The christological dimension of the NT constitutes the ground of "a pattern of divine activity that is expressed in the doctrine of *creatio ex nihilo*."[58] In other words, the early Christians' confession of Jesus as the Son of Man constituted the basis of "the logocentric conception of creation."[59] Equivalently, the cosmic Christology of the NT (John 1:1–14; Col 1:15–19; Heb 1:2–4) speaks of "the integral link between Christ's role in creation and in reconciliation."[60]

I affirm that this cosmic Christology is inseparable from the cosmic pneumatology in the NT. When Christology is cosmic, pneumatology is to be cosmic as well.[61] In the OT, it is usual to portray the creative work of God in terms of wisdom. "At times, wisdom became almost hypostatized as well as feminized, looking quite like a personified agent of God (Prov 3:19; Jer 10:12; Matt 11:19)."[62]

The concept of wisdom in the OT breaks down into the Logos and the Spirit in the NT. Both the Logos and the Spirit, therefore, have cosmic dimensions just like the OT notion of wisdom. According to Moltmann, the Logos Christology is no substitute for Spirit Christology or Wisdom Christology, and must not supplant it.[63] Jesus Christ was empowered by the Spirit as the breath of life for all creatures, and after the cross and resurrection, the Spirit is the Spirit of Jesus Christ. It is the Spirit who makes universal not only the scope of the work of Christ but also the work of Christians for the world. In the NT the Spirit is more often used to describe the work of Christ of the believers in Christ. However, its matrix is the presence of the Spirit who effects the work of Christ in creation in general.[64] Likewise, the logos (the Word) and wisdom are alternatives in the writings of the church fathers like Theophilus of Antioch and Irenaeus.[65]

---

58. McGrath, *Scientific Theology*, 1:155.

59. McGrath, *Scientific Theology*, 1:156.

60. Kärkkäinen, *Creation and Humanity*, 58.

61. For example, for Ambrose, the Spirit creates the world just as the Father does. See his "On the Holy Spirit," 2.6.61.

62. Peters, *God—The World's Future*, 253.

63. Moltmann, *Way of Jesus Christ*, 74.

64. Moule, *Holy Spirit*, 19–21.

65. Theophilus of Antioch, "To Autoclycus," 2:15. Irenaeus, "Against Heresies," 4.7.4.

Likewise, Ted Peters writes, "[l]ike wisdom, the Logos organizes the creation, and like wisdom the Spirit [acts] as the life-giving power . . . Both are universal in scope."[66] According to 1 Peter 3:18, Jesus was put to death in the body and risen in the power of the Spirit. In Romans 8:11, Jesus Christ became the first fruit of the general resurrection. In Romans 8:21–23, the whole of creation awaits the resurrection in the power of the Spirit. The whole of creation awaits the resurrection in the Spirit in whose power Jesus rose from the dead. In that sense, the Spirit, as the pledge of the kingdom of God, is universal.[67]

For this reason, when Spirit Christology is dismissed, Christology loses a significance of the cosmic and kenotic dimensions that constitute the core beliefs in Christ within the biblical and patristic traditions.[68] For the patristic fathers, such as Clement of Alexandria, Origen, the Cappadocians, Maximus the Confessor, and many others, "[t]he Logos in His *kenosis*, His self-emptying, is hidden everywhere" in continuing creation through the ubiquitous life-giving presence of the Spirit.[69] Likewise, Terence Fretheim argues that the eschatological dimension of creation is to be brought back to the center in understanding creation. He contends that in the OT creation is a project that has its beginning, God's continuing providential care, and its consummation.[70] The trinitarian grammar of creation through the cosmic Christ and Spirit in the NT constituted the ground for the doctrine of creation *ex nihilo* against the dualistic Gnostics in the process of Christianity's expansion into the Hellenistic intellectual world of late classical antiquity.[71]

---

66. Peters, *God—The World's Future*, 253.

67. Moltmann, *Way of Jesus Christ*, 45. For his discussion of the relationship between Logos Christology and Spirit Christology, see Moltmann, *Way of Jesus Christ*, 73–78.

68. Pinnock, *Flame of Love*, 91–92.

69. Knight, "Theistic Naturalism and the Word Made Flesh," 60.

70. Fretheim, *God and World in the Old Testament*, 3–13.

71. For example, in the controversy between Valentinians and Irenaeus, Irenaeus affirmed that "God did not enter into or act to redeem an alien world to redeem." McGrath, *A Scientific Theology*, 1:162. Citing Irenaeus, *Against Heresies*, 2.10.2–4. McGrath understands that Irenaeus made a direct connection between creation and redemption. Unlike the dualistic Gnostics, Irenaeus affirmed that the Redeeming God of the NT created the world *ex nihilo*, rather than creating the world with the intractable pre-existing matter. This Christian development of *ex nihilo* is differentiated from the Jewish tradition where *ex nihilo* was one interpretation among many while it is "debatable whether Judaism developed a doctrine of *creatio ex nihilo* at this stage or even later." McGrath, *Scientific Theology*, 1:160. Also, for the diverse approaches to this matter, see http://www.jewishencyclopedia.com/articles/4730-creation.

However, in Christian tradition, there is a tendency to subsume creation under reconciliation. John Calvin, for instance, advanced the idea of *"duplex cognitio Domini."* According to this idea, we have the twofold knowledge of God: the Creator on the one hand and the Redeemer on the other.[72] In separating the saving work of the Son and the Spirit from the non-human realm of God's creation, one runs the risk of making "a duality within the economy of salvation."[73] When this takes place, the saving work of the triune Creator through the mediation of the Son and the Spirit tends to be focused on the salvation of the human souls and become anthropocentric.

I think that this view does not befit the trinitarian nature of the Christian doctrine based on the NT's cosmic Christology and pneumatology. Creation should not be excluded from the trinitarian economy of salvation.[74] The cross and the bodily resurrection of Christ tell us the genuine value of creation. By the same token, Gunton laments the Western inclination "to subordinate creation to redemption" because it transpires that "the status of the material world as a whole is endangered."[75] The genuine value of creation is to be seen within the trinitarian history that encompasses *creatio originalis, creatio continua, and creatio nova.*

Accordingly, when the doctrine of creation *ex nihilo* is understood in a trinitarian framework as discussed above, creation as a whole comes into the focus of the continuous saving economy of the Trinity toward the new creation. That is, the soteriological implications of Christ's cross and resurrection and the Spirit as the pledge of the new creation become central in the doctrine of creation.

For this reason, I agree with Moltmann when he understands the doctrine of *creatio ex nihilo* in a trinitarian grammar as he takes a soteriological approach to creation. In his trinitarian view of creation, Moltmann reclaims a cosmic Christology and a cosmic pneumatology and contends that in consummating the new creation, God's continuously creative presence in the universe is an on-going "messianic" liberation of the universe from the powers of death, violence, and cruelty.[76]

72. Downey, *The Knowledge of God in Calvin's Theology*, 41–52.
73. McGrath, *Fine-Tuned Universe*, 64.
74. McGrath, *Fine-Tuned Universe*, 77–82.
75. Gunton, *Triune Creator*, 165.
76. Moltmann, *God in Creation*, 94–96.

As one can see in the first Genesis creation narrative (1:1—2:4), human beings have a special meaning and purpose as the *imago Dei* within creation as God's vice-regents (Gen 1:26–27). However, God also declares all other creatures as good. Furthermore, they have their own values even before human beings have been created (Gen 1:4, 10, 12, 18, 21, 25). As the ground of all values, God gives them their intrinsic values.[77] If so, it is theologically more plausible to regard the redemptive love of the triune Creator as inclusive of creation as a whole rather than regard creation as merely the background of the reconciliation of human beings, the *imago Dei*.

The Universe as an Emergent Locus of the "Purposeful" Creation of the Triune Creator

I agree with Pannenberg that if the universe is the creation of God, it cannot be fully understood by natural sciences without God. In other words, if the universe can be perfectly understood without God, how can God be the One who creates it *ex nihilo*?[78] In that sense, theology (in particular, a Christian theology of nature) is to embrace and explain "the overall patterns of ordering that are discerned in the universe" under the theme of the triune God while natural sciences seek to provide a detailed explanation of their subject matters.[79]

While the biosphere of the Earth that belongs to the universe is finely tuned for the emergence of life, the history of both is still unfinished, just as theologically speaking, God's creation is not finished until the new creation. Furthermore, as McGrath says, because of the fallen nature of our human minds and the structures and patterns of the world, our knowledge of the universe as God's creation can never be complete.[80]

Therefore, dissonance may consistently appear, but through it, we can reach a deeper level of consonance in a mutual dialogue between natural sciences and theology. That said, before discussing the problem of natural and cosmic evil as well as divine creative and redemptive action in the biosphere and the cosmic construct as its context, I explore how biological evolution on the planet can be seen as the way through which

---

77. Wright, *Mission of God*, 397–400.
78. Pannenberg, *Toward a Theology of Nature*, 16.
79. McGrath, *Scientific Theology*, 3:195.
80. McGrath, *Scientific Theology*, 1:175.

God creates life. I think this task is imperative for building a robust natural and cosmic theodicy because a discussion of "purposeful" creation constitutes a context for the discussion of creative divine action amidst natural and cosmic evil.

Chance, Regularity, and Directionality Inherent in the Universe and Biological Evolution

According to contemporary natural sciences, the chronology of our universe briefly goes as follows: 1) the Big Bang event began roughly 13.7 billion years ago; 2) the formation of the Earth was completed about 4.5 billion years ago, and the congealment of the Earth's crust took place about 3.8 billion years ago; 3) the first life appeared on the earth about 4 billion years ago; 4) the dinosaur roamed around the face of our planet from 180 million to 63 million years ago; 5) *Homo erectus*, the proto-human, thrived between 600,000 and 350,000 years ago; and 6) *Homo sapiens* appeared about 100,000 years ago.[81]

In this chronology, the universe continues to develop and expand in the complex interplay between regularities and chance.[82] Unlike Newtonian and Laplacian mechanistic physics, contemporary physics and biology appreciate the openness of nature to the emergence of novelty and complexity according to contemporary quantum mechanics, chaos theory, and the second law of thermodynamics. Therefore, the cosmos and the biosphere of our planet are continuously self-organizing.[83] Here, in the emergence of higher levels of complexity, the role of non-linear dissipative open systems[84] is significant. The emergent systems interact with each other, and

---

81. Peters, *God—The World's Future*, 133.

82. Peacocke, *Theology for a Scientific Age*, 44–71.

83. Self-organization is a central notion of systems science. It means the ability of a class of systems to change their internal structure and/or their function in response to external circumstances. Self-organization is achieved by the growth of the internal space-time complexity of a system, along with the layered or hierarchical structures or behaviors, through dynamic and spontaneous interactions among developmental systems. The modern concept about self-organization began from the foundation of cybernetics in the 1940s. Yet, later, the idea was adopted in physics and now pervades in biology and other disciplines. Banzhaf, "Self-Organizing Systems." 1–16. http://www.cs.mun.ca/~banzhaf/papers/article3.pdf.

84. A non-linear dissipative system (a thermodynamically open system) behaves contingently. If their excess entropy production (E) is below 0, a system "may or may not resist change during fluctuations." This takes place in *all open systems* in the physical

there emerge new levels of novelty out of chaos in those interactions, indicating that they are interrelated and interdependent.

According to Ilya Prigogine, dissipative systems radically differ from the stabilized systems in equilibrium in terms of energy flow through matter.[85] A closed system is in equilibrium in terms of the flow of energy and matter, but an open system is far from equilibrium. Thus, a new order can spontaneously and irreversibly develop in the system of non-equilibrium.[86] That is, under the right conditions, the fluctuations are not stifled, but rather amplified "so that the system changes its whole structure to a new ordered state in which it can again become steady and imbibe energy and matter from the outside and maintain its new structured form"[87] Here, the newly emerging forms are irreducible to the entities of the lower levels. The novel properties of an emergent form are larger than the sum of the parts that belong to those at a lower level of complexity.

In this process, gradually increasing complexity enables the emergence of self-replicating macromolecular systems that are capable of receiving information from their environment and reacting to external information so as to transform the environment. This means that in the history of the Earth, dissipative systems played a key role in the emergence of living organisms. In the increase of complexity, organisms became able to receive and respond to the information from their environment more effectively by developing sentience, enabling them to survive longer. In increasing survivability, organisms also generally became larger and more energetically intensive.[88]

While a dissipative system's thermodynamic fluctuations in the microscopic level are probabilistic and accordingly unpredictable, they are still not separable from physical and chemical theories that govern the macro-level phenomena.[89] In other words, random mutations in DNA can affect the ability of an organism to procreate. Ultimately, in the

---

levels. Also, "universally all forms of life that we know are open systems, and hence all are subject to these kinds of thermodynamic contingencies." Russell, *Cosmology*, 245.

85. Prigogine and Stenger, *Order Out of Chaos*. Also, see Peacocke, "Chance and Law," 134–37.

86. Prigogine and Stenger, *Order Out of Chaos*, 139–42.

87. Peacocke, "Chance and Law," 135.

88. McGrath, *Fine-Tuned Universe*, 186.

89. Peacocke, "Chance and Law," 124–25.

The Significance of Natural and Cosmic Theodicy

environment, the persistence of novel organisms is subject to the law of natural selection that constrains their survivability in extended duration.[90]

In the same vein, Charles Darwin introduced the mechanism of evolution: random variations and natural selection. Neo-Darwinian synthesis tells us how the random mutations take place in DNA and their results are inherited through the interplay of chance and law.[91] Through the deep time of the universe and the geological and evolutionary time of the Earth, evolution took place through the gradual increase of complexity. However, more recently Stephen Gould and Niles Eldredge also suggested that there was *punctuated equilibrium*, which explains why there are periods with intensive variation within populations and the gaps in the fossil records.[92] In other words, the emergence of higher complexity is that the process should not be considered developmental in a linear manner.

Furthermore, biological evolution through natural selection, at face value, only shows innumerable emergent species' successes and failures in surviving. In other words, natural selection is "directed to the goal of increasing reproductive efficiency."[93] Yet natural selection itself "does not properly claim that more complex organisms will be favoured."[94] At times, surviving species could be more persistent while remaining less developed in terms of complexity.[95]

If so, do contemporary scientific cosmology and evolutionary biology defeat this portrayal of nature as God's purposeful creation? Would it be necessary to contend that evolutionary history is sheerly accidental? First of all, natural sciences do not provide an answer to the "metaphysical" question as to biological evolution's ultimate telos. Moreover, chance events in nature are not purely happenstance. Rather, they are constrained by laws and tend to show directionality in evolution even when the actualization of the laws of nature takes place contingently. According to contemporary evolutionary biology, there is "local adaptive purpose of natural selection."[96] The mutations of DNA randomly take place. Even

---

90. Peacocke, *Paths from Science Towards God*, 73–76.

91. McGrath, *Fine-Tuned Universe*, 171–76.

92. Refer to Gould, *Punctuated Equilibrium*; Eldridge and Gould, "Punctuated Equilibria," 82–115.

93. McGrath, *Fine-Tuned Universe*, 187.

94. Ward, *God, Chance and Necessity*, 69.

95. Schloss, "From Evolution to Eschatology," 71–75.

96. In evolutionary biology, telenomy means the intelligible notion of contingent finality in the process of evolution. For instance, "when an organic structure appears

so, there are certain potential patterns of development constrained by the macro-level environment governed by regularities.[97] The directionality of evolution involves a complex orchestration of random events and regularities.[98] Therefore, one cannot merely predict an endpoint of evolution. However, evolution is not purely random but unfolds within the bounds of regularities.

This long history of evolution can be regarded as having a directionality toward the emergence of *Homo sapiens* through the complex interplay of chance and law. When they emerged in the long history of biological evolution, they are distinct from other species by virtue of their strong individualization, their ability to monitor and alter their environment for their own purposes, their use of language, and their elaborate socialization.[99] More importantly, they are marked by their symbolic thoughts and their reflective self-consciousness, through which they can develop a thematic relationship with God.[100] The emergence of *Homo sapiens* is the result of the soul-making process of evolution full of innumerable trials and errors.

Our Universe Finely-Tuned for Life and Consciousness

Moreover, from a theological perspective, the consonance between the evolution of the universe and *creatio continua* may gain more persuasive force due to the recent scientific notion of "the fine-tuning of the universe" as "the anthropic principle." That is, the universe can be regarded as developing toward the emergence of intelligent, self-conscious, and religious creatures like human beings. To be more specific, the universe is finely tuned in terms of its universal constants and initial conditions.[101]

These universal constants include the four areas: "space and time ('Planck minimums,' speed of light, and so forth); energy (four

---

to be finalized in relation to a certain function." Bailly and Longo, "Causes and Symmetries in Natural Sciences," 198–200 [199].

97. McGrath, *Fine-Tuned Universe*, 184–87; Peters and Hewlett, *Evolution from Creation to New Creation*, 25–28.

98. Peacocke, "Chance and Law," 134–37.

99. Peacocke, *Theology for a Scientific Age*, 72.

100. Peacocke, *Paths from Science Towards God*, 78–81.

101. Spitzer, *New Proofs for the Existence of God*, 50. See for a detailed list, McGrath, *Fine-Tuned Universe*, 119–21. Also, see Davies, "Teleology without Teleology," 157–58.

The Significance of Natural and Cosmic Theodicy

fundamental forces: gravitational, electromagnetic, strong nuclear, and weak nuclear force); and large-scale and fine-structure constants (total visible rest mass and a number of other constants such as the Hubble constant and cosmological constant)."[102] Here, "a critical element has to do with the initial conditions of these constants, which determine the possibility of the emergence of life and consciousness in the universe."[103] Thus, the physicist Freeman Dyson writes, "[T]he more I examine the universe and study the details of its architecture, the more evidence I find that the universe in some sense must have known that we were coming."[104]

However, this is not a crystal-clear signal of the emergence of life and consciousness as one considers that there is not only one possible interpretation. To be more specific, the fine-tuning universe with the anthropic principle is presented in two forms of "the Strong Anthropic Principle" (SAP) and "the Weak Anthropic Principle" (WAP). For those who stick to the SAP, "*Intelligent life must exist in the universe; it is a necessity*," whereas for those who stick to the WAP, "*We can observe the universe from places and times where intelligent life can exist.*"[105]

According to the WAP, we cannot know all kinds of possible laws and initial conditions that can exist in the universe. Nor can we be sure of whether this life-nesting fine-tuned aspect of the universe, as we observe it, applies to restricted regions or to the whole of the universe homogeneously. Yet this stance indicates that the constants cannot vary too much from what we observe. Furthermore, according to this stance, we are not even sure of whether such a current state of the universe is an initial state or if there were other prevenient phases.[106] For these reasons, the WAP does not give a sweeping statement that it is necessary to bear living creatures and self-conscious ones like human beings in this universe.

According to the SAP, intelligent life is necessary for the consistency of quantum mechanics, since some of its formulations rely on the

---

102. Kärkkäinen, *Creation and Humanity*, 140–41. Also, for a recent update on this, refer to "Introduction to the Constants for Nonexperts" of National Institute of Standards and Technology Reference on Constants, Unit, and Uncertainty. http://physics.nist.gov/cuu/Constants/background.html.

103. Davies, "Teleology without Teleology," 157–58.
Cited in Shin, "Non-Anthropocentric Understanding of the Trinitarian Creatorship," 7.

104. Dyson, *Disturbing the Universe*, 250.

105. Murphy and Ellis, *On the Moral Nature of the Universe*, 52.

106. Murphy and Ellis, *On the Moral Nature of the Universe*, 52.

concept of an observer. Ellis and Murphy point out that, in this stance, some problems arise.[107] That is, considering diverging interpretations of quantum mechanics we cannot jump to such a conclusion. Quantum features according to the differing interpretations are not consistent; thus, it cannot necessarily lead to the conclusion of the SAP. Furthermore, even when we accept the necessity of quantum mechanics, we cannot be sure of why it is required and if there had been other prevenient phases.

Hence, it seems that the WAP is more acceptable than the SAP. Even so, I think that it does not weaken the possibility of mutual dialogue between natural sciences and theology regarding the life-nesting universe and its theological implications. There still remains the question of "why" only in certain parts of the universe life forms emerge and eventually self-conscious creatures appear on the scene of evolutionary history. Furthermore, in this scheme, we are not sure of why there exist transient phases that lead to the one phase where self-conscious and religious creatures emerge.

In chapter 5, the most constructive chapter, I discuss that various quantum cosmologies seem to eliminate room for a theological discussion of *creatio ex nihilo*. However, I affirm that they cannot be used to deny the fundamental contingency of our universe as well as the biosphere of the Earth. I discuss in the following chapters that adopting Einstein's special theory of relativity, one can speak of God's continuous creative involvement in spacetime from the perspective of the eschatological new creation.

Theistic Evolution as a "Metaphysical" Choice

If this is the case, one may ask: "Does this prove a divine design?" I think that the contingency of our universe and the biosphere of the Earth alone do not prove the Creator as the triune God as revealed in the economy of salvation. Thus, it does not prove a divine purpose for creation. There are different kinds of naturalisms that can be metaphysically conceived. I discuss here three different sorts of naturalisms: atheistic naturalism, soft naturalism, and methodological naturalism. While naturalism does not make room for immaterial agents within the web of natural causes, neither does it exclusively champion reductive physicalism, nor reductive

---

107. Murphy and Ellis, *On the Moral Nature of the Universe*, 53. Citing Barrow and Tipler, *Anthropic Principle*; Isham, "Quantum Gravity," 99–129.

materialism, since they are metaphysical choices that go beyond the scope of natural sciences.

An ethical or theological meaning-making is not necessarily precluded, but it is to be continuously posited in consonance with sciences' accounts of their subject matters. There can be theological or metaphysical interpretations as to the ultimate purpose for the natural processes.[108] In other words, religious and ethical values supervene on the lower levels of the epistemic hierarchy of disciplines, but the former cannot be entirely reduced to the latter. That said, atheistic naturalism as a *metaphysical* interpretation is one of the options to choose as can be seen in the "atheistic naturalism" of Steven Gould, Richard Dawkins, and Jacques Monod.[109] Without being atheistic or anti-theistic, there still can be "soft naturalism"[110] that neither rejects religion nor accepts a transcendent Creator, as can be seen in the naturalistic ideas of Karl Peters and Ursula Goodenough, who identify the Creator with the process of nature itself.[111] Furthermore, there can be agnostic, yet anti-materialistic, naturalism that is skeptical of the neo-Darwinian reductionistic explanation of the origin of life and evolution while it still may remain atheistic, as is seen in the idea of Thomas Nagel.[112] For Nagel, mind and consciousness is not to be excluded from the realm of science since it is an irreducible and integral dimension of reality.

As discussed above, it is not self-evident that we can speak of the existence of the Creator on the basis of the scientific accounts of the order of nature. Still, as one adopts *methodological* naturalism rather than *metaphysical* naturalism, there can be a genuinely theistic interpretation of nature. For example, in his theistic naturalism, Peacocke affirms that everything in nature evolves in emergence and that the emergent levels of

---

108. Flanagan, "Varieties of Naturalism," 430–32, 444–49.

109. For example, see Gould, *Wonderful Life*; Monod, *Chance and Necessity*; Dawkins, *Selfish Gene*.

110. Haught, *Is Nature Enough?*, 7–8. For Haught, "soft naturalism" is distinguished not only from hard naturalism or scientific naturalism but also from sunny naturalism. "Sunny naturalists hold that nature's overwhelming beauty, the excitement of human creativity, the struggle to achieve ethical goodness, the prospect of loving and being loved, the exhilaration of scientific discovery—these are enough to fill a person's life. There is simply no good reason to look beyond nature for spiritual contentment." Haught, *Is Nature Enough?*, 10.

111. Peters, *Dancing with the Sacred*, 1, 30–37, 47–48. Goodenough, *Sacred Depths of Nature*, 11–12, 171.

112. Nagel, *Mind and Cosmos*.

reality cannot be reduced down to the lower ones.[113] Likewise, there can exist a Creator who creates the world as a whole *ex nihilo* while continuing to create through the established order of nature without violating it.

The continuing creative work of God can be found in a "stronger" version of emergence that all the four interlocutors of this work adopt. That is, first, "new things emerge in natural history, not just new properties of some fundamental things or stuff." Second, "these emergent things exercise their own types of causal power. Such 'downward causation' occurs at many different levels in nature," while the emergent levels are causally irreducible to the lower levels.[114]

On the contrary to weak emergence, according to which the physical closure of reality is ontologically deterministic, the emergence of novelty according to strong emergence does not necessarily have to fall into physical reductionism. As Murphy maintains in her irreducible physical monism, while reality is ontologically physical in that the physical level constitutes the fundamental level of reality, the emergent levels of reality are not causally reductive to the physical level.[115] Likewise, as will be discussed in the following chapters of this work, a reductionistic-deterministic sort of physicalism does not sit well with the self-organizing of life in evolution according to contemporary developmental biology.

That said, even a stronger version of emergence cannot guarantee divine action as it can end up in *reductionistic materialism*.[116] However, I think that when the order of nature is open to genuine emergence, it is metaphysically possible to extend the downward causation to divine action. "Nature is not a codified concept that stays exclusive to only one sort of exposition."[117] Rather, nature is a metaphor that invites a diversity of interpretations. Accordingly, nature can be understood differently by both atheist and theist perspectives.[118]

---

113. I further discuss his idea of emergent evolution in ch. 3.

114. Clayton, *Adventures in the Spirit*, 73. Also, see his *Mind and Emergence*, 4–7. For instance, ants have been found to creatively integrate and use their experiential data in finding their paths to their food even when their surroundings have changed. They learn and unlearn their knowledges of their environment in making choices. For the details, see Zeil et al., "Looking and Homing: How Displaced Ants Decide Where To Go." https://www.ncbi.nlm.nih.gov/pmc/articles/PMC3886322/. Cited in Shin, "Non-Anthropocentric Understanding of the Trinitarian Creation," 8.

115. See Murphy, *Bodies and Souls, or Spirited Bodies?*.

116. Kärkkäinen, *Creation and Humanity*, 322–24.

117. Shin, "Non-Anthropocentric Understanding of the Trinitarian Creatorship," 9.

118. McGrath, *Scientific Theology*, 1:110–32.

In my view, there can be an empirical fit between a scientific theory and a theological doctrine of creation in which each helps the other understand reality more fully by illuminating different levels of reality.[119] That is, natural sciences investigate their subject matters *a posteriori* through the *tradition-mediated* research methods. Likewise, the Christian doctrine of *creatio ex nihilo* is a product of *a posteriori* investigation of reality through christological reasoning within the Christian tradition, as I discussed in the previous section.[120] Given the fact that they constitute different aspects of reality, both need each other as dialogue partners for the sake of a fuller understanding of the creation of God and the Creator.

Polkinghorne's understanding of the relationship between theology and science is grounded in the fact that both theology and science depend on motivated beliefs that are mediated by traditions and by communal discernment and can be put in a mutual metaphorical relationship. "If science and theology are colleagues in the common quest for truth, then they will have cousinly gifts to offer to each other."[121] If both are indeed truth-seeking endeavors, there must be "a mutually respectful interaction between the insights of the two."[122] In that sense, for Polkinghorne, the recognition of "continuities and discontinuities" between science and theology is significant in an interdisciplinary dialogue between theology and science.

Whereas theology (in particular, a Christian theology of nature) embraces and explains "overall patterns of ordering that are discerned in the universe" under the triune God, natural sciences provide the detailed explanation of their subject matters.[123] In this manner, theology and science constitute different levels of the epistemic hierarchy of disciplines, and accordingly, there can be consonance between theology and natural sciences when it comes to interpreting the universe as the triune God's creation.

Noting the fundamental contingency of an evolutionary process that develops indeterminately yet under the constraint of regularities,[124]

---

119. McGrath, *Fine-Tuned Universe*, 57–60.

120. Polkinghorne, *Science and Theology*, 12–33. Also, see the third volume of McGrath, *Scientific Theology*, 3:193–97.

121. Polkinghorne, *Science and Religion in Quest of Truth*, 33.

122. Polkinghorne, *Science and Religion in Quest of Truth*, 22.

123. McGrath, *Scientific Theology*, 3:195.

124. Stoeger, "Immanent Directionality of the Evolutionary Process," 163–90; Davies, "Teleology without Teleology," 151–62.

we can speak of the Creator who continuously and purposefully creates the world. On the contrary, when the Aristotelian idea of the fixity of nature is integrated into the interpretation of Scripture like we see in the traditional doctrine of creation, the idea of continuous creation through evolution can be called into question. However, I think the creation of all things does not have to be a one-time event to be God's purposeful act.[125]

The Fundamental Contingency of Creatures in a Trinitarian Framework of Creation

In this theistic interpretation, the concept of mediated creation is significant. By understanding the trinitarian framework of creation as the Father's work mediated by the Son and the Spirit, one can speak of purposeful divine agency in the contingent development of the universe and biological evolution. To be specific, according to Gunton, creation through the mediation by the Son and the Spirit in a trinitarian framework of creation means that creatures are given by God their relative freedom.[126]

In that freedom, creatures have their contingent agency in temporally finite existence that makes them ontologically distinct from God while being dependent on God since God creates them *ex nihilo*. That is, the Son serves as the principle of differentiation among creatures or independence. The Spirit gives existence and life to contingent creatures while persistently calling them into the unity with the Father through the Son, the principle of creation. This sort of a mediated creation is found in the doctrines of creation of Irenaeus, Athanasius, the Cappadocian Fathers, and Luther, for example.[127]

In a mediated way of creation, creatures are granted independence, contingency, and freedom as finite beings in distinction from other creatures and God.[128] Here the intra-trinitarian nature of diversity-in-unity

---

125. McGrath, *Fine-Tuned Universe*, 104–6.

126. Likewise, for Pannenberg, first, creatures are given independence from God and other creatures in their temporal finitude of flowing time. That is, their temporal existence is unnecessary, and its duration is limited. Second, accordingly, creatures are contingent in terms of their becoming and acting in openness to the horizons of the future. "Only in the process of time can a finite being act and thus manifest itself as the center of its own activity." Pannenberg, *ST* II, 95.

127. Gunton, *Triune Creator*, 66–73, 146–54.

128. I briefly discuss this in Shin, "Non-Anthropocentric Understanding of the

The Significance of Natural and Cosmic Theodicy

in love serves as the ontological ground and the goal of the existence of all creatures. Therefore, creatures' mutual respect of each other's independence-in-dependence becomes a norm of creaturely existence. The mediated creation in a trinitarian framework affirms the genuine value of the material world in contrast to the neo-Platonic emanationism and the Thomistic hylomorphism where creatures are placed in the fixed hierarchy of being in terms of perfection in a soul-body dualistic framework.[129]

In working through the contingency of creatures, God's providential presence in creation is not fully deterministic while all the creaturely potentials are granted by and known to God. God gives creatures the relative yet genuine freedom to lead their lives contingently, which is the way through which God continues to work in creation.[130] This idea of mediated creation significantly contributes to a shift from the ontology of unchanging being to that of being in contingent becoming in the matrix of the creative field of the Spirit who creates *ex nihilo*. Likewise, as Luther maintains, "what is central to Christian theology of creation [is], that creation is to be understood not only as God's address *to* but also *through* the creature."[131]

For Luther, this notion of creation speaks of both God's freedom and love. In God's creation, all things are given their independent and contingent existence by the "generous God" who is "categorically the [O]ne who gives."[132] In providence, God continues to be a faithful Creator by sustaining and working through their relatively independent order and contingency that are ontologically grounded in the rationality of the triune Creator. In that sense, whereas the Greek philosophers regarded contingency as "a defect of being,"[133] in the suggested trinitarian framework of mediated creation, the contingency of creation invites us to explore "contingent rationality" as "a quest for rationality inhering in the order of space and time, not beyond it."[134]

Trinitarian Creatorship," 11. Here, I develop the discussion further by engaging with more theological and biblical resources.

129. Gunton, *Triune Creator*, 147–51.

130. Gunton, *Triune Creator*, 149.

131. Gunton, *Triune Creator*, 149. Citing Bayer, *Schöpfung als Anrede*, 93.

132. Bayer, *Martin Luther's Theology*, 254. Cited in Shin, "Non-Anthropocentric Understanding of the Trinitarian Creatorship," 12.

133. Gunton, *Triune Creator*, 112.

134. Gunton, *Triune Creator*, 112–13. Citing Torrance, *Divine and Contingent Order*, 3–4. For Torrance, whereas God is infinite, creation is finite. Yet creation reflects

This notion of creation as a trinitarian mediated act is significant for understanding the "relation-in-otherness" of creatures, as the Son is the One in whom "all things hold together," (Col 1:17), and the Spirit is the One who "achieves the creation's true plurality by relating the 'many' to the Father through the Son."[135] The Spirit is the One through whom the incarnation of the Son became possible. Likewise, the Spirit serves the mediatory role of relating all the embodied creatures to the Father. The Spirit creates genuine plurality in creation as the Son serves as the principle of creation or the Logos. This idea enables us to shift from the analogy of being to the analogy of relations that renders creation as neither deterministic nor mechanistic, but dynamic and relational.[136]

In this theistic interpretation of nature, God acts creatively in the world through "chance" that is inherent within the "order" of nature. Thereby, *creatio continua* becomes possible by God's act of creating through the interplay of chance and regularities "operating within the created order."[137] Since the order of nature does not exist necessarily but contingently, God gives existence to what exists in duration. In this continuously creative process, God brings into existence the diversity of species and humanity as *imago Dei*. In this approach, one can honor "both God's sovereign freedom and the integrity of the phenomenal universe and its physical laws."[138] Creating the world *ex nihilo*, God continues to be the Creator in *creatio continua*, and evolution can be regarded as the way through which God creates.

I regard this approach as coherent with the purposeful creation of God as depicted in the first Genesis creation account (Gen 1:1—2:4). Whereas in this passage the creation of each kind is immediately dependent on God's creating act, in evolutionary theory diverse species emerge from their predecessors. This discrepancy led to theologians' concern about Darwinian evolution through natural selection. However, we can find God's continuously creative presence in the evolutionary process that is contingent and open to the future.[139] Importantly, the sequential emergence in that process is not alien to the Genesis creation account,

---

the rationality of the Creator even though it does only in contingency.

135. Gunton, *Triune Creator*, 143.
136. Moltmann, *God in Creation*, 75–77.
137. Peacocke, "Naturalistic Christian Faith," 18.
138. McFarland, *Creation and Humanity*, 429.
139. Pannenberg, *Toward a Theology of Nature*, 44–48.

since the creation of different kinds of creatures is dubbed as the "generations of the heavens and the earth" (Gen 2:4). This continuous creation is a trinitarian work as Irenaeus dubs the Son and the Spirit as the *two hands* of the Father in creating the world.[140]

All in all, by affirming *creatio ex nihilo*, we can theologically posit that God continues to create through natural processes that God continuously gives existence. The Father works through the mediation of the Son and the Spirit as his two hands. In this suggested trinitarian grammar, the Son is the Logos or the ground of the order of nature. The Spirit is the One who actualizes the order of the Logos as the cosmic Spirit. Thus, in the presence of the Spirit, the created order of nature brings forth new forms of life in genuine contingency through the interplay of law and chance inherent in the order of nature. Not only does the triune God create the cosmos *ex nihilo*, but God also perfects it through *creatio continua* and *creatio nova*. If so, the self-organizing universe should reflect the goodness and love of the triune Creator just as revealed in the economy of salvation according to Scripture.

A Call for a Robust Natural and Cosmic Theodicy

We meet a grave challenge here. As discussed in the beginning of this chapter, it is known that roughly 98 percent of all species in the history of evolution went extinct.[141] Furthermore, it is manifest that the entire history of evolution is ridden by death, pain, and suffering. According to the second law of thermodynamics, as the increase of entropy is the fundamental cause of death, it becomes the ultimate cause of the pain that results from death. Furthermore, our universe in its entirety as a closed non-linear system will reach the final point of *Freeze or Fry* due to general relativity theory and the second law of thermodynamics. Our planet will meet its end much earlier than the demise of our universe in the far future. Accordingly, I affirm that it is imperative to regard creation as a trinitarian project in which the cross and the resurrection of Christ constitute the soteriological significance for the whole of the creation.

According to Christopher Southgate, in the Christian faith, the doctrine of theodicy should tackle three different dimensions: "ontological,

---

140. Gunton, *Triune Creator*, 54.
141. Peters and Hewlett, *Evolution from Creation to New Creation*, 23, 118.

teleological, and soteriological."[142] First, the pain, suffering, and, death of all creatures should not be considered merely the privation of divine aesthetic perfection like in Augustine's theodicy. Rather, non-human creatures are exposed to real pain and suffering, even though their pain and suffering may be analogical to human beings' understanding. Second, as I discussed in the beginning of this chapter, while pain is the cause of suffering, suffering is experienced in different degrees by the ones who perceive pain. Yet the ultimate cause of both pain and suffering is death and decay that is universal in the life-bearing universe. The ever-increasing entropy is ambiguous in that it is instrumental for good while being at the same time intrinsically evil, as it is an affront to life, too. Then, if God is a loving Creator, the pain, suffering, and death must have purpose for a greater good. If they exist without the boundary of God's purposeful work, the Christian faith in God's all-powerful Creatorship encounters a question of dualism that threatens *creatio ex nihilo*. Third, all the pains and suffering are not teleological as we can see in the extinction of a whole species and the scientifically predicted demise of our universe. Fourth, there is suffering caused by contingent predations, and it is not necessary in the animal world. Finally, the sacrifices of other species necessary for the emergence of *Homo sapiens* raises a question about the goodness of God. If so, there should be the Creator's soteriological presence in the process of evolution of life through providence and the eschatological new creation.[143]

In that sense, I critically sympathize with a *developmental good-and-harm* analysis and a *property-consequence good-and-harm* analysis in constructing a natural theodicy. The former is exemplified by John Hick's developmental understanding of natural evil in his Irenaean-Schleiermacherian theodicy while the latter is represented by the free-will and free-process defenses in the Augustinian theodicy. To be more precise, as I will discuss in chapter 4 in detail, Russell adopts Reinhold Niebuhr's interpretation of Augustine's notion of moral evil and labels entropy as "the unnecessary but inevitable" byproduct of God's good creation.[144] However, such an Augustinian understanding of entropy becomes an insufficient interpretation, once we know that entropy serves an inevitable platform for God's continuous creation. For this reason, Russell finds the

142. Southgate, "God and Evolutionary Evil," 802–23.

143. Here, I further develop and elaborate my theodical argument discussed in Shin, "Non-Anthropocentric Understanding of the Trinitarian Creatorship," 16.

144. Russell, *Cosmology*, 226.

Irenaean theodicy complementary in more fully understanding the nature of entropy from a theological perspective.

For Hick, in understanding the presence of evil in creation merely as the privation of good, the Augustinian theodicy risks impersonalizing the *dynamic* relations among creatures through which birth and growth of new life take place.[145] Augustine does not neglect the empirical aspect of evil in his theodicy. However, evil does not have an ontological status in the context of "the principle of plenitude"[146] that reflects the perfection and goodness of God. Hick is concerned that such a view of evil leads to the problem of absolving God of the ultimate responsibility for what takes place in God's beloved creation.[147]

Thus, evil is a developmental obstruction that God works through, rather than merely the privation of good. While permitting contingent and inevitable existence of evil in creation, God as the One who creates *ex nihilo* brings good out of evil. In that sense, our experience of pain and suffering is instrumental and consequential to our physical and mental growth. God empowers us to learn from the pain and suffering and mature. However, in Augustine's theodicy, this *means-end* argument is not central. In my view, Hick's teleological understanding of pain and suffering is helpful to a theological interpretation of contemporary cosmological and evolutionary theories from the perspective of the trinitarian framework of continuous creation suggested in this work. Unlike Augustine, Irenaeus regards evil as not only contingent but also purposeful in God's creative interaction with creation. That is, through struggling "we have the possibility of maturing into the full manifestation of our relationship to God and of ultimately taking on a genuine likeness to God."[148] Thus, evil is developmental obstruction rather than the privation of good. Schleiermacher took this view and claimed that we gradually get closer to perfection as we mature through struggling with sin: "Our preoccupation with the world."[149] We mature as we attain more and more God-consciousness amidst our struggle with evil, and in that sense, our struggle with pain is an inherent part of our growth. Endorsing

---

145. Hick, *Evil and the God of Love*, 94. Hick discusses this problem of the aesthetic theodicy of Aquinas who follows Augustine's theodical scheme. Hick, *Evil and the God of Love*, 93–95.

146. Augustine, *City of God* 12.4.

147. Hick, *Evil and the God of Love*, 228.

148. Russell, *Cosmology*, 232.

149. Russell, *Cosmology*, 232.

Schleiermacher's idea, Hick affirms that pain and suffering are the necessary features of the soul-making world.

However, I regret that Hick himself did not contribute to establishing a robust evolutionary theodicy. Furthermore, his idea is still anthropocentric as he tends to relegate sentient animals' death and suffering to non-conscious stimuli, even if natural evil is given its place in his theodicy.[150] Furthermore, Hick rarely engages with the problem of evolutionary evil in the light of the trinitarian grammar of creation. Hick also does not consider the existence of unnecessarily excessive pain and suffering that does not have *developmental* values. For example, from the vantage point of individual preys in predation, there are too many prematurely killed lives that suffer excessive pain and cannot live up to their full potentials. As a vivid illustration, we see numerous sea lion cubs that suffer orcas' "unnecessarily" excessive tossing for prolonging their agony, yet there are other kinds of orcas who do not behave in the same manner when hunting prey.[151]

Here, the preys' sacrifice is not only contributive to the lives of other creatures but also embedded in the world where "the existence of a good is *inherently, constitutively, inseparable* from the experience of harm or suffering." This sort of understanding of natural evil can be dubbed as a "constitutive good-and-harm analysis."[152] I agree with Southgate that the suffering of prey raises a theodical question about God's goodness and faithfulness to those *individual* animals since their sacrifice is not voluntary but forced and violent.[153]

Accordingly, I believe that it is imperative to understand the process of evolution and the animal world in general as ridden with pain, suffering, and death, seen through the lens of a *cruciform* creation. The cross of Jesus Christ becomes significant for non-human creatures considering cosmic Christology and pneumatology. Importantly, cosmic Christology is to be applied to creation based on the meaning of the cross that represents not only the *self-giving* and *co-suffering* love of Christ for others, but also the faithful Creator's *saving* immanence in the lives of suffering creatures in light of the bodily resurrection of Jesus.

---

150. Hick, *Evil and the God of Love*, 309–17.

151. Southgate, "Creation as 'Very Good' and 'Groaning in Travail,'" 59–61. Citing Chadwick, "Investigating a Killer," 86–105.

152. Southgate, "Creation as 'Very Good' and 'Groaning in Travail,'" 59.

153. Southgate, "Creation as 'Very Good' and 'Groaning in Travail,'" 60–61, 67.

This approach is imperative as I consider the excessive suffering and massive extinction that individual creatures and their species undergo.[154] Furthermore, the increase of entropy is contingent as I discussed above. In that sense, I think Murphy and Ellis recapitulate this insight by maintaining that "suffering and disorder in biological evolution are necessary byproducts of a *non-coercive* creative process that aims at the development of free and intelligent beings."[155] Here, we see the universe as the locus where the self-giving love of Christ is at work in *creatio continua* through the mediation of the self-organizing universe that bears life, consciousness, and self-consciousness. In so doing, God never gives up on fulfilling the greater good out of pain, suffering, and death.

Importantly, however, Murphy and Ellis avoid romanticizing the pain and suffering in nature in the name of kenotic self-sacrifice for other creatures. Rather, in my reading of these scholars, in Jesus' life, cross, and resurrection, God showed us the end of the victimization of one for other members of a community. In the Christ event, God manifested God's once-and-for-all efficacious self-sacrifice to stop the victimization of the weak.[156] If the OT animal sacrifices find their completion in the cross of Jesus Christ, we can see that God does not perpetuate violence but terminates the infinite cycle of violence through the once-and-for-all sacrifice of Christ. Through the history of evolution, God's Creatorship is redemptive by continuously inviting creation into "the embodiment of a *kin-dom* of mutually loving among people as the *imago Dei* in communion with God, each other, and non-human living creatures."[157]

As I will discuss in the following chapters, I think that the epigenetic and emergent processes, along with genetic mutations and natural selection in neo-Darwinian evolution, can be theologically seen theologically as the loving and faithful Creator's participation in the inevitable suffering of creatures while bringing good out of evil and continuing to redeem creatures into unity with God. Contemporary developmental biologists engage with epigenetic theories, such as self-organization, symbiogenesis, niche construction, and developmental systems theory.[158] According to

---

154. I discuss further God's "self-giving" or "self-sacrificing" and "saving" dimensions of Christ's cross and their implications for natural and cosmic theodicy in chapter 5.

155. Murphy and Ellis, *On the Moral Nature of the Universe*, 247, emphasis mine.

156. Murphy and Ellis, *On the Moral Nature of the Universe*, 189.

157. Shin, "Non-Anthropocentric Understanding of the Trinitarian Creatorship," 18.

158. For a detailed explanation of these alternative factors in evolution, see

these theories, living organisms are not merely passive in their adaptation to their natural environment. Instead, they are able to transform their environment and affect the evolutionary paths of their descendants through reshaping the environmental pressure.[159] In this process, as Pannenberg says, evolution can be an *ecstatic* or self-transcending process toward genuine altruism, love, and community as the Logos constitutes the principle of independence-in-relations. I discuss in the following chapters how these epigenetic processes of evolution can be *seen* as God's special creative action in the matrix of the interplay of chance and regularities that God created *ex nihilo*.[160] However, the universe is constrained by the second law of thermodynamics in its fine-tuning for the creation of life and consciousness.

Furthermore, the universe is destined to end up in a state of thermodynamic equilibrium. If so, I think that an eschatological ontology of creation, based on a resurrection hope, becomes imperative because of the problem of suffering and death inevitable in the process of evolution and ultimately the *Freeze or Fry* of the universe as the nest of all the living creatures. Without the redemption of the whole of the universe there cannot be the redemption of life in it. Therefore, in the eschatological ontology of creation, natural theodicy is to be placed in cosmic theodicy.

God's continuous creation finds its *goal* only in the new creation. Also, as the original, continuous, and new creation is one act of God's creation, the consummation and redemption constitute the point of departure. The primordial goodness of creation according to Genesis 1:31 can be understood in the light of Revelation 21:1 (NIV): "Then, I saw 'a new heaven and a new earth.'" The present creation is where we see in the mirror dimly (1 Cor 13:12). This is not a deterministic account of creation.

Barbour, "Five Models of God and Evolution," 419–42. Considering these alternative evolutionary factors, one may say that natural selection is not the only and primary driving force of biological evolution. According to developmental systems theory, organisms have the power to transform their own environment and affect the paths of the evolution of their descendants. Moritz, "Evolutionary Evil and Dawkins' Blackbox," 143–88. I discuss the theological implications of these factors of evolution in the following chapters.

159. For detailed discussions of these factors at work in biological evolution and its theological implications, refer to Southgate, "Creation as 'Very Good' and 'Groaning in Travail,'" 53–85; Haag, "Nature and Nurture: The Irony of the Sociobiology Debate," 99–119; Moritz, "Evolutionary Evil and Dawkins' Black Box," 143–88.

160. As I discuss in the following chapters, this creative divine action may adopt not only top-down and whole-part causation but also bottom-up causation. I discuss this in relation to the discussed epigenetic processes of biological evolution in detail in chapters 4 and 5.

The Significance of Natural and Cosmic Theodicy 63

Rather, while the cross of Christ shows God's kenotic immanence in the present creation honoring the contingency of creatures, in light of Christ's resurrection, his cross shows us God's co-suffering for *redeeming* creatures, so they can live in genuine God-granted freedom in the peaceable *basileia* of God.[161] In that way, God's creative presence in the world is not only kenotic but also intrinsically eschatological and redemptive.

The Significance of Kenotic-Eschatological Divine Immanence: Trinitarian Panentheism

I think a trinitarian panentheistic view of God's transcendent immanence in creation expresses God's co-suffering yet redemptive immanence through interpreting anew the transcendent immanence of the God of classical theism.[162] I affirm that this move is imperative, as one considers the contemporary scientific cosmology, the theodical dilemma in classical theism, and the biblical portrayal of the dynamic God-world relationship. Considering these essential elements of natural and cosmic theodicy, I critically glean significant insights from the four interlocutors of this work in the following chapters.

The Co-Suffering and the Responsive Love of God

In the broad spectrum of classical theism, God is the Spirit deeply immanent in creation, but not limited by the corporeality of creation. According to John of Damascus of the Eastern Orthodox tradition, God is considered to be "above all existing things . . . [and] infinite and incomprehensible."[163] Hence, God is immanent in creation as the principle of creation while transcending it uncontaminated by the fallen nature of creation. This notion of divine transcendent immanence is found in a different manner in the Aristotelian-Thomistic tradition according to which God is the *prima*

---

161. I further articulate this affirmation in the following chapters, especially in chapter 5, the most constructive chapter.

162. "It has been customary to speak of 'classical theism' as a generic term designating the approaches of traditional postbiblical developments of early Christian theology that sought to express its faith in the biblical God with the help of Greco-Roman philosophical categories and later found its highest sophistication in medieval scholasticism." Kärkkäinen, *Trinity and Revelation*, 228.

163. Kärkkäinen, *Trinity and Revelation*, 230. Citing John of Damascus, *Orthodox Faith*, 1.4.

causa or "the effective first cause of all things or the secondary causes."[164] God is the first cause of all things created as secondary causes. Thus, the eternal God is immanent in every part of creation as "the ultimate formative principle" that is "simple" and "without potentiality."[165] Likewise, in the seventeenth- and the eighteenth-century Reformed scholastic tradition, God was believed to be "the immaterial substance" or "utterly incorporate essence—wholly uncontaminated by materiality"[166] while the secondary causes are dependent on God the primary cause.

These ideas are the product of the Christian tradition's efforts to understand the deep immanence of God in creation as the faithful and loving Creator without dissolving the scripturally-based infinity of God by critically appropriating the philosophical notions and the worldviews foreign to the Bible.[167] Classical theism serves as an example of the Christian tradition's critical interaction with the surrounding cultural and intellectual environments.[168] Yet, rather than rejecting classical theism, I think that its core belief in God's transcendent immanence is to be reinterpreted in our intellectual and cultural world.

When God is regarded as "a single subject" or "the unmoved mover" unaffected by the contingent happenings in history,[169] the loving, caring, dynamic, and relational nature of God of Scripture tends to be eclipsed in a "semi-mechanistic Newtonian" understanding of divine action typical of early modern theology.[170] Likewise, while implying the absolute free-

---

164. Shults, *Reforming the Doctrine of God*, 66.

165. Shults, *Reforming the Doctrine of God*, 16–18[17].

166. Muller, *Post-Reformation Reformed Dogmatics*, 3:271–77, 298–300. Cited in Kärkkäinen, *Trinity and Revelation*, 230.

167. Kärkkäinen, *Trinity and Revelation*, 231–32.

168. Boersma, *Heavenly Participation*, 20–24.

169. Shults, *Reforming the Doctrine of God*,16–18, 66–69; Kärkkäinen, *Trinity and Revelation*, 246–47.

170. Shults, *Reforming the Doctrine of God*, 231.

dom of God, divine omnicausality[171] does not do justice to the biblical portrayal of God's dynamic relationality.[172]

The notion of the unmoved mover has a risk of leading to deism or atheism in the contemporary age of natural sciences in which the nexus of natural causes is believed to be deeply indeterminate or uncertain.[173] In a similar vein, considering the contingent and universal evil (both natural and moral) across the universe that develops by chance and regularities, one may pose a skeptical doubt in the pancausality of God in creation or the all-controlling Creator.[174]

That said, the omniscience and omnipotence of God who creates the world *ex nihilo* is to be reinterpreted in the light of the biblical idea of the *temporal infinity*. That is, while God is responsive to the contingent choices of creatures God incessantly transcends creatures by opening the possibilities for the new future by overcoming the power of the past. In other words, "The Loving, Caring God—Father, Son, and Spirit—is with this creation from 'beginning' to 'end,' providing not only for existence but also the goal and fulfillment."[175]

A Call for Soteriological Panentheism

In my view, the dynamic nature of God's involvement in creation can be represented by a panentheistic vision of creation while appropriating classical theism's essential ideas of the creative and redemptive power of God and creation's fundamental dependence on God. Especially, considering the "relational" and "dynamic" nature of creation according to

---

171. Both Aquinas and Calvin honor the duality of causes: the primary and secondary causes in understanding divine action in creation. Yet, for Aquinas, all creation is in God's foreknowledge of the secondary causes eternally proceeding from the primary causes. Wright, *Providence Made Flesh*, 90. Citing Aquinas, *Summa Theologicae*, 1.14.13. In a similar vein but in his sympathetic critique of Aquinas' notion of divine foreknowledge, Calvin stressed the omni-causal agency of God as an event in creation. For Calvin, believers suffer "except by God's ordinance and command" since there is "no such thing as chance" but all creaturely events are "lodged in the act [of God]." Gunton, *Triune Creator*, 151. Citing Calvin, *Institutes*, 1.16.2–4. For Aquinas and Calvin, "the emphasis on the divine will as the cause of all things effectively suppress creaturely causal efficacy even as it intends to uphold it." Terrence, Providence Made Flesh, 90.

172. Pannenberg, ST II, 52–54; Gunton, "Introduction," 9–11.

173. Kärkkäinen, *Trinity and Revelation*, 230.

174. Migliore, *Faith Seeking Understanding*, 128–29.

175. Kärkkäinen, *Trinity and Revelation*, 231, 242–43.

contemporary quantum and chaos theories, scientific cosmologies, and current system biology, the biblical idea of God's dynamic involvement in the history of the world finds metaphorical consonance with the contemporary scientific worldview. There is no consensus on what the term "in" means as one uses a pan*en*theistic frame of reference in understanding the relationship between God and creatures. Some critics object to adopting it as they read a static overtone into it.[176] Others oppose it by identifying panentheism with pantheism by believing that panentheism removes the genuine *otherness* of both God and creation. [177]

However, I think these are not all the possible forms of panentheism. Rather, a panentheistic vision can posit God and creation in mutual interaction without dissolving the otherness of each other. For example, "dynamic panentheism"[178] is characterized by the "overtones of the Orthodox concept of the active presence of divine energies." This idea is similar to Polkinghorne's understanding of the dynamic immanence of God in creation.[179] Knight illustrates this idea with Polkinghorne's claim that creation is "within the *life* of God," rather than in God.[180] That is, Polkinghorne opposes panentheism by regarding it as dissolving the genuine contingency of creation. However, he accepts the dynamic interaction of God and creation because creation is placed in within the dynamic life of God who engages with contingent creatures.

The mutually interactive and dynamic relationship between God and creation is not foreign to Scripture. In the OT, God is both immediately near to all the creatures and in the unexhausted otherness.[181] While

---

176. For example, see John Polkinghorne's objection to Philip Clayton's approval of John Newton's idea of the absolute space as God's *sensorium* in his panentheism. Polkinghorne, *Faith, Science and Understanding*, 92. Yet, in my view, Polkinghorne does not consider Clayton's ontologically emergent and pluralistic understanding of reality. For his strong emergentism, refer to his *Adventures in the Spirit*, 73–76.

177. For example, see Gunton's identification of panentheism with pantheism in his *The Triune Creator*, 142.

178. Knight, "Theistic Naturalism," 49.

179. Knight, "Theistic Naturalism," 49. Citing Polkinghorne, *Faith, Science and Understanding*, 95. Polkinghorne denies a panentheistic notion of creation's being "in" God due to the possible violation of the contingency of creation. Yet in my view, creation still can be in God, if creaturely contingency and freedom is teleologically granted by God and ontologically dependent on the absolute freedom of God.

180. Knight, "Theistic Naturalism," 49. Citing Polkinghorne, *Faith, Science and Understanding*, 95.

181. Ware, "God Immanent yet Transcendent," 157–59.

the way that God works is hidden to the finite knowledge of creatures (Job 38:4; Isa 45:15, 55:8), the Lord is "a God nearby . . . and not a God far away"; "Do not I fill heaven and earth? declares the Lord" [Jer 23:23-24 (NIV)]. In the NT, similarly, neither God's immediacy nor otherness in creation is dissolved. In John 1:1, God preexists creation as the transcendent Creator. In Acts 17:27-28 (NIV), the all-embracing immanence of God is expressed clearly: "In Him, we live and move and have our being."

Based on these biblical portrayals, cosmic Christology and pneumatology become consequential for conceiving of creation *ex nihilo* in a trinitarian panentheistic framework. As Moltmann affirms, as the universal life force, God's *ruach* is immanent in all creatures: the living, bodily, sexual, ecological, and political dimensions.[182] The Spirit of God is "the power of creation and the wellspring of life."[183] Rather than emerging out of the pre-existing order of nature, the creative Spirit gives existence to all that exists in creation, breathes life into creatures, sustains them, and redeems them from the power of death and evil.

If the Father creates the world through the mediation of the Son and the Spirit, the doctrine of creation is to be formulated in a dynamic, relational, and trinitarian panentheistic vision of creation. In this scheme, the genuine value of God's good creation is celebrated while God's transcendence is not dissolved, because God continues to redeem the fallen creatures and thereby fulfill the eschatological new creation.

This sort of panentheism can be categorized as "soteriological panentheism" according to Niels Gregersen.[184] In this kind of panentheism, the Logos is the principle of creation or the divine pattern by which creatures are brought into existence *ex nihilo*. Creatures can have their independence in communion with other creatures and with God. At the same time, for its fulfillment, creation is not self-sufficient. Creation needs God's soteriological accompaniment for its perfection in the course of its continuous creation. This does not necessarily mean the violation of the established order of nature but rather the fulfillment of creation. According to the earlier church fathers, the "Logos" means not only "*ratio*" (reason or pattern) but also "*sermo*" (sermon or dialogue).[185]

---

182. Moltmann, *Spirit of Life*, 225-28.
183. Moltmann, *Spirit of Life*, 35.
184. Gregersen, "Three Varieties of Panentheism," 24-27.
185. Gregersen, "Three Varieties of Panentheism," 26.

To put it differently, the Logos is both the principle of creation and that of revelation. The hypostatic union of the human and divine natures in the person of the Son provides the ontological ground of the order of nature while never ceasing to redeem creation from the power of death, sin, and evil. That is, the hypostatic union of the human and divine natures in the person of the Son or the Logos serves as both the creative and soteriological principle through which creatures participate in embodying genuine communion of the eschatological *basileia* of God and in "the network of relations" with each other. Creatures are invited into the peaceable network of relations with each other, through the Father's continuing creation by the mediation of the Son and the Spirit.[186] The fulfillment of this trinitarian project is only possible in the eschaton by redeeming the thermodynamic universe as discussed above through God's transformation of the old into the new.[187]

The Logos, the Creaturely Logoi, and the Eschatological Spirit

The Logos finds pluralistic expressions in *logoi* or "divinely given patterns of being" according to the Maximus the Confessor.[188] Those *logoi* represent the full potentials granted by God to each creature. While they do not have to be regarded as a vitalism refuted in the contemporary scientific age, they mean "the beauty and meaning of things," or an individual creature's and a species' nature and what God intends it to be.[189]

According to evolutionary biology, "biological organisms and species are best seen as representing points and peaks within the evolutionary fitness landscapes."[190] These peaks are not predetermined nor static but in constant shift through the dynamic interactions among organisms and their environments and among the diverse species sharing the same habitat. Also, individuals of a species do not represent the same location in a landscape because all of them do not live out the full potentials given to their species.[191]

---

186. Gregersen, "Three Varieties of Panentheism," 27.

187. Gregersen, "Three Varieties of Panentheism," 27. According to Pannenberg, one of the lacunas in theology not to develop a concrete understanding of the joint work of the Son and the Spirit in God's providence. Pannenberg, *ST* II, 109–10.

188. Refer to Louth, "Cosmic Vision of Saint Maximus the Confessor," 188–90.

189. Southgate, *Groaning of Creation*, 61.

190. Southgate, *Groaning of Creation*, 61.

191. Shin, "Cosmic Spirit's Creatorship," 14.

The Significance of Natural and Cosmic Theodicy

As Kallistos Ware explains the notion of the *logoi*, they are what "make [a creature] distinctively itself and at the same time draws it toward the divine realm."[192] Therefore, the *logoi* can mean the full potentialities of each creature and species in the process of biological evolution. Those potentialities are not static but open to the emergence of novelty. Similarly, gleaning from the metaphysics of Gerard Hopkins, Southgate poetically describes each creature as "selving" in its "most characteristic way, and flourishing in so doing."[193] When a creature *selves*, it lives out the best potentials granted to it and its species by the creative Logos and through the life-giving Spirit. In that way, creatures "gain their existence, beauty, and meaning, that which prevents them from reverting to nothingness."[194]

The fulfillment of the *logoi* is not a one-way divine predetermination but continues to be fulfilled by the creatures' participation in the divine call to unity with the loving Creator. This is because each creature, given independence and biological evolution, is called to bring forth genuine freedom that culminates in the emergence of human beings and in their unity with God.

Along those lines, there are creatures whose lives are "fulfilled," "growing toward fulfillment," and "transcending [themselves]."[195] A fulfilled life is "a state in which the creature is utterly being itself, in an environment in which it flourishes, . . . with access to the appropriate energy, sources and reproductive opportunities." A life "growing toward fulfillment" is "not yet mature, but still with the possibility of attaining the 'fulfilled' state." In contrast, a "frustrated" life is "held back in some way from fulfillment." However, God continues to work to create a life "transcending itself" through "some new pattern of behavior, whether as a result of a favorable mutation, or a chance exploration of a new possibility of relating to its own or another species."[196] The ultimate goal of this process finds its place in the eschatological peaceable kingdom of God where all the creatures *selve* in "mutual dependence, cooperation, and shared life" without death and predation.[197] In the Spirit of the risen Jesus,

192. Southgate, *Groaning of Creation*, 61. Citing Ware, "God Immanent yet Transcendent," 160.
193. Southgate, *Groaning of Creation*, 63.
194. Southgate, *Groaning of Creation*, 63.
195. Southgate, *Groaning of Creation*, 64.
196. Southgate, *Groaning of Creation*, 64.
197. Southgate, *Groaning of Creation*, 62. Citing Denis Edwards, *Breath of Life*, 134–35.

we can hope for loving communion without violating creatures' finitude in their relationships with others.

In this continuously creative way, biological evolution, when placed in the theological context of *soteriological panentheism*, can be regarded as the creative work of the Logos and the Spirit in unity as the two hands of the Father, representing God's transcendent immanence that continues to be creative and redemptive within creation. Here, just as one can see in the Palamite tradition, while the *ousia* of God is not enriched by creatures, the diffusive love of the trinitarian hypostases gives existence to contingent creatures in unqualified freedom and invites them to share in "mutual participation and mutual joy" through the interaction with God.[198] The divine energies (*energia*) represent the uncreated activities of the Spirit within creation, through which there comes into existence the genuine plurality of creation. Thus, the uncreated divine energies mean "the indivisible multiplicity of [God's] creative and redemptive work" immanent in the continuous creation.[199]

Likewise, Karl Rahner passed beyond the dominant neo-scholastic concept of grace as the created effect of the Spirit, and built his theology of grace around the idea of "quasi-formal cause."[200] Rahner qualifies formal causality with "quasi" to express that God's grace is fully given and fully efficacious in creation in a creative and redemptive mode, while the Spirit remains the uncreated grace.[201] With this concept, Rahner contends that "a graced person can be as close to the triune God as possible ontologically, while the Spirit remains uncreated."[202]

In a similar fashion, in the proposal of his "classical panentheism", Kärkkäinen argues that the triune God is "not ever really distant from creation, although creatures, since they are unlike God in nature, are necessarily distant from God."[203] In that sense, he goes on to argue, "[i]n

---

198. Ware, "God Immanent yet Transcendent," 168.

199. Ware, "God Immanent yet Transcendent," 165.

200. Aristotle defined four causes: material (the matter of something), efficient (that which produces something), final (the purpose of something), formal (that which makes something to be what it is, the kind of being that it is). Quasi-formal cause means something less than formal causality. That is, according to Rahner, "[n]ot-appropriated relations of a single person are possible, not with an efficient causality, but with a quasi-formal self-communication of God." Rahner, *Trinity*, 4.

201. Rahner, *Trinity*, 4.

202. Rahner, *Trinity*, xiii.

203. Kärkkäinen, *Creation and Humanity*, 78.

The Significance of Natural and Cosmic Theodicy

the Trinitarian grammar, similarly to Christ's mediating work that links together creation, redemption, and eschatological fulfillment, the Spirit's mission relates in its own way to the Trinitarian unfolding of the divine economy."[204] This "intimate nearness and otherness" of God within creation in the discussed panentheistic views stress "God's connectedness and responsiveness to the world."[205]

As many liberation and eco-feminist theologians affirm, the dynamic and relational understanding of God and the God-world relationship is significant not only for understanding the locus of God in the midst of the problems of suffering, inequality, and injustice in human society,[206] but also for the suffering prevalent in creation as a whole including non-human creatures.[207]

In the hope of the new creation, Moltmann goes further to claim the eschatological orientation of the current creation based on the cross and the resurrection of Jesus Christ. For Moltmann, this free creative act of the triune God takes place through the divine self-limiting out of love, honoring the freedom and independence of creatures. This means that the triune God works by the mediation of the contingent creatures and accordingly co-suffers with them in the midst of the inevitable evil as the byproduct for creativity in the finite creation.

For Moltmann, God's self-limitation is not God's self-withdrawal from the process of *creatio continua*. Rather, divine self-limitation means a kenotic mode of creation grounded in the solidarity of the Father and the Spirit with the incarnate Son on the cross. In order to fulfill God's redemptive purpose for creation, God participates in the suffering of creatures through the cross of the Son incarnate. The divine co-suffering is redemptive because God works from the perspective of the eschatological new creation. God is not passively suffering, but actively co-resisting with creatures against the power of death and evil[208] while preserving and working through the established order of nature.

---

204. Kärkkäinen, *Creation and Humanity*, 80.

205. Peterson, "Whither Panentheism?," 396 [395–405]; Johnson, *She Who Is*, 233–36.

206. Cone, *Black Theology of Liberation*, 76–78; Gutierrez, *Theology of Liberation*, 156–57.

207. Johnson, *She Who Is*, 228–30; McDaniel, "Can Animal Suffering be Reconciled with Belief in an All-Loving God?," 161–72.

208. In the same vein, Moltmann affirms that on the cross of Jesus Christ, we meet a "protesting God." Moltmann, *Crucified God*, 226.

The genuine meaning of the cross for creation cannot be grasped without the resurrection hope promised in the "bodily" resurrection of Jesus. Based on this understanding of the relationship between Christ and the Spirit, it is apropos to see Christ's passion as a "birth pang" or "the apocalyptic suffering," in which the Spirit participates in an unquenchable hope for the eschatological new creation.[209] Here, I affirm that God's life-giving and life-sustaining immanence through co-suffering and suffering-redeeming is to be applied to all other creatures in the midst of the inevitable and yet contingent experience of pain and suffering in the face of death and decay.

If God is a monotheistic ground of being for each creature, the Spirit of God is the Giver of Life for each creature that emerges in the process of evolution. Polkinghorne astutely writes, "All creation must matter to the Creator in ways that are appropriate to its nature,"[210] because God is their faithful Creator who brought them to life according to their nature. In arguing this, Polkinghorne emphasizes that all creatures are invited to have their true fulfillment in God because humans are not the only creatures who matter to God in God's creative and redemptive act.

If so, I think that this trinitarian panentheistic portrayal of God is based on the biblical narratives of the saving economy of the triune Creator. This interpretation helps avoid both deism and pantheism, as it acknowledges both God's "deep immanence" in creation and God's inexhaustible transcendence.[211] Echoing this trinitarian grammar, I seek to construct a theologically and scientifically plausible trinitarian panentheistic vision of creation through a mutual interaction between theology and natural sciences, in which the creation, reconciliation, and consummation of the world comprise the history of the trinitarian God that culminates in God's kingdom. God's creation can be termed "the fruit of the loving [triune] God's longing for the other and for that other's free response to the divine love [in a co-suffering but liberative mode]."[212]

---

209. Moltmann, *Way of Jesus Christ*, 151.

210. Polkinghorne, "Eschatological Credibility," 49.

211. Similarly, Gregersen regards this panentheistic immanence of God as a "deep incarnation" of the Logos, implying that the incarnation of the Son is not only meaningful for human beings but also for all creation. Gregersen, "Deep Incarnation," 178.

212. Kärkkäinen, *Trinity and Revelation*, 236.

Inviting the Four Interlocutors in the Task of Constructing a Kenotic-Eschatological Panentheistic Vision of Creation

All four interlocutors, Peacocke, Keller, Pannenberg, and Russell contribute to constructing a robust kenotic-eschatological panentheistic vision. While they present different understandings of the "transcendent immanence" of God in creation and the existence of natural evil in God's good creation, they provide each other with mutually complementing insights. In my understanding, this is because they adopt different methods in theology-science dialogue while affirming the cognitive aspects of theological inquiries in the matrix of epistemic holism. They differ in degree of mutuality in the interaction between theology and science and the ways of interacting with natural sciences in presenting their theodical arguments. Via comparison of the four interlocutors, I find their panentheistic views to complement each other in significant ways. In this constructive work, their understandings of creaturely contingency, divine co-suffering, soteriological special action, and eschatological redemption are put into dialogue.

3

Natural and Cosmic Theodicy of Peackocke and Keller

IN THIS CHAPTER, I critically engage with how Peacocke and Keller theologically present God's transcendent immanence as a creative and redemptive presence in creation through pursuing fruitful conversation between theology and science. Thereby, I explore comparatively how they understand natural and cosmic theodicy. In her dipolar panentheism,[1] Keller portrays God as the responsive lure of love. God is involved in continuous creation through objectively special lures or God's spontaneous responses to the choices that creatures make in actualizing the divinely granted potentialities.

While Peacocke explicitly opposes deism, unlike Keller, he also rejects the Whiteheadian notion of a special lure that would allow special actions of God that are not merely metaphorical but can also be seen

---

1. According to David Griffin and John Cobb, in dipolar (process) panentheism, God has on the one hand an abstract essence and concrete actuality on the other hand. The former includes "eternity, absoluteness, omniscience and independence." The latter includes temporality, relativity, dependency, and constant changing. Cobb and Griffin, *Process Theology*, 7. Griffin writes, "God transcends the finite world in that he is not dependent upon it for his existence, although he is dependent upon the world for part of his actuality, the concrete experiences that he is having" (186). In this sense, God is creative in that God persuades actual entities to make a choice for better goods, but God is responsive because he does not compel them to make the choice that God desires but is open to their choices in metaphysical necessity.

as actually involving objective divine action.[2] In his ENP (emergentist-naturalistic-panentheistic) approach, God is universally immanent in every part of creation while being infinitely transcendent as the One who creates *ex nihilo*. Yet God's continuous interaction with creatures takes place in whole-part and top-down manners without adopting bottom-up and special divine actions.

The similarities and dissimilarities in their ideas of the God's interaction with creation lead to similar yet subtly different understandings of natural and cosmic theodicy. This chapter comprises three main sections: 1. Peacocke's Perspective of Natural and Cosmic Evil in the Context of the ENP scheme, 2. Keller's *Tehomic* Perspective of Divine Action in Creation and Natural/Cosmic Theodicy in Dialogue with Modern Natural Science, and 3. Comparative Analysis. In the third part, I discuss how Peacocke's vision of *creatio ex nihilo* and Keller's *creatio ex profundis* can complement each other from theological, scientific, and philosophical perspectives. In this way, I maintain a "kenotic-eschatological" panentheistic vision of creation based on the co-suffering yet redemptive immanence of God on the cross and the resurrection of Jesus.

This chapter prepares the reader to understand the importance of the doctrine of *creatio ex nihilo* in its inextricable relationship with the new creation as *creatio ex vetere*, and the significance of special divine action in seeking a fruitful answer to the dilemma of the sweeping natural and cosmic evil. In that vein, this chapter bridges chapter 2 and chapter 4 in which I discuss the contributions of Pannenberg and Russell. In chapter 5, I will present how Peacocke and Keller can contribute to the theodical discourses of Pannenberg and Russell.

Peacocke's Natural and Cosmic Theodicy in His Emergentist-Naturalist-Panentheistic (ENP) Scheme

Peacocke's ENP scheme governs his approach to the problem of natural and cosmic evil in the matrix of God's good creation. In his ENP

---

2. Peacocke writes, "I see no need to postulate any *special* action of God—along the lines, say, of some divine manipulation of mutations at the quantum level, or of some special 'lure' of God in the process—to ensure that persons emerge in the universe, and in particular on Earth... [T]he whole process leading to the emergence of persons can be satisfactorily accounted for as a purely naturalistic one and therefore implemented by God's *general* providential ordering of and immanent presence in the world." Peacocke, "Cost of New Life," 33.

framework of creation, God creates the whole of the universe *ex nihilo*. However, God actively limits Godself in God's omniscience and omni-causality in *creatio continua* by granting freedom and contingency to creation for the emergence of diversity and the higher levels of complexity in evolutionary history. In God's self-limitation in *creatio continua*, as revealed in the life and the cross of Jesus, the loving God the Creator co-suffers with creatures that suffer amidst the universal, contingent, and inevitable evil. Yet this compassionate immanence of God is both creative and redemptive as God continues to work toward the emergence of a community of the loving people of God who freely commit themselves to the genuine communion with God, other fellow humans, and all other non-human creatures.

A Demand for "Naturalistic Theism" in a Scientific Age

Peacocke recognizes that contemporary Christians are faced with "a pressing need to describe the realities that Christian belief wishes to articulate in terms that can make sense to [our scientific] culture while expanding its theological significance."[3] Without a continuous attempt to fruitfully engage in dialogue with natural sciences and respond to their challenge through revision, theology cannot be relevant to the contemporaneous scientific worldview. However, their consistent reciprocal dialogue enriches not only our understandings of God but also our understanding of the world, as "God is, in fact, the all-encompassing Reality that Christian faith proclaims."[4]

To be more specific, for Peacocke, in the Newtonian mechanistic worldview, the providence of God became questionable, since in this perspective every occurrence is deemed to follow fixed natural laws, and thus there is no room for a God who works through intervening in those regularities.[5] However, according to contemporary physics, the world of physics no longer has to be regarded as deterministic due to the genuine indeterminacy on the sub-atomic level and the unpredictability inherent in the emergence of complex organisms in dissipative systems. Thus,

---

3. Peacocke, "Naturalistic Christian Faith," 5

4. Peacocke, *Creation and the World of Science*, 17. Also, see his *Theology for a Scientific Age*, 91–98. Here, Peacocke discusses Richard Swinburne's discourse as to "the concept of God" in the philosophy of religion as well as its consonance and dissonance with "God in Christian Belief."

5. Peacocke, "Naturalistic Christian Faith," 17.

such a deterministic worldview is not a necessary metaphysical choice and does not do justice to the expulsion of the Creator God of a monotheistic religion.[6]

Rather, one may believe in God as the Creator of the cosmos while being faithful to the cogency and comprehensiveness of the current scientific view of the world at the same time. While the Judeo-Christian notion of God is neither philosophical nor metaphysical but rooted in religious experience, the notion of the rational Creator of all things—who is "personal, omnipotent, perfectly free, perfectly good"—remains useful for the rational attempt to render all that is intelligible.[7]

However, the perfect *Being* of God is neither static nor atemporal. The reason is that while God as the ground of being in divine supreme rationality and unfathomable richness creates all that is *ex nihilo*, God experiences *Becoming* as the source of law-like regularities and chance.[8] In that sense, Peacocke believes that a monotheistic notion of God, such as the Judeo-Christian version, provides "the best explanation of how the world actually is,"[9] because such a notion of the Creator can provide a locus for discussing the universe intelligibly in coherence and in consistency.

Accordingly, Peacocke advances a naturalistic theology that is consistent with scientific perspectives and with the view of the world implicit in natural sciences.[10] In that way, Peacocke counts scientific naturalism as a platform for contemporary Christians to understand God as Creator and natural processes as God's creation in an intelligible manner. This is because in Christian theology, nature is the theological locus to experience the self-communication of God.[11]

In that sense, Peacocke endorses a scientific naturalism according to which the universe is an extremely complex web of cause-and-effect relations.[12] Every event occurs within this web, having causal antecedents and causal consequences. Furthermore, every event is a common set of

---

6. Peacocke, "Naturalistic Christian Faith," 18–20. Also, in this regard, see his *Paths from Science Toward God*, 99–108.

7. Peacocke, *Theology for a Scientific Age*, 92.

8. Peacocke, *Theology for a Scientific Age*, 101–24.

9. Peacocke, *Theology for a Scientific Age*, 91.

10. Peacocke, "Naturalistic Christian Faith," 8, 17–20.

11. Peacocke, "Naturalistic Christian Faith," 9–10.

12. Peacocke, "Naturalistic Christian Faith," 6–9. Peacocke endorses the naturalistic ideas of David Griffin and Charles Hardwick.

causal principles.[13] In other words, for Peacocke, a notable aspect of these scientific accounts of the natural world is "the seamless character of the web that has been spun on the loom of time; at no point do modern natural scientists have to invoke any non-natural causes to explain their observations and inferences about the past."[14]

However, Peacocke argues such a scientific naturalism does not have to entail atheism. Naturalism rules out only supernaturalism, according to which there is a supernatural being that exists outside the universal web of cause-effect relations and can violate that web. In that sense, Peacocke names his naturalism as *naturalism ns* (non-supernatural), which is distinguished from any full-swing materialistic version of naturalism.[15]

Rather, defining the cosmos as an emergent, monistic, and complex system can lead to the revision of the classical theism rather than its abnegation. One can consider the manner of divine action within the cosmos to be consistent with the manner of the closed cosmos' operation, as is explained by *naturalism ns*. Scientific naturalism as *naturalism ns* can be naturalistic theism, and in this sort, one may see "natural processes characterized as laws and regularities" as the actions of God, who "continuously gives them existence."[16]

In my understanding of Peacocke's naturalistic theism, epistemology forms ontology without dissolving the distinction between the two. Likewise, on the one hand, the eternal and perfect being of God according to classical theism is not rejected as God is the ground of all the potentials to be actualized in creation. On the other hand, the notion of the divine being in classical theism is substantially revised in rumination on the way that the natural order as God's creation operates by law-like regularities and chance.

The transcendence of God is never exhausted in the becoming of creation as the doctrine of *creatio ex nihilo* reflects the "ontological dependence" of creation on God. At the same time, in Peacocke's theistic naturalism, the Christian doctrines including the belief in God as the Creator are subject to radical revision in consistency with natural

---

13. Also, see Griffin, *Process Christology*, 22–24. Griffin interprets special providence as something within the web of natural causes that can be regarded as reflecting strong divine presence according to the Christian vision of reality, rather than direct divine operation in nature.

14. Peacocke, "Naturalistic Christian Faith," 19.

15. Peacocke, "Naturalistic Christian Faith," 5–11.

16. Peacocke, "Naturalistic Christian Faith," 17.

sciences. Based on emergent monism as the overarching metaphysics that also governs Peacocke's research in theology-science dialogue, the process of biological evolution poses constraints on the Christian belief in the way God interacts with nature in the process of *creatio continua*.

This is not only an epistemological but also an ontological statement in my reading of Peacocke's ENP approach. The being of God is not dualistically separated from the emergent whole of reality open to the novelty of the future of creation, but rather, the being of God is regarded as also being in the process of *becoming* in the interaction with the world processes.[17] The being of God is not static but dynamic in interaction with creation while without the former the latter cannot exist.

Furthermore, in our life-birthing universe that is an emergent whole, even though religious language cannot be reduced to the terms of biology and physics, Christian tradition rarely has a right to illuminate the research of natural sciences. For this reason, I acknowledge Peacocke's commitment to metaphysical naturalism while not failing to speak of the Creator as a science-theologian hybrid. This aspect of his ENP approach is reflected in his revision of the doctrine of creation, theodicy, and the incarnation. I turn to these topics in the following sections.

The Universe and the Biosphere in *Creatio ex Nihilo* and *Creatio Continua*

In his employment of *naturalism ns* in a minimal sense, Peacocke sees consonance between the naturalistic understanding of the universe and God's presence in the world as the creative ground of being. For Peacocke, emergent monism and top-down causality serve as the central hermeneutical lens to understand God's creative transcendent immanence within creation and the problem of natural and cosmic evil.

Emergent Monism: The Emergent Whole Created ex Nihilo

Peacocke contends that all the concrete particulars of the world including humans—with their own properties—are "constituted only of

---

17. In that sense, Peacocke finds it useful to distinguish the two poles of "being" and "becoming" in the notion of the nature of God. Peacocke, *Theology for a Scientific Age*, 99–101. However, in my understanding as I discuss in this section, Peacocke's idea of the becoming of God is somewhat passive in God's interaction with creation.

fundamental physical entities of matter/energy at the lowest level."[18] Yet he also affirms that the universe consists of a complex series of the irreducible levels of organization and matter in which "each successive member of the series is a whole constituted of parts preceding it in the series."[19] Peacocke's view of the world as a whole can be labeled as a "layered physicalism", which is ontologically monistic, since "everything can be broken down into whatever physicists deem ultimately to constitute energy/matter."[20] At the same time, however, the distinctiveness of each level is not to be reduced down to the properties of lower levels.[21] In that sense, those upper levels are epistemologically non-reductionist.

In the wake of the hot Big Bang, the interplay of indeterminate quantum events and law-like regularities played a creative ensemble in the causation of matter on the Earth to evolve into more and more complex entities and finally into self-conscious beings like *Homo sapiens*.[22] For Peacocke, as the fine-tuning of the universe takes place at the Big Bang, the anthropic principle may signify the purposeful creation of a "personal" or "supra-personal" Creator.[23] Yet the possibility of other life-bearing universes is not precluded. Furthermore, Peacocke raises a question against the identification of *creatio ex nihilo* with the absolute beginning of time, considering the challenge of the Hartle-Hawking model.[24] For Peacocke, even though the emergent universe is temporal, the absence of the absolute singularity t=0 does not affect the doctrine of *creatio ex nihilo* as it is the belief of the world's ontological dependence on God.[25]

In the emergence of living creatures of higher complexity in this finely-tuned universe, Peacocke recognizes the significance of genuine Heisenberg uncertainty of quantum-scale events, the genuine unpredictability in the operation and interaction of non-linear dissipative systems, and the amplification of unpredictability via the random intersection of

---

18. Peacocke, "Naturalistic Christian Faith," 12.
19. Peacocke, "Naturalistic Christian Faith," 12.
20. Peacocke, "Naturalistic Christian Faith," 12.
21. Peacocke, "Naturalistic Christian Faith," 13.
22. Peacocke, *Theology for a Scientific Age*, 56–61.
23. Peacocke, *Theology for a Scientific Age*, 105–13, 191.
24. Peacocke, *Theology for a Scientific Age*, 69–71.
25. Peacocke, *Creation and the World of Science*, 77–79.

causal chains in the environment.²⁶ Furthermore, emergent evolution does not unfold only by the genuine chance inherent in the process, but also by law-like regularities.

Random mutations in the micro-level make changes in an organism's cells. However, the emergent genetic properties in the cell are bound to natural law-like regularities. While chance in mutations may affect the ability of the organism to procreate in its environment, at this macro-level, it is subject to the law of natural selection for the emergent forms of life to survive in extended duration.²⁷ In the emergence of a new level of complexity, while lower levels place constraints on higher levels, the latter are emergent and cannot be reduced entirely to the former. In other words, "[e]ach level has to be regarded as a cut through the totality of reality . . . in the sense that we have to take account of its mode of operation at that level."²⁸

Physical and chemical principles partly constrain the work of the consciousness of the human-brain-in-the-body, while the latter has its own logic of operation that cannot be explained by the laws applicable to lower levels. Accordingly, Peacocke labels this perspective as emergent monism.²⁹ Peacocke sees that the emergent hierarchy of reality is inherent in the whole of the cosmos, and it represents the interrelatedness among the different epistemic levels of creation: "physical, biological, ecological, human, social, and cultural."³⁰

Creatio Continua *through Divine Whole-Part Influence*

I find that in Peacocke's scheme this emergent nature of the universe is not only applicable "diachronically" to our understanding of the relationships among the different levels in the evolutionary process of nature, but also "synchronically" to our understanding of a whole composed of parts.³¹ In

---

26. Peacocke, *Theology for a Scientific Age*, 55–59.

27. Peacocke, *Paths from Science towards God*, 75–77. Also, see Peacocke, "Biology and a Theology of Evolution," 699–701.

28. Peacocke, "Naturalistic Christian Faith," 13.

29. Peacocke, *Paths from Science towards God*, 48–51.

30. Peacocke, "Naturalistic Christian Faith," 11. According to the biophysicist Harold Morowitz, there are no less than twenty-eight emergent levels. See Morowitz, *Emergence of Everything*.

31. In his *Theology for a Scientific Age*, 214–44, Peacocke distinguishes the four emergent levels of evolution: the physical level (Level 1), the level of living organisms

other words, on the one hand, the world consists of "a complex series of levels of organization and matter, in which each successive member of the series is a whole constituted of parts preceding it in the series."[32]

On the other hand, "new and distinctive kinds of realities at the higher levels of complexity may properly be said to have emerged."[33] Therefore, the universal epistemic hierarchy corresponds not only to how the complex systems have evolved over time out of the earlier and simpler ones, but also to the manner in which different sciences relate to each other in the present condition.[34]

The complexity of a system and our inability to reduce it down to the terms of its parts encourages us to conjecture a whole-part and top-down causation. What Peacocke means by causation here is not a deterministic movement of matter or transmission of energy that takes place in causation in the same level within a living organism. Rather, it is a joint effect between different levels that takes place from the whole to its parts via a downward "transmission of information."[35] This idea of a non-physical causal connection is inevitable because of the relationship between a whole and its parts.

The *interrelatedness* among parts of a complex system *diachronically* results in irreducible noble features of that system over the deep history of the universe and the biosphere of the Earth. *Synchronically*, the way in which a part of a complex system behaves depends on the properties of the whole to which the part pertains, while the former supervenes on the latter.[36] The efficacy of downward causation is inseparable from, yet irreducible to, bottom-up causation that involves the transmission of energy and the movement of matter.

The notion of downward causation is contested among reductionist materialists. They are open to the notion of "weak emergence" according to which new patterns develop out of the fundamentally deterministic web of physical causes. Yet they also propose that the new patterns can

---

(Level 2), the behavioral level (Level 3), and the cultural level (Level 4). He identifies them as the constitutive levels of a human being too.

32. Peacocke, "Naturalistic Christian Faith," 12.

33. Peacocke, "Naturalistic Christian Faith," 13.

34. Peacocke, "Naturalistic Christian Faith," 13.

35. Peacocke, "Naturalistic Christian Faith," 16. Also, see Peacocke, *Theology for a Scientific Age*, 58–59.

36. Peacocke, *Palace of Glory*, 97–98.

exert causal influence on lower levels.³⁷ In contrast, Peacocke does not subscribe to weak emergence because he affirms genuine indeterminacy of sub-atomic events, the genuine unpredictability of the operation of non-linear open systems, and the consequent irreducible novelty of emergent levels that has causal influence on the lower levels.³⁸ Nonetheless, I find problematic that in his idea of supervenience and whole-part constraint Peacocke rejects the bottom-up divine action in interpreting the top-down and whole-part causation in the interaction among the emergent levels of reality.

The Active and Passive Dimensions of God's Creatio Continua

Peacocke defines the universe as an emergent monistic complex system that can be regarded as God's continuous creation. While he revises classical theism, he does not entirely reject it. For Peacocke, God is "the ultimate ground and source of both *law* and *chance*,"³⁹ as we consider the fundamental contingency of the being and becoming of the emergent cosmos. For a theist, God must be seen "as acting creatively in the world often through what we call 'chance' or random processes," while giving existence to what exists in duration, "thereby operating within the created order."⁴⁰ In this ongoing creation, each stage constitutes the "launching pad" for the next one to emerge.⁴¹ Here one can see the Creator unfolding the created potentialities "in and through a process, in which its possibilities and propensities become actualized."⁴²

Peacocke finds this model of God to be more befitting the dynamic and personal interaction between God and creation according to

37. Kärkkäinen, *Creation and Humanity*, 104–5. See also Clayton, "Conceptual Foundations of Emergence Theory," 1–31.

38. Peacocke, "Naturalistic Christian Faith," 14–16. Similarly, Philip Clayton maintains the significance of the idea of downward causation in the context of emergent monism for the following reasons. First, "all that exists in the space-time world are the basic particles recognized by physics and their aggregates." Second, "when aggregates of material particles attain an appropriate level of organizational complexity, genuinely novel properties emerge in these complex systems." Third, emergent properties are irreducible to, and unpredictable from, the lower-level phenomena from which they emerge." Clayton, *Mind and Emergence*, 4–7 [4].

39. Peacocke, *Paths from Science Towards God*, 77.

40. Peacocke, "Naturalistic Christian Faith," 18.

41. Peacocke, *Theology for a Scientific Age*, 156.

42. Peacocke, "Naturalistic Christian Faith," 18.

Scripture. Here, God can be regarded as the Creator who has gifted the universe with "a 'formational economy,' which is the set of all of the dynamic capabilities of matter and material, physical and biotic systems."[43] God is always the Creator because God continuously gives existence to the created order of nature that brings forth the new. God acts everywhere in space and time "holistically affect[ing] the state of the world at all levels."[44]

After the emergence of *Homo sapiens*, God's top-down/whole-part constraint or influence on the world-as-a-whole is actualized in each level mostly by the operation of human beings,[45] since they are "the emergent reality which is located at the apex of the systems-based complexities of the world."[46] Then, God would be conceived as "acting in the world in a whole-part manner by influencing human personal experience, an influence that thereby affects events at the physical, biological, and social levels."[47] Peacocke postulates "divine whole-part influence at all levels, but with increasing intensity and manifestation of divine intention from the lowest physical level up to the personal level, where it could be at its most concentrated and most focused."[48]

What is noticeable here is that when Peacocke mentions divine influence in particulars, it does not mean a *localized* event of God's agency at a particular time and place. Rather, it means God's presence in a particular event of creation through holistically influencing creation by

---

43. Peacocke, "Naturalistic Christian Faith," 19. Citing Van Til, "Creation," 349, 151. Following Van Til, Peacocke regards the fine-tuned universe as sufficiently equipped with potentialities for the creation of life and consciousness. Peacocke denies God's objectively special action considering the history of the universe that is long enough to create life and consciousness through natural processes. Peacocke, "Cost of New Life," 26. However, in my view, special divine actions do not have be necessarily compromised even when the interplay of chance and regularities are sufficient for creating life and consciousness in the *deep* history of the universe.

44. Peacocke, "Naturalistic Christian Faith," 46.

45. Divine top-down causation through influencing human persons implies that the divine agency is non-dualistic since this sort of top-down causation is historically the result of the evolution of materials and non-conscious living organisms. In likening God's personal agency to human beings', Peacocke recognizes that there is discontinuity between God's interaction with the world and the interaction between the human body and mind, which is related to the human finitude. Peacocke, *Theology for a Scientific Age*, 144–46.

46. Peacocke, "Naturalistic Christian Faith," 46.

47. Peacocke, "Naturalistic Christian Faith," 46.

48. Peacocke, "Naturalistic Christian Faith," 46–47.

giving it existence and vitalizing the interaction among its particulars in a whole-part influence.[49]

Therefore, I acknowledge that there are both *passive* and *active* aspects of God's creative presence in the world in Peacocke's idea. On the one hand, the traditional notion of God who "sustains the world in its general order and structure" is "enriched by a dynamic and creative dimension."[50] On the other hand, unlike the traditional idea of God who can perform supernatural miracles and has the power to communicate divine revelation through special providence, after giving existence to the self-organizing universe, God is dependent on the law-like regularities and chance. As Charles Kingsley puts it: "God indeed makes 'things make themselves.'"[51]

I think Peacocke does not yield to deism in his scheme even though it may appear deistic due to its passive aspect. While Peacocke emphasizes with Gordon Kaufman and Maurice Wiles that God's action influences the world as a whole, he strongly stresses, "[God's] maintaining and supporting interaction [with the world] is a continuing as well as an initial one."[52] Peacocke sees God as the Creator who actively continues to sustain the emergent evolutionary process through the necessity and chance inherent in the universe with which God endowed the universe.[53]

All in all, the Creator is both personal and supra-personal,[54] in that the Creator communicates the divine intention and purpose in the creative act. However, the creative act is by the mediation of "the [inbuilt] propensities for an increase in complexity, which is the basis for an increase in organization in living organisms, itself as the basis of the emergence of consciousness and so of self-consciousness."[55]

God as person can be regarded as creating the world without violating the natural order yet by way of the necessity and chance built into

---

49. With regard to Peacocke's detailed account on divine whole-part divine agency as holistic interaction, also see "God's Interaction with the World" (chapter 5) of Peacocke's *Paths from Science to God*, 91–115.

50. Peacocke, "Biological Evolution," 359.

51. Peacocke, "Naturalistic Christian Faith," 18. Citing Kingsley, *Water Babies*, 248.

52. Peacocke, *Theology for a Scientific Age*, 163.

53. Peacocke, *Theology for a Scientific Age*, 117–19.

54. For Peacocke, since God also transcends the personal in creation, God is also supra-personal as God is infinite and immanent in all that is.

55. Peacocke, *Theology for a Scientific Age*, 156.

the universe "*ab initio*."⁵⁶ Here, Peacocke rejects objectively special action of God in creation. In other words, without objectively particular or localized divine action,⁵⁷ God holistically interacts with the world by transmitting information to the world-as-a-whole to influence the world in general and its constituents in particular.⁵⁸ In my view, Peacocke presents a way to explain the personal Creator's transcendent immanence in the inherent openness of the natural order in consistency with emergent monism and naturalistic theism. However, as I discuss in the assessment of his scheme later in this chapter, I think his theistic naturalism does not have to be incompatible with special divine action in *creatio continua* and the new creation.

Peacocke's Kenotic Panentheistic Vision of Creation

Peacocke's emergentist monism, theistic naturalism, and divine whole-part influence constitute the ground of a panentheistic vision of the world as God's creation in which God continues creative work "in, with, and under" the natural processes of the world.⁵⁹ He believes that this view can be theologically acceptable when it does not dilute the ontological distinction between God and creation. Thus, Peacocke discusses how both God's immanence and transcendence can be preserved in his panentheism.

Peacocke explains how God's transcendence can be compatible with immanence by employing the metaphor of a human person's action. That is, God's agency within creation is analogous to an embodied person's agency. A person does a certain action through the body, and the action can be described in terms of physiology and anatomy at the bodily level. Yet the person's intention of doing the action transcends the languages of physiology and anatomy. As a person transcends the body, God transcends the world even though the world expresses divine action.⁶⁰

---

56. Peacocke, "Biological Evolution," 363.

57. For Peacocke, the sheer "given-ness" of the potentialities "*ab initio*" in the universe enables him to speak of God's co-suffering in God's continuous creativity, but he precludes not only radical transformation, such as resurrection, but also special divine action in an objective sense. Peacocke, "Biological Evolution," 371–72. See Polkinghorne's critique of Peacocke's idea of downward causation without special action in his *Scientists as Theologians*, 39.

58. Peacocke, *Theology for a Scientific Age*, 157–60.

59. Peacocke, *Theology for a Scientific Age*, 158.

60. Peacocke, "Naturalistic Christian Faith," 23.

I appreciate Peacocke's idea of God's transcendent immanence. However, as I will discuss later in this chapter, considering the contingent nature of natural evil, I think Peacocke needs to consider more seriously the soteriological presence of God through special divine action that Peacocke is reluctant to include in his panentheistic vision of creation. Furthermore, special divine action in *creatio continua* is to be ontologically grounded in the eschatological fulfillment of creation through redeeming creation from the power of death and evil.

Natural and Cosmic Theodicy in Peacocke's ENP Scheme

For Peacocke, this kenotic version of panentheism is more acceptable than classical theism because the former better addresses the problem of evil. That is, in classical theism, God is allegedly immune to the suffering of the world. However, in this panentheistic view, God is in and with the world that suffers. God experiences the pain and suffering undergone by creatures in the course of evolution of life.[61]

The Inevitable and Contingent Presence of Natural Evil in Creation

Concerning the universal prevalence of pain, suffering, and death in the course of evolution, Peacocke sees both positive and negative aspects of natural evil. First, the ubiquity of pain, suffering, and death in the world of living organisms not only may preclude a species or an individual from flourishing but also may serve to stimulate creatures to acquire more and more complexity for survival and better procreation in natural selection. This is because the increase in complexity that led to the emergence of consciousness was the consequence of the interplay of the emergence of novelty and the increase of entropy in the thermodynamic universe.[62] Second, in that vein, natural evil contributed to the diversification of living organisms in the interplay of chance and law.[63] Third, in the finite universe ("finite in the sense of the conservation of matter-energy"), new patterns can come into existence "only if old patterns dissolve to make a place for them."[64]

---

61. Peacocke, "Naturalistic Christian Faith," 25.
62. Peacocke, *Theology for a Scientific Age*, 125–26.
63. Peacocke, *Theology for a Scientific Age*, 119–21.
64. Peacocke, *Theology for a Scientific Age*, 62.

Considering the inevitability of natural evil with both positive and negative aspects, on the one hand, Peacocke celebrates God's "joy and delight in creation,"[65] which is marked by the diversity and richness of life. This is intended by God *ab initio*. On the other hand, in his panentheistic vision, Peacocke regards God as co-suffering with creatures amidst their pain, suffering, and death. Peacocke appreciates the cosmic dimension of Christ's cross as God's participation in the suffering of creatures.

In the kenotic presence of God, on the one hand, God has a particular purpose of bringing about the greater good of the emergence of the human beings who freely love each other, other creatures, and God in genuine communion with God. On the other hand, this mechanism takes a free process that entails inevitable pain and suffering resulting from the uncertainties created by the contingent behaviors of creatures. Accordingly, I think that Peacocke's natural theodicy is both *free-process theodicy* and *developmental good-and-harm theodicy*.

For Peacocke, in continuous creation God brings good out of evil through the inherent creativity of the universe. Here God co-suffers with suffering creatures. Yet God never ceases to create emergent novelty. Nonetheless, there seems to be no room for special providence as objectively particular divine action and the eschatological new creation. This is because of the way Peacocke understands the incarnation, the resurrection, and the new creation in the context of his naturalistic view of special providence. In other words, in his naturalistic theism, Peacocke denies God's special providence as objectively particular divine action and the eschatological redemption of creation by regarding them as supernatural.

Special Providence Reduced to General Providence

For Peacocke, in downward causation, God is equally present in all things created. However, human beings find some sequences of events in the natural surroundings or in human history to be more meaningful. Peacocke affirms that such special occasions take place only in the psychological level when people think that "God unveils his meaning more than in others." Peacocke acknowledges the possibilities of experiencing the patterns of events which "reveal God's meanings most overtly, effectively, and distinctively"[66] without divine intervention in the natural order. Yet

---

65. Peacocke, *Theology for a Scientific Age*, 113–15 [114].
66. Peacocke, *Theology for a Scientific Age*, 181.

they could take place only through God's continuous whole-part constraint and top-down causation.⁶⁷

In the same manner, miracles are not so much physical and biological as psychological, social, and cultural in nature. Therefore, in order for a certain pattern of events to be registered as miraculous, there have to precede certain attitudes toward the scientific possibility of such events along with the preunderstandings of God's interaction with the world that makes such events possible.⁶⁸

In that sense, Peacocke regards special providence such as the incarnation and resurrection as placed in the context of God's general providence. To be specific, Peacocke affirms that the divinity and humanity of Jesus are to be seen in the context of our understanding of his life, death, and the resurrection as interpreted through the lens of the ENP approach. That way, Jesus Christ's divinity has no contradiction with the biological level of his existence, which is his complete humanity. Here, there is no conflict between Christology from above and Christology from below. His humanity is, in and of itself, the expression of the divine transmission of information and the *logos* into the developmental process of the cosmos. His divinity is a new reality that emerges in the process of the expression of the God-transmitted information through the evolution of humanity.⁶⁹

In his life and death, "Jesus' will was fully open in submission to the divine will, such that in his historical person, there emerged a unique new reality, the God-imbued human being."⁷⁰ This emergent reality in Jesus manifested the divine being, insofar as it is expressible in a human form—"the manifestation of a self-offering love which is manifested in

---

67. Peacocke writes that "the particular events or clusters of events, whether natural, individual and personal, or social and historical, (a) can be socially and significantly revelatory of the presence of God and of the nature of his purposes to human beings; and (b) can be intentionally and specifically brought about by the interaction of God with the world in a top-down causative way that does not abrogate the scientifically observed relationships operating at the level of the events in question." Peacocke, *Theology for a Scientific Age*, 182. Here, I agree with Peacocke that special divine action should not violate the God-established order of nature. Yet I find it problematic that Peacocke does not consider the elements of discontinuity between the present and the new creation as the *transformation* of the former. Likewise, as I discuss later, *creatio ex nihilo* should be the ground of the possibility of God's particularly focused action in a bottom-up manner throughout *creatio continua* too, unlike Peacocke denies it.

68. Peacocke, *Theology for a Scientific Age*, 181–83.

69. Peacocke, "Naturalistic Christian Faith," 39.

70. Peacocke, "Naturalistic Christian Faith," 36.

the life, suffering, and passion of Jesus."[71] By this new reality in Jesus characterized by those divine features of the encounter with him, his followers were led to perceive a dimension of transcendence that could be identified only as divine.[72]

Peacocke's emphasis on Jesus's continuity with other human beings and the incarnation in an emergentist framework leads him to affirm that in Christ, one can see "the distinctive manifestation of a possibility always inherently there for human beings in their potential nature." As an example for the destiny of the rest of humanity, Jesus was wholly open to God, so that God's presence could be "clearly unveiled to the rest of humanity in a new, emergent and unexpected manner."[73] In this idea of the incarnation, while special providence is a matter of human persons' fulfillment of their inherent divinely granted potentials and epistemological maturity, one can hardly find room for objectively particular divine action in the incarnation.

This exemplary nature of Jesus Christ reaches culmination in his resurrection as an occasion of the generalization of Jesus' full unity with God in the psychological and possibly-existing higher levels.[74] Peacocke posits that since the historicity of the empty tomb tradition is not sufficiently credible, and as we consider the fate of the physical composition of our bodies after death, the bodily resurrection is not relevant to the future of humanity and the rest of creation. Yet Peacocke affirms that it is improper to dismiss the resurrection of Jesus as merely psychological hallucination because of "the variety of the same witnesses and the witnesses' willingness to suffer and die for their belief."[75] It can be an objective event without being bodily, and this is possible for Peacocke within the emergent hierarchy of reality.[76] That is, Jesus' *personal* resurrection includes the special contents of the life, teaching, and death of Jesus and their influences on the lives of the current believers in the resurrection of Jesus. Likewise, the event also includes the transformation of the witnesses of the resurrection as well as those witnesses' incipient discernment of the presence of God to them and so in Jesus.[77]

71. Peacocke, "Naturalistic Christian Faith," 36.
72. Peacocke, "Naturalistic Christian Faith," 38.
73. Peacocke, *Theology for a Scientific Age*, 187.
74. Peacocke, *Theology for a Scientific Age*, 280–83.
75. Peacocke, "Naturalistic Christian Faith," 33–34.
76. Peacocke, *Theology for a Scientific Age*, 279–80.
77. Peacocke, "Naturalistic Christian Faith," 33.

> The core of resurrection faith is that already within the temporal order of existence, a new beginning of a life in unity with God, is possible, and is also anticipatory of what human life has in it to be as divine creation; and that this has been made apprehensible and available in the life of Christ as effective power for overcoming whatever obstructs a life fully open to God.[78]

The resurrection of Jesus could be described as an emergent event, in which the disciples experienced the possibility of a new level inherent in this creation through Jesus.

While gleaning significant insights from the contemporary revival of the theology of the cross, Peacocke also appropriates the ideas of the theologians of hope such as Moltmann, Pannenberg, and Braaten. However, what strikes me is that while Peacocke appropriates their ideas, he dismisses their understandings of the eschaton as the future of God that redeems and affirms the *material* world.[79] Rather, he presents a disembodied *transcendental* notion of the new creation.

Those theologians of hope stress that the unfolding of history is the work of the Spirit as the pledge of the eschatological kingdom (or *basileia*) and that the eschaton is the fulfillment of creation through the transformation of this world. Therefore, the coming of the future of God in the present includes God's objectively particular action within the universe as an emergent whole without violating the established order of nature, given that it is in genuine openness to novelty.

In Peacocke's appropriation of their eschatological ideas, the eschatological reality is not a radically new divine event, but is rather built into the universe that is divinely endowed with God-given propensities, and it can take place here and now. These propensities are open to the random future yet constrained by the inbuilt propensities of nature that can be theologically deemed to be God's general divine ordering of the world. This takes place through the emergence of higher complexity and finally the emergence of a community of the loving people of God who freely commit themselves to the genuine communion with God, other fellow humans, and all other non-human creatures.

In my view, if the bodily resurrection of Jesus proleptically shows us God's eschatological fulfillment of the divine purpose for the present creation rather than replacing it or violating it, it also shows us that God's *creatio continua* through general providence is not exclusive to divine

---

78. Peacocke, "Naturalistic Christian Faith," 35.
79. Peacocke, *Theology for a Scientific Age*, 344–46.

special action. However, for Peacocke, *visio Dei* as the eschatological fulfillment of creation does not involve any redemptive action of God. Rather, it results from the emergent evolution that develops through the potentials God granted it *ab initio*. Likewise, Peacocke rejects the idea of special divine lure or special divine action. In that way, Peacocke's panentheism, in my view, represents a *modalistic expression* of a trinitarian way of God's act of creating through emergent evolution. The regenerative and emergent evolution expresses the trinitarian aspects of the loving Creator in a modalistic manner.[80] Yet Peacocke does not consider the three Persons of the Godhead to be fulfilling the eschatological telos of creation from the vantage point of the new creation as *creatio ex vetere* or the transformation of the old.

A "Future-less" yet Hopeful Fulfillment of Creation

Peacocke's theodicy is not anthropocentric because God redeems the world in God's faithfulness through sustaining the self-organizing universe in God's self-limitation. However, his eschatology does not seem to affirm the genuine value of non-human creatures and the physical cosmos as good creation without which the community of the people of God cannot emerge. Furthermore, God is not faithful to creation to the extent that God redeems the victims of biological evolution by natural selection. Nor is there objectively special divine action en route to the fulfillment of the new creation. Peacocke finds God's faithfulness to creation in God's co-suffering with creatures. However, Peacocke does not consider seriously the historical possibility and the cosmic implications of the bodily resurrection of Jesus Christ.

For Peacocke, in the life, death, and resurrection of Jesus, we see "a concentration of the activity of the immanent Creator to bring created personal-ness out of materiality into the divine life." Likewise, "[f]rom the perspective of the Christian revelation, the ultimate destiny of humanity is to be 'in God,' to be vouchsafed that beatific vision so nobly expressed in the last stanzas of Dante's *Paradiso*."[81] In other words, in the future of creation, the non-human creatures and the cosmic construct as their nest do not have a resurrection hope. Only the personal or spiritual have that

---

80. For a similar assessment of Peacocke's trinitarian thinking, see Buxton, *Trinity, Creation and Pastoral Ministry*, 28–30.

81. Peacocke. *Theology for a Scientific Age*, 344.

hope. In that sense, I think Peacocke's eschatology becomes transcendental, and therefore, goes against his holistic idea of the universe.

Peacocke affirms that theology is to go beyond natural sciences in speaking of for the hopeful future of the universe in the face of the scientifically predicted cosmic demise. Yet he falls into agnosticism as he attempts to place the bodily resurrection of Jesus within the bounds of his ENP scheme. [82] He does not consider that the bodily resurrection in the Christian tradition implies God's affirmation of the material world and life in it as a whole.

As a result, his idea of a *personal resurrection* ends up as the continuation of one's personhood or self without the resurrection of one's physical body. But the problem is that personhood or self cannot be separated from one's body. That is what Peacocke as an emergent monist believes: the mental level of a person cannot exist without his or her physical body even though the former is not reduced to the latter. Related, his interpretation of the resurrection is problematic in that it also gives no hope to non-human embodied creatures as well as the entire universe at large; there is no hope for the future-less universe that will end up in *Freeze* or *Fry*. Let us now move to consider Keller's theodicy.

Natural/Cosmic Theodicy in Keller's *Tehomic* Perspective

For Peacocke, God is deeply immanent within creation as the ground of being while fulfilling the purpose of creation through the contingent becoming of creatures in the emergent-monistic universe. In that process, God co-suffers with creatures suffering due to inevitable natural evil as a byproduct of the person-making creation. The mode of God's creative act is top-down/whole-part influence or constraint.

Unlike Peacocke, Keller in her process theology emphasizes God's particular and responsive lure at every occasion in responsive love. God is also transcendent as the infinite source of possibilities open to the world. For Keller, however, God does not have the power to give existence to creatures and sustain them, but rather can only influence every occasion as the incessant divine lure. Thus, she does not see the bodily redemption of the creatures in the immanence of the faithful Creator.

Before engaging in a comparative study of Keller's and Peacocke's theodical arguments, I first discuss Keller's methodology and the doctrine

---

82. Peacocke. *Theology for a Scientific Age*, 344–46.

of creation as the context of her natural and cosmic theodicy, and then move on to consider the way she understands creative divine action amid natural and cosmic evil.

Process Panentheism as a Metaphysical Framework in Theology-Science Dialogue

For Keller, considering the universal presence of evil prevalent in both human and non-human realms of creation, Calvinistic understanding of the divine action in the world cannot resolve the problem of theodicy in a theologically persuasive way. She writes, "Calvin is right that God is not sitting in a watchtower, impassively awaiting the blowback. God is there in the midst of every event. Calvin, however, assumed that to *participate* in an event is to *control* it."[83]

While Keller discerns God's panentheistic immanence in the world (similarly to Peacocke), she rejects divine action as God's intervention in a causal system or network of creatures. The biological evolution within the self-organizing universe is to be seen as the way God is present in the creative process without intervening in its natural processes. At the same time, similarly to Peacocke, God is also transcendent by incessantly providing new potentials for the world in continuing development. While not dissolving God's transcendence into the free processes of nature, Keller celebrates the integrity of the natural order as God's creation.

For Keller, God is immanent as the irreducible infinity by incessantly transcending what exists in the created world. Thus, God and creation are not in a *binary* or *dualistic* interaction. Rather, God remains the matrix of the infinite possibilities for the continuous creation of the universe that never ends. In this inseparable entanglement between God and creation, God's purposive creation of the cosmos is endlessly actualized in and by the cosmos itself. Thus, in understanding the ineffable notion of the divine infinity, Keller adopts the metaphor of *the cloud of the impossible* that consistently becomes possible while incessantly opening the horizons of novelty to emerge in creation.

God's influence of love or the infinite desire (*eros*) for life is in the process of "absolution, dissolution, and resolution" through the responses of creatures to the divine lure. This is universal in all emergent levels of creation. Here, I find Keller's *non-binary* understanding of the

83. Keller, *On the Mystery*, 81.

God-world relationship to be in parallel with Peacocke's non-dualistic or *naturalistic* notion of the divine whole-part causation. However, Peacocke identifies God as the creative ground of being for the existence of the emergent process of the universe that develops through the pre-given rich potentials to be contingently actualized.

Yet Keller sees God as a continuously responsive *lure* for the world processes to actualize themselves according to her *dipolar* panentheism. That is, when one says that God wills something, to will is not to be counted as the same as to cause. Rather, God's willing is to be God's "wanting, desiring, and urging", [84] or "eros".[85] God's initial lure continuously works persuasively through persistently responding to the contingent choices and acts by creatures.

Keller names her idea of creation as non-dualistic since the evolution of the material world is never possible without the creativity of God. However, I think this idea is still dualistic in that creation is not in God, but rather, they are *co-eternal*. In contrast, in Peacocke's concept of divine downward influence, God as the ground of being in absolute freedom to create provides creation with its in-built propensities, and in God's self-limitation, continues to give it existence. Hence, it can continuously operate by chance and law to fulfill the divine *telos* since its sustenance is contingent if chance is an actual factor in its operation.

For Keller, while God lures creation into developing diversity and the higher levels of complexity within a self-organizing creation, God works at every level of the emergent hierarchy of creation through the responsive lure.[86] Those potentials are not built into the universe but there is spontaneous mutual interaction between creation and God. Keller sees God as the One who responsively interacts with creatures, by opening up new creative potentials for the creatures, so that they can break through the chaos of the world that represents both pain and suffering and yet the womb of new potentialities. Here, Keller brilliantly engages with the resources of modern natural sciences, process theology, various medieval and postmodern thinkers.

---

84. Keller, *On the Mystery*, 99–101 [100].
85. Keller, *On the Mystery*, 99.
86. Keller, *On the Mystery*, 23–24.

The Apophatic Entanglement of the World in Keller's Engagement with Contemporary Natural Sciences

Keller engages with chaos theory, self-organizing complexity theory, quantum indeterminacy, and superstring theory. These scientific theories indicate the indeterminacy and continuous creativity of evolutionary process[87] and interdependency among creatures.[88] Superstring theory, one of the most recent theories in physics, suggests that the microscopic landscape is "suffused with tiny strings whose vibrational patterns orchestrate the evolution of the cosmos."[89] According to this theory, the development of the cosmos is characterized by continuous pulsations of the microscopic strings. What we learn from this theory is the unending rhythmical movements in the microscopic level of the cosmos.

Chaos theory, on the other hand, engages with complex physical systems, which are extremely sensitive to initial conditions.[90] There are two hallmarks of chaotic systems. First, the equations describing a system are highly interdependent. This creates the second hallmark, namely, the system is highly dependent on initial conditions. Accordingly, even a small change in the system can result in a large effect on the later condition of the system. Since it is impossible to measure all the initial parameters exactly, the trajectory of the system's operation is inherently indeterminate. That is, this theory is represented by the interdependence among constituents of a system and the uncertainty of the possible conditions of its stages of development.[91]

Coupled with superstring theory, algorithms of chaos mathematics "depict not some formless disorder but the complex forms of flow, too complex precisely in their fluidity, to be captured in linear formulae."[92] In the highly complex interrelatedness and indeterminacy, this cosmos evolves as a self-organizing creation and is understood as an organism

---

87. Keller, *On the Mystery*, 47–52, 149–52. Here, Keller focuses on chaos theory in her discussion of indeterminacy and interrelatedness in the creativity of creation. Also, for her engagement of quantum mechanics, see chapter 4 ("Spooky Entanglements: The Physics of Nonseparability") of Keller's *Cloud of the Impossible*.

88. Keller, *On the Mystery*, 22–24. Also, see her chapter 5 ("The Fold in Process") as well as chapter 4 ("Spooky Entanglements") of her *The Cloud of the Impossible*.

89. Keller, *On the Mystery*, 49.

90. Keller, *On the Mystery*, 52.

91. Keller, *On the Mystery*, 149–51.

92. Keller, *On the Mystery*, 51.

that is in the process of continuous creation through "the interplay of chance and natural law."[93]

In that sense, as Ilya Prigogine and Stuart Kauffman hold, our cosmos is in the continuous process of the emergence of complexity and order in nonlinear systems at the edge of chaos.[94] "Every beginning is a beginning-again."[95] For this reason, Keller affirms this cosmos is to be regarded as having inherently open-ended interactivity.[96] As to the open-ended interactivity, in her most recent writing, Keller brings into her attention quantum indeterminacy, superposition, and non-separability, while appropriating these up-to-date scientific resources in rendering her process theism more intelligible to the contemporary reader. Keller engages with the works of Karen Barad and Henry Stapp who contribute to bridging process metaphysics with quantum theory.[97] Thereby, Keller discusses that the world is continually in the state of *becoming* in interdependence, and all its constituents are "intra-active" rather than interactive.[98]

Here, Keller explains that the parts of a whole are in the process of mutual creation via ontologically inseparable interaction. In coherence with this discussion, Keller draws upon the philosophy of Gilles Deleuze in developing Whitehead's process ideas.[99] Whitehead affirmed that all entities in the world are *mutually conditioned* by their relations. He writes that "when an entity is objectified by another, it is present in the latter."[100]

---

93. Keller, *On the Mystery*, 61.

94. Keller, *On the Mystery*, 61–63.

95. Keller, *On the Mystery*, 48.

96. Keller, *On the Mystery*, 81. Also, see Keller's detailed account on *counter-apocalyptic* and *inconclusive* eschatology in her *Apocalypse Now and Then*, 273–310.

97. Chapter 4 ("Spooky Entanglements: The Physics of Nonseparability") of Keller's *Cloud of the Impossible*.

98. Keller, *Cloud of the Impossible*, 120–22. In her more recent essay on the theological import of the inseparable entanglement in the quantum level, Keller regards the body of Jesus as the locus of the Supreme Entanglement through all creatures–both inorganic and organic, and across all the levels of complexity–are interdependent and intertwined. In the body of Jesus, they find their ultimate model of relating to each as their differences do not dilute their interdependence. Keller, "Tingles of Matter, Tangles of Theology," 111–35.

99. Moving on to chapter 5 of the book ("The Fold in Process"), Keller further develops the discourse of the interrelatedness as well as ontological and epistemological unpredictability through her dialogue with Deleuze.

100. Griffin, *Process Christology*, 179. Citing Whitehead, *Religion in the Making*, 91, 149.

Deleuze elaborates this point by contending that all identities are brought into being by differences.[101] Therefore, identity does not precede difference logically or metaphysically. Rather, identity consistently emerges in the waves of differentiation. "Enfolding and unfolding" endlessly ensues. In that sense, simplicity does not mean a state of static unity, but it is ontologically inherent in the complexity of nature. Simplicity and complexity are not opposite, but they are like the two sides of a coin dialectically.[102] All identities are inherently in "an apophatic entanglement."[103]

The Entangled Universe as God's *Creatio ex Profundis* in *Creatio Continua*

For Keller, the discussed contemporary scientific discoveries are significant in our understanding of God's relationship with the world if the world is God's creation where God manifests Godself. For this reason, the Genesis creation narrative as to the creation of diverse species is to be re-read in the light of "the current scientific metaphor of self-organizing complexity" as an interpretive device.[104]

In Keller's *re-reading* of the Genesis creation narrative, the hermeneutical key is the fact the cosmos is in the constant process of contingent self-organization. To be specific, "*Tohu va bohu*" in the first verse is literally translated as "waste and wild".[105] Being a playful poetic repetition, however, it also connotes a creative vibration. *Tehom* in the second verse is translated into "the oceanic deep" that was later translated into Greek as *abyssos* that means chaos.[106] These two terms seem to bear a close analogy to the indeterminate and rhythmical waves of the strings on the microscopic physical level. In the language of quantum mechanics, one quantum event is in both particle- and wave- forms in superposition.[107]

The creative indeterminacy and interdependence inherent in the cosmos can be metaphorically expressed as chaos. Here, chaos is the

---

101. Keller gleans these ideas from Deleuze, *Fold* and *Difference and Repetition*.
102. Keller, *Cloud of the Impossible*, 168–72.
103. Keller, *Cloud of the Impossible*, 34.
104. Keller, *On the Mystery*, 46.
105. Keller, *On the Mystery*, 48.
106. Keller, *On the Mystery*, 49
107. Keller, *Cloud of the Impossible*, 13–40.

"womb" of the cosmos.[108] The current dialectic of order and disorder is created *ex profundis* (or out of chaos). "Ruach Elohim" in Genesis 1:4, which is translated as "the spirit/breath/wind of God", needs to be seen in correspondence to "the whirlwind of God" in the book of Job 38:1 as well as "the uncontainable wind blowing in truth, flowing as living water" in the gospel of John 3:8.[109] Based on these accounts, Keller holds that God continually creates through self-organizing systems that are open to the genuine novelty of the future while conditioned by the past occasions of their developmental processes in intertwined relationship with each other.[110] In this regard, God is the creative and responsive *eros*.[111]

I find that Keller's understanding of God's continuous creation through the self-organizing complexity of the universe does not consist in the metaphysical ground of being like in Peacocke's. Rather, Keller affirms that there was no time when the universe was not self-organizing in the context of her doctrine of *creatio ex profundis*.[112] In the interaction with the others, God is also perennially constrained by the dipolar metaphysic rather than imposing self-limitation on Godself to give freedom to creatures after *creatio ex nihilo*. Yet God is still infinite in that God primordially provides all possibilities and continues to open new futures in responding to the contingent actions of creatures.[113]

In that sense, with Nicholas of Cusa, Keller conceives of God as *posse ipsum* for all things that exist in their relations and interdependence that continue in the continuous process of absolution and dissolution and knowing and unknowing.[114] Furthermore, with Jacques Derrida, Keller contends that by challenging an actualized occasion God is there at the actualized occasion as "the possibility itself of deconstruction" for the

108. Keller, *On the Mystery*, 56.
109. Keller, *On the Mystery*, 49.
110. Keller, *On the Mystery*, 61–62.
111. Keller, *On the Mystery*, 98–100.
112. Keller, *On the Mystery*, 48.
113. Keller, *Cloud of the Impossible*, 187–89.
114. Keller, *Cloud of the Impossible*, 47. Citing Nicholas of Cusa, "On the Summit of Contemplation," 295. Furthermore, drawing upon his idea of "knowing ignorance" or *docta ignorantia* [cited from Nicholas of Cusa, "De Visione Dei," in *Nicholas of Cusa*, 252.], Keller discusses the infinite God who is both continuously known and unknown as God indwells in all creatures that are in incessantly becoming new via interrelation with each other. God's Truth here is impossible to be known but is to be continuously sought after within creation. God provides the infinite possibilities of becoming. Keller, *Cloud of the Impossible*, 15–19.

sake of God's self-transcendence in relation to others.[115] In that vein, "In the dense matrix of relatedness ... creative newness is not disconnection, but new connection."[116] In the cosmos, there is a matrix of cosmic interrelations that bottom into an infinite depth. This depth of interrelations implies both the past of the relations and their open-ended/unpredictable future in the course of incessant *intra-action*.

The *depth of relations* per sciences lacks the *interpersonal* relatedness of God. However, it can be theologically translated into "the depth of the God-self, the creative womb of all that is."[117] In this frame of reference, while God is the One who is manifest in creaturely occasions, God still opens new possibilities for the creation without end. It is an individual creature "here/now" that incessantly emerges "within the matrix of all creaturely relations" going through deconstruction and reconstruction.[118]

Keller agrees with Barbour that, in response to the past concrescence of occasions, God is a "structuring cause" who opens up for creatures "the range of possibilities within which creatures act."[119] Nonetheless, unlike Peacocke who maintains *creatio ex nihilo*, Keller does not regard the range of the possibilities as that which God continues to provide through the in-built potentialities inherent in the universe since God does not create the world *ex nihilo*. Rather, the open possibilities lured by God imply that the creativity of this world is conditioned by both God and the world co-eternally.

In my view, it is no wonder Keller does not find the significance of the anthropic principle in her identification of evolution as the locus of *creatio continua*. In this respect, the divine freedom to create "depends upon the responsive freedom of the creatures, [and] the lapping and overlapping of influences flowing upon the face of the deep."[120] The open-ended interactivity is a metaphysical principle under which both God

---

115. Keller, *Cloud of the Impossible*, 46. Citing Derrida, *Specters of Marx*, 59.

116. Keller, *On the Mystery*, 106.

117. Keller, *On the Mystery*, 99. In that sense, Keller also writes, "To collapse God into the sheer impersonality of Process might undo the anthropomorphism, but it is not Whitehead's solution, God is rather a metaphor of the relation to the infinite process. And God, thus, provides a primordial locus of all possibilities, which begin to lose their sheer abstraction already by being housed, tabernacled." Keller, *Cloud of the Impossible*, 188.

118. Keller, *On the Mystery*, 99.

119. Keller, *On the Mystery*, 62. Citing Barbour, *When Science Meets Religion*, 164.

120. Keller, *On the Mystery*, 89.

and the world make their ways along the incessant process of dissolution and resolution. I appreciate Keller's proposal of God's honoring creation's freedom and contingency in God's spontaneously responsive love. However, as I discuss later in this chapter, I regret Keller's God is not powerful enough to be responsible for the universal, inevitable, and contingent evil for which God's act of creating is ultimately responsible.

Keller's Natural / Cosmic Theodicy in *Tehomic* Perspective

As discussed above, Keller's *Tehomic* perspective draws upon diverse theological, philosophical, and scientific resources to find consonance between a Christian doctrine of creation and the contemporary natural sciences. In this context, Keller engages with her natural and cosmic theodicy. I now turn to Keller's understanding of the presence of the sweeping prevalence of pain and suffering in nature as well as the cosmic evil.

A Dialectical Ontology of Chaos

As discussed above, the cosmos in general is in constantly creative formation out of the never-dissipated chaos. There is the incessant emergence of order and new lives in a nonlinear system. Hence, chaos is both good and evil. I think this resonates with Peacocke's understanding of the pain and suffering in nature as both positive and negative for the same reason. On the one hand, chaos both threatens the stability of lives in the cosmos and threatens the sustenance of lives. In that sense, it can be identified with evil to the human eye. Keller locates the identity between chaos and evil in Scripture. "Biblical scholars draw on divine warrior motifs in Isaiah and the Psalms to make a case that the biblical God does create through violence, that chaos is evil, and that God creates and redeems not from nothing but from the struggle with the sea monster, sometimes called Leviathan."[121] Interestingly, Keller here does not discuss the presence of the universal entropy as *death* and *decay* as natural evil. Yet entropy and chaos share a similarity in that they both signify disorderliness and threats to the stability of life, and thus they both can be interpreted as natural evil.

---

121. Keller, *On the Mystery*, 57. As to *chaoskampf*, see Keller, *Face of the Deep*, 111–14, 215.

At the same time, in modern natural sciences, disorderliness or chaos can be seen not only as evil but also as good for the cosmos since there is the birth of a new life at the edge of chaos. The goodness of chaos also appears in different parts of Scripture. That is, in the Genesis creation narrative, *Tehom*, the oceanic depth is analogous to the state of chaos, but it can be regarded as "the very *womb* of the world."[122] Therefore, for Keller, the watery chaos in the creation account does not mean an evil to be vanquished by a good God. This interpretation is supported by Psalm 104 in which the sea monster Leviathan is celebrated as a playmate of God, and the ocean is not depicted as something to be conquered, but as the place where diverse lives flourish.[123]

All in all, for Keller, chaos in the universe is not only evil but also good. At first glance, Keller's view of evil looks like that of a "developmental good-and-harm theodicy". In a developmental good-and-harm theodicy, God is ultimately responsible for the existence of evil as God creates all that is *ex nihilo*. In this scheme, evil as an inevitable byproduct of God's good creation functions as a developmental hindrance in creation's growth into God's goodness. Thus, "God is 'ultimately ordaining sin and suffering' and hence, bears the ultimate responsibility."[124]

In contrast, for Keller, God does not permit the entry of evil into creation. Rather, God is with God's creation in loving interaction in the face of incessantly crashing waves of chaos without a temporal beginning and end.[125] Thus, there is "a cosmic liturgy: divine lure, creaturely improvisation, and divine reception."[126] Here, chaos is co-eternal with the *omni-amorous* God and God as the infinite love does not force but lures the chaos into order.

Along similar lines, God can be identified with the *Abba* who was in Jesus' suffering on the cross.[127] Yet the co-suffering of God has a creative and redeeming power because God's co-suffering with Jesus means

---

122. Keller, *On the Mystery*, 58.

123. In Keller's scheme, death, suffering, and pain in nature is reduced to disorderliness in which all the organisms are interrelated and create new lives through the endless waves of dissolution and resolution. Chaos serves as the *womb* for new lives without considering the problem of God's faithfulness to each creature victimized in the process as well as the heat death of the cosmos.

124. Kärkkäinen, *Creation and Humanity*, 198.

125. Keller, *On the Mystery*, 72–74.

126. Keller, *On the Mystery*, 62.

127. Keller, *On the Mystery*, 83–87.

the unclosed horizons of the hope for reconciliation and healing as God raises Jesus in the resurrection. However, God is an incessantly empowering power rather than a telos-fulfilling power of the eschatological new creation. Likewise, amid chaos, God lures creation to form new lives and the potentials of life-affirming love and justice in the world. God's co-suffering of Jesus means God's deep immanence in the world including the non-human creatures as one considers "our interdependence as creatures of an intricately interwoven creation."[128] Thus, for Keller, the notion of God's omnipotence is to be replaced with the notion of a non-coercive, responsive, and creative love in a continuous process.

This may sound like God's free decision to limit Godself similarly to Peacocke's kenotic idea of creation. However, in Keller's scheme, death, suffering, and pain inherent in nature tend to be reduced to a matter of "co-eternal chaos" in which all organisms are interrelated and are re-organized into new lives through the endless waves of dissolution and resolution. God is a creative lure while either positive or negative response to the lure is the contingent choice of creature. I agree with Keller that the dissolution of an organism is necessary for the birth of a new life and thus serves as the womb for new lives. If God is the omni-amorous richness of possibilities for a new future, God is to be seen as a non-coercive lure as well as a co-suffering persuader. However, I think the chaos as the womb of life itself is to be regarded as God's own creation *ex nihilo*, as Peacocke affirms, based on theological, philosophical, and scientific reasons that I will discuss in the next section.

Furthermore, for that reason, I think we are to consider seriously the eschatological new creation by considering God's faithfulness to each individual creature and its species that are victimized in the process of evolution and in the heat death of our universe. In my view, Keller's idea of God as the com/passionate lure fails to fulfill the ultimate responsibility of a faithful God we see in the bodily resurrection of Jesus. Keller places special providence in the matrix of her idea of divine lure of creatures into a new ordered life, beauty, and diversity in God's non-coercive yet creative love.

128. Keller, *On the Mystery*, 106.

Special Providence in the Matrix of Chaos

In Keller's idea of *creatio ex profundis*, God is always particularly present in creation by providing specific potentials for creatures to actualize in specific contexts. As the initial lure of God grounds all the possibilities for the world to continue to form, God can be responsive to each occasion of creation. In that sense, I think the miraculous can be seen as God's personal response to the needs of creatures without violating the established order of nature.

This is intelligible to the modern mind of a scientific age. Keller's perspective is also faithful to the dynamic-and-creative love of God presented in Scripture. God is the loving Creator who became manifest in Jesus' life-affirming table fellowship of love that empowered and gave genuine hope to the marginalized and the hopeless. Be that as it may, one may ask how we would render the genuine meaning of Easter as a bodily death-overcoming event if we adopted Keller's view of God's *endless* co-suffering yet life-luring presence in creation. With Keller, how could we speak of the eschatological redemption of creation that is central to Christian theodicy? Also, what could we speak of a hopeful future of the cosmos in the face of the scientifically predicted demise of the universe?

In my reading of Keller's writings, while she affirms the autonomy of theology and natural science, the consistency between the two disciplines leads to the identification of special divine actions, such as Jesus Christ's incarnation and his resurrection, with the "root-metaphors" taken to interpret natural events in the context of the Christian vision of reality.[129] This is obvious in Keller's understanding of the resurrection of Jesus and

---

129. Griffin also argues in a similar way that special revelation is not only subjective but also objective, while its distinguished meaning cannot be acknowledged without the prevenient Judeo-Christian vision of reality. Griffin, *Process Christology*, 16–18. A vision of reality is a system of coherent root metaphors, or in Ian Barbour's terms, "the total matrix of life and thought of a community." Barbour, *Myths, Models, and Paradigms*, 67. A religious model is a construct that people use to account for an observed pattern of events in the inner world of human experience. Some are the interpretation of experience, while others are the expression of people's moral attitudes. In both cases, models are intended to disclose certain aspects of human life. Thus, an "empirical fit" between religious models and their corresponding experiences is to be communally tested. Barbour, *Myths, Models, and Paradigms*, 60–63. When the models are highly reliable, they lead to the construction of metaphysical systems that stay with people longer and with a stronger impact in their world views and ways of life. Barbour names these cases "root metaphors." Barbour, *Myths, Models, and Paradigms*, 65. For a more detailed account of a religious model (or parable), paradigm, and root-metaphor, see McFague, *Metaphorical Theology*, 108–11.

its eschatological implication. For Keller, Jesus' Christ-ness does not lie in his identity as the Son of God that is historically confirmed by his bodily resurrection. Rather, Jesus is "a Christ-process" in that Jesus himself lived out a life that actualized the *basileia* of God—the loving, life-affirming, and just rule of God—in his ministry and life for the poor and the oppressed.[130] What makes Jesus a Christ is his "priority of love and option for the poor"[131] that belongs to the *basileia* of God.

Whereas Keller does not explicitly deny the historicity of Jesus' resurrection, she apparently seems to neither acknowledge nor pay special heed to it. She interprets the event as a metaphor for endlessly continuing transcendence (both objective and subjective) in our lives here and now. To put it differently, Keller understands Jesus' resurrection as "some kind of psychic-somatic contact with the *dead* young rabbi."[132] "Jesus died and came alive again in the narrative of the risen Christ. The Christ-symbol is alive *only* to the extent that it is *embodied in process*."[133] In this respect, Jesus "died as a parabler [of the *basileia*] of God, and rose as *Parable*."[134] Jesus spoke of God's *basileia* through the parables that both reveal and conceal the *basileia* of God. His resurrection means the incessant revelation and embodiment of his parables of the *basileia* of God. This embodiment of God's rule of love and justice proceeds without end in the open-ended interactivity among creatures. In this interpretation, the incarnation of Jesus is to "get redistributed as *intercarnation*."[135]

Keller regards special divine action in the matrix of *creatio ex profundis*. God's special revelation via Jesus's life, death, and resurrection is counted as special because of Jesus' total openness to the creative and responsive lure of God. This is equally possible for all other creatures in God's incessant act of luring. For this reason, Keller coins "Christographics" to substitute for the traditional term Christology as the latter stresses the uniqueness that separates Jesus from others.[136]

---

130. Keller, *On the Mystery*, 133–55.
131. Keller, *On the Mystery*, 142.
132. Keller, *Apocalypse Now and Then*, 91.
133. Keller, *On the Mystery*, 154, emphasis mine.
134. Keller, *On the Mystery*, 155.
135. Keller, *Cloud of the Impossible*, 296, emphasis mine.
136. Keller, *Cloud of the Impossible*, 288–300. According to Griffin, the particularity of divine revelation in Jesus's message, cross, and resurrection is commonly possible for every other human being. Thus, it is not particular but general in terms of the kind and intensity of divine information. However, it is special in that it took place in

For Keller, God invites every creature to be part of the actualization of God's *basileia* here and now. The reality of the *basiliea* of God is contextual in nature. In other words, it appears in a mode of open-ended "closing" and "disclosing." Whereas countless differences are not sublimated into colorless oneness, the identity appears out of irreducible distinctiveness. An identity is in constant becoming in the relentless emergence of distinctiveness.[137] Furthermore, there is no linearity in the flow of time. Because all of the past occasions do not close but disclose unactualized novelty, there is rather a spiral of times in the unfolding of new occasions in ongoing intertextual dialogue. Thus, Keller denies the eschatological fulfillment of creation.

In that sense, there is no all-closing apocalypse at the end of the linear flow of time.[138] Accordingly, there is no beginning of a new creation; nor will there be final overcoming of natural and cosmic evil.[139] Thus, Keller is not interested in seeking mutual interaction between theology and science on the fulfillment of a new creation as *creatio ex vetere*.

Comparative Assessment of Keller's and Peacocke's Natural and Cosmic Theodicy

Comparative Assessment of the Methods in Theology-Science Dialogue

In the comparative analysis of Peacocke's and Keller's perspectives, I find their theodical ideas to complement each other in significant ways. Put differently, in his emergent-naturalistic-panentheistic (ENP) perspective, Peacocke conceptualizes God as teleologically creating the universe *ex nihilo* and continues to be creative in it through the free process of God's purposeful creation. In that sense, God is both active and passive while God fulfills the purpose of creation. In that process, God faithfully co-suffers with creatures suffering in the inevitable byproduct of natural evil. However, Peacocke's God rarely work through special lures.

---

the context of Jewish monotheism and its apocalyptic anticipation that enabled Jesus to fully open himself to the hope of the kingdom of God. Griffin, *Process Christology*, 206–32.

137. Keller, *Apocalypse*, 1–35.
138. Keller, *Apocalypse*, 84–138.
139. Keller, *On the Mystery*, 170–76

Keller portrays God as a spontaneous and responsive (or special) lure immanent in creation by providing creatures with the possibilities to actualize in the emergence of novelty based on their past and present and in interrelations with other creatures. In my view, she does not dismiss the purposiveness of the evolutionary character of the universe. This is because she distinguishes the "initial" lure of God (God's purposive act) and the "subjective" lure of an occasion.[140] An actualized occasion is the fruit of an entity's subjective response to the divine purposive lure.

However, the actualization of the purposive lure is not grounded in the free process of necessity and chance that God endowed the universe with via *ex nihilo* (coupled with divine self-limitation). Likewise, in the case of Jesus as a *Christ-process*, Jesus was in *particular* cultural and historical circumstances as he responded to the divine lure. Furthermore, Jesus was received as the Son of God in the Jewish apocalyptic tradition that was a particular cultural context. For us here and now, the belief in Jesus as Christ consists of how we respond to the tradition. Jesus is "one particular Christ-process" that serves as a parable for the coming of other messiahs in other contexts.[141] The *basileia* of God has not been fully actualized with the coming of Jesus; it is still in process. The entitlement of Jesus as a Christ does not lie in his identity as the Son of God and the Son of Man that originates from the "bodily" resurrection, the confirmation of his message of the *basileia* of God.

In contrast, while Peacocke explicitly opposes deism, he rejects the Whiteheadian notion of a special lure in the world occurrences that would imply special divine actions that can be objectively particular within God's general providential ordering.[142] He also denies any eschatologically transformative action of God beyond general providence like the bodily resurrection of Jesus.[143]

Nonetheless, in my view, this does not mean that Peacocke denies special providence per se. He acknowledges the experience of divine special act as ontologically actual. However, Peacocke sees it as an "emergent" entity that is part of God's general act of creation through a whole-part

---

140. For the concept of the initial aim and a subjective aim, see Griffin, *Process Christology*, 181–86. Cobb and Griffin, *Process Theology*, 22–29.

141. Keller, *On the Mystery*, 152–55.

142. Barbour, "Remembering Arthur Peacocke," 96.

143. Furthermore, as discussed in the previous section, Peacocke grounds the emergence of the community of the loving people of God in the whole-part constraint by God *ab initio*.

constraint, rather than an objectively divine particular action. God actively continues to sustain the emergent evolutionary process through the necessity and chance inherent in the universe with which God endowed the universe *ab initio*.

By the same token, for Peacocke, Jesus' life, teaching, and cross are the manifestations of the *agapic* love of God. They mean Jesus' unity with God and the possibility for the same in the lives of all other humans and other non-human creatures via God's faithfully continuous whole-part constraint and top-down causation. That reality comes to pass through the fulfillment of the propensities embedded in the free process of nature in which all creatures are interrelated and affect each other. The resurrection of Jesus represents the apex of the process of becoming in total unity with God that is part of the divine general ordering of the world, which is also exemplary for all other creatures.

It does not mean that God's *direct* or objectively particular influence is on the crucified Jesus and his resurrection. Like Keller, Peacocke contends that the interpretation of the resurrection belongs to the psychological, social, and cultural levels or one that is above them, if there is any upper level in the epistemological hierarchy. Special providence emerges as a level in or above the psychological level as it belongs to God's general ordering of the world created to participate in unity with God. This notion of the resurrection coheres with Peacocke's idea of the eschaton as an emergent state of spiritualized unity with God "out of material" as I discussed in the first section of this chapter.

What, however, differentiates Peacocke from Keller is that for him *creatio ex nihilo* is the context where one understands the emergence of consciousness, self-consciousness, and the community of people seeking to embody the *basileia* of God in self-humbling and mutual respect. As the emergence of *Homo sapiens* is one of the branches of the humongous tree of evolution, one cannot find the history of biological evolution predetermined. Nonetheless, the potentials for their emergences are created and granted by God *ab initio*.

For that reason, in my understanding, Peacocke's idea of divine action in creation is more teleological than Keller's. While Keller's process panentheism also has a teleological aspect due to the initial lure of God, metaphysically, the world in response to God's lure is co-eternal with God. That is, God does not have the power to bring the world into existence *ex nihilo*; but, the poles of the material and the spiritual (or mental) are metaphysically applied not only to the world but also to God.

Here I find a difference between Keller and Peacock, as astutely pointed out by Ted Peters: "In contrast to Whiteheadian panentheism [followed by Keller], for whom God's limitations are metaphysically required, Peacocke is a classical theist who holds that God is all powerful. Any limitation on God's power is the result of God's free decision, not a requirement by anything external to God."[144]

Both Peacocke and Keller take up methodological naturalism when engaging with natural sciences. According to Paul De Vries, "methodological naturalism"[145] does not preclude the possibility to posit a Creator because the theological subject matter goes beyond the subject matters of natural sciences. In contrast, metaphysical naturalism abnegates the possibility to speak of the existence of a Creator.

Peacocke and Keller do not accept metaphysical naturalism in its full-blown sense. Nonetheless, in their quite "assimilationist"[146] approaches, both of them have a *metaphysically naturalistic* bent. Peacocke regards God's creative act as a *kenotic* divine action via downward causation limited to the evolutionary course established *ab initio*. Keller sees God's creative act as co-suffering yet life-luring immanence without endorsing the purposefulness embedded in creation in its beginning. Here, they focus on the theology of the cross, while not simply dismissing the meaning and importance of the resurrection of Jesus Christ. Nevertheless, in their metaphysically naturalistic tendency, their perspectives are not fully faithful to the genuine meaning of the *bodily* resurrection of Jesus Christ. Likewise, both Keller and Peacocke do not agree with the possibility of the eschatological new creation as a *radically transformative* divine act as part of special divine providence.[147]

For Keller, Jesus' resurrection means the incessant revelation and embodiment of his parables regarding the *basileia* of God. This embodiment of God's rule of love and justice proceeds without an end in the open-ended interactivity among creatures and between God and each creature.

144. Peters and Hewlett, *Evolution from Creation to New Creation*, 138.

145. De Vries, "Naturalism in the Natural Sciences," 388–96; Numbers, "Science without God," 320n2.

146. Similarly, Polkinghorne also regards Peacocke's approach as assimilationist although he does not dissolve the uniqueness of the Christian beliefs in his emergent-monist idea of reality. For Polkinghorne, Ian Barbour's approach also seeks mutual dialogue, but gravitates toward an assimilationist position due to his process metaphysics where both God and the world processes are placed in synthetic integration. For this comparative work, refer to his *Scientists as Theologians*.

147. Russell, *Cosmology, Evolution, and Resurrection Hope*, 45–49.

In this respect, for Keller, the history of the cosmos remains open-ended, just as it does not have a beginning with God's *creatio ex nihilo*.[148]

Thus, Keller's effort to resolve the problem of evil is not convincing. God is suffering with creatures in the face of uncertainties, chaos, dissipation, and death while empowering them to stand back up from failures. Yet Keller's God does not have the power to eventually eliminate evil while continuing with creatures to incessantly overcome the threats of chaos. However, chaos is sort of the womb of the creatures' existence, without which God cannot create them. The metaphysically pre-existing dipolar relationship between God and creation enables the emergence of higher complexity from the "interiority" of the material world toward the self-consciousness of human beings that live out the reality of the *basileia* of the loving Creator in their relationships with other creatures in top-down causation.[149] In that sense, in my view, Keller understands evolution in a strong sense. However, all the material world is open to divine influence in God's *creatio ex profundis* (or out of chaos) rather than *ex nihilo*.

Accordingly, Keller believes that in this creative process, God's inability to eradicate evil does not have to do with the goodness and the creating power of God since both God and the world are subject to the dynamic of the responsive co-creating process between God and the world from the very beginning. However, one may ask if her theodicy is fruitful when God as the faithful Creator does not have the capacity to overcome the power of death that runs across the history of evolution, especially when the creation is ridden with excessive forms of evil in its history and faced with the cosmic demise.

On the other hand, Peacocke does not reduce the eschatological new creation to a dialectical metaphor of endlessly continuous "enfolding and unfolding" as Keller does. Peacocke sees the new creation as an emergent phase of creation in God's teleological ordering of the world, yet only via God-given necessity and chance inherent in the universe. Still, the eschatological novelty remains the consummation of God's purposeful creation via whole-part causation.

---

148. Keller, *On the Mystery*, 173–76.

149. According to Ian Barbour, the "interiority" of the material world comprises *mental* and *physical* poles, while the mental capacities of conscious and self-conscious animals differ from the basic responsiveness of non-sentient creatures and the material spheres of the universe. Yet the universe as a whole has a mental pole in diverging degrees. Barbour, "Remembering Arthur Peacocke," 92–93.

Likewise, Peacocke regards the resurrection of Jesus as an emergent event in which Jesus is manifest as fully in unity with God. Thus, it can be objective even when it is a non-bodily event. This is because his resurrection consists in the psychological level or even higher levels of the emergent hierarchy of reality since Easter is an event that Jesus' followers experienced collectively as a large group of people. Here, one can see that Peacocke tries to "wrestle more thoroughly with the actual scientific ideas and seek a fuller integration with theological ideas."[150] However, at the expense of this move, in Peacocke's ENP scheme, there is no hope for the eventual overcoming of suffering, pain, and death in the face of the sweeping prevalence of natural evil and the scientifically predicted cosmic death. Also, in Peacocke's scheme, there can rarely be God's *objectively special* action in creation in spontaneous response to the suffering of creatures.

In sum, it seems to me that neither Peacocke nor Keller addresses properly the problem of natural and cosmic theodicy. Their *assimilative* integration of theology with natural science is misguided. In Keller's interpretation, God appears to be the *loving-yet-somewhat-limited* Creator. In Peacocke's interpretation, God's fulfillment of creation is not faithful enough to the non-human creatures as well as our universe as the life-nesting construct. Thereby, neither scholar properly presents God as the all-determining eschatological reality as the Creator and Redeemer of the entire cosmos, as was proleptically manifested in the resurrection of Jesus Christ.

I affirm that Peacocke's and Keller's views of consonance between theology and natural science is important for a fuller understanding of the world as God's creation because there are overlapping concerns between the two counterparts. Furthermore, based on the fact that the historical Jesus was a human being like all others, I agree with Keller and Peacocke that the investigation of the meaning of Jesus as the Christ is to begin from below rather than from above, and that it is also to be constrained by physics, biology, psychology, and sociology.

This approach *from below* is also imperative from the theological point of view, since the traditional christological affirmations began to be formulated based on the disciples' experiences in their traditional, historical, and personal settings. In addressing the problem of sin and evil, Christ is to be seen as a particular human person. Furthermore, his vicarious suffering is to be seen as a representative action on behalf of

---

150. Peters, "Science and Theology: Toward Consonance," 31.

other human beings and for the fulfillment of all other creatures' creation by liberating them from the sting of death and evil. In order to fulfill this, Jesus Christ is to be a particular human person with generic properties, rather than the Logos who has a general human nature.[151] Reminding the reader of this point of agreement, in the next section, I make constructive suggestions of the kenotic yet eschatological mode of the triune Creator's immanence in creation.

Reaffirming the Fundamental Contingency of Creation: From a Theological Perspective

The cosmic dimension of Christ and Spirit in the biblical traditions and the corresponding trinitarian doctrine of *creatio ex nihilo*, along with philosophical and scientific reasons, makes it necessary to reconsider in a sympathetic and critical manner Keller's *Tehomic* panentheism.[152] If Jesus' resurrection means the promise of the eschatological redemption of creation, one should believe in the ontological dependence of creation on God the Redeemer. According to Alister McGrath, the trinitarian grammar of creation of the NT constituted the basis of developing the doctrine of *creatio ex nihilo* in Christianity's expansion into the Hellenistic intellectual world of late classical antiquity. For instance, in the controversy between the Valentinians and Irenaeus, Irenaeus claimed that "God did not come into an alien world to redeem," and he made a direct connection between creation and redemption. Unlike the dualistic Gnostics, Irenaeus affirmed that the Redeeming God of the NT created the world *ex nihilo*, rather than creating the world with the intractable pre-existing matter.[153]

Robert Jenson argues that, in the OT, God is the one who brought Israel out of Egypt as they were left with the threat of death without any hope for the future. In the NT, the same God is the one who raised Jesus from the dead, and is the one who fulfills the reality of Jesus' resurrection in our own reality. In these saving acts of God, God is not bound to the past, but overcomes the past and fulfills Jesus' triumph over death. Scripture portrays God as "the power of the future."[154] God is open to future threats posed by contingent creatures, but at the same time, God

---

151. Crisp, *Revisioning Christology*, 123.
152. Crüsemann, "Scripture and Resurrection," 90.
153. McGrath, *Scientific Theology*, 1:161–63 [162].
154. Jenson, *Triune Identity*, 23.

takes the initiative in making history contingently toward the fulfillment of the new creation.[155]

It is true that as McGrath argues, the language of the OT creation narratives jumbled together with the languages of "ordering" and "making." There are the interchangeable phrases of "bringing into being," "imposing forms," and "assembling a structure."[156] Yet, in the Pauline literatures and the gospels of the NT, there is a christological dimension to the doctrine of creation which differentiates it from the OT's vision of creation. Christology points to "a pattern of divine activity which is expressed in the doctrine of *creatio ex nihilo*."[157]

While there is the mixed use of the language of "ordering" and "making" in the OT, the resurrection of Jesus made manifest creation's ontological dependence on God's providential immanence in all aspects of nature and history. This Christian development of *ex nihilo* is differentiated from the Jewish tradition where *ex nihilo* was one interpretation among many (even though it is "debatable whether Judaism developed a doctrine of *creatio ex nihilo* at this stage or even later").[158] In the Christian tradition, the cosmic Christ and Spirit, as well as the eschatological hope for God to be "all in all" in creation, is the basis of the monotheistic faith of Judaism in the OT.[159]

I understand that Keller is mindful of the cases in which *creation ex nihilo* is counted as one-time and absolutely top-down divine action

---

155. Jenson, *Triune Identity*, 23–25.

156. McGrath, *Scientific Theology*, 1:142.

157. McGrath, *Scientific Theology*, 1:155.

158. McGrath, *Scientific Theology*, 1:160. Also, for the diverse approaches to this matter, see http://www.jewishencyclopedia.com/articles/4730-creation.

159. As Pannenberg discusses in his earlier book, *Revelation as History*, divine revelation takes five steps: (a) intuitive mantic forms, (b) visions of deities, (c) manifestations of divine names, (d) the revelation of divine wills, and (e) prophetic revelations. The earlier stages are shared by natural religions that do not take divine revelation as the fulfillment of successive divine promises. Yet in the developmental processes, religions tend to move in the direction of historical, apocalyptic (universal), and monotheistic ideas of God. Likewise, in the Christian tradition, one can find a gradual development into the confession of divine revelations of a monotheistic and eschatological God confirmed in particular historical events and eventually in the history of Jesus Christ. The apocalyptic beliefs in Later Judaism concretized in the history of Jesus and fulfilled in the historical event of Jesus' resurrection, while inviting believers to the credible hope for the universal redemption. In this manner, the Christian faith takes revelation as an *indirect* historical revelation and as open-ended toward the eschatological consummation of history.

in the beginning of the world because such interpretations of creation tend not to honor the contingency of creatures and the absolutizing of one voice over others as the Truth.[160] However, as I discussed in chapter 2, a doctrine of creation in a trinitarian framework implies that the triune Creator continues to create the world through the mediation of the self-organizing universe created *ex nihilo*. This creation is ontologically grounded in the genuine *otherness-in-unity*.

There can be no creature without God's whole-part creative influence. God gives existence to creation, sustains its existence, and continues to be actively creative within continuous creation. Furthermore, since the divine essence is love, the triune God is in dynamic interaction with creatures. The Spirit mediates the inter-personal relationship between the Father and the Son[161] as well as the relationship of creation with the Father through the incarnate Son. Hence, God as an interpersonal and communal Being can "internalize" all the varied experiences of the world, bathe them in infinite love, and transmit them back to other experiences in the form of the continuous divine special lure or information.[162] In other words, if the trinitarian Being of God is regarded as the ontological ground of the diversity-in-unity of creation, *creatio ex nihilo* is not necessarily exclusive to the freedom, the plurality, and the diversity of creatures, something Keller is concerned about.

Life and Death Contingent on God's *Creatio ex Nihilo*: From a Philosophical and Scientific Perspectives

Like Moltmann contends, our *active* experience is always mediated via our communities, society and historical contexts, and thus is simultaneously *passive*. Creaturely finite experiences are placed in the infinite field of the creative Spirit that experiences our joys and suffering, and the Spirit persistently calls us into the hope for the eschatological new creation that embraces the whole of creation.[163] In that sense, I wonder if Keller's God is comprehensive enough to explain the fundamental contingency of the fine-tuned universe, the sheer *given-ness* of the directionality in the

---

160. Keller, *On the Mystery*, 47–48, 174–76.

161. In that sense, Philip Clayton affirms that God is to be "always *internally related within the divine being*" as the Trinity. Clayton, *Adventures in the Spirit*, 181.

162. Clayton, *Adventures in the Spirit*, 177–84.

163. Moltmann, *Spirit of Life*, 31–40.

development of the universe and biological evolution. Unlike Peacocke, Keller does not see the novelty that emerges in evolution as a result of the universe's self-organizing that is teleologically endowed with necessity and chance that is contingent on the creative act of God. Likewise, while God is also in the process of being created by the creaturely responses to the divine lure, God only lures new lives to emerge out of co-eternal chaos.[164] For that reason, God is not accountable for the problem of death, suffering, and pain within creation.

However, according to the second law of thermodynamics, destruction, death, and resulting pain and suffering are constitutive of the birth of a new life and the emergence of new species in the history of evolution. If so, the divine creative lure is not only responsible for life that emerges at the edge of the pre-existing chaos but also for the inevitable destruction of an existing order. The potentially excessive increases of entropy are to be seen as belonging to the creative divine lure too. Put differently, the evolution of life does not begin with a creaturely subjective response to the divine lure in co-eternal chaos, but with the divine creative influence that inevitably results in that state of chaos. Suffering and pain within nature come "from the *normal* operation of natural processes" that characterizes the self-organizing universe that is fundamentally contingent and not necessary.[165]

Drawing upon superstring theory, Keller affirms that our thermodynamic universe consists of many regions endlessly interlacing without beginning and ending. For that reason, she also affirms the necessity of chaos or the mechanisms of dissolution and resolution, for which God cannot be accountable. This idea may cohere with the "ekpyrotic" and "eternal inflation" scenarios for our universe's life. That is, the hot Big Bang of our universe is not the absolute beginning of the entire spacetime of our universe, but rather one of the "gateways" into another four-dimensional membrane or slice of the more-than-four-dimensional universe. Our universe is regarded as only one of many membranes within a larger universe that can be compared to an island in interaction with many other islands. According to the ekpyrotic scenario, our universe is one of the two membranes that "repeatedly collide, and move apart, and collide again." According to the "eternal inflation theory," the Big Bang of

---

164. For example, Keller, *Cloud of the Impossible*, 312–16.
165. Southgate, *Groaning of Creation*, 24.

our universe is only the formation of our "island" while the formation of other islands continues incessantly.[166]

Like multiverses theories, this theory's problem is the lack of empirical evidence and therefore, it remains highly speculative. But even if this theory were correct, it would not seem to eliminate the fundamental contingency of our universe that the doctrine of *creatio ex nihilo* affirms. According to the research of Arvind Borde, Alexander Vilenkin, and Alan Guth, those spacetimes within an island are to be regarded as having begun at some point in the past with an established set of constants that is fundamentally contingent because it has a beginning in the past. The islands are known to have begun to expand with low entropy in an average Hubble expansion greater than zero just as ours. The fine-tuning of those constants for no apparent reason cannot be outright explicated. In the same vein, even the existence of many islands and multiverses demands the notion of a singularity in the past to explain why they exist.[167] All in all, considering the fundamental contingency of the way that our thermodynamic universe exists, Keller's dualized approach to creativity and chaos is not persuasive.

Questioning the Boundary of the Universe as a Causal Link with Divine Influence *Ab Initio*

In my view, Peacocke needs to consider the possibility of special divine action if he holds on to the ontological causal gaps in the sub-atomic level. While working in the top-down/whole-part causation or constraint, God can still work at a particular moment without violating the order of nature. According to chaos theory, "vulnerability to small disturbances is simply diagnostic of that sensitivity to the circumstance that means that the system must, in fact, be treated holistically."[168]

However, as Russell points out, contemporary scientific cosmology depicts the universe as "boundless" in the three models: "spherical" or closed, "flat," and "hyperbolic." If so, the only way that one may see the "dotted boundary" of the universe open to the divine top-down information[169] is to understand the boundary as "the three-dimensional curved

---

166. Spitzer, *New Proofs for the Existence of God*, 19–21.
167. Spitzer, *New Proofs for the Existence of God*, 33–37.
168. Polkinghorne, *Scientists as Theologians*, 39.
169. Peacocke does not speak of a causal joint where God is involved in continuous

hypersurface of the universe considered at a specific moment of proper time J (i.e., the age of the universe)."[170] If that is the case, God is to be seen as present everywhere and at every point of the hypersurface in which point-like quantum events take place in indeterminacy. What Peacocke means by the whole-part constraint is God's bottom-up action through mediation of a system as a whole at a certain slice of spacetime. Then, the top-down agency should not be pitted against particular and spontaneous bottom-up causation in the quantum level as long as God is personal or supra-personal, something even Peacocke himself affirms.

As God created the world as a whole *ex nihilo*, in the universe that is probabilistically open to different possibilities in the emergence of novelty, God can be regarded as continuing "actively" to influence the world to create particular effects. Therefore, as Polkinghorne asserts, through more mutual dialogue between Christian tradition and scientific cosmology, one should not preclude "the possibility of some instances of quasi-localized causality, such as we presumably exercise within our bodies and perhaps as God does within terrestrial history."[171]

The Significance of Divine "Top-Down-through-Bottom-Up" Causation

Peacocke is reluctant to interpret quantum events as the locus of *objectively* special divine action. The reason is that if quantum events are ontologically indeterminate according to the Heisenberg interpretation, their outcomes should be unpredictable even to the knowledge of God. This genuine unpredictability in the indeterministic quantum level would be "a limitation of the knowledge even an omniscient God could have of . . . the future trajectory . . . of the system," and so would prevent God from being able to act in the system to implement the divine will.[172]

---

creation as one of physical causes. Rather, the divine information is given by the inherent propensities established in the Big Bang event.

170. Russell, "Arthur Peacocke on Method in Theology and Science," 150.

171. Polkinghorne, *Scientists as Theologians*, 39. For Polkinghorne, the *quasi-localized* divine action is the way that a whole-part constraint is carried out in response to the actions of the free processes of nature. However, unlike Russell, Polkinghorne adopts chaos theory and suggests a modification of its classical equations by considering the genuine indeterminacy of nature.

172. Peacocke, "God's Interaction with the World," 279.

However, I think Peacocke's judgment of God's knowledge of the world is misguided in that he misunderstands the meaning of God's omniscience. What I mean is that if creatures are granted contingency, their actions cannot be fully predictable even when they are constrained by the law-like regularities. As Peacocke rightly argues, God can know reality as the way it is with creatures' potentialities yet to be actualized contingently at each moment.

Therefore, God's omniscience should not be understood in a deterministic way as in the Augustinian-Thomistic tradition. Similarly, I think that the traditional notion of God as the *actus purus* is to be reformulated in terms of God as the "Persons-In-Mutual-Communion." The divine communion of infinite love extends to divine immanence in *creatio continua* that is open not only to joys but also to suffering throughout the contingent unfolding of history.[173]

Nonetheless, I think these revised meanings of omniscience and *actus purus* do not prevent God from actively continuing to work in creation through special providence. Even though God cannot foreknow how a future state will be determined "based on God's knowledge of the present just prior to the quantum event,"[174] God still can know all the possibilities available to it. God as the ground of being can be *present* to all those potentialities, and they are not outside the knowledge of God who is infinite in and beyond creation.

In quantum mechanics, due to the superposition of a quantum system as represented by the wave Ψ, it is only probabilistic to predict the result of the collapse of the wave function. However, the unpredictability or indeterminacy is not the absence of the calculation of the odds. The probabilities are calculated from the wave function. Therefore, I think, as Russell points out, if even scientists can calculate the odds, "surely God can know them exactly."[175] This idea still coheres with the concept of divine omniscience in the classical tradition since it means God's knowledge of "the future in its own present actuality"[176] rather than knowing a future state based on the present.

In other words, all the available potentialities are within the bounds of divine knowledge of the world as God's creation. In the

---

173. Edwards, *Jesus the Wisdom of God*, 123–25 [124].
174. Russell, *Cosmology*, 134.
175. Russell, *Cosmology*, 171.
176. Russell, *Cosmology*, 134.

Thomistic understanding of providence in terms of determinative divine knowledge,[177] the notion of divine omniscience "does not endorse 'divine omni-determinism,' but rather establishes a meaningful notion of divine knowledge that is in keeping with the indeterminacy of nature."[178] If that is the case, I think that it is theologically more plausible to say that God as a personal Creator can act in *particular ways* in particular circumstances with divine purposes throughout dynamic interaction with creation in its continuous becoming(s).

Keller rightly endorses the infinite *eros* or lure for life present at all the moments of evolutionary history. On the contrary, Peacocke regards divine action as limited to a top-down influence without a special lure or a special divine action objectively taking place in the sub-atomic level. However, I think that an objectively particular divine action in the contingent order of nature is viable theologically and scientifically as discussed above.

In his critique of Peacocke's understanding of divine action, Keith Ward contends that if God is believed to have created the world *ex nihilo* through "the strongest possible causal influence," God is to be believed to be able to act in particular ways in personal interaction with creation. That said, special divine action can be in concurrence with the established order of nature, rather than violating it every now and then.[179] This claim coheres with the idea of the miraculous according to the Christian tradition. That is, miracles perfect nature through general and special providence as well as the fulfillment of the new creation.[180]

To perceive an event as a miraculous or revelatory, one requires the theological notions of a Creator and creation. These ideas are gleaned from a tradition, a culture, and a society. The psychological and social levels are embedded in the emergent hierarchy of reality, and thus cannot be isolated from its inextricable relationships with the lower levels.[181] If the top-down and whole-part causation can be actualized from the fundamental level of physics in the emergence of novelty, there can be objectively particular divine action that involve bottom-up divine action. A bottom-up divine

177. Gunton, *Triune Creator*, 180–82.
178. Kärkkäinen, *Creation and Humanity*, 176.
179. Ward, "Personhood, Spirit, and the Supernatural," 155.
180. In that vein, the resurrection is more than a *supernatural* miracle, according to Russell. It is not God's improvisational violation of the order of nature, but it is a proleptical event of the fulfillment of the telos of creation as a whole. The event is "more than a miracle." Russell, *Cosmology*, 128–29.
181. Clayton and Knapp, "Divine Action and the 'Argument from Neglect,'" 188–90.

action can take place in the nerve systems and ultimately at the quantum level that is not entirely deterministic but rather probabilistic.[182] Hence, Peacocke's vision of whole-part (top-down) divine causation is to be reinterpreted as "top-down-through-bottom-up" causation.[183]

Peacocke argues that "mental properties are . . . epistemologically irreducible to physical neurological ones."[184] I agree with him because, like the collective behaviors of a flock of birds influence the behaviors of the individual birds, the cultural and religious aspects of human life affect individual persons' ways of acting in the world. The emergence of a higher level is unpredictable, and so is also top-down influence. Along those lines, Lynn Rothschild contends that "life can never be truly understood from only a reductionist perspective."[185]

However, there are objections and concerns as to the non-reductionist emergent perspective. For example, Paul Davies' concern is that strong emergence overdetermines Newtonian systems.[186] For Niels Henrik Gregersen, even strong emergence does not remove reductionism, because all emergent properties are also resultants and as a result, reductionism survives.[187] For Jaegwon Kim,[188] physicalism is undented by emergence considering causal overdetermination and causal closure.[189]

Nonetheless, I argue in this project that while the physical level generates emergent properties, they cannot be explained fully in the physical terms. For instance, according to the experiments by Benjamin Libet, "electrode stimulation of a particular cortical region correlates only with specific behaviors or memories." However, such an analysis cannot explain away the data of human cultural production and the data of human behaviors.[190] If so, the physical level is affected by the mental level while

182. Murphy and Ellis, *On the Moral Nature of the Universe*, 216–18.

183. Russell, "Peacocke on Method in Theology and Science," 151.

184. Peacocke, "Emergence, Mind, and Divine Action," 267.

185. Rothschild, "Role of Emergence in Biology," 163.

186. Davies, "Physics of Downward Causation," 46.

187. Gregersen, "Emergence," 285.

188. Unlike Davies and Gregersen, Kim is a rigorous atheistic materialist. Yet even Jaegwon Kim says that "Physicalism is not the whole truth, but it is the truth near enough," Kim, *Physicalism, or Something Near Enough*, 6.

189. Kim, "Non-Reductivist's Troubles with Mental Causation," 208–9. Kim's thought evolves toward granting the possibility and need for a sort of mental causation within the bounds of his overall reductionist scheme. In that sense, he calls his proposal *conditional physical reductionism*. Kim, *Physicalism or Something Near Enough*, 4–6.

190. Clayton, *Adventures in the Spirit*, 96.

the mental phenomena themselves cannot take place without a causal link in the fundamental level of physics.[191]

Ultimately, if God is more than a person or supra-personal, God can be seen as purposefully omnipresent across the emergent processes as a whole through the ontological openness to novelty in nature. I think that bottom-up causation in particular cases should not be ignored in speaking of top-down causation and whole-part constraint. Rather, "downward causation in the world is always mediated by ordinary physical forces."[192] The whole-part constraint and top-down information should be regarded as particularly constrained by the bottom-up constraints from the fundamental level of reality (i.e., quantum level).[193]

This coheres with Russell's critique of Peacocke's notion of the boundary of the universe because the universe is unlimited according to general relativity. As Russell says, the dotted boundary fundamentally consists in the quantum level at a specific slice of spacetime. Considering this problem, Murphy asks Peacocke: "If God acts immanently and everywhere in quantum events, selecting one of the possible outcomes for each, is that not also an instance of downward causation?"[194] Bottom-up special divine action is to be a specific way that divine downward information works in creation if God is truly both immanent and transcendent.

If the fundamental contingency of the universe means that it is created *ex nihilo*, divine special action is to include the eschatological redemption of creation, provided God is the faithful and loving Creator. The bodily resurrection of Jesus is an exemplar that shows how God will perfect creation rather than temporally sustain or break the order of nature God created. We cannot presumptuously pinpoint a *causal joint* of divine action as divine action is always mediated through created causes while being immanent in yet transcending them.[195] However, it is theologically plausible to understand divine action as inclusive of its general, special, and eschatological modes.

---

191. Ritchie, *Divine Action and the Human Mind*, 125 27.

192. Murphy, "Emergence, Downward Causation and Divine Action," 129.

193. Whereas Kim affirms that the physical causal closure is self-sufficient, Murphy and Brown contend that, due to the causal efficacy of the higher levels, they cannot be entirely reduced to the physical level, even though the former supervenes on the latter. Thereby, they reject "the atomist-reductionist-determinist world view." Murphy and Brown, *Did My Neurons Make Me Do It?*, 235–36.

194. Murphy, "Emergence, Downward Causation and Divine action," 131.

195. Edwards, "Discovery of Chaos and the Retrieval of the Trinity," 172–75 [173].

A Call for God's Soteriological Presence in Evolution and the Cosmos

In this work, I contend that when we see the continuation of the acute pain and suffering in God's good creation, we are bound to ask, "Why does God not alleviate the pain and suffering in continuous creation?" In so asking, one may end up with a nonpersonal notion of God like Wesley Wildman. From his "argument from neglect," Wildman affirms that God who does not reduce pain and suffering in nature "does not pass the test of parental moral responsibility."[196] He goes on to argue that "[w]e must conclude that God has a morally abysmal record of inaction or ineffective action."[197]

At first glance, this may look like a plausible answer. However, as Hick rightly points out, just as we cannot know if our universe is the best type of the world to possibly exist,[198] we cannot grasp the worst type of evil that we could ever experience. Comparably, even though we can grasp that a life-birthing universe like ours is within a narrow window of the possibilities, we cannot accurately pinpoint that there is a better type of a universe with less pain and suffering than ours.[199] Furthermore, we do not fully understand how the universe operates when the dark matter makes up the majority of the composition of it. Likewise, our meaning-making is open-ended as the new horizons of the future befall us. Ultimately, if our universe is God's creative project, it is yet to be fulfilled.

Hence, we cannot pass judgment that God has been inactive in alleviating the pain and suffering in creation. On the contrary, following Philip Clayton and Steven Knapp's carefully thought-out response to Wildman, God can still work in particular ways while staying in *consistency* with the created order of nature. In that way, God can still be faithfully active as the loving Creator in the face of the different occasions of suffering and pain in creation. God is compassionate toward suffering creatures while not violating what God has established.[200]

In his emergent monism, Clayton tends to separate downward causation from bottom-up causations as he understands the emergence of

---

196. I glean Wildman's theodicy from Clayton and Knapp, *Predicament of Belief*, 45.

197. Clayton and Knapp, *Predicament of Belief*, 45.

198. Hick, *Evil and The God of Love*, 160–66.

199. See Russell, "Physics, Cosmology, and the Challenge to Consequentialist Natural Theodicy," 126–27.

200. Clayton and Knapp, "Divine Action and 'the Argument from Neglect,'" 179–94. For a similar argument of Southgate, see Southgate, *Groaning of Creation*, 73–75.

consciousness irreducible to the physical substrates of the brains. However, "emergent levels of reality might be ontologically distinct insofar as they are somehow more than their substrates and exhibit novel causal powers, but they still exist in ontological continuity with their lower-level substrates."[201] Similarly, Nancey Murphy contends that downward causation cannot take place "without overpowering the lower level."[202]

That said, as Keith Ward rightly argues, we can conceive of God who "could act to heal and save from harm on occasion and to the extent that does not undermine the general structure of reality."[203] As Russell argues, this takes place through "bottom-up-in-whole-part" divine action. In this manner, one can regard God as luring creatures away from preventing others from living their God-given full potentials or their *logoi* or the specific expression of the Logos for individual species and individual creatures. A faithful God would not stay aloof from creatures when they suffer from "starvation, pain, and abandonment to a premature death." In their God-granted contingency and freedom, they can respond to the divine active information.[204]

We could theologically interpret the emergence of the various types of altruism in the world of animals as God's providential guidance in evolution. Altruism may be regarded as the gradual development of the "transcendence of mere self-interest,"[205] rather than as evolutionary strategies that reinforce creatures' egoistic DNA. When the "cooperation" among the animals takes place within the same species and across species, it happens within a larger context of *competition* over the limited amount of resources.[206] Nonetheless, we can still posit God who persistently lures animals to genuine *self-transcendence* and toward genuine altruism that emerged in the life, teaching, and cross of Jesus. In the self-giving life and cross of Jesus, one can see that mutual altruism is not the end of the emergent history of sacrificial love. Creatures are observed

---

201. Ritchie, *Divine Action and the Human Mind*, 129.
202. Murphy, "Emergence, Downward Causation and Divine Action," 120.
203. Ward, *Rational Theology and the Creativity of God*, 208.
204. Southgate, *Groaning of Creation*, 64.
205. Southgate, *Groaning of Creation*, 66.
206. Southgate, *Groaning of Creation*, 65–66. According to William Hamilton's formula (rB>C), only when actual benefit of a sacrificial act is larger than the resulting cost, animals behaves in a sacrificial manner. Hamilton, "Genetical Evolution of Social Behavior I," 1–16. For that reason, Robert Trivers names such an act as "reciprocal altruism." Trivers, "Evolution of Reciprocal Altruism," 35–37.

to act in a way that benefits others at the expense of one's well-being. "In the behaviors of ants, fish, rodents, canines, elephants, primates, and other animals we find examples of creatures acting for the good of others at some cost to themselves."[207] Rather than regarding all of the altruistic behaviors merely as ultimately self-centered, one is to understand that the reality of nature shows the mixture of diverse intents for altruistic behaviors.[208] Joshua Moritz points out that moral awareness demands the four elements: *"knowledge, rationality,* and *independence."* A moral agent should be "able to make sense of the world in which they act, anticipate the consequence of the action, and consider alternative possibilities."[209] These attributes are found not only in human beings but also in subhuman creatures. In evolutionary history, these attributes had gradually developed even before the appearance of *Homo sapiens.*[210]

In my view, this gradual emergence of consciousness and morality involves not only general providence but also special divine action. On the contrary to Peacocke, I think that in the face of the vast continuum of natural evil, God's *inability* to work in objectively particular ways (i.e., special lure) in *creation continua* does not answer the theodical question of why there is evil prevalent in the biosphere. Rather, it should be

---

207. Oord, *Uncontrolling Love of God,* 71–73 [72]. Citing Axelrod, *Evolution of Cooperation*; Bowles and Gintis, *Cooperative Species*; Dukatin, *Cheating Monkeys and Citizen Bees.* Humpback whales are known to help out individuals of entirely different species when they are under attack by their few predators, killer whales. Research continues to find out the reason of this sacrificial behavior that does not fall in the category of mutual altruism. According to Schulman-Janiger and her colleagues, some humpbacks may act in this way as reaction to previous trauma. "Two of the 16 whales she identified as exhibiting interventionist behavior had the marks of previous attacks by killer whales on their fins. These scars could have come from being attacked when they were calves themselves, or from injuries sustained while defending their offspring." Learn, "Killer Whales are Bullies, and Humpback Whales are Bouncers."

208. Oord, *Uncontrolling Love of God,* 75–76. Also, for Moltmann, our experience of the self is always inseparable from our experience of sociality. One's independent being is formed and transformed in interdependent relationships with others. One's independent being appears against the background of the "all-embracing horizon of the world." Therefore, their relational being has both "a transcendent and inward side." The Spirit, the Creator constitutes the ontological ground of the creatures' differences-in-unity, and is experienced by them in their mutual relationships with each other. Moltmann, *Spirit of Life,* 34–38 [36].

209. Moritz, "Contingency, Convergence, Constraints, and the Challenge from Theodicy in Creation's Evolution," 311.

210. Moritz, "Contingency, Convergence, Constraints, and the Challenge from Theodicy in Creation's Evolution," 319–24.

Natural and Cosmic Theodicy of Peackocke and Keller

theologically more plausible to regard God as continuing to influence the world in particular ways and spontaneously; this is what Keller and many other process theologians affirm with the idea of the divine lure as the embodiment of the love of God.

Furthermore, if God created the universe as a whole *ex nihilo*, I think God is to take responsibility for the individuals that fell victim to their predators who took their lives prematurely and violently causing lots of pain. If the creation of human beings is the culmination of God's creation through Darwinian evolution, other animals that vanished in the scene of evolution should not be treated like a "ladder . . . kicked away when the summit is reached."[211] Furthermore, our universe as a life-bearing nest should be redeemed so it will continue to be the locus of God's fulfilling the purpose of creation rather than ending up in *Freeze or Fry*.

If *creatio ex nihilo* is a project in the anticipation of its fulfillment, it demands the new creation. God is to redeem the whole of creation including the cosmos, so that all the victimized creatures become the *end* of God's creation, rather than merely the means to the flourishing of others including humans. Thereby, the primordial goodness of creation according to Genesis 1:31 can be understood in the light of Revelation 21:1 (NIV): "Then, I saw 'a new heaven and a new earth.'" The present creation is where we see in the mirror dimly (1 Cor 13:12). The cross of Jesus shows God's kenotic presence in the present creation, but in the light of his resurrection, this indicates God's act of redeeming in divine freedom that liberates God's creation from suffering.

As N. T. Wright affirms, the resurrection of Jesus is to be taken as God's vindication not only for the peaceable kingdom of God that Jesus preached and lived out, but also for God's faithfulness to Jesus himself and the others whom he represents before God.[212] On the contrary, John Dominic Crossan believes that Jesus' gospel of God's coming reign is found in Jesus' own life and the cross. For him, Jesus' resurrection is a metaphorical expression of the early Christians' faith in his gospel.[213] I agree with Crossan that the self-giving presence of God in Jesus shows us the kingdom of God. However, I believe that the presence of evil and the victimization of the innocent, as well as the exploitation of the weak, should not have its place in the kingdom of God where God will be all in all.

---

211. Gunton, *Triune Creator*, 169. Also, for St. Francis' Christ-like loving of nature as an example, see Santimire, *Travail of Nature*, 111.

212. Wright and Crossan, "Resurrection," 43–47.

213. Wright and Crossan, "Resurrection," 45–47.

Without God redeeming the life of Jesus himself, how could he have claimed to be the Son of Man or the Messiah who ushers in the advent of the kingdom of God? God should be faithful to Jesus and creation if the divine essence is truly love. Along those lines, I think that God's love for creation demands God's responsibility to fulfill its universalization in the eschatological new creation. Thus, it should not be shrunk down to the question: "Do you believe in a miracle?" as the resurrection of Jesus is about the whole of creation that will participate in the mutual love between the Father and the Son through the bond of the Spirit. Resurrection faith is about the justice and faithfulness of God, without which no theological doctrine of God can survive. As discussed above, in the Christian tradition, the new creation as *creatio ex vetere* constitutes the basis of *creatio ex nihilo*.

Furthermore, since the new creation is the consummation of God's creation in the independence-in-unity grounded in the mutual love of the trinitarian Creator, *creatio continua* is interpreted as God's kenotic participation in the history of biological evolution through the interplay of chance and regularities and that of life and entropy.

The Call for the Reconsideration of the Historicity of the Bodily Nature of Jesus's Resurrection and Its Eschatological Implications

According to Kärkkäinen, "[t]he various objections to the historicity of the resurrection usually rest on one of the three main lines of argumentation: first, that there is no access to such historical knowledge; second, that there is no analogy for such resurrection; and third, that there is no evidence."[214] The first objection is represented by Willi Marxsen's objection to the historicity of Jesus' resurrection. According to Marxsen, instead of the history of Jesus' resurrection, we can only access to the disciples' beliefs as to the event. This approach represents a positivistic fashion of understanding an occasion in natural science. Thus, it does not befit the historical studies that deal with one-time past events. Hence, Wright contends that "ruling out as historical that to which we do not have direct access is actually a way of not doing history at all."[215]

---

214. I am indebted to Kärkkäinen, *Christ and Reconciliation*, 125–33 [128] as to the three mainline objections to the historicity of the resurrection of Jesus Christ.

215. Wright, *Resurrection*, 16.

The second objection is represented by Ernst Troeltsch's "principle of analogy." According to him, historians can speak of only the things that have a certain analogy to our experience. However, because the resurrection does not occur in our normal experience, we cannot speak of Jesus' resurrection as a historical event.[216] This principle is "a nuanced restatement of Hume's famous objection to miracles in general."[217] Troeltsch's claim is also problematic, since, being a one-time event "does not disqualify it from being a historical event. Nor does the historicity of the event call for an indubitable certainty after Cartesian epistemology."[218] As Wright argues, "the rise of the Church thus constitutes in itself a counterexample to Troeltsch's general point."[219]

This is because the emergence of the church is a historical event that is "derived from the resurrection of Jesus, and has no analogy in the history of religions and our experience."[220] The emergence of the Christian faith in Jesus as Christ is distinguished from the belief in the Son of Man according to both the second-Temple Judaism and the contemporaneous Greco-Roman pagan philosophies and religions. This is because the Christian faith in Jesus as Christ radically modified the messianic hope and promoted the eschatological hope in God's overcoming the past through redeeming creation by fulfilling the Shalom of God's kingdom, rather than placing the hope in this-worldly freedom, hope, and security achieved via strong rulers.

The third objection is represented by post-Bultmannian NT studies and the work of Crossan. The first group builds a hypothetical tradition-history of the resurrection narratives and believes that there is no real evidence of Jesus' resurrection. Wright counterargues that those efforts are unfruitful since "[w]e simply do not know very much about the early church," and historians are to pursue investigating the matter in a critical realistic manner not excluding the credibility of its historicity as a credible option.[221] However, for the lack of real evidence of the resurrection, Crossan establishes a hypothetical view of the resurrection narratives' shaping process as merely the product of political power games. On

216. Troeltsch, "On the Historical and Dogmatic Methods in Theology [1898]," 728–53.
217. Wright, *Resurrection*, 17.
218. Kärkkäinen, *Creation and Humanity*, 129.
219. Wright, *Resurrection*, 18.
220. Kärkkäinen, *Christ and Reconciliation*, 129.
221. Wright, *Resurrection*, 19.

the other hand, N. T. Wright contends that there is plenty of historical evidence about "coherence and unity of the views of resurrection along various early Christian communities."[222]

Unlike Peacocke's and Keller's views of the resurrection of Jesus, there are reasons to count the bodily resurrection of Jesus as historically credible based on the two traditions of Christ's reappearance and his empty tomb.[223] Based on these traditions, according to N. T. Wright, early Christians regarded the resurrection neither as Jesus' "perceived status in the ongoing church," nor as his "heavenly and exalted status," nor "the passage of the human Jesus into the power of God," but instead affirmed his "bodily resurrection."[224] The eschatological resurrection is neither resuscitation nor shining like a star as can be seen in Daniel 12, but a *bodily transformation* just like Jesus' proleptic example.

Early Christians spoke of the spiritual yet bodily presence of the risen Jesus. The commonly shared accounts of Jesus' resurrection according to the NT Gospels speak of the bodily nature of the risen Jesus, rather than identifying his dying on the cross as his exaltation to the heavenly Father.[225] There are the accounts about the temporal interval between his death and Easter. Furthermore, in the Pauline literatures, there is the new notion of the *two-phased* resurrection: the first for Jesus and the last for all others in Christ together.

The fact that something does not cohere with the currently accepted beliefs motivated by the natural sciences does not mean that it is necessarily unhistorical. A one-time past event might not be repetitive in history, but it still can be acknowledged as historical in the sense that it actually took place as a public event through *indirectly* supporting evidence. This is not only applicable to the problem of Jesus' bodily resurrection but also generally to the research of the natural sciences. Polkinghorne rightly points out that scientists are to be seen as critical realists, since, in establishing a theory, they involve well-motivated beliefs when they

---

222. Kärkkäinen, *Christ and Reconciliation*, 130.

223. In his *Systematic Theology*, 2:356–59, Pannenberg substantiates the historicity of the resurrection of Jesus through the two traditions. Henceforth, *ST* II. In the same vein, Kärkkäinen also writes, "The two main pillars of evidence for the historicity of the resurrection are the appearances of Jesus to a great number of eyewitnesses and the empty tomb tradition. Rather than visionary experiences as in hallucinations or other psychological projections, there are good reasons for maintaining the appearances as actual encounters." Kärkkäinen, *Christ and Reconciliation*, 130–31.

224. Wright, *Resurrection*, 209.

225. Wright, "Jesus' Resurrection and Christian Origins," 615–35.

establish the theory.[226] The existence of the unseen entity is not directly evinced, but a scientific supposition of its existence can bear high feasibility thanks to other identified things that indirectly support its existence.

On the basis of the NT narratives about the appearances of the risen Jesus and his empty tomb, Polkinghorne affirms that the resurrection is not an expression about something other than what took place to the embodied person of Jesus. In his "bottom-up" critical realist approach, Polkinghorne argues that it is credible to believe that the resurrection is a historical event.[227] By tracing the historical link between the resurrection and the early church's confession of Jesus as the eschatological Redeemer, Polkinghorne argues that the confession of Jesus as the Lord and the Son of God can be seen as a well-motivated belief.

In contrast, both Peacocke and Keller deny the christological and eschatological significance of the empty tomb tradition by *naturalizing* or *psychologizing* the reappearances tradition. As to the reappearance tradition, Peacocke regards it as an emergent reality within the levels of psychology and sociology in the context of God's creation as holistic top-down causation.

Keller also reduces Jesus' resurrection event to the disciples' psychological encounter with the dead young man Jesus and sublimates it into Jesus' continuous influence on the generations to come. Peacocke does seriously consider whether Jesus' resurrection is bodily or not based on his presupposition that the event is essentially spiritual that cannot be reduced to the lower emergent levels. However, he gravitates toward its interpretation as a non-bodily but personal event. Jesus' person can still influence other persons without being *physically* embodied.

Neither does Keller seriously consider the historical possibility of the bodily resurrection of Jesus. That said, she regards Easter as exemplifying creatures' continuous embodiment of the initial divine lure to the *basileia* of God through their subjective and collective responses. Both Peacocke and Keller share the belief that Jesus' resurrection is his *exaltation* by his followers, an opinion widely shared by many twentieth-century biblical theologians who dismiss the historical validity of the tradition.

Like Kärkkäinen contends, "the empty tomb tradition was not contested by the contemporaries . . . Had the claim to the empty tomb been a fabrication, how could the preaching about the resurrected Christ have taken place in Jerusalem, the place of execution and burial?"

226. Polkinghorne, *Science and Religion in Quest of Truth*, 16–19.
227. Polkinghorne, *Science and Religion in Quest of Truth*, 117–24.

Accordingly, he affirms that for this reason, "not only the resurrection but also the empty tomb is a public event."[228] This claim is supported by N. T. Wright's argument that while the reappearance traditions tell us about the trans-physical nature of Jesus' risen body rather than a spiritualized one in which his body is abandoned, without the good news of the empty tomb, the disciples could not stop mourning after Jesus' crucifixion. Also, the empty tomb itself without the reappearances of the risen Jesus could not be sufficient because as the narratives in Matthew say, there were the cases when buried bodies were stolen.

Furthermore, as Polkinghorne appositely argues, the credibility of the empty tomb tradition is reinforced when we consider that the eyewitnesses of the empty tomb were women and the traditions speak of Joseph of Arimathea, a particular person's name, as the one who buried the body of Jesus. The former can be seen as a credible evidence for the resurrection of Jesus because, even though in the ancient world, women were not counted as capable of being dependable witnesses in a court of law, Scripture uses them to support the truthfulness of Jesus' resurrection.[229] The latter reinforces the belief in the historicity of Jesus' resurrection since the particular person's name could not have been honored, if Jesus' body had been stolen as the rumor at that time said.[230]

Noteworthy is also the fact that even though Paul does not mention anything about the empty tomb of Jesus, he believed that Jesus was alive. This also constitutes another credible support of the bodily resurrection of Jesus. "A first-century Jew, taking a psychosomatic view of the nature of human personality, would have been very unlikely indeed to have believed so, if he also thought that there was a corpse lying in a tomb."[231] Based on this evidence, Polkinghorne argues that the belief in the *bodily* resurrection as an actual historical event is "not without serious motivation to which a truth-seeking bottom-up thinker should be prepared to give careful consideration."[232]

If these are *motivating* data, one can have a credible hope for the universal realization of the bodily resurrection that embraces the whole of creation. This is because, in the early Christian faith, the understanding

228. Kärkkäinen, *Christ and Reconciliation*, 85.
229. Polkinghorne, *Science and Religion in Quest of Truth*, 123.
230. Polkinghorne, *Science and Religion in Quest of Truth*, 123. One can find helpful accounts in Brown, *Virginal Conception and Bodily Resurrection of Jesus*, 92–124.
231. Polkinghorne, *Science and Religion in Quest of Truth*, 123.
232. Polkinghorne, *Science and Religion in Quest of Truth*, 123.

of Jesus' resurrection was inseparable from the apocalyptic anticipation of the resurrection at the eschaton (as evident in 1 Corinthians 15). If the bodily resurrection of Jesus is an event of historical credibility, we may anticipate that God will redeem all other human beings. In so doing, God does not violate the established order of nature but fulfills it. As Revelation 21 says, the redeeming effect reaches to every corner of creation: human, non-human, and cosmic dimensions. The cosmic Christology of the NT does not leave out non-human creatures in God's economy of salvation.

If the eschatological presence of God in Jesus is the harbinger of the new creation, it participates in creatures' suffering and helps redeem them from the powers of death, violence, and cruelty. We anticipate the fulfillment of the promise of the new creation here and now, placing the hope in the faithfulness of the loving Creator manifested on the cross of Jesus and in his resurrection. The new creation does not originate merely from the potentialities embedded in the universe.

Rather, the new creation is God's radically redemptive act, even though it is not the second creation *ex nihilo*. It is rather the fulfillment of the original and continuous creation through the transformation of the present one. God is in, with, and under the present creation as the faithful companion in God's infinite compassion. God is powerful to redeem the world from the hold of death, violence, and cruelty.

If this is the case, I think that Peacocke and Keller must give credence to the historicity of the bodily resurrection of Jesus Christ. I also affirm that thereby they must reconsider the possibility of the new creation as an eschatological event of God's redeeming the whole of creation. This is so, if God is faithful to individual creatures and species that suffer the inevitable pain, suffering, and decay. The belief in the bodily resurrection is imperative when one considers God's love and providential care for the entire creation including non-human creatures. Furthermore, without the redemption of the physical cosmos as a whole, there cannot be the new creation or the eschatological transformation of creation: the new earth and the new heaven.

Toward an Eschatological Ontology of a Trinitarian Creation: a Kenotic-Eschatological Panentheistic Vision of Creation

"God's *ruach* is the life force immanent in all the living, in body, sexuality, ecology, and politics"[233] (Job 33:4, 13; Ps 104:29). These accounts present the Spirit of God as "the power of creation and the wellspring of life."[234] They speak of the "immanent transcendence" of the Spirit.[235] The Spirit is working in creation as "the vitalizing principle, the lure to self-transcendence, and as the inspirational power of ecstasy."[236]

In the life-giving presence of the Spirit, it should be noted that the Spirit's presence does not reject, but rather celebrates the co-creative participation of creatures: "Let the land produce . . ." [Gen. 1:11 (NIV)]. The work of the Spirit is cosmic and thus is the redeeming presence of Christ within creation in the inherent linkage between the Spirit Christology and the logos Christology as discussed in chapter 2.

In *creatio continua*, the contingency of creation is preserved. Yet in the openness to the future, the preservation of creation's contingency means God's continuing fulfillment of its *telos* through divine general and special ordering of nature. The Father's creation is created "in" Christ through the transcendent immanence of the Spirit. The triune Creator is in dynamic interaction with creation through continuing creation. Therefore, the triune God is immanent in creation while transcending it as its Creator.

In this divine companionship throughout the present creation as a trinitarian project, God compassionately participates in the suffering of creatures as seen on the cross of Jesus. The co-suffering is not only a moral exemplar that demonstrates genuine solidarity with the weak and *kenotic* ethics of self-giving, but also a promise-giving co-suffering for the new creation as promised in the bodily resurrection of Jesus Christ. In this vein, Moltmann understands the doctrine of *creatio ex nihilo* in a trinitarian grammar as he takes a soteriological approach to creation. In his trinitarian view of creation, Moltmann contends that towards the fulfillment of creation in the new creation, God's continuously creative

---

233. Moltmann, *Spirit of Life*, 225–26.
234. Moltmann, *Spirit of Life*, 35.
235. Moltmann, *Spirit of Life*, 35.
236. Pannenberg, "Working of the Spirit in the Creation," 23.

immanence in the universe is an on-going *messianic* liberation of the universe from the powers of death, violence, and cruelty.[237]

If so, I think as Peters and Hewlett affirm, creation is to be seen as "created from the future, not the past."[238] If God is a personal Creator, there needs to be coherence in the divine action from the beginning through the fulfillment of creation in which the eschatological purpose is reflected. God is not bound by the past but opens a new future as the power of the future. Therefore, the primordial goodness of creation according to Genesis 1:31 can be understood in the light of Revelation 21:1 (NIV): "Then, I saw 'a new heaven and a new earth.'" The present creation is where we see in the mirror dimly (1 Cor 13:12). The cross of Jesus Christ shows God's kenotic presence in the present creation through *teleological* and *soteriological* divine accompaniment through the operation of the created causes. The resurrection of Jesus Christ means that the Spirit as the pledge of the eschaton is present in creation. The Spirit is both the source of life and its beauty and diversity through continuously giving and sustaining existence to creation where life flourishes. The flourishing of life inevitably entails pain, suffering, and death. God not only co-suffers with the loved creation but also is at work stereologically by redeeming it from the power of pain, suffering, and death.

That said, in the next chapter, I discuss how the teleological and soteriological immanence of the triune Creator can be understood in the mode of "bottom-up-in-whole-part" causation in the eschatological ontology of creation thorough dialogue with Pannenberg and Russell. As one can see in the bodily resurrection of Jesus as a proleptic event of the new creation, the eschatological new creation is not an emergent result of the universe with the potential propensities embedded *ab initio*. Rather, the eschaton is the fulfillment of God's good creation, as discussed above. It means the transformation of the present creation (or *creatio ex vetere*) in continuity and discontinuity with the present creation. It does not replace or violate what God has created in the present world, but rather brings it to completion by fulfilling the *perichoretic* communion of the triune Creator through the creatures' participation in that communion.

Both Pannenberg and Russell find the eschaton or the redemptive new creation as the ontological basis of the fundamental contingency of *creatio ex nihilo* and *creatio continua*. God's kenotic creation means God's

---

237. Moltmann, *God in Creation*, 94–98.
238. Peters and Hewlett, *Evolution from Creation to New Creation*, 160–64 [160].

non-coercive luring of life, consciousness, and self-consciousness through co-suffering. Yet God's kenotic creation is not exclusive to God's *saving* presence. The present creation is both the creative and soteriological accompaniment of the triune Creator with creatures as co-creators. Here the eschaton is the source and goal of the created spacetime as the locus of *creatio continua*. In that sense, not only *creatio continua* but also *creatio nova* is placed in mutual interaction between sciences and theology.

4

Natural and Cosmic Theodicy of Pannenberg and Russell

As KELLER AND PEACOCKE argue, special providence can be perceived only through a certain prevenient notion of God and a pre-understanding of the Creator's creative agency. Our understanding of God in creation is always finite and limited as well as conditioned and formed or *embedded* in certain cultural contexts that condition our understanding of things in our reality. In that vein, our knowledge is always *perspectival* and remains developing rather than remaining as a fixed substance. Our knowledge of God and creation is inherently both substantive and relative, and thus it is open to critical realistic investigation. As Peacocke and Keller affirm, God's creation is finite and open to new hermeneutical horizons. I appreciate their understandings of reality from the perspective of epistemic holism.

Yet, in my view, while special revelation and special providence are perceptually subject to the recognition of the human mind through faith as a metaphysical construct for interpreting reality, it is not necessary to exclude the possibility of God's special activity through both usual and unusual events in nature. Keller endorses the spontaneous and responsive agency of God in creation but tends to reduce the meaning of the eschaton to a subjective interpretation of the continuous *counter-apocalyptic* processes of the world. In his idea of divine influence on the world as a whole, Peacocke tends to dissolve special divine action into creation's general ordering. Likewise, he regards the eschaton as an emergent level of reality that *transcends* all material levels below.[1]

In both views, the material world and the victims of biological evolution do not have an eschatological hope. Likewise, Keller denies God's absolute ability to give creatures relative freedom and contingency and then sustains it. For Keller, *creatio continua* cannot be a process of faithfully fulfilling the divine purpose of creation that is fundamentally contingent. Rather, in the face of the waves of dissolution, God only opens new possibilities for creatures in reciprocal and spontaneous responses. While Keller endorses God's creative presence in all levels of the emergent hierarchy of reality as a responsive lure, Peacocke, in his idea of divine self-limitation, denies the objective status of special divine action as bottom-up causation by positing the sufficiency of the whole-part constraint that God creates *ab initio*.

While seeking to be faithful to both the transcendence and the immanence of the Creator according to Scripture, they do not seriously consider the significance of the trinitarian narrative of God's *Redemptive* Creatorship according to Scripture. As Kärkkäinen points out, a Christian theology of nature is essentially trinitarian. In the trinitarian Creatorship the infinite Creator becomes involved in *creatio continua* in a relational, dynamic, and redemptive mode through the mediation of the contingent agents of the finitely created world.[2]

In this trinitarian framework, creation is not subsumed under redemption, but creation becomes a redemptive project. Here, by granting creatures their contingency, God who creates *ex nihilo* becomes a "co-agent" and "co-sufferer" in *creatio continua*.[3] Yet this is not God's self-emptying of the eschatological Redeemership. God works in both special and general ways to persistently fulfill the eschatological consummation within creation.

In that regard, seeking hypothetic consonance between the self-organizing universe and creation, both Pannenberg and Russell value the significance of the faithful Creatorship and Redeemership of the triune Creator. God not only grants creation its contingency but also sustains it

---

1. Yet in chapter 5, I will also include how Keller's idea of *counter-apocalyptic* eschatology can help to further nuance the contingency of creation for Russell's and Pannenberg's eschatological ontology of creation by appropriating it in a trinitarian panentheistic framework of creation.

2. Kärkkäinen, *Creation and Humanity*, 9–10.

3. Migliore, *Faith Seeking Understanding*, 135–36 [136].

and fulfills its eschatological *telos* of it through the new creation. As the consummation of a trinitarian creation, the new creation is not only the *goal* of creation but also the *basis* of *creatio ex nihilo*.

To advance this argument, I first discuss Pannenberg's *sub ratione Dei* method in a theology-science dialogue. This paves the way for my discussion of Pannenberg's trinitarian and eschatological ontology of creation in his interpretation of the universe and the biological evolution on our planet as presented by contemporary scientific cosmology and evolutionary biology. In this context, I discuss Pannenberg's ideas of divine creative and redemptive action amidst natural and cosmic evils.

Next, I explore Russell's CMI method in theology and science, which I find similar to Pannenberg's but more updated with cosmological and physical theories. While Pannenberg presents the roles of the Son and the Spirit as the two hands of the Father in creation and suggests that it coheres with contemporary sciences' description of our life-bearing universe, Russell complements Pannenberg's trinitarian doctrine of creation through updating it with the resources from quantum mechanics, the special and general theories of relativity, and contemporary quantum cosmology. Furthermore, Russell affirms more mutual interaction between theology and science when it comes to the role of the new creation as *creatio ex vetere* in developing physical, cosmological, and biological research programs. These efforts for seeking *hypothetical consonance*[4] is vital to our understanding of this universe and the biosphere of the Earth as God's creation.

While theological statements of creation are to be in coherence with scientific theories as they engage different dimensions of the same reality, theology is not assimilated to sciences while seeking *deeper consonance* in an open-ended dialogue. Thereby, like Pannenberg, Russell places natural theodicy in the matrix of cosmic theodicy since the fate of the universe is significant as the life-nesting construct without whose redemption there cannot be the redemption of living creatures.

Next, I place Pannenberg and Russell in dialogue, discussing the significance of both the co-suffering and the redeeming immanence of the triune Creator in the present creation, seeking a robust *kenotic-eschatological* vision of creation. Russell not only updates Pannenberg's theology-science dialogue but also enriches Pannenberg's overly rationalistic idea of the Spirit as an all-embracing creative field. This chapter

---

4. I discussed in depth this idea in chapter 1.

paves the road for chapter 5 in which I construct my trinitarian idea of kenotic-eschatological panentheism by appropriating the triune Creator's *co-protesting* immanence in creation. In chapter 5, the kenotic insights are gleaned from Keller and Peacocke to further nuance the co-suffering Redeemership of the triune Creator in this chapter.

Pannenberg's Natural and Cosmic Theodicy in His *Sub Ratione Dei* Scheme

For Pannenberg, theological statements about creation have both epistemic continuity and discontinuity with contemporary natural sciences. He writes that "[i]f the God of the Bible is the Creator of the universe, then it is not possible to understand fully or even appropriately the processes of nature without any reference to that God."[5] Accordingly, a theological understanding of the world as God's creation can be put in mutual interaction with natural sciences. In the following subsections, I discuss how Pannenberg engages with the contemporary physical, evolutionary, and cosmological theories in his understanding of divine action as God's original and continuous creation and eschatological consummation of the creation. The following subsections are significant, in that they provide the context and the grounds for my discussion of Pannenberg's view of God's dealings with evil in the context of his dialogue with modern natural science.

Pannenberg's Method of Mutual Coherence "*Sub Ratione Dei*"

Pannenberg regards the task of theology as engagement with God as the unifying unity of all reality *sub ratione Dei* in a scientific manner. As such, for Pannenberg, theological statements have "scientific and intersubjective validity,"[6] meaning that theology is a branch of science. Even though there are unique characteristics in a theological quest for the truth, Pannenberg thinks that principles applicable to sciences in general also can be adopted by theology for the examination of its statements because he regards history in general as the sphere of divine self-revelation.

---

5. Pannenberg, *Toward a Theology of Nature*, 16.
6. Pannenberg, *Theology and the Philosophy of Science*, 326.

Pannenberg points out that some of Heinrich Scholz's items are outmoded and do not befit the irreducible discrepancies among sciences.[7] Moreover, Scholz's items are the standards formulated to fulfill logical positivism. Nonetheless, there are undisputed minimum requirements that are explicit statements and thus still in use for the process of testing scientific statements about the state of an affair.[8] Pannenberg presents the "minimum" postulates suggested by Scholz: (1) the postulate of propositionality, (2) the postulate of control, and (3) the postulate of coherence.

The Postulate of Propositionality

Theological statements can be regarded as scientific when they "typically say something about a state of affairs for which they claim truth, i.e. correspondence with the state of affairs which is the object of the statement."[9] For Pannenberg, every religious statement is not only affective but also cognitive since they are "assertions about divine and divinely instituted realities."[10]

Theology needs to engage with the objects that exist independently from the assertions. This task is significant for theology to be scientific since without this the assertions about religious experience end up as fictitious stories. The existence of the object independent from a statement about it means that the object has "verifiability through sense observations accessible to anyone at any time."[11] When this is guaranteed, a theological statement gains objectivity and can be engaged with by use of scientific methods. For a theological assertion of God as the "all-determining reality" to be scientific, such a reality of God should be shown to be implicit in all finite beings. All things are to be studied *sub ratione Dei*. This implicit fact is proven true when it is "made explicit in the anticipatory experiences of the totality of reality."[12]

---

7. Pannenberg, *Theology and the Philosophy of Science*, 326.
8. Pannenberg, *Theology and the Philosophy of Science*, 326.
9. Pannenberg, *Theology and the Philosophy of Science*, 327.
10. Pannenberg, *Theology and the Philosophy of Science*, 327.
11. Pannenberg, *Theology and the Philosophy of Science*, 327.
12. Pannenberg, *Theology and the Philosophy of Science*, 330.

The Postulate of Control

In this quest for the truth, imposing a dogmatic authority upon a theological statement is improper because "it is impossible to regard the question of the divine authority of Scripture and Christian doctrine as settled in advance."[13] This is because what we have currently is not a closed statement but is to be treated as a problem that still invites further elucidation and verification in the unfolding of history. If the objects of a theological statement are exterior referent, the verity of the statement is proven when it is put to test as a hypothesis or a problem. Otherwise, the theological statement becomes an expression of subjective attitudes.

Even though subjective or existential elements in theological statements are inextricable from their objective elements, they can still be tested through the communal discernment within a tradition and through inter-traditional dialogue, given that God is the all-unifying reality of the world processes. Is the knowledge of God then just the objective knowledge of God without considering the significance of a subjective act of knowing? Pannenberg agrees with Eberhard Jüngel that our knowledge of God is impossible apart from the faith tradition as it is context-based.[14] Yet Pannenberg counterargues that our new self-understanding required by the true knowledge of God still requires the priority of God's revelation of Godself for us to know the content of that revelation.[15] In other words, there is still something apart from our experience.

Pannenberg, therefore, claims that our ideas of God need to be examined as indefinite hypotheses. All experience of meaning is inevitably "hypothetical" because it is "based on an anticipation of the totality of reality which is still incomplete in the process of reality."[16] In this view, Pannenberg draws upon the Popperian principle of verification through "trial and error" involved in a quest for truth.[17] If theology as the science of God decided to adopt a dogmatic method, "it would remain trapped in the difficulties of positivism and also of subjectivism."[18]

---

13. Pannenberg, *Theology and the Philosophy of Science*, 330.

14. See Jüngel, "*Nihil Divinitatis, Ubi Non Fides*," 232–33.

15. Pannenberg, "Den Glauben an Ihm Selbs Fassen und Verstehen: Eine Antwort," 355–70.

16. Pannenberg, *Theology and the Philosophy of Science*, 333.

17. Pannenberg, *Theology and the Philosophy of Science*, 37.

18. Pannenberg, *Theology and the Philosophy of Science*, 299.

The Postulate of Coherence and Consistence

A proposition or an assertion entails a logic related to many other states of affairs. That is, "[t]he individual state of affairs does not become the object of assertion in isolation, or it is not distinguished from others in isolation."[19] Therefore, by setting propositions that are coherent with other things that are related to them, a person can make an argument stronger. In scientific theology, however, the fulfillment of this postulate is more difficult than in other disciplines because of God's reality as the all-unifying reality. If God can be completely verified within a finite limited logic, the Godhead loses its nature as the ground of all finite beings. For this reason, Pannenberg claims an indirect approach. In other words, because the manifestation of God's reality is only historical and eschatological, the religious assertions about a divine reality and action can be "tested by their implications for the understanding of finite reality, to the extent that the object of the assertions is God as the all-determining reality."[20]

In that vein, Christian theology must continuously carry out this examination of the inner logic of "consistency" along with its "coherence" with other disciplines. This establishment of coherence is inevitably made through an *implicit* anticipation of the ultimate reality available at its time, since the totality of reality remains incomplete.[21] Therein is the happy circularity of verification and anticipation in a provisional mode.

Creatio Ex Nihilo as the Absolute Beginning of Creation of the Universe and Life

For Pannenberg, the whole cosmos is God's finite creation that is dependent on God as the One who creates it *ex nihilo* as a trinitarian project. In that sense, there is unity between *creatio originalis* and *creatio continua*. The universe can be theologically regarded as God's contingent creation with its finite beginning and its development through the interplay of chance and law-like regularities. The expanding universe as a whole is finite with temporal sequences in its history as the standard Big Bang model explains. It is finite with its beginning, even though its size is

---

19. Pannenberg, *Theology and the Philosophy of Science*, 331.
20. Pannenberg, *Theology and the Philosophy of Science*, 332.
21. Pannenberg, *Theology and the Philosophy of Science*, 333.

known to be unlimited. Furthermore, all the living creatures on the Earth and in the universe are predicted to end in the far future.[22]

For Pannenberg, as the Big Bang event indicates that the cosmos began with time but not within time, the cosmos is to have an endpoint. Pannenberg also discusses Hawking's idea of the absence of a sharp beginning of our universe's time. Although in this quantum cosmology there could be no singularity t=0, even "imaginary or subjective time" objectively takes shape as "a sequence of events" and there should be a boundary between our time and eternity.[23] In that sense, the doctrine of *creatio ex nihilo* should not equate the singularity t=0 as the point of the original creation as the Pope Pius XII affirmed. Rather, it means the contingence of the finite universe on God the Creator as every moment in its history cannot exist as the emergence of a new event.

After the universe's beginning, its history unfolds in openness to a future that is genuinely indeterminate but constrained by regularities. This understanding of creation echoes Israel's faith in God's continuation of contingent saving act in the OT as well as the promise of the new creation revealed in the bodily resurrection of Jesus in the NT. The belief in the covenant of the saving God is extended to the belief in the entire world's dependence on God in all occurrences.[24]

The belief in "the unlimited freedom of the act of creation" coheres with the Israelites' experience of the contingent salvific history of God.[25] In the NT, the God of Israel is the God of Jesus who raised him from the dead as the harbinger of the peaceable *basileia* of God that will be fulfilled in the new creation. Therefore, Pannenberg regards *creatio continua* as God's redemptive and creative act while honoring the independence of creatures. *Creatio continua* has a consummating point that is the fulfillment of the eschatological kingdom of God. Thus, the whole process of creation makes sense only in the eschaton.

If the eschatological consummation is the point from which God's creation of the world is put into purview, then the beginning of the world "loses its function as an unalterably valid basis of unity in the whole process [of creation]."[26] This means that everything is not predetermined in

---

22. Pannenberg, *Systematic Theology*, 2:158–59. Henceforth, *ST* II.
23. Pannenberg, *ST* II, 154–56.
24. Pannenberg, *ST* II, 9.
25. Pannenberg, *ST* II, 13.
26. Pannenberg, *ST* II, 146.

the beginning, but creation is historical or open to genuine novelty in its unfolding until the consummating point in the eschaton. In the same vein, Pannenberg regards the beginning of the universe as "merely the beginning of that which will achieve its full form and true individuality only at the end."[27] Theologically, we hypothetically can have a resurrection hope beyond the *Freeze or Fry* of the universe because the new creation is a cosmically fulfilled reality that embraces the whole and all the parts of the universe rather than suspending the order of nature. It remains hypothetical since it is yet to come. In this eschatological ontology, for the hopeless temporal finitude, the eschaton or the futurity of God can be the standpoint from which the whole process of creation is understood as God's good creation.

The Arrow of Time, the Priority of the Future, and Proleptic Divine Action in *Creatio Continua*

For Pannenberg, the second law of thermodynamics in physics provides critical insight into the "irreversibility" of time and the contingency in the development of the universe and the evolution of life. The principle "traces back the irreversibility of time in its future orientation to differences between past and future in the structure of time, e.g., the facticity of the past and the indeterminacy of the future."[28]

Pannenberg finds a tension between the laws of nature characterized by repeatability and the irreversible flow of time according to the second law of thermodynamics. The laws of nature are essentially contingent and open to novelty. They are formed by the patterns of events that were originally contingent before becoming regular. Natural laws are not unchangeable but are open to reform down the road as they are the approximation of reality.[29] They are no longer independent of time.

In the causal relationship between A and B, without the first occurrence of B and regular repetition of A and B in their causal relationship, A and B cannot be considered a pattern. In that sense, "the connection between the two is constituted from B." This means that the sequential relation between the two is not self-explanatory, but contingent. Thus, one can regard "the laws of nature as themselves grounded on contingency

---

27. Pannenberg, *ST* II, 146.
28. Pannenberg, *ST* II, 97.
29. Pannenberg, *Toward a Theology of Nature*, 77–78.

and functional within open systems—i.e., these laws describe realities that did not always exist and will at some point in time cease to exist, and therefore the laws are historically relative."[30]

The indeterminacy of the future is instrumental to the irreversibility of time as supported by quantum mechanics along with the second law of thermodynamics.[31] According to the Copenhagen interpretation of quantum mechanics, future occurrences are not predetermined, but they are indeterminate in the fundamental physical level. Such indeterminacy "stands in contrast to the past as the realm of the factual, as well as the present as the point that possibility becomes factual."[32] This is because the outcomes of measurements can be reported only in probabilistic terms. The statistical regularities are only the abstraction of the contingent events in the subatomic level. Furthermore, the decisions of the experimenters in their scientific observation are bound to historical relativity because of the finitude of their knowledge of reality that is susceptible to revision down the road.[33]

Here, unlike Peacocke and Keller, Pannenberg affirms that the irreversible continuum of time is always seen "on the basis of the end" through a backward bridge-building, rather than a forward expanding development.[34] This idea metaphorically coheres with the biblical ontology of the created time as the advent of the future of God in the present. In Scripture, there is the priority of the future in the unfolding of history as God makes promises and fulfills them from the point of a future.[35]

Likewise, even though physicists are interested in the predictability of the future based on past events, it is possible only along the lines of statistical probabilities. In that sense, the regularities of the universe such as its fine-tuning (or the anthropic principle) may imply the purposeful directionality of God's creative act. Nevertheless, those regularities are to be regarded as having come into existence *contingently* at the beginning of God's creation of our universe.[36]

---

30. Buller, *Unity of Nature and History in Pannenberg's Theology*, 65–66.
31. Pannenberg, "Theological Questions to Scientists," 43–44.
32. Pannenberg, *ST* II, 99.
33. Pannenberg, *Toward a Theology of Nature*, 96–97.
34. Pannenberg, *Toward a Theology of Nature*, 106.
35. For Pannenberg's understanding of the historicity of creation, see his *Theology and the Kingdom of God*.
36. Pannenberg, *ST* II, 69–70.

I notice that when Pannenberg emphasizes the priority of the future, he also acknowledges the impossibility to speak of the global simultaneity since Einstein's introduction of special and general theories of relativity. Those theories demonstrate the problems of the relativity in the observing and measuring of an object because "determining time depends on the speed of light" and measuring time is also "relative to the standpoint of an observer." However, one can still speak of a relative simultaneity[37] that is "simply that of what is not simultaneous in itself." However, it does not make simultaneity illusionary altogether, because "the temporal sequence of events is not affected."[38] In understanding the sequence of events in every frame of reference, there is the present that bridges the past and the future. Thus, there is the priority of the future in all frames of reference.

Like Augustine, Pannenberg regards the present as a bridge between the past and the future, hinting at eternity as "the undivided present of life in its totality."[39] However, unlike in Augustine's interpretation of eternity, Pannenberg argues that "we do not expect a disappearance of the distinctions that occur in cosmic time, but the separation will cease when creation participates in the eternity of God." This is because "if God positively willed the world and all its creatures, the same applies to the temporal form of their existence."[40] In the same vein, for Pannenberg, as Revelation 10:6 says, Christ is the faithful Creator and Redeemer for all that is in "the heavens, the earth, and the sea." The temporal sequence of creation finds its ultimate fulfillment in the eschaton rather than being obliterated as if it had no purpose after all. If so, the present creation is a continuous process of fulfilling the eschatological purpose of creation.

From the perspective of the eschaton God is proleptically present in *creatio continua* that finds its consummation in the eschaton.[41] Here, Pannenberg regards the eternity of God as honoring the contingent creatures because the eternity is not rigidly immutable but open to the emergence of novelty in the temporal processes of creation. Pannenberg finds its ontological ground in the trinitarian differentiation-in-unity of God.[42]

37. Pannenberg, *ST* II, 90–91 [91].
38. Pannenberg, *ST* II, 155n434.
39. Pannenberg, *ST* II, 92.
40. Pannenberg, *ST* II, 95.
41. Pannenberg, *ST* II, 145.

42. Pannenberg, *Systematic Theology*, 1:403–6. Henceforth, *ST* I. In that vein, Pannenberg names it "differentiated unity." Pannenberg, *ST* I, 405. Pannenberg's idea of

Pannenberg contends that the future of God constitutes the ontological ground of the genuine contingency and freedom of creatures. Here the notion of a mediated creation through the Son and the Spirit is significant. God creates the world out of the mutual faithfulness and love between the Father and the Son by the mediation of the Spirit. Creation is the expression of God's free and constant faithfulness to creatures rather than the atemporal eternity that relegates the temporal processes of creation to the second category.[43] Accordingly, while eternity is a temporal structure with distinctions in unity, it finds fulfillment in the eschaton. God's eternity means *omni-temporality*.[44]

However, the created time is God's creation rather than emanation from God. While Pannenberg gleans from Plotinus the idea of eternity as the ontological basis of temporal transition within creation, he reappropriates Augustine's teaching that God freely created time with all the creatures in the world.[45] As the Lord over the beginning of time and its duration, the loving Creator grants contingency to finite creatures and continues to act creatively in and through the contingent created order of nature.

For Pannenberg, the proleptic presence of God in the present creation is not only temporal but also spatial. Drawing upon Einstein's theory of general relativity, space means the simultaneity of the different occurrences in their interrelations. Here, Pannenberg follows Leibniz's idea of space as relations on the contrary to Newton.[46] Pannenberg regards space as "the order of togetherness of simultaneous phenomena"

---

prolepsis does not necessarily make *creatio continua* necessary, like some of his critics claim. For these critiques of Pannenberg's eschatological ontology of creation, see Gilkey, "Pannenberg's *Basic Questions in Theology*," 53. Rather, in my view, as Roger Olsen says, since Pannenberg posits the dynamic distinction-in-unity of the Trinity as the ground of *creatio ex nihilo*, the reality of the eschaton is to be regarded as "unity-in-distinction." Olsen, "Wolfhart Pannenberg's Doctrine of the Trinity," 185. In the same vein, Christiaan Mostert agrees that, in Pannenberg's idea of the eschatological totality, creatures' independence and their differences created in *creatio continua* are not eliminated. Without the creaturely differentiations, the eschatological whole cannot be fulfilled, since the eschatological future is the ontological ground of the past and the present. Mostert, *God and the Future: Wolfhart Pannenberg's Eschatological Doctrine of God*, 88, 93. For a similar account by Cornelius Buller, see his *The Unity of Nature and History in Pannenberg's Theology*, 122–25.

43. Pannenberg, *ST* II, 52–54.
44. Pannenberg, *Historicity of Nature*, 163–74.
45. Pannenberg, *ST* I, 413n168. Citing Augustine's *Civitas Dei*, 11.6, 12.15.
46. Pannenberg, *ST* II, 87–91.

and time as "the order of their sequence." Here, while he sees the distinct treatment of space and time as an approximation of spacetime, he finds time more fundamental than space.[47] As the eternity of God constitutes the source of the distinctions of time, the triune Creator also takes up different finite spaces into unity in the matrix of the Infinity of the triune Creator. God transcends them rather than abnegates them.[48]

The Force Field: A Scientific Metaphor for the Contingent and Holistic Creation

For Pannenberg, as discussed above, creation's genuine openness to novelty shows that the whole process of the cosmos' continuous creation is to be seen from the perspective of the future as the eschaton constitutes the ground of the being and becoming of creaturely existence. For this reason, *creatio continua* is placed in God's whole-part causation from the perspective of the new creation.[49] Creation as a whole and all its parts are contingently created "from the perspective of the eschatological future, that is, from the divine eternity, which constitutes the *unity* of the irreversible sequence of history."[50] Thus, the Spirit is the all-unifying reality.

In that vein, God continues to create the world spontaneously through creating the laws of nature and through the mediation of the established order of nature.[51] Pannenberg speaks of spontaneous and particular yet holistic divine action in the history of continuous creation. If divine creative action is not only contingent but also regular and holistic, it means that God honors the regularities inherent in the patterns of natural events. Pannenberg stresses the regularities of natural phenomena along with their unpredictability and particularity because there would not have been emergent novelties in duration and stability without the consistency of the environment. Thus, the regularities of nature represent

---

47. Pannenberg, "Eternity, Time and Space," 98.
48. Pannenberg, *ST* I, 414; *ST* II, 85–90.
49. Pannenberg, "Theological Appropriation of Scientific Understandings," 257–59. Drawing on the idea of Wilhelm Dilthey, Pannenberg emphasizes the significance of the creative field of the Spirit as the infinite One that is present in all the independent finite creatures. The Spirit unifies them without being dissolved into the sum of the finite parts. Also, see his *Metaphysics and the Idea of God*, 23–35, for his understanding of the immanent transcendence of the Infinite in the finite.
50. Grenz, *Reason for Hope*, 88, emphasis mine.
51. Pannenberg, *ST* II, 69–72.

"the expression of the unity and continuity of the divine faithfulness surrounding contingent events."[52]

Yet, as discussed in the previous subsection, the regularities are dependent on God as they are not necessary but contingent.[53] Our current laws of nature are only approximations and need to be revised when new observations are made. This means that natural laws are both originated and subject to time. For Pannenberg, this does not mean only the epistemic gap in our knowledge of creation, but also its contingency and openness to God's formative and transformative work from the point of the eschaton.[54]

Considering the coherence between the contingency and regularities inherent in the natural order and the eschatological immanence of the Creator, Pannenberg devotes significant attention to Michael Faraday's model of a time-space-energy force field.[55] He believes that the scheme provides a consequential metaphorical tool for understanding the all-embracing creative Spirit in the created spacetime that is open to the novelty of the future.

In the OT, the *ruach* of Yahwe is "the source of all that is and the enlivening breath of life for creatures that exist, move, and act on the Earth (Gen 2:7, Ps 104:30, Job 33:4)."[56] However, in modern physics, there has also been a tendency to reduce energy and forces to masses and material—making the notion of the Creator irrelevant.[57] Furthermore, in contemporary evolutionary/developmental biology, the life of a cell is regarded as self-organizing, self-sustaining, and reproducing without any room for theology to speak of as a transcendent power operating in all of the processes.[58] On the contrary, for Pannenberg, these deterministic and materialistic ideas do not cohere with the contemporary non-mechanical understanding of the physical level and the epigenetic understanding of living organisms' openness to self-transcendence through interaction

---

52. Grenz, *Reason for Hope*, 114. See Pannenberg, *ST* II, 72.
53. Pannenberg, *Toward a Theology of Nature*, 76–80.
54. Pannenberg, *Toward a Theology of Nature*, 83–85.
55. Pannenberg, *Toward a Theology of Nature*, 81–102.
56. For the all-embracing breath of life or the Spirit, see Pannenberg, *ST* I: 401, 413, 414, 416, 420, 421, 445; *ST* II: 20–21, 23–24, 33–35, 47, 61, 77, 102, 135, 171–74, 270–74.
57. Pannenberg, *ST* II, 79–80.
58. Pannenberg, *ST* II, 77.

with their environment according to contemporary biology.[59] The work of the Spirit can be compared to the whole-part information of the environment on living creatures.

According to Michael Faraday's field theory, the collection of energy is prevenient in the force field, and it is essential to the formation of matter and the interrelations among the bodily elements within it.[60] Hence, Pannenberg finds this theory helpful in providing a point of contact between natural science and his theological discourse on the creative immanence of the Spirit in the cosmos rather than directly identifying the theological idea with the physical theory.[61]

Pannenberg agrees with Jeffrey Wicken's suggestion for a corrective update of Faraday's theory by paying more heed to the mutual interaction between the field of energy and the material elements according to contemporary physics. On the one hand, the field is constituted by "the material elements and movements that occur in it."[62] On the other hand, the field conversely "regulates the elements relating to it."[63] Polkinghorne also points out that Faraday's field theory is outdated since Faraday regards particles as "the singularities of the cosmic field." When a field represents the movement and momentum of energy, the energy is not extricable from its particles as if the field were immaterial or spiritual.[64]

For this reason, Polkinghorne critiques Pannenberg's adoption of Faraday's field theory in his conceptualization of the Creatorship of the Spirit. I think both Wicken and Polkinghorne are right that Pannenberg needs to engage with more updated field theories if both reality and those theories about it are merely the abstractions of the work of the Spirit.[65] As Pannenberg himself contends, there needs to be continuous mutual interaction between theological and scientific presentations of reality in pursuit of coherence. It is consistent with Pannenberg's own principles to update where this coherence lies in light of scientific advances.

However, in my reading, for Pannenberg, Faraday's force-field theory is helpful "strictly for theological reasons." The theory adopted in his

59. Pannenberg, *ST* II, 115–29 (See, especially, 123–24).
60. Pannenberg, *ST* II, 80.
61. Pannenberg, *ST* II, 101–2.
62. Pannenberg, *ST* II, 101–2.
63. Pannenberg, *ST* II, 101. Citing Wicken, "Theology and Science in the Evolving Cosmos," 45–55, especially, 52.
64. Polkinghorne, "Fields and Theology," 795–97.
65. Pannenberg, *Toward a Theology of Nature*, 39–41.

pneumatology is carries metaphorical significance. He does not physicalize the Spirit like Wicken contends.[66] For Pannenberg, there is metaphorical continuity and discontinuity between the Stoic idea of *pneuma* and Faraday's notion of the force field. To be more precise, according to the Stoics, pneuma is "a very fine stuff that permeates all things, that holds all things in the cosmos together by its tension (*tonos*) and that gives rise to the different qualities and movements of things."[67] Likewise, Faraday's field concept "suggests the idea of dynamic movement, of force, together with spatial and temporal extension, but without requiring a material element serving as a medium of field dynamics."[68]

However, according to Max Jammer, the latter has its conceptual root in the former while they are not identified. Pannenberg agrees that both schemes are the finite "approximation" of reality while they are to be open to revision when they are finite representations of the larger context of reality that goes beyond any scientific theory and philosophical-theological views.[69] Hence, both the notion of *pneuma* and Faraday's notion of the force field cohere with the contingently and holistically creative, all-pervading Spirit of God according to Scripture who actively creates and enlivens every creature.

Accordingly, Pannenberg regards the Spirit as comparable to the Stoic notion of the all-creating *pneuma* rather than the Platonic notion of "*nous*" or "the cosmic reason that absorbs human reason."[70] Here, Pannenberg clarifies that the Spirit as a creative field is personal. The Spirit is "experienced primarily as a will that manifests itself in history as the will of a holy power and hence as personal, rather than a divine intellect or a divine self-consciousness."[71] Without anthropomorphizing the

---

66. See Pannenberg's essay, "Theological Appropriation of Scientific Understandings," 428. Also, for a similar clarification of Pannenberg's idea of the metaphorical relationship between Faraday's field theory and the creative Spirit of God, see Gutenson, *Reconsidering the Doctrine of God*, 196–200.

67. Pannenberg, *ST* II, 81.

68. Pannenberg, "Theology and Science," 307.

69. Pannenberg, *Toward a Theology of Nature*, 15–19, 37–41. Pannenberg writes that "[t]o be sure, even a cosmic field conceived along the lines of Faraday's thought as a field of force would not be identified immediately with the dynamic activity of the divine Spirit in creation. In every case the different models of science remain approximations in that they are all conceived under the point of view of natural laws, of uniform structures in natural processes." Pannenberg, *Toward a Theology of Nature*, 40.

70. Kryst, *Quest Profundus*, 91.

71. Pannenberg, *Metaphysics and the Idea of God*, 41.

all-pervading Spirit, Pannenberg does not depersonalize the Spirit as the creative field just to address the problem of the traditional idea of the Spirit as the absolute consciousness that bypasses the dynamic and cosmic Creatorship of the Spirit.[72] That said, while "by nature, the creative working of the divine Spirit cannot be regarded as conditioned by the resultant creaturely phenomena," Pannenberg still finds metaphorical coherence between the force field and the creative field of the Spirit.[73]

All in all, based on the biblical notion of the Spirit as the power of the future who raised Jesus from the dead,[74] Pannenberg maintains that the force field model can be adopted as a metaphorical tool for understanding reality "from the perspective of the eschatological future, that is, from the divine eternity, which constitutes the unity of the irreversible sequence of history."[75] From this whole-part approach, Pannenberg understands all things as constituted by their eschatological future that grounds all the contingent occurrences of the present creation.

Here, I see that Pannenberg's engagement with the natural sciences' theories in his theology is not an assimilation of theology to natural science. Rather, for Pannenberg, there is to be a continuing mutual conversation between the two counterparts by respecting both consonance and dissonance between the two. In this way, both can cooperatively seek to reach a fuller understanding of creation. This is based on the hypothesis that the universe explored by natural sciences explore is the creation of God that theologians investigate *sub ratione Dei*.

Emergent Evolution: Creation in Independence-in-Dependence

For Pannenberg, the cosmos is seen as the work of the all-embracing creative field of the Spirit who continues to create the universe through the harmonious whole of the self-organizing creative systems.[76] They are

72. Pannenberg, *ST* II, 83.

73. Pannenberg, *ST* II, 101.

74. In Pannenberg, *ST* II, 356–59, Pannenberg thoroughly substantiates the historicity of the resurrection of Jesus through the two traditions. For example, "[t]here is no trace of any contention against Christians that the body was still in the tomb" Pannenberg, *ST* II, 358. In chapter 3, I discussed the historical credibility of the bodily resurrection of Jesus.

75. Grenz, *Reason for Hope*, 88.

76. "In a modern perspective, self-organization is characteristic of life on all levels of evolution. It accounts for the spontaneity in all forms of life, and it is in the principle

based on the concepts of the irreversibility of time, contingency, law-like regularity, and fields of force. In this contingent self-organizing universe, the creation of independent creatures is the goal of the creative work of the Spirit as the all-embracing force field. Pannenberg regards God as the ontological ground of the contingency of creatures; therefore, "by nature, the creative working of the divine Spirit cannot be regarded as conditioned by the resultant creaturely phenomena."[77] However, at the same time, "for the sake of the creatures, this working [of the Spirit] can adjust itself to the conditions of their existence and activity and thus give them room to affect the field structure of the Spirit's working."[78] While creatures are given independence from God in their contingent being and becoming, that *independence* is relative being granted by God in God's absolutely free act of creation.

In that sense, once having created the universe *ex nihilo*, the Spirit as the creative field is working in creation as "the vitalizing principle, the lure to self-transcendence, and as the inspirational power of ecstasy."[79] The Creator Spirit does not reject, but rather (based on the biblical teachings) invites the co-creative role of creatures: "Let the land produce . . ." [Gen 1:11 (NIV)]. Therefore, for Pannenberg, the contingent development of the universe and biological evolution mean the triune God's creative work through honoring the creaturely independence.

Creatures are independent from God and other creatures since their existence and actions are finite, having limited duration in time, as opposed to the infinity of God. Their limited existence in terms of their being and becoming is contingent rather than necessary.[80] In their limited duration, they have relevant freedom to choose to contingently act while they learn to be more mature as the horizons of the future open to them. "Only in the process of time can a finite being act and thus manifest itself as the center of its own activity."[81] Only on this finite condition can

---

of spontaneous self-organization that we have to perceive the roots of human subjectivity. Self-organization is the principle of freedom and superabundance in the creative advance of evolutionary process." Pannenberg, *The Historicity of Nature*, 96.

77. Pannenberg, *ST* II, 101.

78. Pannenberg, *ST* II, 101.

79. Pannenberg, "The Working of the Spirit in the Creation and in the People of God," 23.

80. Pannenberg, *ST* II, 95–96.

81. Pannenberg, *ST* II, 96. For Pannenberg, in the new creation, creatures in temporal finitude will be interrelated in co-presence and make the eschatological whole.

creatures have their own experience in their independent existence in relation to God and others. Thereby, they may make contingent choices that alienate them from the goodness of God in their temporal limitedness and the resulting finitude of their existence.

God brings into existence *ex nihilo* the life-bearing universe in its fundamental contingency and continues to bring living creatures into being and becoming in their independence alongside, over, and against God and other creatures in *creatio continua*. Their independent existence enables creatures to develop over time.[82] This course of creation is expressed in the concept of emergent evolution in which self-organization characterizes all levels of its evolution.[83] The self-organizing process "accounts for the spontaneity in all forms of life, and it is in . . . the creative advance of the evolutionary process."[84]

In the harmony of chance and law-like regularities, the succession of forms within creation from the outset involves conflicts, destruction, and reconstruction. This process moves on toward the emergence of complex organisms that can organize themselves and eventually the emergence of the human beings who can thematically conceive of the Infinite or the totality of meaning.[85] For Pannenberg, the development of the life-nesting universe and the emergent evolution of life is the continuous creative work in the universe through the concert between the inherent law-like regularities and chance. As discussed above, the contingency of the continuous creation through emergent evolution is grounded in God's free act of creating the cosmos *ex nihilo* from the perspective of the eschaton if it is the goal of creation to fulfill.

Ironically, entropy takes an ambiguous position by being analogous to evil as it means dissipation, death, and decay against life, while inevitably becoming a medium for the emergence of novelty and the creation of diverse and complex forms of life.[86] Furthermore, our universe is whole is held victim to an eventual demise according to the second law of thermodynamics. It is "part of the cost of the development of independent

---

Hence, temporal limitedness through death is not a necessary condition of creaturely finitude. Even in the absence of death, creatures of different tenses can dynamically interrelate with each other but remain ontologically dependent on the Infinite God as the field of all the novel possibilities. Pannenberg, *ST* II, 95–97.

82. Pannenberg, *ST* II, 127–29.
83. Pannenberg, *ST* II, 127–29.
84. Pannenberg, *Historicity of Nature*, 96.
85. Pannenberg, *ST* II, 127–33.
86. Pannenberg, *ST* II, 115–36.

creaturely forms within the natural order that regulates the general process of the universe."[87] The increase of entropy is inevitable due to the limited amount of energy within open systems that interact with each other. The history of the universe is also constrained by the universal entropic principle and is subject to a heat death because it is a closed system.[88]

Furthermore, like Keller and Peacocke, Pannenberg sees the increase of entropy not only as inevitably required by creation for bringing forth life and consciousness but also as unpredictable due to its contingency. In other words, Pannenberg notices that indeterminacy is universal in the operation of the cosmos in the constraint of the second law of thermodynamics. This implies that there always remains the possibility for natural forces to "close themselves against the future of God," become closed and self-centered system, and end up as "demonic forces."[89]

The contingent increase of entropy constitutes the ground of the genuine independence of creatures in evolution toward the emergence of the moral consciousness and freedom to choose. Hence, such an unpredictable nature of entropy is unnecessary and inevitable. Accordingly, Pannenberg posits that natural evil is a constitutive part of the free process of the life-bearing universe. God honors the genuine contingency of the order of nature.

However, unlike Keller and Peacocke, Pannenberg regards the process of creation as a trinitarian project in which God affirms the value of the material world through both general and special providence throughout *creatio continua*. Ultimately, in the new creation, God will ultimately overcome the power of pain, suffering, and death. For Pannenberg, continuous creation is the process of the triune Creator's fulfillment of the eschatological goal through the mediation of the Son and the Spirit by whom creatures are given contingency and independence that find fulfillment in the new creation.

The Self-Actualization of the Triune Creator: Creation and Redemption in Unity

The existence of entropy is ambiguous in that it enables not only life but also death, pain, and suffering across the good creation of God. The existence of natural evil is not only unnecessary and inevitable, its increase

---

87. Pannenberg, *ST* II, 97.
88. Pannenberg, *ST* II, 157–61.
89. Pannenberg, *ST* II, 108.

is contingent. In his trinitarian framework of creation, Pannenberg presents the self-organizing universe as an emergent whole open to the continuously creating and enlivening breath of the triune Creator while not lost meaninglessly in the sway of entropy. Furthermore, God is faithful to fulfill the genuine freedom of creatures by persistently luring them to participate in the eschatological kingdom of God. In the creative field of the Spirit, independent creatures are brought into self-transcendence through the emergence of novelty in evolution in their openness to the future. In this process, the *logoi* of creatures are brought into conformity with the Logos, which will be consummated only in the eschaton.[90]

Creatures' openness to the future in their temporal structure finds theological coherence with the creative field of the Spirit who works from the perspective of the eschaton. The Spirit at work in continuous creation means the trinitarian Creator's cooperative participation in the history of creation by respecting the divinely ordained order of nature. In the all-embracing field of the creative Spirit, the work of chance and the law-like regularities of the order of nature can be interpreted as the cooperation of the Logos and the Spirit.

To be specific, the independence of creatures from God and others is that which allows for self-identity. "In order to be in a meaningful and loving fellowship with God, creatures are to have a sense of self which ontologically originates in the self-differentiation within the Godself."[91] For the creation of an independent creature in its distinction from all others and from God, we need a principle of such distinction, which we find in the self-distinction of the Son from the Father.[92]

The Logos, hence, serves as the principle of "self-distinction" in the immanent Trinity that is inseparable from Jesus' self-differentiation from the Father. The latter constitutes the epistemological pathway to the doctrinal formulation of the former.[93] We see the Son's self-differentiation from the Father through Jesus's humble self-differentiation from the *Abba* as well as from creaturely lives in retaining his own finitude. We see this in his message, life, and ministry focusing on the pursuit of the peaceable *basileia* of God. Jesus' cross is the climactic locus of his self-emptying.

---

90. Grenz, "Wolfhart Pannenberg: Reason, Hope, and Transcendence," 81–82.
91. Shin, "Non-Anthropocentric Understanding of the Trinitarian Creatorship," 10.
92. Pannenberg, *ST* II, 25–35.
93. Pannenberg, *ST* II, 429–31.

In his resurrection God confirms the coming of God's *basileia* in Jesus as the Son's incarnation. In his interpretation of Romans 1: 18–32, the central problem of human existence is their refusal to honor and acknowledge God by accepting their creaturely finitude.[94] In contrast, in Jesus' humble self-differentiation from the Father, one can find Jesus' acceptance of his own finitude in differentiation from the Father yet in loving unity with the Father through the bond of the Spirit.

Jesus' acceptance of his creaturely finitude differentiated from the Father defines the *differentiated unity* among all creatures through which they can participate in the loving communion of God's kingdom. "As [Jesus] is united to the Father as the Son precisely in his self-distinction from him, he vicariously reconciles in his own person the independence of humans and all creatures to God."[95]

The creaturely existence of Jesus does not merely manifest the self-differentiation of the eternal Son from the Father, but his creaturely existence "actualizes" it in the course of his life.[96] Jesus' life, ministry, and cross are his own self-emptying in his willful acceptance of his finitude in his relationship to the Father. "[I]n the concept of the divine Logos we cannot separate the eternal dynamic of self-distinction (the *logos asarkos*) from its actualization in Jesus Christ (the *logos ensarkos*)."[97]

Along these lines, Iain Taylor contends that for Pannenberg the *logos asarkos* is not an abstract and atemporal being or "something to be discovered or located outside Jesus." Rather, it takes concrete shape in "[*logos*] *ensarkos* . . . [who is] really, powerfully and dynamically present in [the] individual historical human being [of Jesus]."[98] This means the inner-trinitarian relationship that is "active in se," rather than rigidly immutable.[99] The economic Trinity is the actualization of the free and constant faithfulness of the inner-trinitarian relationship.[100]

For Pannenberg, the relationship between Jesus and the Father represents "the cosmic structure and destiny of all creaturely reality."[101]

---

94. Pannenberg, *ST* II, 262–63.
95. Pannenberg, *ST* II, 450.
96. Pannenberg, *ST* II, 23–26, 389–93.
97. Pannenberg, *ST* II, 63.
98. Taylor, *Pannenberg on the Triune God*, 72.
99. Taylor, *Pannenberg on the Triune God*, 88.
100. Taylor, *Pannenberg on the Triune God*, 86.
101. Pannenberg, *ST* II, 24.

The Logos or the Son serves as the principle of the independence and plurality of all the creatures in their unity,[102] and the Spirit is the cosmic creative field that gives existence to all creatures and lures them into self-transcendence as the ecstatic power of the eschatological future.[103] "The universal Logos is active in the world only as he brings forth the particular *logoi* of specific creatures."[104] In that sense, through the creative cooperation of the Logos and the Spirit, the gestalt of each creature is not static but is open to an eschatological fulfillment, while the historicity of nature finds its fulfillment in the emergence of human beings as the *imago Dei*. In a *backward* manner, emergent evolution finds its meaning therein. Nonetheless, all other creatures in the history of evolution do not have their end in the emergence of human beings but in the triune God, the loving Creator who is faithful to redeem all creatures.[105]

"Spontaneous and Gracious" Divine Action in Evolutionary History

Creatio continua is the spontaneous and gracious redemptive action from the horizons of the eschatological new creation as the fulfillment of the divine purpose of creation. To be more specific, "theology should think of God rather as the origin of freedom, as the reality which makes possible the subjectivity of man."[106] Likewise, in creation in general, "[w]ith the eschatological future God's eternity comes into time and it is thus creatively present to all the temporal things that proceeded this future. Yet the eschatological future is still the *creative origin* of all things in the contingency of their existence."[107] Such a creative presence of God honors the genuine independence of creatures.

In that vein, Pannenberg advances a doctrine of preservation that respects both God's purposeful creation of the universe *ex nihilo* and the contingent creativity of the universe as the medium through which God continues to create rather than maintaining what has been completed.[108]

102. Pannenberg, *ST* II, 61–63.
103. Pannenberg, *ST* II, 76–84.
104. Pannenberg, *ST* II, 63.
105. Pannenberg, *ST* II, 52–54.
106. Pannenberg, "Speaking about God in the Face of Atheistic Criticism," 109–10.
107. Pannenberg, *Systematic Theology*, 3:531. Henceforth, *ST* III.
108. Pannenberg, *ST* II, 34.

Along those lines, God's continuous creation proceeds in *concursus* with the creative order of nature through God's "participation in the independence of [the] lives of [God's creatures], even though the intentions of creaturely conduct may deviate from the norm of the Son to the Father."[109] Both preservation and *concursus* mean that God's omni-causality is not deterministic but works through the independence of creatures. In seeking independence there may be creatures' "revolt against the limit of finitude, in the refusal to accept one's own finitude."[110] In the excessive increase of entropy, autonomous creatures may go against the ecstatic lure of God through which life's genuine participation in the *basileia* of God is fulfilled. They may rather defy the spiritual origin of all life due to their self-centeredness.

As proleptically promised in the resurrection of Jesus, the history of creation is regarded as a purposeful project with an ultimate goal yet to be fulfilled. God's "world government" is "providence in its orientation to a goal."[111] This is a spontaneous temporal process of God's fulfillment of the inner-trinitarian faithfulness that we can see in the relationship between the *logos asarkos* and the *logos ensarkos*. In that sense, "[i]n the light of the eschatological future, the process of the divine economy in the history of salvation is . . . a process of God's spontaneous and gracious offering himself for communion with his creatures so that they may participate in his eternal life."[112] In preserving the creative contingent order of nature and working in concert with it as the faithful Creator, God "will bring the creation into perfect communion with [Godself]."[113]

As the ecstatic lure of the eschaton, the Spirit's creative work is also redemptive as the "spontaneous and gracious" power of the future that works in and through creatures like the persuasive lure of the Creator according to Alfred Whitehead.[114] This idea of the transcendent immanence of the Spirit in the course of creation takes both the general and special ordering of creation toward the fulfillment of the new creation. Therefore, Pannenberg defines miraculous divine action as unusual occurrences within the created order of nature, and they take place as the

---

109. Pannenberg, *ST* II, 58.

110. Pannenberg, *ST* II, 171.

111. Pannenberg, *ST* II, 57.

112. Pannenberg, "Divine Economy and Eternal Trinity," 84.

113. Taylor, *Pannenberg on the Triune God*, 81.

114. Pannenberg, *ST* II, 16, 53–54. Unlike Whitehead, Pannenberg stresses the ontological priority of the field of the Spirit that gives existence to creation.

result of both God's general and special ordering of nature.[115] Likewise, the bodily resurrection of Jesus and the new creation is not the violation of the order of nature but the fulfillment of the *logoi* of creatures by participating in the *basileia* of the triune Creator.[116]

The eschatological reality is a promised reality that breaks into the present so that every creature is lured to participate in it.[117] In this eschatological providence, creatures interact with their environment that nurtures them yet transcend themselves and their environment. They are ecstatic in their emergent evolution within the creative field of the Spirit. Thereby, they have emergent novelties (i.e., self-direction, self-consciousness, altruism, and the conceptualization of the Transcendent). This newness is vital to the contingency of the environment that keeps being shaped through the complex dynamics of the interdependent creatures.

Natural selection neither drives evolution alone nor excludes the activity of the Creator. In that sense, the independence of the emergent creatures of higher complexity and novelty does not mean the grim determinism advanced by "the early mechanistic interpretation of Darwinism."[118] Rather, Pannenberg affirms "the gift of newness and freedom" inherent in the history of evolution.[119]

Here, Pannenberg deploys a holistic approach to divine action. The creative field of the Spirit constitutes the ontological ground of the fundamental contingency of the smallest particles in the space-time-energy force field. The contingent sub-atomic events give rise to the law-like regularities.[120] Theologically, the bottom-up events can be regarded as the work of God from the perspective of the eschaton or the all-unifying reality in a whole-part constraint. Furthermore, the Spirit is in eschatological immanence through the mediation of emergent evolution as a persuasive lure rather than a unilateral force. The Spirit lures living creatures into self-transcendence toward the fulfillment of the eschatological new creation. In that sense, the Spirit is in a top-down causation in *creatio continua*.

---

115. Pannenberg, "Concept of Miracle," 759–62.
116. Pannenberg, *ST* II, 601.
117. Pannenberg, *ST* II, 31–35.
118. Bradshaw, *Pannenberg*,153.
119. Bradshaw, *Pannenberg*,153.
120. For this reason, Pannenberg considers the law-like regularities to be ontologically contingent as discussed in the previous subsections.

The Triune Creator Faithful to Save: Seeking Deeper Consonance in the Face of Cosmic Evil

In conceiving the fulfillment of *creatio continua*, theology can hypothetically go beyond what natural sciences provisionally predict about the end of the universe and also can inspire scientists in their research programs as to that matter. In *creatio ex nihilo*, if the history of the universe is ontologically dependent on the absolute freedom of God, so is the consummation of its history. There is the correspondence between *creatio ex vetere* and *creatio ex nihilo* if God is the triune Creator who fulfills creation as a purposeful project. In other words, the eschaton is "the creative beginning of the cosmic process" rather than the end of the world processes. Thus, the new creation fulfills the project of *creatio continua* through transformative liberation from the power of death, sin, and evil. This is reflected in the continuity and discontinuity between the embodied person of Jesus before and after Easter.[121]

The contingent nature of the cosmos can be seen as being in an open-ended path to the fulfillment of the *basileia* of God whose reality took place proleptically in the resurrection of Christ. This does not mean that faith overrules the investigations of natural sciences. Rather, it means that while acknowledging the scientific prediction of the demise of the universe, one can still engage in mutual interaction or seek coherence between theology and scientific cosmology through which the natural order is given hope for its far future when there seems to be no hope.

According to modern thermodynamics, it is predicted that there will be a point of thermodynamic equilibrium.[122] Pannenberg notices that "a temporal end of the universe parallel to its temporal beginning is conceivable in modern physics," and therefore, this universe is temporally finite.[123] However, Pannenberg also points out that this scientific prediction

---

121. Pannenberg, *ST* II, 144–46.

122. Pannenberg, *ST* II, 158.

123. Pannenberg, *ST* II, 158. Pannenberg does not agree with the "static" universe theory advanced by Hermann Bondi and Pascual Jordan as they claim that in the long range of time the universe remains static due to the constant medium density of matter in the universe. Pannenberg agrees with C. F. von Weizsäcker that there is an arrow of time inherent in the expanding universe, in that the expansion of the universe involves the increase of matter by leaps, the irreversible processes of the origination of new forms through concentrated consumption of energy, and the resulting increases of entropy. Pannenberg also disagrees with William Bonnor's model of the oscillating universe since it lacks empirical data. Pannenberg, *Toward the Theology of Nature*, 91–96.

conflicts with the eschatological hope for the new heaven and earth since there will be neither any life nor its cosmic environment remaining after the cosmic demise. Thus, it is theologically problematic, considering the bodily resurrection and exaltation of Jesus Christ. Hence, Pannenberg stresses both continuity and discontinuity between the end of the present creation and the new creation, based on the trans-physical reality of the bodily resurrection of Jesus. Pannenberg writes that "[w]ith the completion of God's plan for history in His kingdom, time itself will end (Revelation 10:6f), in the sense that God will overcome the *separation* of the present from the past and the future . . . in distinction from eternity."[124]

Yet there will be a new kind of temporality through a process of transformation that fulfills the telos of creation: the *independence-in-relation* of all creatures in genuine freedom and love in the creative field of the Spirit. The Lordship or deity of the triune God will be confirmed when the peaceable kingdom of God is fulfilled by the cooperative Creatorship of the Son and the Spirit.[125]

Pannenberg sees that there is radical discontinuity between how we scientifically understand the present creation and how we anticipate the eschatological new creation. Nonetheless, just as God's new creation takes place through the transformation of the present creation as an emergent whole, in the end, physics will have its own descriptions of the reality of the world as will theology. They will find perfect coherence with each other in explaining the way the world is.[126]

In that regard, when Pannenberg engages with Frank Tipler's physical conceptualization of the possibility of the eschaton, he calls for a mutual and open-ended interaction between theology and science without reducing the resurrection hope to the power of computer technology or the furthest developed intellect that can process all the information about the universe and living creatures to regenerate them. Such a *physicalized* eschatology reduces contingently emerging living organisms and human cultures merely to the virtual realities deterministically processed by a computer. Furthermore, Tipler reduces the eschaton merely to the fulfilment of the finite human ideals of the kingdom of God. For Tipler, the Omega Point takes place as a process of emergence from below. Yet he does not regard the process as the proleptic presence of the eschaton or as

---

124. Pannenberg, *ST* II, 95. Emphasis mine.
125. Pannenberg, *ST* I, 331.
126. Panneberg, "Concept of Miracle," 761–62.

the redemptive immanence of God that is not only in continuity with the present creation but in radical discontinuity with it, like what proleptically took place in the resurrection of Jesus.[127]

Natural and Cosmic Theodicy in the Resurrection Hope for Creation

All in all, God brings into existence creatures independent from God in "the temporal form of existence," and only in the process of time do they act as finite beings apart from other creatures and God as "the center of [their] own activity."[128] Finitude is characteristic of the segments of time and space which are the necessary conditions for the duration and identity of a creature.[129] Creatures contingently emerge in evolution by the interplay of chance and law and in temporal finitude so that they can have their own independence. The universal sway of entropy represents the inevitable byproduct of the contingent natural order that is necessitated by God's intention to create subjective entities in independence.[130]

For Pannenberg, natural evil is also contingent. Its excessive increase is also unnecessary and inevitable in cultivation of the genuine independence of creatures. Natural evil contingently becomes worse when creatures "seek to maintain autonomy and thus to aim at a radical independence."[131] "We see this on the ascending line of forms of life, and it reaches a climactic point in human sin, for among us the relation to God has become thematic."[132] In that sense, "[i]f the Creator willed a world of finite creatures and their independence, then he had to accept their corruptibility and the possibility of evil as a result of their striving for autonomy."[133]

In this cosmic order, complex order spontaneously emerges out of chaos by increasing entropy in the environment, and this contingent act is necessitated by the emergence of humanity with intellect, free will, and genuine ecological self-transcendence to other creatures and God in the

---

127. Pannenberg, *ST* II, 159–61. Pannenberg, "Theological Appropriation of Scientific Understandings," 266–70.

128. Pannenberg, *ST* II, 95–96 [95].

129. Pannenberg, *ST* II, 95–96 [95].

130. Pannenberg, *ST* II, 97.

131. Pannenberg, *ST* II, 172.

132. Pannenberg, *ST* II, 173.

133. Pannenberg, *ST* II, 173.

awareness of the Infinite. For Pannenberg, human persons are created to responsibly make ethical choices, knowing that they are finite before God and in relationships with other creatures. Yet many non-human creatures also have certain degrees of independence in their living and moving by making choices that may lead to the excessive increases of entropy.[134] Accordingly, there is an analogy between how, in the universal finitude that limits their life and resources, both human and non-human creatures' revolt against their finitude.

For this reason, God's free decision to create the world as an entropic one "carried with it the risk of a misuse of creaturely freedom"[135] or the risk of the abuse of God-given freedom to conform to the reality of the kingdom of God.[136] In this respect, God did not will the existence of evil, and God does not take pleasure in it, and it is not an object of his purposeful creation. Nevertheless, evils are inevitable phenomena "as the condition of the realizing of his purpose for the creatures."[137] Accordingly, I think Pannenberg's understanding of evil in nature is both "developmental good-and-harm theodicy" and a "property-consequence good-and-harm theodicy."[138]

The eschatological horizons of the future constitute the ontological ground of the independence and freedom of creatures via preserving the regularities of nature and yet continuing to create emergent novelties in *concursus* with the order of nature. The eschatological *world government* as divine action in the present creation deploys various types of divine action through the mediation of the created agents. En route to the eschatological fulfillment of creation, God does not leave creation alone to run its course without the particular guidance of the Creator. Rather, God's creatorship is both general and special as well as eschatological.

In Pannenberg's theodicy, natural and cosmic evils ultimately do not have a place in the new creation. It is credible to believe that the resurrection of Jesus is a historical but uniquely divine event in which the whole of the world is called to participate in a hope for the trinitarian

134. Pannenberg, *ST* III, 559–61.
135. Pannenberg, *ST* II, 166.
136. Pannenberg, *ST* III, 643.
137. Pannenberg, *ST* II, 173. According to Gunther Wenz's interpretation of Pannenberg's view of evil, it originates in "the risk that is not externally added to the creative act of God, but one which is inherent to the determined completion of the act of creation." Wenz, *Introduction to Wolfhart Pannenberg's Systematic Theology*, 104.

138. I discussed the different types of natural theodicy in chapter 2.

fulfillment of the new creation in the cosmic level. This is the end of the talons of time but not the end of life. It is the coming of eternity into time and thus the beginning of the totality of life where no past is lost and no future becomes a threat to flourishing. The triune Creator of the infinite love becomes all in all.[139]

Natural and Cosmic Theodicy in Russell's CMI Approach

Like Pannenberg's coherence-seeking *sub ratione Dei* model, Russell's Creative Mutual Interaction model engages with science-theology dialogue both in terms of consonance and dissonance in pursuit of mutual coherence. In such a mutual conversation, "theology can indeed offer creative suggestions in the form of questions, topics, or conceptions of nature which scientists might find helpful in their research and as judged by their own professional criteria."[140]

In his CMI approach, Russell presents natural and cosmic theodicy based on mutual dialogue between theology and natural sciences whereby he honors the integrity of both disciplines. Russell seeks mutual interaction between the doctrine of *creatio ex nihilo* and contemporary Big Bang models. In *creatio ex nihilo* as a purposeful project, God continues to be creative and redemptive in God's objective and particular action within the anthropic-thermodynamic universe and biological evolution. Ultimately, "The Thermodynamic-Anthropic Principle"[141] is placed in the hypothetical matrix of God's eschatological consummation of creation that is proleptically revealed in the bodily resurrection of Jesus.

Russell gleans the trinitarian and eschatological ontology of creation from Pannenberg when he bases the fundamental contingency of creation in *the priority of the future* that is ultimately rooted in the transformative power of the eschaton. Russell's contributions serve to update Pannenberg's engagement with natural sciences. Furthermore, in his understanding of the bottom-up NIODA (Non-Interventionist Objective Divine Action), Russell gleans a holistic idea of creative divine action from Pannenberg's whole-part approach to divine causality according to his idea of the Spirit as the eschatological force field. Yet I think Russell's *theopaschitic* understanding of the cross of Jesus and the co-suffering of

---

139. Pannenberg, *ST* III, 642–43.
140. Russell, *Cosmology*, 4–24 [21].
141. Russell, *Cosmology*, 259.

God in creation helps to enrich Pannenberg's concept of the force field of the Spirit that tends to be overly rationalistic.

Creative Mutual Interaction between Theology and Natural Sciences

Like Pannenberg, Russell believes that natural sciences and theology can mutually interact with each other since the theological-philosophical notion of *contingency* is central to both disciplines. Hence, Russell believes it can be useful for creating *consonance* between science and theology while *dissonance* is not dissolved in mutual interaction between theology and science because each discipline has its subject matters and corresponding research programs.[142]

In this mutually constructive dialogue, Russell finds it fruitful to employ Imre Lakatos' idea of a scientific theory as a research program. Russell understands scientific theories and theological doctrines in a metaphorical relationship. In Lakatos' view of "the structure of scientific webs,"[143] or a research program, a hardcore theory that unifies the entire program in coherence is not easily falsified by simple demonstrations of counter-evidence. Rather, they lead to adding and modifying auxiliary hypotheses while holding onto the hardcore theory of the paradigm.

For Lakatos, within a research program, auxiliary hypotheses and their data are bi-directional in a hypothetico-deductive manner while the auxiliary hypotheses are in the reciprocally supporting connections within the hardcore theory.

> The data follow (quasi-deductively) from the auxiliary hypotheses, and the auxiliary hypotheses from the core theory. In that sense, the data that support an auxiliary hypothesis are theory-laden within the larger context of the paradigm. However, in virtue of that very fact, they support the auxiliary hypotheses and the core theory in turn.[144]

Moreover, auxiliary hypotheses may reinforce or be buttressed by other auxiliary hypotheses as well. For this reason, on the one hand, according to Murphy and Ellis, this program works in the midst of the

---

142. Russell, *Cosmology*, 14–16.
143. Murphy, "Evidence of Design," 410.
144. Murphy, "Evidence of Design," 410–11. For the details of his theory, see Lakatos, "Falsification and the Methodology of Scientific Research Programmes."

problems of circularity and relativism that arise in the coherence-oriented research programs via coherently integrating novel facts in their relation to higher levels of knowledge.[145] On the one hand, a good paradigm or a "progressive" research program fulfills its positive heuristic by occasionally predicting novel facts and successfully addressing novel facts through integrating more coherent auxiliary hypotheses. On the other hand, a research program becomes "degenerative" when it fails to predict, corroborate, and incorporate those novel facts. In this case, all or most of the auxiliary hypotheses are "added in an ad hoc manner." [146]

Appropriating these insights, Russell finds this Lakatosian method to be not limited to the research programs of natural sciences. He affirms that it is applicable to theology in that theology can be regarded as a scientific discipline, based on the fact that the Christian tradition critically engages with religious data that are communally discerned, organized, and developed. In other words, "[b]oth science and religion make cognitive claims about the world using Hempelian hypothetic-deductive method that incorporates a form of Popperian falsification placed within a contextual and historicist framework complete with metaphysical commitments and criteria of theory assessment."[147] Both scientific and theological communities organize observation and experience through relevant models that are "analogical, extensible, coherent, and symbolic, and expressed through metaphors which refer even if only partially."[148]

However, Russell does not dismiss the marked discrepancies between theological and scientific data. Theological data are different from scientific data in terms of their function because the former serves non-cognitive functions that are missing in the latter, "such as eliciting attitudes, personal involvement, and transformation." Furthermore, in natural sciences, "theories tend to dominate models, whereas in religions models are more influential than theories."[149] That is, in theology, a doctrine is more likely than a scientific theory to be revised by the addition of auxiliary hypotheses in the face of recalcitrant novel facts that are introduced by other disciplines within an epistemic hierarchy. However, this is not one-way traffic in view of the holistic nature of reality. Theological

---

145. Murphy and Ellis, *On the Moral Nature of the Universe*, 10–13.
146. Murphy, "Evidence of Design," 412.
147. Russell, *Cosmology*, 5.
148. Russell, *Cosmology*, 5.
149. Russell, *Cosmology*, 5.

data can contribute to the construction of a scientific theory by providing a philosophical or metaphysical grounding in choosing a research method or a hypothesis over others when there are alternative ones backed by equivalent evidential observations.

Besides these distinctive characteristics,[150] religion also includes elements not found in science such as story, ritual, and revelation.[151] As the community of scientists rest on its foundations of bedrock that include "the assumptions that underlie and give rise to the empirical method," the community of Christian theologians have the foundations that include the living encounter with God through worship, scripture, tradition, reason, and experience.[152] As Barbour points out, while religious data are less objective than those of natural sciences, the former still have cognitive content with empirical import due to the tradition-mediated process of choosing among different tenets of faith, self-criticism of one's own basic belief, and communication among different traditions or paradigm communities.[153]

Thus, they have the status of historical data and can be objective to a certain degree rather than being totally reduced to merely existential and subjective statements like in the "two-worlds" perspectives. Russell affirms that theological data are both historical and hermeneutic and that accordingly they are "a marvelous mixture of changing and unchanging commitments and beliefs negotiated through a variety of interpretive principles and traditions based on a text that is both given and created, both permanent and highly fluid."[154]

By virtue of these similarities and dissimilarities, theology and natural sciences can be placed in a metaphorical and creative interaction, and through their reciprocal interaction they can contribute to each other in their honest search for truth, without dissolving certain differences between the two approaches. In so doing, Russell critically appropriates Peacocke's "epistemic holism," affirming that theology constitutes the top level of the epistemic hierarchy of disciplines in which a higher level is

---

150. For a detailed comparison between theological/religious data and scientific data, also see Barbour, *Myths, Models, and Paradigms*, 142–50.

151. Russell, *Cosmology*, 6–7. For the similar argument as to the discontinuity between the empirical data of religion and natural sciences, refer to the subsections of this chapter on Pannenberg's methodology in theology-science dialogue.

152. Russell, *Cosmology*, 23.

153. Barbour, *Myths, Models, and Paradigms*, 144–46.

154. Russell, *Cosmology, Evolution, and Resurrection Hope*, 66.

constrained by the lower levels and that the former has emergent properties that cannot be reduced to the latter.[155]

Yet like Pannenberg, Russell believes that theology can also contribute to the construction of scientific theories, while the former is constrained by the latter based on his "holistic" epistemology. In my understanding, this is supported by his eschatological ontology of creation based on the hypothesis of the new creation as "the potentially real" state of creation yet to be fulfilled. The eschatological transformation as a communally discerned motivated belief can provide philosophical tools in constructing and selecting a scientific theory.

Because of the non-reductionist, emergent, and pluralistic ontology of the universe, theology can engage in mutual interaction with natural sciences. This is the case particularly when the philosophical concept of contingency constitutes an underlying assumption for both natural sciences' empirical research and theology's investigation of God's creative and redemptive act indirectly revealed in history. Therefore, in his Lakatosian research program, Russell seeks to reach a deeper level of consonance between natural sciences and theology in terms of understanding the universe as God's creation through ongoing dialogue in the face of emerging dissonance from the contemporary natural sciences.

Eternity in Time: The Trinitarian Ontology of Time

I now move on to Russell's discussion of natural and cosmic theodicy. Before engaging with the deliberation, I first discuss Russell's eschatological ontology of creation as a metaphysical framework in placing theology and science in dialogue in rendering the universe and the biosphere on the Earth as God's purposeful and good creation.

Like Pannenberg, Russell affirms that the faithfulness of God does not mean only God's compassionate accompaniment with creatures along the paths of biological evolution that are red in tooth and claw, it also means God's power to fulfill the eschatological new creation. Accordingly, Russell finds useful Pannenberg's idea of the divine eternity characterized by *duration*, *co-presence*, and *prolepsis*.[156] For Russell, these features do not

---

155. Resonating these non-reductionist monist views, Russell favors the term "emergent ontology" over "emergent monism" to avoid the risk of being a "causal reductionist" while sticking to epistemic holism. Russell, *Cosmology, Evolution, and Resurrection Hope*, 103–7.

156. Russell, "Time and Eternity," 46–47.

belong to the new creation only but need to be in this creation even in both continuity and discontinuity. That is, as the bodily resurrection of Jesus proleptically reveals the radical transformation of the present, there should be continuity between the present creation and the new creation as preconditions indicate the "transformability" of the present creation or the "preconditions" for the new creation as *creatio ex vetere*. Here, Russell notices the God of *ex vetere* is the God of *creatio continua*.[157]

In chapter 1 to chapter 8 of his *Cosmology*, while he chooses ontological indeterminism as a "philosophical" interpretation of quantum events, Russell values the theological concept of contingency according to the doctrine of *creatio ex nihilo* as the cognitive element that gave rise to modern natural sciences. Natural sciences began to develop by seeking to understand the rationality of nature when it was regarded as reflecting the *logos* of the Creator based on the doctrine of *creatio ex nihilo*.

However, in chapters 9 and 10 of *Cosmology* and in his *Time in Eternity*, Russell connects *creatio ex nihilo* and *continua* with the new creation while placing the ontological priority on the latter. In other words, God's creative presence in the present creation has the eschatological fulfillment as both its goal and its source. In that sense, like Pannenberg, Russell also affirms that while both creation and New Creation belong to "a single divine act of creation *ex nihilo*," there should be an inextricable relation between the present creation and the new creation "in which the eschatological future 'reaches back,' and is revealed in the event of the bodily resurrection of Jesus."[158] Likewise, even though the reality of the resurrection of Jesus is not yet universal, the eschatological future has a causal priority over the past and the present because it is the eschatological consummation of history that gives meaning to each moment.[159]

Gleaning from Ted Peters, Wolfhart Pannenberg, and Karl Rahner, Russell uses a trinitarian ontology of creation as his metaphysical framework in his theology-science dialogue and his natural and cosmic theodicy. In the rise of modern natural sciences, the Christian belief in *creatio ex nihilo* and the Logos as the ground of contingent natural phenomena become central. Furthermore, based on the trinitarian revelation according to the Christian tradition, God's creation unfolds in the creative

---

157. Russell, *Time in Eternity*, 180.
158. Russell, *Time in Eternity*, 180.
159. Russell, *Time in Eternity*, 117–22.

immanence of the Spirit towards the eschatological new creation.[160] For Russell, the significance of the cross and the resurrection of Jesus is a communally discerned well-motivated belief that can be placed in mutual dialogue with the theories empirically established by scientific traditions.

The "Unbounded" Finitude of the Universe in Creatio ex Nihilo

Before engaging with Russell's discussion of natural and cosmic theodicy, I first analyze his understanding of the coherence between *creatio ex nihilo* and the singularity t=0 according to the contemporary Big Bang models because *creatio continua* through "theistic evolution" is placed in the larger context of *creatio ex nihilo*. Then, I explore his discussion of divine action in the limit of "the thermodynamic Anthropic principle" in *creatio continua* and the problem of natural evil.

Russell provides significant insight into how the philosophical-theological concept of contingency, or the dependence of the finite world on something beyond itself,[161] relates to the singularity of an absolute beginning of time, or t=0.[162] In this metaphorical dialogue, Russell finds contingency to be an essential underlying core assumption for both the doctrine of *creatio ex nihilo* and contemporary scientific cosmology.[163]

For Russell, contemporary Big Bang cosmology gives rise to a serious challenge to locate an initial singularity t=0 and directly correlate the *sharp border* of time or the absolute beginning of time to the theological notion of *creatio ex nihilo*. To be more specific, the standard quantum model or the Hartle-Hawking model presupposes a pre-existing state of "absolute no-thing" where the integration of time and space takes place. Here, the "quantum tunneling effect" gives rise to an "imaginary time" where only the internal time of each point-like quantum event exists without an external time that arises from the relations among those events due to the "fuzzy" paths among the events in quantum fluctuation.[164]

This imaginary time smoothly "transitions" into the "phenomenological" or "physical" time of the Einstein domain. In that sense, the Hartle-Hawking model denies a point of absolute singularity but

---

160. Russell, *Cosmology*, 102–3, 191–93, 264.
161. Russell, *Time in Eternity*, 35–37.
162. Russell, *Time in Eternity*, 39.
163. Russell, *Time in Eternity*, 52.
164. Russell, *Time in Eternity*, 95–103.

rather posits the infinite state of the universe while considering a kind of phenomenological or physical time originating from quantum gravity. Phenomenological or topological time arises smoothly from the "imaginary" time. Russell regards the former as the "temporal" Einstein domain governed by general relativity and the latter as the "timeless" Hawking domain governed by quantum gravity.[165] The two distinct domains have a "transitional domain" between them. For Russell, the transitional domain is still non-temporal in differentiation from the Einstein domain.[166] Hawking advanced this model in an atheistic overtone, arguing that there is no room for the Creator in his scheme in which there is no initial point t=0 and infinite quantum gravity gives rise to the time-space field of the Einstein domain.[167]

Russell's bridge is now populated with *two-way* traffic: contrasting the *creatio ex nihilo* tradition with the Big Bang model *without a sharp beginning*. Russell does so by redefining the finite beginning of the Einstein domain by correlating the transitional domain to the broadened theological concept of contingency. In so doing, one may still regard the universe's possibly infinite size and time as existing in *unbounded* finitude by utilizing the various modes of contingency available in the Christian tradition rather than directly correlating the finitude of creation to a sharp edge of time at its beginning.[168]

In the Christian tradition, the doctrine of *ex nihilo* rejects the Neo-Platonist notions such as moral and metaphysical dualism as well as pantheism.[169] The *creatio continua* tradition rejects the belief that God is not continuously involved in the world after the instant of creation.[170] These doctrines highlight God's free and unconditioned action as the sole source of creation and creation's continuous dependence on God for its existence.

165. Russell, *Time in Eternity*, 79, 94. Russell warns that the relationship between the two is in ongoing debate, and if quantum gravity is "to be the fundamental theory replacing general relativity, God's relation to the universe as a whole will need to be reinterpreted in terms of the complex role and status of temporality and finitude in quantum gravity." Russell, *Time in Eternity*, 79.

166. Russell, *Time in Eternity*, 107n70.

167. Russell, *Time in Eternity*, 97–103. See Peacocke's discussion of Hawking's theological conclusions and his critique in *Theology in a Scientific Age*, 133–35; also, Ellis and Stoeger, "Introduction to General Relativity and Cosmology," 33–48.

168. Russell, *Cosmology*, 35–38, 97–103.

169. Russell, *Cosmology*, 34–35.

170. Russell, *Cosmology*, 35.

Based on these ideas, one may construe different kinds of contingency. To be more concrete, *ontological* contingency applies to the sheer given-ness of an existing thing or its fundamental contingency. *Empirical* contingency applies to the particular characteristics of a temporally finite thing in existence. Russell also distinguishes between two main types of contingency: *global* (which applies to the universe as a whole) and *local* (which applies to different parts of the universe). These categories of contingency show that our universe is contingent not because of its finitude in terms of duration and size. Rather, contingency is a holistic idea.[171]

Besides these categories, "nomological" contingency means the contingency of the laws of nature. First, Russell means by this sort the "first instantiation" of a law of nature. There were only some of a basic set of the laws of nature manifest in the "beginning," and new forms emerged in their first instantiation from the pre-existing set of laws. In this case, nomological contingency is a "mild" sort.[172]

The second category of nomological contingency is an "aggressive" one which refers to something that is "radically new" and unprecedented like Christ's bodily resurrection. This sort proleptically points to "a transformation of the present nature *beyond* what emergence refers to."[173] In that sense, Russell names it the "FINLONC" (First Instance of a New Law of the New Creation).[174] This aggressive nomological contingency implies the ontological dependence of the universe on God who gives existence to it and redeems it through its transformation as a whole. Therefore, "the meaning of contingent processes that begin with a first instance in nature will only be fully clear at the end of history (that is, eschatologically)."[175]

These categories of contingency lead to different ways of understanding the contingency of our universe in its beginning.[176] That is, *creatio ex nihilo* constitutes the hardcore hypothesis with a series of auxiliary hypotheses about the different modes of the finitude of the universe that are based on the empirical observations.[177] With this scheme, while challenging the strict identification between the singularity t=0 with *creatio*

---

171. Russell, *Cosmology*, 35–36.
172. Russell, *Cosmology*, 37–38.
173. Russell, *Cosmology*, 37.
174. Russell, *Time in Eternity*, 51, 181.
175. Russell, *Cosmology*, 37–38.
176. Russell, *Cosmology*, 80–84.
177. Russell, *Cosmology*, 78–79.

ex nihilo, he also rejects Hawking's atheistic presupposition of no need for speaking of a Creator due to the quantum gravity that gives rise to the temporal domain. In contrast, Russell contends that in a "smooth transition" from the timeless domain to the temporal one, God still can be posited as the source of the universe's ontological origination. Furthermore, the transition itself has empirical origination, even when there is no sharp border of time like in the standard Big Bang model.[178] That is, God can be "the Creator of the transition to temporality."[179]

In the doctrine of *creatio ex nihilo*, God creates out of *no-thing* (*ouk on*), rather than creating "out of 'nothing' of any sort" (*me on*).[180] In the Hartle-Hawking model, what is presupposed to exist is a *preexisting set of laws of nature*, rather than a preexisting space-time. Thus, there is actually no thing that exists co-eternally with God. Hawking understands the indefinite phase of the quantum tunneling as the absolute no-thing that does not require a creator. For Russell, the preexisting transitional phase and the pre-existing laws of nature therein are *ontologically contingent*, even though one may not have access to their empirical origination.[181] Furthermore, that smooth transition from imaginary time to the Einsteinian time marks a certain phase that denotes the beginning of time. Thus, it is empirically contingent.

The existence of the Hawking domain may provide the cause for the existence of the fine-tuning of the universe or the anthropic principle.[182]

178. Russell, *Cosmology*, 78–79.

179. Russell, *Cosmology*, 101.

180. Russell, *Cosmology*, 96. For a detailed explanation of this notion, see Tillich, *Systematic Theology*, 1:186–89, 253–54.

181. Russell, *Cosmology*, 97. Also, Russell points out that the ontological status of the natural laws is controversial because as Stoeger argues, they are descriptive rather than prescriptive. They are not counted as having "an ontological standing on their own." *Cosmology*, 108n84.

182. Regarding the *global* and *ontological contingency* of the fine-tuning, there are two interpretations: (a) cosmic design and (b) Many-Worlds. Russell's response is constructive as he suggests a series of meta-levels that includes multiple universes within a cosmic design. In other words, he attempts to navigate between choices (a) and (b) without understanding them as an "either-or" dichotomy. To be more precise, Level 1 includes different regions of the universe with varying constants under the same set of physical laws, like the WAP proposes. In Level 2 or the first meta-level, there can be the multiverse that includes many universes with different physical laws. The multiverse, however, has an idiosyncratic formal logic that governs the physical laws of the different universes. In Level 3 or the second meta-level, there can be a higher system with different subordinate logical systems. Under the higher category all the

Then, the emergence of life and intelligence on our planet can still be contingent if the Hawking domain is categorized as a global ontological contingency. Here, both the beginning of the Einstein domain and the quantum fluctuation are regarded as contingent since the Einstein domain is the result of the quantum domain which is also fundamentally contingent.

If so, the ontological contingency of the openness of nature should not preclude the metaphysical question of divine action. Rather, we can theologically posit that "God relates directly to each three-geometry, supplying its existence *ex nihilo*."[183] This direct presence of God in the mediated manner is also applicable to his understanding of the divine action in "the origin of life, mind, and spirit, without needing to look solely for a sharp discontinuity between domains of nature (for example, the inanimate/animate distinction)," which "potentially signals divine agency."[184] In this view, Russell defines the quantum fluctuation and the imaginary time before the emergence of the Einstein domain as ontologically contingent rather than temporally contingent like Pannenberg asserts. Still, there can be a beginning of time as a transitionary phase despite the fuzzy paths of the events therein that cannot be deemed temporally sequential.

Creatio Continua through Evolution: A Holistic Divine Action

For Russell, the broadened notion of contingency based on *creatio ex nihilo* makes metaphysical room for theology to speak of the creative presence of God in the "beginning" of the fine-tuned universe within the context of contemporary quantum cosmology. The contingent beginning of the universe through God's "unmediated" creation *ex nihilo* is important, for it enables us to speak of God's continuous creative work in *creatio continua* through the "mediation" of the self-organizing universe. Both the cosmos and living creatures are finite and fundamentally contingent on the Creator.

God sustains regularities in *creatio continua* after *creatio originalis*. In *creatio continua*, new creatures appear in evolution in "their first instantiations" (FINLONs). This idea coheres with Pannenberg's idea of the temporal contingency of the regularities of nature. Yet Russell places

---

logical systems may operate. Other meta-levels could also exist above the third one. Russell, *Cosmology*, 49–52.

183. Russell, *Cosmology*, 102.

184. Russell, *Cosmology*, 101.

the empirical contingency of the Einstein domain within the ontological contingency of the Hawking domain. Despite this discrepancy, the contingency of creation ontologically originates in the eschaton that constitutes the basis of novelty that emerges anew in *creatio continua*. Like Pannenberg, Russell regards the whole of creation and "all its parts" as contingent and open to novelty in the matrix of *creatio ex nihilo*.[185]

We know that only a small subset of imaginable universes could produce life.[186] The fine-tuning of the universe or the biopic principle shows us that the existence of our universe is contingent.[187] In all of the universe's parts, God remains "objectively" (both in "general" and "special" providence) present in *creatio continua* through the inherent interplay of "chance and law." God can work in particular ways in the history of the universe and the biosphere through "'created natural gaps' in the causal regularities of nature."[188]

In that vein, QM-NIODA (Quantum Mechanics-Based Non-Interventionist Objective Divine Action) is foundational to a conceptualization of theistic evolution. The collapse of the wave function may be seen as occurring by the co-operation of divine and natural causes. That is, identifying the evolutionary process as *creatio continua* is not equal to reducing God's present work to statistical deism. In Russell's view, "bottom-up causality, relying on quantum indeterminism could hold for God's action throughout the history of the universe, including the evolution of life through genetic mutation and natural selection."[189]

In this process, God can be regarded as acting *directly* but in a *mediated* mode in the microscopic levels of nature to bring forth the *indirect* results in the macroscopic level. The direct action in the quantum level is regarded as mediated because a particular measurement is consistent with the probabilistic character of quantum mechanics.[190] Yet God can

---

185. Russell, *Cosmology*, 14–16.

186. Russell, *Cosmology*, 46–52. Also, for the high improbability or rarity of a fine-tuned universe, see Murphy, "Evidence of Design," 421–24.

187. Russell, *Cosmology*, 46–48.

188. Russell, *Cosmology*, 214.

189. Russell, *Cosmology*, 252.

190. Russell, *Cosmology*, 122–24, 178–81. Mediated divine action, for Russell, means divine action "in, through, and together with the processes of nature." Hence, divine action, both special and general, takes place in concert with the order of nature that God created *ex nihilo* in an unmediated fashion. Russell, "Divine Action and Quantum Mechanics," 355n9.

be seen as directly working in the quantum level because it is the most *fundamental* physical level that is open to genuine indeterminacy according to the Heisenberg interpretation.

Russell adopts ontological indeterminism as a philosophical choice in understanding the chance events in the quantum level. Even though the wave function Ψ in a quantum system follows determinism according to Schrödinger's equation, when the irreversible interactions between quantum systems take place, it becomes indeterministic due to the superposition of several potential states. Ontological indeterminism is supported by Fermi-Dirac statistics qualitatively different from Bose-Einstein statistics,[191] as well as the nonlocality and the holistic entanglement of the indeterminate quantum world.[192]

For Russell, quantum events are not episodic like Polkinghorne argues. They are not only "micro-macro" (i.e., the absorption of a photon by the retina) but also "micro-meso" (i.e., the capture of an electron by an interstellar dust particle) as well as the irreversible "micro-micro" (i.e., proton-proton scattering in the presence of heavy nuclei) interactions. In other words, the irreversible quantum events are "comprehensive" rather than "episodic." Therefore, they are "pervasive."[193] The measurement

191. Electrons and protons are fermions, and photons and gravitons are Bosons. Both Bose-Einstein (BE) statistics and Fermi-Direct (FD) statistics are used to explain the indeterminacy of those particles of the quantum world. However while, at low energy states with low temperature, BE statistics still works in resemblance to classical forms, FD statistics works in a strikingly different manner. This shows that the macroscopic world where Boltzmannian statistics applies and points to classical determinism is actually the product of the operation of the quantum world where indeterminacy and regularities work together. Russell, *Cosmology*, 157. For a detailed explanation of FD and BE statistics, refer to Penrose, *Emperor's New Mind*, 605–9.

192. In quantum mechanics, according to the "superposition" principle, a particle in the quantum level is probabilistically both here and there as it is impossible to measure both the position and the momentum of the particle due to its wave/particle duality. Per Copenhagen interpretation the impossibility of the measurement is actual rather than originating from a measurement device's defect. It is also named "a standard interpretation" following Werner Heisenberg, Max Bonn, and other physicists who stick to the view of ontological indeterminism. I also discuss other alternative interpretations later in this chapter. According to Bell's theorem, when an atom decays, the spins of the two electrons from the atom do not have any influence on each other but they are observed to be inseparably correlated to each other. This phenomenon is named "nonlocal correlation" or "nonlocality" of electrons. For a further detailed account, refer to chapter 7 of Polkinghorne's *Quantum World*.

193. Russell, *Cosmology*, 171–73. For the pervasiveness of divine action in quantum events and the descriptive nature of the laws of nature in the macroscopic level, see Murphy, "Divine Action and Natural Order," 340–42.

problems do not limit the irreversibility of the disruptive nature of the superposition in the interaction of different quantum systems. The indeterminate nature of the quantum level is comprehensive to the extent that it may be regarded as "ubiquitous" because it can be "related to the sudden disruptive aspect of quantum processes that can occur anywhere."[194]

God's direct action at the quantum level creates indirect effects in its amplification at the macroscopic level where the general features of the world are sustained according to classical physics.[195] In other words, divine action in the fundamental sub-atomic level makes effects in the levels above through indirect causation that begins from the quantum level. The indirect causation of divine action forms the regularities of nature that follows classical physics in the macroscopic level. Because the indirect causation includes the result of special divine action in the fundamental level, it can involve both general and special providence.

Based on these notions of divine action, Russell puts forth a theological hypothesis that genetic mutation, in the context of biological evolution via natural selection, can be theologically construed as special providence. In the course of evolution, genetic variations or mutations take place with the help of the "combination of law and chance that characterize physical and biological processes." Theologically speaking, based on the contingency of these events, evolution can be interpreted as "God's way of creating life."[196]

In this creative process, the indeterminate quantum events play a fundamental role in collaboration with classical and ecological sources.[197] The classical factors can be counted as the results of classical processes such as hydrodynamics, thermodynamics, statistical mechanics, and chaotic systems, etc. Along with these quantum and classical sources, there are also environmental factors, such as ecological and geological variables that come into play in mutations and their phenotypic expressions. All these factors are interwoven in gene mutations and their phenotypic expressions.[198]

---

194. Russell, "Divine Action and Quantum Mechanics," 375–76 [376]. In this indeterminate interpretation of quantum mechanics, Russell prefers the term "pervasiveness" to "ubiquity" because the NIODA is focused on the disruptive moments of the wave functions in quantum mechanics.

195. Russell, *Cosmology*, 181–84.

196. Russell, *Cosmology*, 215.

197. Russell, *Cosmology*, 217–19.

198. Russell, *Cosmology*, 218–19.

I think that Russell's consideration of these factors along with bottom-up causation coheres with his consideration of whole-part, top-down, and lateral causalities that are involved in the course of emergent evolution as holistic divine action.[199] Theologically, one may affirm God "acts in, with, under, and through these processes as immanent creator, bringing about the order, beauty, complexity, and wonder of life."[200] There cannot be the genuine openness of nature without the indeterminacy in the fundamental level of physics. Chance in all these events is neither anomalous nor external to nature. Rather, it is a natural aspect of the created order.

Russell recognizes historical relativism and diversity in the philosophical interpretations of quantum mechanics. Leaving room for the possibility that other philosophical interpretations (i.e., epistemological unpredictability, idealistic interpretation, instrumental interpretation) may gain more persuasive force in the scientific community, Russell takes a "what if" approach.[201] Yet whichever case it may be, the statistically unpredictable nature of the physical level in interaction with the emergent levels above can no longer be considered classically deterministic. Rather, it is deeply indeterministic and holistic.[202]

All in all, I see Russell develop a coherence-seeking case for divine action in accordance with methodological naturalism.[203] On the one hand, neither theology nor science should posit God as a natural cause.[204] On the other hand, Russell proposes that the appropriate understanding of divine action honors the Judeo-Christian understanding of God as continuously active in *creatio continua*.[205]

---

199. Russell, *Cosmology*, 124. In lateral causation, causes and effects are in the same epistemic level. In response to Michael Dodd who regards QM NIODA as making God as a finite cause among causes, Russell engages with Thomas Aquinas' rich and multifaceted notion of miracle and explains how QM NIODA presents God as continuously working via the mediation of created causes universally in a holistic manner. Russell, "What We've Learned from Quantum Mechanics," 150–58.

200. Russell, *Cosmology*, 212.

201. Russell, *Cosmology*, 164.

202. Russell, *Cosmology*, 160, 189.

203. Russell, *Cosmology*, 169.

204. Russell, *Cosmology*, 122–23.

205. Russell, *Cosmology*, 116.

The Universal, Unnecessary, and Inevitable Presence of Natural and Cosmic Evil

For Russell, divine action in both general and special ordering of creation is in coherence with the trinitarian redemptive presence in creation like in Pannenberg's doctrine of creation. Such a dynamic view of God's participation in the finite creation represents God's faithfulness and goodness for creation as revealed in the Incarnation, especially when the present creation involves unnecessary, universal, and inevitable natural and cosmic evils.

When the emergence of higher levels of complexity in biological evolution is constrained by more fundamental branches of physics, such a creative process can take place thanks to the fundamental constants of the anthropic principle.[206] This finely tuned construct of the universe serves biological evolution thanks to the universal presence of the second law of thermodynamics that characterizes the expansion of the universe as a whole. Life and consciousness could not have appeared in this universe without this *cosmic construct* that enables the temporally sequential emergence of the diverse species within the finite biosphere with limited resources. Russell regards the entropic principle as required by the diversity and beauty of God's creation.

Accordingly, there is the need for a robust evolutionary theodicy and ultimately a cosmic theodicy. Also, this is imperative when one considers the heat death of the universe as an unavoidable result of the second law of thermodynamics.[207] In presenting his natural and cosmic theodicy, Russell gleans substantive insight from both Augustine and Irenaeus. By tracing the precursor or precondition of evolutionary evil in physical and cosmic levels, Russell adopts Niebuhr's reinterpretation of the Augustinian notion of the original sin as "unnecessary but inevitable evil." In his holistic view of the universe, Russell argues that one may find the precondition of moral evil "at the level of physics, specifically thermodynamics, where we find universal contingent processes throughout nature."[208]

---

206. Russell, "Physics, Cosmology, and the Challenge to Consequentialist Theodicy," 123.

207. Russell, "Physics, Cosmology, and the Challenge to Consequentialist Theodicy," 123–24.

208. Russell, *Cosmology*, 226.

However, for Russell, a metaphorical relationship between entropy and natural evil based on the Augustinian-Niebuhrian concept of evil is faced with a dilemma when we find that entropy is an inevitable part of evolution used by God as a means to continue creation.[209] While in the Augustinian-Niebuhrian theodicy, disorder and decay represent "the privation of good," in the physical and biological spheres, the disorder and decay serve as the birthplace of biological evolution.

As a metaphor, entropy can have both positive and negative meanings. The dual meaning of entropy is heuristic in that it leads us to re-evaluate and appropriate the Irenaean-Schleiermacherian-Hickian theodicy.[210] In that theodicy evil is a hindrance to growth, but at the same time it also signifies the creative role of entropy in evolution, while the Augustinian-Niebuhrian perspective underscores "the brokenness of existence as our modes of interdependence."[211]

However, Russell points out that the gravest challenge to this idea of evil as developmental hindrance is the excessive suffering and its attempt to justify the suffering by a *means-end* argument.[212] Excessive predation and the resultant extinction in the animal world are not justified by the emergence of human beings, which makes theistic evolution anthropocentric, and thus is contradictory to God's faithfulness to God's creation as a whole, according to Scripture.

Therefore, Russell affirms that the Irenaean theodicy applied to evolution as creation is not in and of itself redemptive.[213] Such a suffering-ridden creation requires a theology of the cross as God's co-suffering in creation and an eschatological hope in the world of non-human creatures.[214] Furthermore, the transformation of the cosmos as a whole is to be considered in eschatology when the universe is finely-tuned in a way that entails not only the inevitable and contingent increase of entropy but also the heat death of our universe. Hence, an eschatology that affirms the genuine value of creation is indispensable in natural and cosmic theodicy.

---

209. Russell, *Cosmology*, 235.

210. Russell, *Cosmology*, 235.

211. Russell, *Cosmology*, 235.

212. Russell, *Cosmology*, 262.

213. Russell, *Cosmology*, 262.

214. Russell, *Cosmology*, 263–66. For Russell, God's eschatological Redeemership is not exclusive to God's compassionate presence amongst suffering creatures.

The New Creation of the Entire Cosmos: Affirming the Value of Every Living Creature and the Life-Bearing Cosmos

In his trinitarian ontology of creation, Russell affirms that the Father suffers the death of the Son for creation. The loss of Fatherhood on the cross does not mean the defeat of God over the power of death but gives us the hope of the new creation as the Father raises the Son Jesus from the dead in the power of the Spirit. The triune God is on the cross of Jesus, giving the resurrection hope for *creatio ex vetere*.[215] The development of the life-bearing universe and the emergent evolution take place in a trinitarian project through the mediation of the Son and the Spirit. All the creation is placed in the providential care of the loving Creator.

Accordingly, Russell claims the need for the universal bodily resurrection that includes not only humanity, but also each individual creature of every species. Each creature must be "taken up into the voluntary suffering of Jesus Christ on the cross and through it the voluntary suffering of the Father." Since the whole of creation is under the power of pain, suffering, and death, a benevolent God's faithfulness should reach all the creatures suffering in *creatio continua*. The resurrection must be universally meaningful to non-human creatures as well. [216]

As the emergence of life is dependent upon the construct of the finely-tuned and thermodynamic universe, Russell moves away from an eschatological focus upon the Earth alone on the contrary to Teilhard de Chardin's anthropocentric and Earth-centered view of the Omega Point.[217] Russell adopts a perspective that includes the whole of the cosmos—a "cosmic interpretation" of eschatology.[218]

The scientific cosmology, depending upon Einstein's special and general relativity, presents three models for the expansion of the universe: closed, open, and flat. The latter two models posit the expansion of the universe as infinite. As discussed in detail in chapter 2 of this work, these two models commonly predict the cosmic death (*Freeze or Fry*) that this universe is faced with in the far future.[219] Therefore, the current scientific Big Bang cosmology and Christian eschatology challenge each

---

215. Russell, *Time in Eternity*, 44, 69–70, 80.
216. Russell, *Cosmology*, 266.
217. Russell, *Cosmology*, 289.
218. Russell, *Cosmology*, 280–81.
219. I discussed the so-called *Freeze or Fry* of our universe in chapter 2 of this book.

other when it is believed that the whole cosmos will be the dwelling place of God in God's *basileia* as the resurrection of Jesus proleptically shows the continuity and discontinuity between the present creation and the new creation.

However, this does not mean that either one is to be falsified away by the other counterpart in an irresolvable conflict.[220] In this tension, Russell assumes that "if theology does have cognitive content, . . . it too must somehow be taken seriously as making empirical, even competitive, claims about nature."[221] The belief in the bodily resurrection of Jesus, based on the empty tomb tradition and the reappearance traditions, is to be taken seriously as a *proleptic* event of the cosmic transformation that entails both continuity and discontinuity between the present creation and the new. The event is where the triune God becomes *all-in-all* in God's good creation, and creatures lead their true independence-in-relation through the embodiment of the trinitarian life of God.

Creation and the New Creation in Continuity and Discontinuity

For Russell, natural theodicy is ultimately cosmic theodicy. The theodical dilemma of God's good creation is resolved only in the new creation. Therefore, in the new creation as a cosmic event, each slice of spacetime is given ultimate meaning from the eschatological perspective yet to be fulfilled. Russell affirms that in "a single divine act of creation *ex nihilo*,"[222] the eschatological future has a causal priority over the past and the present moments of the cosmos and the living creatures in it.[223]

Therefore, Russell engages with the five core themes discerned from Pannenberg's concept of eternity: (1) flowing time (a past/present/future structure or "p-p-f" structure), (2) the co-presence of every event of nature and history in eternity, (3) duration as temporal thickness, (4) a single global future for creation in the new creation, and (5) the proleptic "reaching back" of the eschatological future to a moment in this creation.[224]

As the new creation is not a second *creatio ex nihilo*, but rather the transformation of the present universe, these five elements become

---

220. Refer to chapter 6 of Russell, *Time in Eternity*.
221. Russell, *Cosmology*, 289.
222. Russell, *Time in Eternity*, 15.
223. Russell, *Time in Eternity*, 117–22.
224. Russell, "Time and Eternity: Special Relativity & Eschatology," 52–55.

essential to "reconstructing" eschatology on the one hand and suggesting new directions for scientific research programs on the other hand. The central issue at stake here is as follows:

> We would expect that time as understood by physics is not only a characteristic of this universe as God's creation, but that it will in some ways be a characteristic of the new creation. Yet we would expect that in the new creation, our experience of temporality will no longer be marred by the loss of the past and the unavailability of the future.[225]

The new creation is the beginning of a sort of *transformed temporality*. There will be temporality, but without the loss of the past and the unavailability of the future. If eschatology includes cognitive elements of reality, there can be mutual interaction between eschatology and physics. Therefore, Russell first seeks to reconstruct Christian eschatology based on what we know about the temporality of our universe. Then, he creatively suggests possible directions for future research in physics and cosmology in the light of the religious data according to the reconstructed eschatology. Particularly, he does so by reconstructing the eternity as "co-present flowing time."[226]

In this task, Russell notes that the concept of flowing time is one of the most controversial notions in contemporary philosophy of time. First, the greatest challenge arises from the special theory of relativity due to the loss of the global present and the resulting concept of the block universe.[227] Russell also acknowledges the challenge to flowing time from the analytic philosophers of time.[228] Yet Russell defends the concept of flowing time through reconceiving it in response to those challenges by developing his reconstructed ontology of flowing time: namely, "a multidimensional (or spacetime), inhomogeneous ontology, and relational" notion of time. In this understanding of time, while time is not composed of tense-less relations as in a "B-theory of time" or a block time theory,

---

225. Robert Russell, "Eschatology and Scientific Cosmology," 112.

226. Russell, *Time in Eternity*, 317–54.

227. For example, see Isham and Polkinghorne, "Debate over the Block Universe," 135–44.

228. For example, for John McTaggart, there can be no genuine flowing time because, based on the special theory of relativity, there cannot be the simultaneous present as a property. Russell, *Time in Eternity*, 132–34. Also, because there is "the tangle of conflated ontological assignments" at each slice of spacetime, there cannot be a tense as a property. Russell, *Time in Eternity*, 138.

time is relational yet with tenses in inhomogeneity. Russell advances a "relational A-theory of time" with tenses as relations, rather than as properties.[229] This is a *modified* A-theory of time because Russell understands tenses as relations like B-theorists of time, whereas A-theorists believe tenses to be properties of flowing time.

Even though there could be the elements of continuity in the present creation, the new creation transcends the present creation because the former is the consummation of the latter. As Pannenberg rightly points out, the infinity of the eschaton is not the sum of the slices of spacetime in *creatio continua*, but *transcends the sum of them* while giving meaning to its each moment. In that vein, Russell holds on to the "III-2" ontology of flowing time, according to which not only the present but also the future states are "potentially real."[230]

By not being dissolved into its part, the whole does not eliminate the independence of its part.[231] Yet Russell agrees with Pannenberg that a tradition-mediated Christian eschatology (i.e., the doctrine of *creatio ex vetere*) can provide *metaphysical* inspirations to scientists in their developing scientific research programs while they stick to the research methods proper to the subject matters of their studies. Therefore, even though there is no positive way to explain away how the cosmic transformation will take place in the eschaton, we can still seek the intelligibility of the preconditions of the new creation in a *negative* sense.[232] In the following two subsections, I discuss Russell's proposal of the preconditions of the new creation in his CMI approach. Russell contributes to Pannenberg's research program in theology-science dialogue by presenting more robust interaction between science and theology.

Scientifically Reconstructing Eschatology: The Preconditions of Eternity as Co-Present Flowing Time

For Russell, flowing time, despite the challenge of the global present according to the special theory of relativity (SR), can be maintained. Before

---

229. Russell, *Time in Eternity*, 134–50.

230. Russell, *Time in Eternity*, 126–27. This contrasts with the III-1 ontology of flowing time that affirms the actuality of the present only. For example, William Craig writes that "[a]ccording to presentism, future times do not exist and past time no longer exists." Craig, *Time and Eternity*, 169.

231. Pannenberg, *Metaphysics and the Idea of God*, 116–17.

232. Russell, "Eschatology and Physical Cosmology," 307.

discussing eternity as co-present flowing time, the notion of flowing time is important when the eternity of the *basileia* of God is what affirms the history of creation in both continuity and discontinuity. As SR challenges the notion of the global present, it does not necessarily mean that one should end up with relativism[233] while accepting the loss of the global present in the special theory of relativity. According to SR, the two initial frames of reference in a uniform motion never have an absolutely shared present.

However, the relative objectivity of the sequence of events is preserved when it is observed in the two different frames of reference.[234] While the different frames of references are relativized depending on the speed of light, they constitute multiple dimensions of spacetime. Russell neither supports absolutism nor relativism, but he celebrates relativity based on his trinitarian ontology of time.[235]

Even when there is no global present, considering the irreversibility of time according to the second law of thermodynamics and the ontologically indeterministic nature of the quantum level, future has more ontological weight than present and past. All the tenses are not equally real like the block universe scheme proposes.[236] The notion of flowing time and the priority of future are significant for natural and cosmic theodicy. That is, the eschatological redemption of creation means God's contingent saving act. Furthermore, the eschatological fulfillment of the faithful God's eternity is the co-presence of tensed events rather than the dissolution of creation into the atemporal eternity.

That said, since the eternity is the ontological ground of the flowing time of *creatio continua*, the p-p-f structure of the created time is to be preserved in the eschatological new creation. The re-conceived notion of flowing time constitutes a precondition of the transformed temporality of the new creation. In the new creation, the different moments of the p-p-f structure torn apart by the talons of time of the present creation will become present to one another without "the conflation of all moments

---

233. Russell, *Time in Eternity*, 313–16. For example, when a person runs with a pole toward and through a barn at a velocity nearly half the speed of light, the contraction of the pole takes place from the frame of reference of an observer inside the barn. Meanwhile, time dilation takes place from the frame of reference of an observer running with the person observed. However, the fact is that the person could run through the barn with the pole without damaging either the barn or the pole. Russell calls this phenomenon "the pole-in-the-barn paradox." Russell, *Time in Eternity*, 248–59.

234. Russell, *Time in Eternity*, 240–58.

235. Russell, *Time in Eternity*, 313–16.

236. Russell, *Time in Eternity*, 125–34.

of time into a single timeless now."²³⁷ Like Pannenberg, Russell regards co-presence as neither timeless eternity nor the endlessly continuing succession of "separated" temporal moments. It is "one of duration, but a duration that includes co-presence."²³⁸ Hence, each present has its past and future, and the tenses represent the relations among the events rather than their unchangeable properties.

In order to illustrate this counterintuitive idea of co-presence by the medium of what we know about the present creation, Russell adopts the metaphor of the "open stacks" library.²³⁹ This metaphor gives us a glimpse into the new creation as there can be the retrieval of any past events causally related to a present event. In the co-present flowing time, without the loss of the present and the past, there will be "multiple prolepses." The infinite future states remain potentially real states. Yet without the fear of death, evil, and suffering, one can experience the richness of temporality and hermeneutical plurality through infinitely dynamic interconnections among tenses.²⁴⁰

The global future in the new creation does not mean a monotonous and undynamic reality but rather a spontaneous interrelation among independent creatures without the loss of the past and the fear of the inestimable future occurrences.²⁴¹ Russell maintains the dynamic "p-p-f" relations and the inhomogeneity of flowing time in the co-presence of all tenses. This is imperative for addressing the question of free will, divine action, and theodicy.²⁴²

Hence, Russell *reconstructs* the idea of the eschatological co-presence that is still ontologically contingent on God, in light of physics, mathematics, and cosmology. Gleaning from Pannenberg the idea of the dialectical relationship between the finite and the infinite, Russell defines the meaning of the infinite as the consummation of the finite and contends that the whole is larger than the sum of its parts. Here, Georg Cantor's notion of the "transfinite" is helpful.²⁴³ Pannenberg adopts Hegel's

---

237. Russell, *Time in Eternity*, 319.
238. Russell, *Time in Eternity*, 319.
239. Russell, *Time in Eternity*, 154–57.
240. Russell, *Time in Eternity*, 67–70, 347–51.
241. Russell, "Time in Eternityy," 53–54.
242. Russell, "Time in Eternity," 53–54. Russell defines the eternity as "the fractal library of histories" characterized by relationality, multidimensionality, and inhomogeneity, open to the future novelty. Russell, "Time in Eternity," 54.
243. Russell, *Time in Eternity*, 207–23. In my understanding of Russell's use of this

twofold categories of the finite and the infinite. The infinite represents history in its totality. This is the fulfillment of the economic Trinity in creation, which is the self-actualization of the immanent Trinity.

However, the consummation of creation through the trinitarian self-actualization of God does not mean a pantheistic identity of God and the world. Creation is still distinct from God, just as the Son as the principle of creation is distinct from the Father. Yet Pannenberg does not posit a third category that distinguishes the infinity of creation from that of God. For Russell, Georg Cantor's mathematical idea of the "transfinite" is significant here, because with the help of the notion it is possible to distinguish the infinity of the kingdom of God from the triune God or the "absolute Infinity." There can be a sequence of so-called "transfinite numbers" within an absolutely infinite set without bounds. They are considered infinite because they are uncountable.

Paradoxically, however, they are still finite because they conceptually form a sequence of numbers. Hence, they are infinite by transcending all countable sets of natural numbers while they are still finite. This means that the transfinite is both finite and infinite. While the transfinite are infinite, they still are transcended by the Absolute Infinite that lies beyond any possible transfinite sets of numbers. Therefore, this threefold distinction of the finite, the transfinite, and the absolute infinite articulates the continuity and discontinuity between the infinity of creation and the absolute Infinity of God.

Russell also adopts the "non-Hausdorff manifold space" to help in understanding the concept of "co-present flowing time" as the transfinite as opposed to the divine infinity. "Hausdorff-manifold space" is comparable to the temporality of the present creation with the loss of the past and the inaccessibility of the future. However, with non-Hausdorff manifolds as an analogy, one can conceptualize the co-presence of different fragments of temporal duration. While their distinction is preserved, they are overlayered in unity. In other words, there can be "temporal distinctions without separation."[244]

Russell also explains co-presence in flowing time by use of an infinite "fractal-like" structure.[245] When A is past to B, and C is future to

---

idea, it is metaphorical because the new creation is not merely physical consummation of every space-time slice. Rather, *creatio ex vetere* includes the ethical level of the emergent hierarchy of nature.

244. Russell, *Time in Eternity*, 167.
245. Russell, *Time in Eternity*, 145–56.

B, one can overlay the two events C and B at a present moment. If the slices of space-time past to the matching point of B and C become infinite, every slice of spacetime past to the matching point can be identified except for B and C. This is because the temporal gap between each moment gets closer to zero. Here, B and C are not identical. Thus, the time past to B (tB<B) and the time past to C (tC<C) are uniquely related to B and C. However, those past moments can be "identified without being conflated." This makes an identity between two temporal connections without the dissolution of their distinction. This sort of branching of time can continue infinitely.[246]

This manner of co-presence finds another metaphor in non-separability or entanglement at the quantum level.[247] Quantum non-separability may provide a useful analogy for the eternity as differentiated unity.[248] As space and time are inextricable because they constitute one four-dimensional continuum, "eternity" and "omnipresence" are inextricable. The entanglement of the quantum world may give us a partial hint as to how co-present flowing time will come to pass.

Regarding the notion of prolepsis, Russell also uses Penrose's diagram for Schwarzschild black holes[249] to illustrate an incident of a person falling into a black hole and quickly entering the same singularity which all of creation is approaching. There are two perspectives of time represented in this illustration. For the individual who enters a black hole, the remote future becomes the immediate future while remaining the remote future for the individual outside of the black hole.

In a nutshell, by employing these mathematical, physical, and cosmological schemes, Russell reconstructs eternity as co-present flowing time, based on the fact that God is faithful to creation and the new creation will be a fulfilled creation in which God will be all in all. God sustains the p-p-f structure of flowing time in the new creation, while the concept of co-presence constitutes discontinuity between the present and the new creation.

---

246. Russell, *Time in Eternity*, 162–72.
247. Russell, *Time in Eternity*, 172–79.
248. Russell, *Time in Eternity*, 178–79.
249. Russell, *Cosmology*, 185–90.

Seeking Deeper Consonance: Eschatology Inspires Natural Sciences

Despite the discontinuity between the present creation and the new, natural sciences can glean inspirations from this reconstructed Christian eschatology. A scientifically reconstructed eschatology can illuminate the future directions of research as the former constitutes a philosophical matrix for interpreting the latter. Such a mutual and creative interaction is important since this cosmos is the locus where the new heaven and earth will be embodied.

For instance, "duration, flowing time, and prolepsis" constitute major components in a scientifically reconstructed eschatology as discussed above. In reverse, eschatology may serve the development of scientific research programs.[250] To be specific, Russell suggests that a "multidimensional, relational, and inhomogeneous" spacetime interpretation of flowing time can be an option better than a neo-Lorentzian interpretation of time without violating SR.[251] Even though there are diverse frames of reference due to "time dilation" and "the contraction of an object's length," they do not require "a unique axis of absolute simultaneity" [252] to understand time as flowing time. Those plural frames of reference may be regarded as representing diverse aspects of one objective event. It can be likened to the trinitarian plurality-in-unity of the Creator.[253] In special relativity, we can still have a causal invariant with which every observer in relative motion can agree. In other words, there remains an *objective* sequence of phenomena that their diverging perspectives commonly share.

Also, the future of the temporal sequence is open to multiple potential realities. In that vein, Russell suggests that the current studies in string theory could help to explain the "intrinsic physical extension" of an object whereas physicists have understood fundamental particles as "point-like objects."[254] String theory has the potential to help us under-

---

250. See chapters 5 and 6 of Russell, *Time in Eternity*.

251. Russell, "Time in Eternity," 50.

252. Russell, *Time in Eternity*, 309. The idea of the unique axis is advanced by William Craig, for example.

253. Like Russell, Pannenberg also maintains the priority of the future in special relativity. However, Pannenberg gives priority to temporality over spatiality of an event when he understands the sequences of events in flowing time. Russell's contribution is to appreciate the multiplicity of frames of reference according to the theory of special relativity in his trinitarian ontology of spacetime.

254. Russell, *Time in Eternity*, 331–35.

stand the fundamental particles in a new way. Thereby, there can be a better way to explain the duration of time in openness to genuine future.

Furthermore, if a physicist seriously takes the eschatological ontology of time, she or he may pursue investigating the possibilities of "forward moving and backward moving waves" in the electromagnetic field by believing in the possibility of "prolepsis."[255] In so doing, one may choose to investigate whether there can be a temporally symmetric characteristic in electromagnetism. It suggests "something like the preconditions in nature that are suggestive of . . . 'the causality of the future.'"[256]

Comparative Assessment of Natural and Cosmic Theodicy of Pannenberg and Russell

For both Pannenberg and Russell, the eschatological ontology of creation is the context of natural and cosmic theodicy. Ultimately, the flowing time of *creatio continua* is the process of the triune Creator's eschatological fulfillment of the good and purposeful creation. In this section, I comparatively assess their methodology, their understandings of general and special providence, and natural and cosmic theodicy in their trinitarian ontology of creation.

Mutual Dialogue between Theology and Science: The Cosmos as God's Good Creation

First of all, I appreciate Pannenberg's and Russell's methods in theology-science dialogue because they speak of the universe as God's creation in a metaphorical manner. They both engage in mutual interaction between the two disciplines while pursuing hypothetical consonance. Natural science's framework of meaning is metaphorical as one can see in the hypothetic-deductive fashion of scientific reasoning in contemporary natural sciences. Likewise, Christians are continuously called to discern God's presence in their lives situated in the world and to test their faith in communal discernment.

In a scientific model, a scientist proposes a hypothesis as to a certain aspect of an observed entity depending on other observed phenomena that serve as its indirect proving grounds. The design of a model is theory-laden

255. Russell, *Time in Eternity*, 342–47.
256. Russell, *Time in Eternity*, 347.

and paradigm-laden, in that a scientist's observation and interpretation is influenced by existing theories and paradigms. Further, the reality of the observed world is not deterministic. The observation of an entity is inherently spatiotemporally relative. In other words, the indeterminacy is also universally inherent in nature according to quantum mechanics.[257]

However, this does not mean that natural sciences are to be seen through the lens of relativism. Rather, even when scientific observations are paradigm/theory-laden, there are still elements of truth that are not totally dependent on paradigms. That is, as Barbour points out, in scientific models as metaphors, the distinction between theoretical language and observational language exists, even if it is relative and subject to shifting, because it is context-dependent.[258] Accordingly, naïve realism, positivist perspectives, and relativism are to be rejected.[259]

On the other hand, religious beliefs are not only affective and ethical, but also cognitive, laden with truth claims based on reliable information gleaned from experiences in history and communally tested. That is, as Keith Ward maintains, one needs to regard Scripture as the result of a process "beginning with primary revelatory data—alleged, fallible revelations by God to humans in seven main forms: public events, inner experience, theoretical hypotheses and reflections, narratives, moral evaluations, writings coming out of liturgical practices, and those arising out of the social practices of the communities."[260]

Furthermore, Scripture is to be seen as "a cumulative consequence of a process composed of such data and formed in a Canonical Matrix."[261] Here, while Ward distinguishes the data of religious experience from the hard data of the natural sciences, he sees scriptural accounts and their canonization as the product of communal discernment of whether various religious experiences actually represent divine revelation. If such a discernment tests the validity of a religious truth claim, it involves coherence as a core standard as it includes more and more novel data to integrate.

If a religious tradition is compared to a scientific research program, it becomes positive and heuristic when the following is included in its

257. Barbour, *Myths, Models, and Paradigms*, 1–3.
258. Barbour, *Myths, Models, and Paradigms*, 43–44.
259. Barbour, *Myths, Models, and Paradigms*, 34–38.
260. Murphy, "Evidence of Design," 415n12. Murphy cites what Keith Ward said in his correspondence with her.
261. Murphy, "Evidence of Design," 415–16n12. Also, see Ward, *Religion and Revelation*, 278–80.

general picture: "(1) assessment of the coherence of the experience with accepted teaching, (2) fruits in the life of the individual and the relevant community, with particular emphasis on unity, (3) independent confirmation from experiences of others involved."[262] The New Testament itself demonstrates these characteristics of communal discernment because on the one hand, it calls for testing prophecies and teachings. On the other hand, "the very existence of the New Testament is due to the fact that these writings, when circulated among the early churches, were consistently judged to be in harmony with the teaching of Christ, either through the apostles or through the Spirit."[263]

Such a testing process is not exclusive to the birth and canonization of the New Testament in the early phase of Christianity. Traditions are "enormously complex tangles of concepts, beliefs, and practices of all kinds that make up communities' cultures."[264] For this reason, as Alasdair MacIntyre argues, a tradition is "an ongoing argument about how to interpret and apply its classical text."[265] In the face of insoluble antinomies to integrate in harmony with its core beliefs, a religious tradition continues to ask "whether the alternative and rival traditions may not be able to provide resources to characterize and to explain the failings and defects of their own tradition more adequately than they, using the resources of the tradition, have been able to do."[266]

If this is the case, with all their distinct features and marked differences, there is a certain sort of similarity between the Christian and scientific communities as they both are built on traditions. Also, both are built on authority that is open to revision rather than closed. In the scientific community, there is ongoing dialogue with new discoveries that contradict the accumulated tradition that is represented by scholars who are recognized as authoritative.

For Christian churches, the authority is the gospel of Jesus according to Scripture that continues to be tested and re-interpreted by the diverse experiences of contemporary Christians. In that vein, Lesslie Newbigin writes that "the Christian community, the universal church, embracing more and more fully all the cultural traditions of humankind, is called to

---

262. Murphy, "Evidence of Design," 416–17 [417].
263. Murphy, "Evidence of Design," 417.
264. Kelsey, *Eccentric Existence*, 17.
265. MacIntyre, *In Whose Justice? Which Rationality?*, 12.
266. MacIntyre, *In Whose Justice? Which Rationality?*, 166–67.

be that community in which a tradition of rational discourse is developed which leads to a true understanding of reality, because it takes as its starting point and as its permanent criterion of truth the self-revelation of God in Jesus Christ."[267]

When a scientific research program is taken as a tradition with its truth claims to reality, a theological tradition can converse with the scientific research program in pursuit of consonance between the two in a holistic view of reality. Pannenberg rightly affirms that if the universe is posited as the creation of God, the universe cannot be fully understood without the concept of God. Furthermore, if God is the Creator of the universe, God cannot be properly understood without a proper understanding of the universe which stages God's trinitarian history.

Thus, under the metaphysics of the unity of reality, Pannenberg advocates mutual interaction between theology and natural/social sciences. While scientists perform research by use of methodology proper to their subject matters, theologians can inspire natural scientists in their development of their research programs through theological/metaphysical insight. On the other hand, theologians are to engage with the new discoveries and theories of natural sciences *sub ratione Dei*.

Likewise, in a very similar way to Pannenberg's methodology, but with significantly unique contributions, Russell suggests two-way traffic on the bridge between natural sciences and theology. In his CMI approach, Russell develops a Lakatosian research program where constantly emerging dissonance may lead to a deeper level of consonance. Therein, Russell appreciates Pannenberg's trinitarian metaphysics of creation and his understanding of "divine action in both creation (and thus providence) and redemption in terms of the Spirit of God."[268] Yet Russell reconstructs Pannenberg's contributions to theology-science dialogue through more thoroughly engaging with contemporary quantum mechanics, quantum cosmology, and theories of relativity.

On the Finite Beginning of the Life-Nesting Universe

Russell and Pannenberg affirm that we can believe with Augustine that time came into being with creation, rather than affirming that creation

---

267. Newbigin, *Gospel in a Pluralist Society*, 87–88.

268. Russell, *Cosmology*, 191–93 [193]. Also, see chapter 6 of Pannenberg's *Toward a Theology of Nature*.

began in time.[269] There can be an empirically contingent beginning of the spacetime of our universe. "While the past has to be finite for the theistic doctrine of *ex nihilo* to work (or else the universe is eternal), that does not necessarily presuppose a beginning in time."[270] By creating the cosmos at its absolute beginning, God becomes the Lord of *creatio continua* in the course of biological evolution and cosmic development that is contingent thanks to the interplay of chance and regularities.

Yet both Pannenberg and Russell recognize that the beginning of time is not necessarily identified with a sharp "singularity" t=0. The infinite state of the universe is clearly denied by the closed universe model in which not only the beginning but also the end of the universe is affirmed. However, according to the Inflationary (Hot) Big Bang models developed since the 1980s, the absolute singularity or t=0 remained unsettled while the Planck time ($10-43$ seconds after the Big Bang) was depicted as undergoing an exponentially rapid expansion before settling down to the expansion rate supposed by the original Big Bang model.[271] Moreover, a variety of the quantum cosmologies were introduced more recently, and among them, there are mixed stances about the question of whether the universe is infinite or finite.

As discussed above, the standard quantum model or the Hartle-Hawking model presupposes a sort of an absolute no-thing (the integration of time and space) where "the quantum tunneling effect" gives rise to an imaginary time. This imaginary time emerges later into a phenomenological or physical time.[272] In that sense, the Hartle-Hawking model denies the absolute singularity and posits the infinite state of the universe without the need for a Creator.

For both Pannenberg and Russell, however, this quantum cosmology does not abnegate the finite beginning of this universe. They believe in the absolute beginning of our universe, even though they affirm the temporally finite beginning of our universe in divergent manners. As the central content of the doctrine of *creatio ex nihilo* is about the contingency of creation,[273] the universe and all its parts do not exist necessarily, but

269. Augustine, *City of God* 11.6.
270. Kärkkäinen, *Creation and Humanity*, 126–27.
271. Russell, *Time in Eternity*, 57–59.
272. Hawking and Hartle, "Wave Function of the Universe," 2960–75. Also, see chapter 8 of Hawking and Mlodinow, *Brief History of Time*.
273. Pannenberg, "Doctrine of Creation and Modern Science," 9. Also, see Tillich, *Systematic Theology* 1,196. For a similar discussion, and see Gunton, *Triune Creator*, 111–14.

they have finite beginnings in their duration even when they are deemed to be infinite in size.[274]

Russell clarifies the loosely defined concepts of contingency in his efforts to place contemporary big-bang cosmology in dialogue with the theological discourse on *creatio ex nihilo* and *continua*. In his engagement with the Hartle-Hawking model, Russell identifies the anthropic principle as ontological, global, and nomological contingency. The sheer given-ness of the finely tuned universe is fundamentally contingent even when it is dependent on the pre-existing laws of nature in the Hawking domain. The existence of the Hawking domain is fundamentally contingent as it gives rise to a specific type of the universe in the Einstein domain that is finely tuned for the existence of life and consciousness.

Like Russell, Pannenberg welcomes the significance of the weak anthropic principle as it may express the purposeful directionality embedded in creation at its beginning.[275] Here, Pannenberg gravitates toward the standard Big Bang model, as he posits "a sequence of events" as imaginary time, as if it were like the time of the Einstein domain even when the Hawking domain is timeless.[276] In the same vein, Grenz points out that Pannenberg tends to reduce space to time.[277]

I agree with Russell that one can theologically regard the timeless Hawking domain as the locus of direct divine action to create the Einstein temporal domain. He or she can posit God as having created a set of timeless potential realities among which God chooses for use in creation of the spacetime of the Einstein domain in smooth transition rather than at a sharp singularity. Furthermore, one can consider God to be the Creator who is active in *creatio continua* by using the laws of nature that God created in the Hawking domain.

In that vein, I think that Pannenberg's scientific understanding of the time-space-energy field needs to be updated in light of contemporary quantum physics and the special theory of relativity.[278] For example, Polkinghorne underscores the significant features of quantum mechanics, such as superposition, non-locality, and entanglement. Russell adds a *"meonic"*

---

274. Davies, *Edge of Infinity*, 130–50.
275. Pannenberg, *ST* II, 74–76.
276. Pannenberg, *ST* II, 156–57.
277. Grenz, *Reason for Hope*, 115.
278. Russell, "Contingency in Physics and Cosmology," 23–43; Russell, *Cosmology*, 193.

interpretation of *creatio continua* in and through the "filled" quantum vacuum fields based on the aforementioned quantum cosmology.[279]

This view might seem to limit the freedom of God in continuing to create the world. Yet I do not think so. The existence of quantum gravity before the emergence of the Einstein spacetime is fundamentally contingent just as discussed in Russell's interpretation of the multiverses as God's contingent design. Likewise, our universe is characterized by the irreversibility of time and the indeterminacy of the subatomic level throughout the course of biological evolution and the development of the universe. Therefore, Hawking's atheistic affirmation cannot stand to reason based on the absence of a sharp singularity t=0 as a point where God directly creates the universe *ex nihilo*. With the ontological contingency of the Hawking domain, one may posit the global and empirical contingency of our universe.

In affirming *creatio ex nihilo*, the temporal beginning of our universe is important because without it we cannot speak of God's objective divine action in particular occasions within *creatio continua*. Such a creative work of God in the beginning enables God to be actively immanent through general and special ordering of the world in *creatio continua*. One can regard the transitional emergences in the physical and biological levels as both are empirically and ontologically contingent. Furthermore, the Creator who gave existence to creation can fulfill the eschatological purpose through *creatio ex vetere*.

Peacocke understands *creatio ex nihilo* as a doctrine of the ontological dependence of the world on God. Yet he does not seriously consider the significance of the finite beginning of time.[280] On the contrary to Peacocke, I agree with Peters who contends that "[t]o reduce *creatio ex nihilo* to a vague commitment about the dependence of the world upon God—though accurate—does not help much."[281] As Hegel rightly affirmed against Kant, for our experience to be contingent in our temporal existence, an event experienced in time requires temporal finitude. There

---

279. Russell, *Cosmology*, 193. An atom tends to be regarded as empty space. However, the empty space is mostly not actually empty, but just looks that way since electrons and photons are not in interaction with the existing physical stuff, such as the quark and gluon field fluctuations. For a succinct explanation, watch https://www.youtube.com/watch?v=J3xLuZNKhlY.

280. Peacocke, *Creation and the World of Science*, 78.

281. Peters, "On Creating the Cosmos," 288.

should be a beginning as well as an ending in a temporal limit.[282] Beginnings that involve transitions are still finite.

The Contingent yet Inevitable Presence of Natural Evil

The perennial theodical dilemma is that this continuing creation in the matrix of *creatio ex nihilo* requires the problem of entropy as a principle of creation. Both Pannenberg and Russell regard the law of entropy as theologically comparable to natural evil that is universal and unnecessary but inevitable. Hence, in my view, both Pannenberg and Russell adopt both *developmental good-and-harm* theodicy and *property-consequence good-and-harm* theodicy.

As a result of *creatio ex nihilo*, natural and cosmic evil is contingent. However, the contingent existence of entropy is inevitable in our life-bearing universe. Let's suppose constants c_1 and c_2 fall in life-bearing regions. "If as [John] Leslie [in his Design vs. Many-World debate] claims, the domains within which c_1 and c_2 fall are much smaller than the distance to the next set of domains, then God had little choice in determining the values c_1 and c_2."[283] These constants include those of the second law of thermodynamics because the expansion of the universe itself relies on them from the Big Bang event in its finitude. This is necessary for the existence of temporally finite beings that are distinguished from God's temporal infinity.[284]

Furthermore, Russell considers John Barrow's research team's recent contribution to answering the question of whether there could be some regions of our universe with the constants of nature that would lessen suffering and pain to some degrees. They "[have] finally offered substantial evidence that the fine structure constant may be growing slightly in time, perhaps to the extent of 5 parts per ten million per billion years."[285]

---

282. Hegel, *Hegel's Philosophy of Nature*, 34–37.

283. Russell, "Physics, Cosmology, and the Challenge to Consequentialist Natural Theodicy," 127.

284. However, I agree with Pannenberg that, in the new creation, finitude does not have to involve temporal cessation. Once they have spatiotemporal independence, in their continuous duration of the new creation, they can continue to exist in independence yet in diversified unity with other creatures. Even in the present creation, in our temporal finitude, we anticipate the future and remember the past as distinct from the present. Pannenberg, *ST* III, 593–602.

285. Russell, "Physics, Cosmology, and the Challenge to Consequentialist Natural

I think that this is theologically meaningful because the high improbability of a life-bearing universe like ours may support a hypothesis of a Designer more than when there are equivalent probabilities for a life-bearing universe and a non-life-bearing one.[286] Then, it is highly improbable to conceive of God's creation without the increase of entropy when it has to bear not only life but also genuine free-willed creatures.

Creatio Continua as Holistic Redemptive Presence of the Triune Creator

Divine creative action is not self-evident as we see it ridden with death, pain, suffering, and extinction throughout the history of biological evolution. Moreover, our universe is predicted to end up in *Freeze or Fry* by contemporary big-bang cosmology. There are also the cases in Darwinian evolution where we wish the contingently violent predations could be fewer and less than we actually see.[287] Therefore, in the face of these universal natural and cosmic evils, we find it necessary to seek the general and special divine action in the midst of the theodical dilemma of the universal evil in God's good creation.

As Ernst Conradie points out, the excessive increases of entropy, unnecessarily violent predation, and parasitism are contingent elements of God's continuous creation. The diversity of life emerges and flourishes through the inevitable process of "eating and being eaten."[288] The existence of the thermodynamic principle is at creative work through regeneration of new lives. However, this continuous generation of life

---

Theodicy," 128.

286. Murphy, "Evidence of Design, 422–23, especially n23.

287. For example, according to biologist John Alcock, the male desert beetle *Tegrodera aloga* will "run to a female and wrestle violently with her in an attempt to throw her on her side." Yet, surprisingly, the male beetles are also observed to be "perfectly capable of courting potential partners in a decorous manner." Alcock, *Triumph of Sociobiology*, 209. Cited in Moritz, "Evolutionary Evil and Dawkins' Black Box," 182–83. Considering the contingent action of animals, Moritz argues that the paths of evolution are contingently alterable by animals' choices in their predatory habits. Citing Whitfield, "Phylogeny and Evolution of Host-Parasitoid Interactions in Hymenoptera," 129–51.

288. Conradie, "Eat and/or Be Eaten." In this article, in comparatively engaging the works of Edward Farley, Sallie McFague, and Norman Wirzba, Conradie claims that natural evil can be seen in the framework of kenotic and regenerative creation while God calls creatures into subjective embodiment of the love of the Creator.

inherently involves the contingent and unnecessary increases of entropy that lead to different degrees of the pain and suffering of creatures. In that sense, Southgate affirms that the regeneration of new life in evolution is not enough. He calls for the theological conceptualization of God's soteriological action in evolutionary history and the eschatological fulfillment of God's good creation.[289]

Accordingly, for Pannenberg, the Spirit as the life-giving field is the eschatological power or influence that enables the ecstatic self-transcendence of creatures to higher levels of complexity in evolution. In this process, the Son is the creative principle of self-differentiation. At the same time, the eschatological Spirit lures creatures toward ecstatic lives that befit the new creation through special providence. Likewise, Russell affirms that "both creation and New Creation are part of a single divine act of creation *ex nihilo*" by the triune God.[290] Accordingly, there should be an inherent continuity between the present creation and the New Creation. In general providence, God continues to be creative in the universe through the interplay of chance and regularities. This creative process is not exclusive to special providence. As the ground of genuine novelty, the eschaton is both in continuity and discontinuity with *creatio continua*.

I affirm God's general and special providence in *creatio continua*, especially in the face of the contingent nature of evil universal in creation. Both Pannenberg and Russell consider diverse kinds of divine action including not only bottom-up special divine action, but also whole-part and top-down divine influence in continuing to redirect the history of the universe and the biosphere of the Earth.

Such a continuous divine creative action is an epigenetic and self-transcending process from which genuine novelty emerges.[291] For Russell, the universe as a whole is constrained by the second law of thermodynamics, yet it does not end up as a selfish-meme-driven process, but rather gives birth to life that emerges with novel properties like moral

---

289. Southgate, *Groaning of Creation*, 24–25, 60–77.

290. Russell, *Time in Eternity*, 15.

291. According to Ted Peters, "epigenesis" means "the transformative dynamism in cosmic and evolutionary history," or "the possibility, though, not necessity, of emergence" of new things not reducible to the lower levels of complexity. Here, Peters refers to a strong sense of emergence in contrast with sociobiologists who use the same term to refer to "the genetic leash on cultural creativity." Peters and Hewlett, *Evolution from Creation to New Creation*, 162.

values such as altruism.²⁹² Genetic mutations take place in the course of evolution through the mediation of the "combination of law and chance that characterize physical and biological processes." Theologically, based on the contingency of these events, evolution can be regarded as "God's way of creating" new life and novel properties.²⁹³

Indeterminate quantum events play a fundamental role in collaboration with classical sources and ecological sources. Namely, "[s]ources of variation in organisms that may include: point mutations, including base-pair substitutions, insertion, repair, recombination; radiative physical mutagens, including X-rays and ultraviolet light; and crossing over."²⁹⁴ These quantum sources are in cooperation with classical sources, such as "chemical mutagens, mechanical/physical mutagens (including physical impacts), and chromosome segregation."²⁹⁵ These classical factors can be counted as the results of classical processes such as hydrodynamics, thermodynamics, statistical mechanics, and chaotic systems, etc.

Along with these quantum and classical sources, organisms interact with their environmental factors, such as ecological and geological variables that come into play in mutations and their phenotypic expressions.²⁹⁶ All these diverse causal factors are interwoven in gene mutations and their diverse phenotypic expressions. The diverse phenotypic expressions may mean creatures' diverse ways of interacting with the environment and other creatures. Theologically, one may affirm that God also "acts in, with, under, and through these processes as immanent Creator, bringing about order, beauty, complexity, and wonder of life" throughout *creatio continua* that will be fulfilled in the eschatological new creation.²⁹⁷

Likewise, Pannenberg maintains an idea of epigenetic evolution like Russell, while not ignoring the fate of the entire universe as is dictated by the second law of thermodynamics. The entropic principle enables the emergence of life as well as conscious and self-conscious creatures

---

292. Russell appreciates Moritz's discussion of the preconditions of morality or *proto-morality* in the pre-human stages of evolution. Yet Russell still emphasizes that the entire cosmos and evolutionary history are ridden with death and suffering. For that reason, the eschatological hope for the resurrection is required. Russell, "Groaning of Creation" 125–26.

293. Russell, *Cosmology*, 212.

294. Russell, *Cosmology*, 218.

295. Russell, *Cosmology*, 218.

296. Russell, *Cosmology*, 218–19.

297. Russell, *Cosmology*, 212.

capable of relating to others and God interpersonally.[298] In this creative process, the universe is likened to the eschatological force field. The Son and the Spirit are at work in creation through the whole-part constraint from the perspective of the new creation. In *creatio continua*, bottom-up divine action is continuously at work while respecting the top-down and whole-part causalities of independent creatures. Through this creative divine lure, biological evolution becomes emergent and epigenetic.[299]

Bottom-Up Special Action as a Viable Theological Interpretation

For Pannenberg, in the creative field of the Spirit, God's eschatological *governance* works as special divine action while divine action takes place in the modes of preservation and cooperation since God's creation is contingent as a whole and in all its parts. Hence, the eschatological horizons of the future of God work in *creatio continua* in a whole-part manner, but they work from the fundamental level by contingently creating and influencing the smallest physical particles from the bottom and upwards in creating and preserving law-like regularities and living creatures in duration.

Likewise, for Russell, *creatio continua* through biological evolution is constrained by the cosmological and ecological conditions (in accordance with the constants of the finely-tuned universe), but fundamentally, the development of our universe and the emergence of life and consciousness through evolution on our planet becomes possible through the fundamental openness of the physical level. Thus, while being mediated by the created order of nature, QM-NIODA serves as God's direct and spontaneous action that leads to diverse indirect effects that reflect God's special intentions.

Pannenberg also regards the fundamental physical level as a creative field open to the emergence of genuine novelty in the development of the regularities of nature and in the emergent evolution in the biosphere of our planet. However, his metaphor of the Spirit needs to be updated in interaction with quantum mechanics and cosmology as well as the flowing time reinterpreted through special relativity. While Pannenberg affirms that not only the whole but all its parts are contingent in his doctrine of *creatio ex nihilo*, and ultimately in the hope for the eschatological

---

298. Pannenberg, *ST* II, 133–34.
299. Pannenberg, *Toward a Theology of Nature*, 44–49, 56–58.

redemption of creation as a whole, he prefers Faraday's force field theory to quantum mechanics as a dialogue partner with the doctrine of divine providence. Even though there is both consonance and dissonance between theology and natural sciences, theologians are to seek mutual coherence between the two counterparts continuously. In that sense, I think that once Pannenberg affirms the fundamental contingency of creation and all its parts, he needs to consider the pervasive nature of quantum events like Russell does.[300]

In his understanding of bottom-up causation from the quantum level, Russell acknowledges the historical relativity in philosophical interpretations of quantum mechanics.[301] As long as it is a philosophical choice to believe in the ontological indeterminacy of quantum events, such a choice can be inspired by metaphysical or theological frameworks, while the latter do not predetermine the former.

I think that in a critical realistic approach, one does not have to subscribe to Niels Bohr's sharp distinction between quantum objects and classical objects since his interpretation of quantum event holds "two separate and unrelated ontologies."[302] For Bohr, theories are only instrumental rather than ontological. The complementarity of the particular and wave-like attributes detected in the quantum level represents the deficiency of a detecting apparatus.

As Barbour points out, according to the studies of "decoherence" in quantum mechanics, when a measurement event takes place, "the coherence of a quantum state is lost when information about it is available through interaction with the laser pulses . . . The transfer of information, not consciousness, is the essential future of the 'collapse of a wave

---

300. Russell's critique of Polkinghorne's idea of the episodic nature of quantum events applies to Pannenberg's preference of Faraday's force-field theory to quantum mechanics. Russell, "Divine Action and Quantum Mechanics," 375–78.

301. For instance, Russell discusses the alternative interpretations: the deterministic interpretation such as "neo-realism" of Einstein and Bohm's idea of "hidden variables" as well as holistic approaches advanced by von Neumann, Wheeler, Wigner, and Stapp who claim "consciousness creates reality." Russell, "Divine Action and Quantum Mechanics," 365. Russell also discusses the recent studies on "decoherence" that attempt to explain how a coherent quantum wavefunction gives rise to the phenomena of classical physics. He also considers instrumentalist interpretations like Bohr's as well as stochastic modifications of the Schrödinger equation like Abner Shimony's. Russell, "Divine Action and Quantum Mechanics," 364–67.

302. Wegter-McNelly, "Atoms May Be Small, But They're Everywhere," 103. For the allegedly instrumentalist understanding of the complementarity of a quantum event, see Bohr, "Causality and Complementarity," 83–91.

function' during an observation."[303] If so, the classical objects and quantum objects are not ontologically separate, but rather, the ontological state of quantum events is to be taken seriously while being regarded as open to revision in continuous research of the subject matters.

In a similar vein, I think Barbour is right that idealist interpretations (i.e., John Wheeler) are not plausible since "it is not mind as such that affects observations, but the process of *interaction* between the detection apparatus and the micro-system."[304] Like Russell, Barbour maintains that since quantum events are irreversible they may be open to many interpretations, but that rather than philosophical idealism, critical realism is a better option to choose because the objectivity of the event is not dissolved in human consciousness.

The measurement of a quantum wavelength collapse is not only mental but objective.[305] As Russell claims, while it is philosophically unsettled, the measurement events are irreversible and the interpretation of ontological indeterminism can be one of the philosophical options if the irreversibility of quantum events is not episodic but pervasive. The effects of quantum phenomena do not include only micro-macro interactions, but also micro-meso and micro-micro interactions as discussed in the previous section. Furthermore, if the quantum world is nonlocal according to Bell's theorem, the quantum world is to be regarded as universally indeterminate in inseparable entanglement.[306]

As Russell contends, therefore, the measurement events of the quantum level are open to other interpretations (both theistic and atheistic) because the irreversibility of quantum events are theoretically inexplicable in the current studies of quantum mechanics.[307] It is not known how, at the moment of decoherence, a certain state of quantum superposition is selected among many at a moment of measurement while others

303. Barbour, *When Science Meets Religion*, 78–81 [80].

304. Barbour, *When Science Meets Religion*, 80.

305. Clayton, "Tracing the Lines," 215–17. An observer's measurement of quantum events actually affects the process of the measurement, which implies that it involves various dimensions of reality "from physical to mental." Kärkkäinen, *Creation and Humanity*, 103.

306. Polkinghorne discusses Einstein's life-long resistance to "the spooky nature" of superposition and how Bell's theorem contributes to putting it to rest in chapter 7 of his *Quantum World*. However, contra Polkinghorne, I agree with Russell that the quantum wave function collapses and their effects are not episodic, if they are not limited to the micro-macro interactions like in the measurement events.

307. Russell, "Divine Action and Quantum Mechanics," 366.

are not. Accordingly, the interpretation of a measurement event remains philosophically open-ended.[308] Furthermore, due to the relativistic nature of a measurement, it is to be regarded as the observer's participation in the event from one's frame of reference.[309]

In this *holistic* understanding of a quantum event and its observer, assuming the objective status of a quantum event should not lead to speculating infinite splitting of the world. I think that like Roger Penrose contends, Everett's many-worlds interpretation is misguided because it presupposes the existence of "many-minds" in a measurement event. If there exist an infinite number of different regions of the universe that come into existence at the observation of the collapse of a quantum wave function, there are to exist the infinite number of different states of an observer's mind. However, this does not cognitively make sense.[310]

Russell points out that none of the alternative interpretations "return us to an entirely classical view of the world."[311] Russell points out that even the deterministic interpretation of Bohm, the biggest challenger of an ontologically indeterminate interpretation, is not entirely classical but semi-classical. Bohm's determinism is rather highly non-local and non-mechanical, "simply not found in a classical sense of determinism one can take from the Newtonian picture."[312]

---

308. Recently, there is a research into the study of decoherence, named "Quantum Darwinism," according to which there is a sort of footprint in the macroscopic level imprinted by quantum wave functions and in the environment some of their superposed states survive as "pointer states" because they best fit with their environment. However, it is still unknown why a certain state is selected while others are not. The singularized states are called "pointer states" because they are regarded as "encoded" in the "possible" states of a pointer on the dial of a measuring device. For the recent researches in this area, see https://www.quantamagazine.org/quantum-darwinism-an-idea-to-explain-objective-reality-passes-first-tests-20190722/. There is also a criticism that decoherence studies in general fall in a circularity charge due to their recourse to a boundary condition. The proponents of decoherence studies posit a single wavefunction in the beginning of the universe. Yet contemporary quantum cosmologies regard the initial conditions of the universe as fuzzy. Kastner, "'Einselection' of Pointer Observables," 56–58.

309. Barbour, *When Science Meets Religion*, 78–81.

310. Penrose, "Quantum Physics and Conscious Thought," 105–20.

311. Russell, "Divine Action and Quantum Mechanics," 366.

312. Russell, "Divine Action and Quantum Mechanics," 398–403 [403]. Also, refer to Russell, "Physics of David Bohm and Its Relevance to Philosophy and Theology," 135–58. According to Russell, in Bohm's formulation, not only classical (local and mechanical) aspects but also quantum potentials (nonlocal and non-mechanical aspects) are carried within Schrödinger's term $\nabla^2 \Psi$. While Bohm's formulation is

Similarly, in seeking an alternative interpretation that reconciles classical physics with quantum physics through modifying classical formalism, as Kirk Wegter-McNelly suggests, I think Russell could also consider Event-Enhanced Quantum Theory (EEQT), a proposal labeled by Philippe Blanchard and Arkadiusz Jadczyk. The theory modifies the classical formalism "only minimally by introducing a means of identifying and including 'classical' subsystems within the wavefunction as well as a clear method for coupling them to quantum subsystems."[313] This idea is built on the "notion of irreversibility tied to macroscopic interactions with classical subsystems."[314] Thus, while this scheme is placed within the classical formalism, it allows for the randomness of the timing of a wave function collapse.[315]

Yet irreversible quantum events invite diverse philosophical interpretations because of the unpredictability and entanglement of the quantum world. As discussed above, none of them brings us back to classical determinism as Russell contends. Then, considering the fundamental contingency of creation according to *creatio ex nihilo*, *ontological indeterminism* remains a plausible option while being open to continuous scientific investigations.

There is criticism of this view based on the difficulty to explain how quantum events are not averaged out in the macroscopic level when quantum mechanics is related to chaos theory.[316] However, even though "quantum chaology" is unresolved, without relating quantum mechanics to chaos theory, one may still see the outcomes of the amplification of quantum events in the macroscopic level.

For instance, according to George Ellis, there are localized firings in "the large arrays of neurons" that lead to "a holistic response from a region of the brain."[317] Similarly, there are localized firings in the microtubules that are amplified to macroscopic effect.[318] Russell also adds that

---

deterministic, it is not so in a strict sense. Russell, "Divine Action and Quantum Mechanics," 398–401.

313. Wegter-McNelly, "Atoms May Be Small," 106–8.

314. Wegter-McNelly, "Atoms May Be Small," 106.

315. Wegter-McNelly suggests that here a Ψ-collapse is still random and not entirely classical in this scheme. Thus, he suggests that Russell may consider it in his QM-NIODA. Wegter-McNelly, "Atoms May Be Small," 107.

316. For example, Koperski, "God, Chaos, and the Quantum Dice," 545–60.

317. Ellis, "Intimations of Transcendence," 472.

318. Ellis, "Intimations of Transcendence," 472.

one may see "biological amplifiers" as expressing "the effects of quantum mechanics within genetic mutations" in cooperation with many other factors including classical ones.[319]

Furthermore, the contingency of the quantum gravity of the Hawking domain serves as the ground of the fundamental contingency of the Einstein domain. Here, the genuine openness of the quantum level is amplified in the higher levels of complexity and the world of classical physics emerges smoothly from the quantum gravity of the Hawking domain. The degrees of independence grow through the emergence of higher complexity within the environment that operates by the interplay of chance and regularities. The bottom-up causation is universal from the beginning of the universe and through the development of the universe as well as the evolution of life. The contingency of the life-bearing universe coheres with the belief of *creatio ex nihilo*.

The Significance of Top-Down Causation in Special Divine Action

While Thomas Tracy sees that God's objectively redemptive presence takes place in certain moments, Russell contends that God is working bottom-up everywhere if the universe as a whole and all its parts are created *ex nihilo* and contingently open to novelty from the fundamental level. Yet God grants freedom to respond to divine lure once there comes into existence certain degrees of independence in living organisms.[320]

Russell claims that top-down causation through sudden mental inspiration may involve special divine action that is amplified from the quantum level of the neural systems.[321] The top level of complexity at a given stage in evolutionary history is ontologically open. Thus, the openness in each stage cannot exist without the openness of the stages (including the pre-animate era) prior to the given one. Therefore, top-down causation through free will involves the ontological openness of the quantum level that transitions into the classical world.[322]

These effects of quantum indeterminate events in the macroscopic level are adopted by Russell too. Russell, "Divine Action and Quantum Mechanics," 359–60.

319. Russell, "Divine Action and Quantum Mechanics," 359.
320. Russell, "Divine Action and Quantum Mechanics," 382–89.
321. Russell, *Cosmology*, 121.
322. Russell, "Divine Action and Quantum Mechanics," 361–63.

I think that Russell would extend this to non-human consciousness because he acknowledges precondition of moral evil in pre-human phases of evolution by endorsing the independence of the top-down agency that gradually grows throughout biological evolution.[323] God is creative in all levels of reality by directly working from the quantum level. Therefore, God inspires creatures in bottom-up causation in God's whole-part influence.[324] Yet God grants freedom to creatures in their actualizing divine inspirations in a top-down manner. Top-down causation originates from God's direct bottom-up causation in the quantum level.

Pannenberg, too, finds this contingent creative process to be metaphorically expressed in Faraday's classical force field theory. However, he sees that bottom-up causation is required by the overall whole-part constraint of the eschatological horizons of the future of God in the present creation. That is, the beginning of the formation of regular patterns does not exist without the contingent patterning of the regularities from the bottom-level of physics. The Spirit is the spontaneous and gracious lure throughout the history of the universe and the ecstatic process of emergent evolution. Through bringing life into existence, the ecstatic lure of the Spirit persistently works as the eschatological "wind of life" or lure to the embodiment of the eschatological community of the people of God.[325]

I agree with Russell and Pannenberg that the history of the universe and life is a holistic work in which bottom-up causation and top-down/whole-part causation are inseparable. The fundamental level's indeterminacy is demanded by the openness of the universe and living creatures to divine action in any stage of cosmological development and biological evolution. Once sentience and primitive consciousness emerge in the scene of evolutionary history, top-down causation is in need because bottom-up causation does not explain what takes place in nature.

A purposeful action can be understood in a bigger teleological picture in the time development of quantum events. The relations among the events and the emergent properties of creation (i.e., symbolic meanings) do not have to be reduced to the lower levels as affirmed in the substance ontology maintained by reductionistic philosophers. Yet as Murphy contends in her critique of Peacocke's whole-part approach, without God's action from the bottom in "selecting" among many potentials, there cannot

323. Russell, "Divine Action and Quantum Mechanics," 386–87.
324. Russell, *Cosmology*, 121–22.
325. Pannenberg, "Working of the Spirit," 23.

be top-down causation that specifically takes place within an emergent whole.[326] That is, "selection among lower-level causal processes" in the emergence of a higher level of complexity requires "some sort of causal effect on the lower-level entities."[327]

If there are different degrees of conscious and independent agency among non-human creatures in the process of the gradual development of consciousness, one may conceive of special divine action that takes a top-down causation (information) or a "special divine lure." Yet bottom-up causation is inseparable from top-down causation (or lure) since making a contingent or free choice involves different bottom-up sequences of events that take place in the brain.[328]

The selection among the sequences may be partially caused by God if the fundamental level of physics is causally indeterminate as long as God respects the contingency and freedom of creatures. In the top-down causation of conscious and self-conscious creatures, bottom-up divine action can take place from the neural systems of the centralized brains and ultimately from the quantum level, which is not entirely deterministic but probabilistic.[329] Conscious animals' top-down causation may be theologically seen as being lured by the Spirit who continues to be creative through preservation, cooperation, and governance within creation as a purposeful project.

All in all, based on the epigenetic schemes of self-organization and developmental systems theory, emergent evolution is not entirely confined to the central masterplan of DNA in a bottom-up manner, like Richard Dawkins contends. Rather, biological evolution is subject to the dynamic interaction between an organism and its environment.[330] As we look at the emergence of the various types of altruism in the world of animals, theologically, we could interpret it as God's providential guidance in evolution, and the gradual development of "the transcendence

---

326. Murphy, "Emergence, Downward Causation and Divine Action," 119–20, 128–31.

327. Russell, "Divine Action and Quantum Mechanics," 128.

328. Murphy and Brown, *Did My Neurons Make Me Do It?*, 282–83. Especially, in the human level, top-down causation is value-ridden with "symbolic representation, abstract concepts, and, especially, moral concepts." Murphy and Brown, *Did My Neurons Make Me Do It?*, 283.

329. Murphy and Ellis, *On the Moral Nature of the Universe*, 216–18.

330. For this account, see Moritz, "Evolutionary Evil and Dawkins' Black Box," 143–88.

of mere self-interest."³³¹ It is unnecessary to categorize it as evolutionary strategies that reinforce their egoistic DNA.

When animals cooperate within the same species and across species, the altruistic behavior is placed within a larger matrix of competition over the limited resources in a shared environment. While in symbiosis or cooperation, animals cooperate for better survival together, in "symbiogenesis" an organism can be enabled to rapidly acquire higher levels of complexity through horizontal sharing of cells via the process of food's digestion.³³² These take place mostly through predation, but on the cellular level, symbiogenesis implies interdependent and mutual relationality among creatures in their self-transcending development, rather than the *selfish meme* rooted in the genes. From the cellular level of an organism's complexity, one may theologically regard God as persistently luring creatures to genuine "self-transcendence" and accordingly toward the emergence of genuine altruism, which may be hidden as a goal to be fulfilled throughout creation's journey toward participation in unity with the triune Creator.

In that vein, Timothy Ingold echoes this claim by arguing that in the "interlacing" matrix of lives in the biosphere as "meshwork," an individual creature's flourishing cannot exist apart from the existence of other creatures within its ecological environment.³³³ In the same vein, Thomas Oord contends writes that when Dawkins regards every altruistic behavior in nature through the lens of the selfish gene's eye view it is ignored that our universe is all interrelated and "isolating my good entirely from the good of others is impossible." It is hard to categorize an altruistic behavior's intent in a clear-cut manner. Then, creatures' sense of community and morality may gradually originate from the pursuit of

---

331. Southgate, "Creation as 'Very Good' and 'Groaning in Travail,'" 69.

332. Margulis and Sagan, *Acquiring Genomes*, 6–14, 41, 72. For a detailed discussion of this theory, also see Moritz, "Evolutionary Evil and Dawkins' Black Box," 165–72. Endosymbiogesis or "living together inside" has been known to be common in the development of evolutionary novelty. For example, according to the experiment done by the lab of Kwang W. Jeon at The University of Tennessee, a possible species change was observed when "new bacterial symbionts became integrated in the host amoeba such that the hosts became dependent on the symbionts within a few years." Furthermore, "the presence of endosymbionts has caused changes in several phenotypic characters of the host cells." Jeon, "Amoeba and x-Bacteria," 118. Cited in Moritz, "Evolutionary Evil and Dawkins' Black Box," 167.

333. Ingold, *Being Alive*, 68–71.

their self-centered flourishing and even at the expense of others.³³⁴ Yet this is not the end of this creative process. Such a self-transcending evolution may gradually become more and more mature in the emergence of consciousness and the embodiment of life-affirming communality and solidarity.³³⁵ I further pursue these epigenetic ideas of evolution through engaging with the contemporary developmental theories in biology in the next chapter. In so doing, I suggest a holistic notion of divine action in the history of evolution from a trinitarian perspective of creation.

The Cross as the Trinitarian *Theopaschitic* Co-Suffering

Despite the possibilities of selection-neutral genetic mutations and evolution, the epigenetic self-organizing of creatures is placed in the second thermodynamic structure of our universe where all living organisms are bound to predation, death, pain, and suffering. Moreover, the increase of entropy is contingent as I discussed in the previous subsections.

If pain, suffering, and death are unnecessary but universal and inevitable in our soul-making or person-making universe, I believe that God should not stay aloof from the pain and suffering of creatures. If God is the loving Creator, the cross of Christ the Son should mean the trinitarian participation in the suffering of creatures. Yet in the light of the resurrection, God's co-suffering is to bring good out of evil while continuously luring creation to participate in the peaceable *basileia* of God. Only in that way can we say that God is both faithful and loving as Scripture witnesses.

According to the OT, the *ruach* of God gives life to creatures and sustains their life; *nephesh* (or breath of life) is shared by all animals and human beings embodied and given life by the divine breath of life (Gen 1:20, 21, 24, 30; Prov 12:10; Eccl 3:18–21). The *ruach* of God gives life and sustains the *nephesh* of all living creatures. Therefore, God's providential

---

334. Oord, *Uncontrolling Love of God*, 71–76.

335. Ted Peters questions the necessity of the selfish-gene meme in understanding altruism that emerges in evolutionary history and upholds the possibility of cultural evolution governed by *the theology of the cross* and *the ethic of a sacrificial (agapic) love* in the human level. Peters, "Evolution of Evil," 19–52. For example, in the human level, neo-Darwinian evolutionary theories cannot answer the questions: "[W]hy parents allegedly driven by the selfish gene toward inclusive fitness give up their children before insuring they have reached reproductive age?," "Why is it that genetically proximate parents abandon children and genetically distant parents invest themselves in raising these children?" Peters, "Evolution of Evil," 26.

care is upon not only humans but also other creatures (Ps 36:6). Such an understanding of creation in unity is not exclusive to the OT. In the NT, there is an integral link between Christ and the Spirit in a complementary model of Logos Christology and Spirit Christology.

"While it is true that the Spirit is a cosmic energy everywhere in creation, the NT speaks of Christ's Spirit, which bespeaks particularity."[336] Further, "[w]herever the cosmic and universal Spirit is at work there is always reference to Christ, and through Christ also to the Father."[337] The *universal* presence of the Spirit is to be understood in the light of the *particular* person and work of Jesus Christ. Based on this understanding of the relationship between Christ and the Spirit, it is apropos to say that the passion and resurrection of Jesus Christ carry a cosmic meaning. In Christ, the whole of creation is regarded as undergoing a *birth pang* and anticipating the eschatological fulfillment of the peaceable kingdom of God.

That said, I am concerned about the overly rationalistic tendency that seems to loom in Pannenberg's theological method. Pannenberg is certainly concerned about the universality of the Christian affirmations in mutual discourse with other spheres of academia and other religions. In so doing, he does not seem to pay sufficient attention to God's presence in the suffering creation. This lies in his understanding of the cross of Jesus Christ.

In Pannenberg's theology of the cross, Christ's atonement is placed in the whole span of the history of Jesus that is marked by the mutual self-differentiation between the Father and the Son. It constitutes the ground of the creation of independent creatures during the creative field of the Spirit in the process of divine creation of the universe. I agree with his affirmations as to the need for the revision of the traditional doctrine of Christ's exclusive substitutionary atonement. However, at the same time, I propose that Pannenberg needs to regard the cross of Jesus the Son as an event of the trinitarian suffering.

To be more precise, for Pannenberg, as the Father hands over His Lordship to the Son Jesus, He makes His own deity dependent on the mission of Jesus. Therefore, Jesus' cross bears a trinitarian relevance.[338]

---

336. Kärkkäinen, *Christ and Reconciliation*, 206.

337. Kärkkäinen, *Christ and Reconciliation*, 206.

338. Pannenberg, *ST* I, 313–14. Pannenberg acknowledges the deity of the Father is "affected" and "questioned" by the suffering and death of Jesus because the intra-trinitarian life is actualized in the economic Trinity. "[I]n their intra-trinitarian life, the persons depend on one another in respect of their deity as well as their personal

If the mission of Jesus is to herald the *basileia* of God where the deity and Lordship of the Father is confirmed, Jesus' cross should be relevant to the deity of the Father as the all-determining reality. The truth-claim doubted on the cross of Jesus is relevant to the truth-claim of the Father being the Lord of all creation.

Nonetheless, for Pannenberg, the cross means the death of the Son Jesus, but the death is only attributed to the human nature, but to not his divine nature. [339] Pannenberg writes that "on the cross the Son of God certainly died and not just the humanity that he assumed. Nevertheless, the Son suffered death in his human reality and not in respect of his deity."[340] For Pannenberg, this understanding of the cross is important because it helps to avoid "reverse monophysitism"[341] by keeping intact the Lordship of the Son endowed by the Father from being conquered by the cross. By not attributing the death of Jesus to his divine nature, Pannenberg is consistent with his idea of Jesus' self-distinction from the Father. As the death of the Son is in Jesus' human nature, his death is *not* attributed to the divinity of the Father while the Father co-suffers the death and pain of the Son in his "sym-pathy."[342]

On the contrary to Pannenberg, if one believes in the incarnation as God's genuine assumption of the flesh in the affirmation of the material world, one should see the suffering of Jesus on the cross as the death of the Son in a *theopaschitic* sense. To be more precise, as Gregory of Nazianzus says, If the Son had not assumed our perishable flesh, he would not have been able to "heal us from our fleshly perishing and our sinfulness and lead us into participation in the divine nature in our unity with the Son."[343] For that reason, as Gregory of Nazianzus maintains, "that which God has not assumed he has not healed, but what has been united with God is saved."[344] In the same vein, according to Martin Luther, "God so loved us as to be willing to pay the price of His only, dearest Child. Him

---

being." Pannenberg, *ST* I, 329,

339. Pannenberg writes, "Jesus was affected by the suffering and death on the cross in person, i.e., in the person of the eternal Son." Pannenberg, *ST* I, 314.

340. Pannenberg, *ST* II, 388–89.

341. Pannenberg, *ST* I, 314.

342. Pannenberg, *ST* I, 314.

343. Gregory of Nazianzus, Epistle 101. Cited in Shin, "Spirit's Pathetic and Redemptive Presence in Global Capitalism," 36.

344. Atkinson, *Martin Luther*, 182. Citing Gregory of Nazianzus, *Epistle* 101:7. Cited in Shin, "Spirit's Pathetic and Redemptive Presence in Global Capitalism," 36.

He sent into our misery, hell, and death, and let him drain these to the dreg."[345] Luther's notion of *communicatio idiomatum* (or the exchange of properties) means that "God in his nature cannot die ... [However,] now that God and man are united in one person, it is called God's death when the man who dies is one substance or one person with God."[346]

In other words, "[t]he attributes of both natures are predicated of the whole person of Jesus 'in concrete,' so that the attributes of the one nature are shared with the other." Accordingly, "mortality, which is exclusively of the human nature, is now attributed to the divinity via the communication of properties" in the concrete human person of Jesus, the Incarnate Son.[347] In my view, the kenotic ideas in the writings of Luther and Gregory of Nazianzus are significant for the entire creation. When considering not only the inevitable but also the contingent nature of death, pain, and suffering universal across creation, a faithful and loving God is to be regarded as co-suffering with creation in redeeming creation through fulfilling the eschatological new creation.

Here, contra Pannenberg, in the distinction between the Son and the Father one can still speak of the Father's co-suffering of the death of the Son without falling into *patripassianism*, the death of the Father. Like Moltmann contends, the Father's suffering of the Son's death is different from the death of the Son because the Father suffers the loss and abandonment of the Son on the cross rather than the death of the Father Himself.[348] Yet not only the Father is affected by the death of the Son, the death of the Son is *"the death of the Fatherhood of God."*[349]

As I discuss in the next chapter by engaging with Eberhard Jüngel's doctrine of the Trinity, the Father's identification with the Son's suffering on the cross shows the Father's faithful love for the Son. Yet the Father's co-suffering should be differentiated from the death of the Son as the Father raises the Son in the power of the Spirit in the resurrection of Jesus.

Russell also adopts *theopaschitic* interpretation of the cross while identifying it with *patripassianism* in the sense that the Father suffers the

---

345. Atkinson, *Martin Luther*, 182. Citing Luther, *Weimarer Ausgabe*, 10/3:161.

346. Luther, "On the Councils and the Church," 104.

347. Ngien, *Luther's Theology of the Cross*, 215. For similar accounts of Luther's discussion of the divine suffering of the Son on the cross, see Rittgers, *Reformation of Suffering*, 117; McGrath, *Christian Theology*, 223. Cited in Shin, "Spirit's Pathetic and Redemptive Presence in Global Capitalism," 36.

348. Moltmann, *Crucified God*, 241–44.

349. Moltmann, *Crucified God*, 212, 243. Emphasis mine.

death of the Son.[350] Yet, in my understanding, when Russell maintains *patripassianism* in his understanding of the cross of Jesus, he does not identify the suffering of the Son with that of the Father as the same sorts. Rather, "the Father who suffers the death of the Son acts anew at Easter to raise Jesus from the dead."[351] Therefore, I think Russell does not fall in the heresy of *patripassianism* according to which the differentiation of the Father and the Son is dissolved. Rather, the Father's identification with the Son does not negate the differentiation of the two Persons in the intra-trinitarian life of mutual love.

In my view, in a *theopaschitic* understanding of the cross, one can speak of the co-suffering of the Spirit in solidarity with suffering creatures. It is not surprising that the lack of God's *theopaschitic* co-suffering in Pannenberg's understanding of the cross[352] leads to his understanding of the Spirit as a creative field. While Pannenberg profoundly deploys the metaphor of a force field in his understanding of the holistic whole-part constraint of the eschaton in the work of the Spirit, he rarely discusses the *pathetic* dimension of the Spirit who co-suffers with creatures through *creatio continua*.[353]

In contrast with Pannenberg, I think that the Spirit, who binds the Father and the Son in love, suffers the pain that the Father and the Son share on the cross.[354] Christ's passion as the trinitarian suffering is to be seen as the ground of the understanding of the pathetic presence of the Spirit in *creatio continua*. If the Spirit is the one who fulfills the eschatological reality proleptically revealed in the Christ event, the Spirit's creative work must be a temporal process of protesting natural and cosmic

---

350. Russell, *Cosmology*, 266.

351. Russell, "Groaning of Creation," 140.

352. I agree with Jonathan Case that Pannenberg's "coordination of the death of the Son and the death of the human being remains somewhat unclear." Case, "Death of Jesus," 13.

353. I discuss the eclipse of the cosmic meaning of the cross as the trinitarian suffering of God in Pannenberg's doctrine of creation in my article, "Church as a Messianic Fellowship in Jürgen Moltmann's and Wolfhart Pannenberg's Public Ecclesiology," 23–37. In the article, through a comparative study, I analyzed how Pannenberg's Christology is related to his doctrine of creation, pneumatology, and ecclesiology, critiquing his notion of the church as a messianic community that does not include active solidarity with the poor and the marginalized as the essence of the church.

354. Moltmann, *Spirit of Life*, 62.

evil in solidarity with suffering creatures. The Spirit after the crucifixion and resurrection of Jesus is "the Spirit of the crucified and risen Christ."[355]

The New Creation as a Redeemed Ecological Community

I think Pannenberg's idea of the eschaton is ecological and pluralistic since he sticks to the unity of creation grounded in the unity-in-distinction of the triune Creator. Creatures are called into their "embodied" existence in independence-in-dependence. Similarly, for Russell, the relationality and multidimensionality of the spacetime of the cosmos implies the ecological dimensions of the present creation and the new creation.

In my view, a *replacement* model of the new creation does not do justice to the biblical portrayal of God's renewal of heaven and earth (Rev 21). God completes and fulfills *creatio continua* rather than the idea that "God's creation will have to be replaced by something completely new."[356] In that sense, Conradie suggests an *elevation* model of the new creation. He suggests that the new creation is God's consummating or ennobling of the present creation. This idea of the new creation contrasts with God's replacing the present creation or *restoring* it to its primal state. The latter two understandings of the new creation end up in body-spirit dualism and the denigration of the temporal development of the processes of the material world as one can see in the eschatological visions proposed by the young-Earth creationists.[357]

The further details of how the creative processes of biological evolution will continue in the new creation should be highly speculative, going beyond our conceptual capability. Polkinghorne believes in God's

---

355. Kärkkäinen, "How to Speak of the Spirit among Religions," 123.

356. Conradie, "What is the Place of the Earth in God's Economy?," 83.

357. Conradie, "What is the Place of the Earth in God's Economy?," 88–89. For example, Henry Morris affirms that the Earth's atmospheric environment dramatically changed from its perfect state by the removal of the antediluvian vapor canopy. In the eschaton, God will eventually restore the ideal antediluvian state of the Earth's atmosphere through a premillennial tribulation and the last catastrophe that accompany an extreme drought and a fiery holocaust. Through the tribulation judgment and the last catastrophe, God will create the perfect heaven and earth again. Morris, "Biblical Eschatology and Modern Science," 291–99. In my view, Morris does not engage with our universe's scientifically predicted heat death with sufficient integrity. Furthermore, Morris rarely considers that the book of Revelation's apocalyptic passages not only speaks of the passing of the evil in the present creation, but also are intended to give a promise for the present creation's fulfillment through the radical transformation.

faithfulness and hopes for the resurrection of his loved pets in the new creation. Yet Polkinghorne claims that it is proper to anticipate God's redemption of creatures by their types.[358] In my view, Polkinghorne may be right if he limits his argument to simple organisms, considering those individuals' minimal capacity to enjoy their independent life or feel intense suffering.

However, as Southgate points out, "with sophisticated mechanisms of perception and the processing of pain," more complex creatures are "individual centers of experience that are subject to intense suffering . . . [and] sometimes experience little or nothing of the fulfilled life."[359] As Moritz contends, from the most elementary organisms to the animals of high levels of complexity, animals make *active choices* in different degrees, which may lead to the unnecessarily excessive suffering in their lives and in those of other animals. If so, the faithful and loving God, who gave rise to their dynamic and contingent lives, is to be the Redeemer of those who could not live out their fulfilled *selving* due to contingent natural evil. Like Moltmann says, Christ is not only *Christus Evolutor* but also *Christus Redemptor*.[360] In that vein, I agree with Russell and Pannenberg that God's life-giving and redeeming immanence is to be applied to all creatures that could not fulfill their *logoi* amidst their pain, suffering, death, and decay.

Questioning the Possibility of Embodied Renewal in the New Creation

That said, I affirm that there is not only the soteriological special divine action but also a promise for the redemption of non-human creatures (Isa 11:6–9, 65:25; Rev 5:13–14). As Moltmann affirms, the eschatological *perichoretic* interdependence of all creatures is to be seen as the final goal of *creatio continua* if Christ's resurrection is not only the promise for humans but for all other creatures *in flesh* based on the cosmic dimension of Christ and the Spirit according to Scripture. This is supported by the Johannine prologue that "the Word that became flesh in Jesus is involved in the whole of God's creative activity."[361] In the Pauline literature, the

---

358. Polkinghorne, *Science and the Trinity*, 152.
359. Southgate, "Creation as 'Very Good' and 'Groaning in Travail,'" 77–78.
360. Moltmann, *Way of Jesus Christ*, 301–5.
361. Cobb, "All Things in Christ?," 174.

eschatological resurrection is not the termination of the history of the present creation. Instead, the new creation means a transition from *soma psychikon* to *soma pneumatikon* or "the transformation of [our] bodies into glorified bodies (cf. Phil 3:21)" rather than the "immortality of the soul."[362] Therefore, Ted Peters points out that what Paul contrasts in 1 Corinthians 15 is not a fleshly and a glorified body, but "a psychic body" and "a spiritual body." Here, it is to be noted that the Spirit is the ontological ground of the ensouled body, and thus the latter fulfills and completes the eschatological purpose of the former, rather than replacing it.[363] If so, this eschatological event implies the renewal of the whole of creation awaiting the arrival of the new creation.

While there is discontinuity between the present creation and the new creation, there is also continuity. In that sense, in the light of the economic Trinity, Peters and Hewlett affirm that creation is to be seen as an emergent whole "created from the future, not the past."[364] God is not bound by the past but opens a new future as the power of the future. Therefore, the primordial goodness of creation according to Genesis 1:31 can be understood in the light of Revelation 21:1 (NIV): "Then, I saw 'a new heaven and a new earth.'" The present creation is where we see the mirror dimly (1 Cor 13:12). The cross of Christ shows God's kenotic presence in the present creation, but this means God's act of redeeming in divine freedom that liberates God's creation from suffering in the light of the bodily resurrection.

Some theologians raise a doubtful question as to the possibility of the bodily resurrection of creatures after the decay and decomposition of creatures' bodies and the regeneration of a new life through the reconstitution of the physical and chemical residues from the decomposed bodies.[365] I understand that the bodily resurrection of Jesus differs from the resurrection of the victims of biological evolution through which the physical bodies of the victimized creatures have decomposed and disappeared.

Yet one should notice that the bodily resurrection of Jesus is not just the resuscitation of his body but God's radically new act of transforming his life as an *embodied* person in continuity with his life before his crucifixion. In that sense, while there is an inconceivable discontinuity

---

362. Green, "Bodies—That Is, Human Lives," 170.
363. Peters, "Resurrection," 308–10.
364. Peters and Hewlett, *Evolution from Creation to New Creation*, 160–64 [160].
365. Schwarz, *Eschatology*, 286–90.

between the present and the new creation, I think that, as Polkinghorne discusses, the idea of the input of pattern-making information helps to conceive of the transition from the new creation into the new creation not only in discontinuity but also in continuity.[366] That is, the input of information makes the emergence of their irreducible attributes and functions possible when the physical stuff of the universe is constituted into the entities of higher complexity.

Likewise, in the transformation of the present creation into the new creation, the information of the all the slices of spacetime in the current creation can be regarded as remembered in the mind of a faithful God, and God will transform and re-infuse the information in the event of the new creation. It involves certain elements that sound nonsensical to the scientific understandings of the possibilities of natural phenomena, yet as Pannenberg and Russell affirm, if the new creation is the fulfillment of the current creation, there should be elements of continuity as "transformability" in the emergence of life and consciousness in the present creation.[367]

For Pannenberg, this sort of pattern-making information is "*eidos*" as the soul is the vital principle of an embodied life in his non-body-mind-dualistic but monistic scheme of the irreducibly pluralistic creation of God. Even though individual parts of our bodies continue to change and are replaced even in our current lives, there is a unifying whole that defines our identity amidst those changes.[368] God can use such information when God redeems those creatures victimized in evolution. In the same vein, Russell names the new creation "the inverse of emergence."[369] The event constitutes the holistic horizons of unifying backward all the separated slices of spacetime into the eschatological co-present flowing time.[370]

---

366. Therefore, Polkinghorne regards the input of active information as "pattern-bearing" in his dual-aspect monism. Reality is the monistic whole that operates by both bottom-up causation and top-down causation. Polkinghorne, "Eschatology," 36–37.

367. Russell, *Time in Eternity*, 180.

368. For Pannenberg, *eidos* or the soul as the vital principle of the body is not atemporal but historical and specific rather than abstract. He gleans this idea from Origen and Aquinas. Pannenberg, ST III, 575–76. Citing Origen, *Principia*, 2.11.2, 2.10.3 and Aquinas, *Summa Contra Gentiles*, 2.58. For a similar account of the identity of a creature that keeps changing over time, see Schwarz, *Eschatology*, 288–90.

369. Russell, *Cosmology, Evolution, and Resurrection Hope*, 106–7 [107].

370. Likewise, by use of the notion of "the input of active information," Polkinghorne maintains that the new creation is a co-present flowing time that is actualized through the divine act of "carrying over" the information of all the vector spaces of

The Cosmos as a Life-Bearing Nest Transformed in the New Creation

I think that without addressing the problem of the cosmologically predicted demise of the universe and the Earth, we cannot have a hope for the future of this cosmos. Furthermore, God's *creatio continua* loses its purposive meaning and thus ends up as a happenstance without any direction. For this reason, in contrast to Keller and Peacocke, both Russell and Pannenberg take the historical credibility and the cosmic implications of the *bodily* resurrection of Jesus seriously. The body of Jesus represents the entire history of the life-bearing universe that is finely tuned to bring forth life and consciousness. Moreover, as Gerald O'Collins says, "the material world will share in the glorious destiny which Christ's resurrection promises to all men and women." As one considers the interrelatedness of humans and the natural environment, a resurrection of life without a "new environment" would look more like the "immortal existence of souls."[371]

Both Peacocke and Keller discuss divine freedom without violating the natural order but in divergent metaphysical frameworks.[372] Yet they do not take the cosmic implications of the bodily resurrection of Jesus seriously. Accordingly, they do not consider the possibility for mutual interaction between scientific cosmology and eschatology. In contrast with these two interlocutors, Pannenberg and Russell affirm that if there were no general resurrection, Jesus could not have been resurrected. However, as we can credibly posit the bodily resurrection of Jesus as a historical event, we can hope for not only the resurrection of non-human creatures but the renewal of the whole of the cosmos as a life-bearing construct.

While considering the challenge from theology to science, Russell affirms that natural sciences can contribute to theology if the new creation is regarded as a reality in both "continuities and discontinuities" with the present creation.[373] This task is possible because the natural sci-

---

the present world alongside each other in the new creation. Likewise, the resurrection appearance of Jesus is the intersection of the vector spaces of his pre-crucifixion life and that of the new creation. Polkinghorne, "Eschatology," 38–41 [39]. Russell rarely explains the new creation in the language of whole-part and top-down information.

371. O'Collins, *Jesus Risen*, 154–55.

372. I comparatively investigated their perspectives in detail in chapter 3 of this book.

373. As Russell argues, theology-religion dialogue on the matter of the resurrection hope is more about the "dissonance" between the two counterparts. Russell, *Cosmology, Evolution, and Resurrection Hope*, 106–7. Also see *Cosmology*, 4–24.

ences explore the fundamental structure of the present universe based on methodological naturalism.

Pannenberg engages with Tipler's physical conceptualization of the possibility of the eschaton. Thereby, he calls for a mutual and open-ended interaction between theology and science without reducing the resurrection hope to the potentialities embedded in the universe.[374] I agree that a physicalized eschatology cannot be accepted as a viable proposal. First, it reduces consciousness and life down to information processed by computers and makes the emergence of higher complexity diminished to the bottom-up causation in the physical level. Second, such a scientized proposal ignores the fact that the infinity of God is not only immanent but also transcendent of the sum of the finite.[375]

However, Pannenberg does not concretely present the possible mutual interaction between the two dialogue partners like Russell. While Pannenberg provides a trinitarian notion of the relations of tenses, Russell substantively reconstructs it in the light of contemporary physical theories based on the continuity and discontinuity between the present creation and the new creation. I appreciate Russell's and Pannenberg's eschatological vision being inclusive of the cosmos as a whole rather than focusing on a terrestrial or anthropocentric vision of the *basileia* of God.

For Karl Rahner, the ultimate end of evolutionary history is human beings' intimacy with God in the risen Christ, while the created order of the cosmos finds its meaning in the eschatologically redeemed humanity and ultimately in the humanity of Christ.[376] Furthermore, for Rahner, cosmic Christ, being immanent in self-transcendent evolutionary history, makes evolution a simply-given part of the grace-filled creation of God.[377] Rather than challenging the inevitable victimization of creatures in evolutionary history, Rahner focuses more on God's self-communication through creatures' self-transcendence in the course of evolution and its consummation through humanity's unity with God.

---

374. Pannenberg, *ST* II, 158–61.

375. In that vein, Polkinghorne contends that, according to a physical eschatology, human beings become "computers made of meat" produced within the current evolving process. Polkinghorne, "Eschatology," 33.

376. For a detailed analysis of cosmic Christ according to Rahner, refer to Edwards, *Jesus and the Cosmos*, 93–108.

377. Rahner, "Fragmentary Aspect of a Theological Evaluation of the Concept of the Future," 235–41.

Hence, Moltmann contends that Rahner fails to draw attention to the victims of Darwinian evolution.[378] In response to Rahner, Moltmann argues that Christ is to be regarded as the Redeemer of evolution. Nonetheless, even though he advances cosmic eschatology, his eschatology is more focused on political and ecological justice. Moltmann rarely engages in dialogue between theology and science on the radical transformation of the cosmos as a whole *beyond* the cosmic heat death.[379] In contrast, while Russell and Pannenberg recognize the limitations of natural sciences in conceiving of the new creation, they argue that there can be consonance between theology and science on the topic even partially.

In the next chapter, while appreciating Russell's suggestion of the *non-zero-sum* relationship[380] between the created and divine causation, according to which *creatio ex vetere* fulfills the genuine freedom of creatures, I appropriate a *qualified* notion of divine self-limitation. Thereby, I contend that the cross and the resurrection of the Son mean the triune God's *co-protesting* or *co-resisting* against the power of death and evil in solidarity with creatures beyond co-suffering solidarity. Furthermore, I call for a more holistic divine action in the new creation. Based on these ruminations, I constructively present a trinitarian kenotic-eschatological panentheistic vision of creation.

---

378. Moltmann, *Way of Jesus Christ*, 297–303.

379. For Polkinghorne's similar critique of Moltmann's eschatology, see Polkinghorne, *God of Hope and the End of the World*, 142–43.

380. Russell, "Divine Action and Quantum Mechanics," 387n87. For Russell, God's agency in the quantum level does not compete with the causes of nature. God is the ontological ground of the indeterminacy of quantum events. While God is present in all the quantum events as they are God's creation *ex nihilo*, God can particularly work without intervening in the order of nature (354–55, 387–88).

5

Envisioning a Kenotic-Eschatological Panentheistic Framework of the Trinitarian Creation

IN THIS CHAPTER, BASED on the comparative investigation of the four interlocutors' theodical schemes, I present a kenotic-eschatological panentheistic vision of the trinitarian creation. In so doing, I focus on the meaning of the cross for creation. The event is the locus of the trinitarian co-suffering. It becomes redemptive in the light of the bodily resurrection of Jesus. In the trinitarian solidarity with creatures suffering from contingent and inevitable natural evil, the Father works through the Son and the Spirit *within* creation. Creation participates in the new creation as the trinitarian self-fulfillment in creation. Toward the fulfillment of that purpose, the triune Creator indwells in creation in redemptive and co-suffering solidarity with creatures through both general and special divine action.

As discussed in chapter 4, unlike Pannenberg, Russell affirms the triune God's *theopaschitic* solidarity with creation suffering from death, evil, and sin. However, Russell is cautious about the concept of God's self-limitation when it involves the lack of divine omniscience and redemptive action. Russell regards divine freedom as the ground of the creaturely contingency and freedom. Therefore, he is concerned that the theological scheme of divine self-limitation makes creaturely freedom and divine freedom *compete* with each other. Accordingly, Russell disagrees with

Peacocke that the future states are unknown to God because of the genuine indeterminacy in the unfolding of history.

Even mathematicians know the available possibilities for a wave function's collapse at a superposition. In that sense, I think that God can know every potential future state in its actuality if the ultimate goal of time is the eschatological future of God. Therefore, I agree with Russell that it is theologically improper to speak of *kenosis* or God's self-emptying in the Incarnation as God's limiting Godself in terms of God's knowledge of creation and God's special divine action. Like Gunton claims, if God grants genuine contingency to creatures, their freedom should be genuine yet dependent on God's absolute freedom to create the world *ex nihilo*.

Yet, considering the freedom and contingency of creatures, I think that God can personally interact with creatures through the interplay of chance and law-like regularities inherent in nature. While the eschaton is in God's mind as the basis of *creatio ex nihilo*, it is not fully determined but in contingent development in flowing time. This does not mean that there are potentialities in creation unknown to God.

Rather, while not denying the omniscience and omnipotence of God, one can still speak of divine self-limitation in a qualified sense. That is, God fulfills the trinitarian creation by retracting from divine infinity some subsets of actualities to potentialities for creatures to actualize them. Creatures can do so by responding to the creative and redemptive lure of God or God's eschatological co-protest against evil. In contending this panentheistic idea, I invite the insights of Keller and Peacocke to enrich the *non-zero-sum* scheme of the God-creation relationship advanced by Russell and Pannenberg. Furthermore, I discuss how in the new creation as *creatio ex vetere* God holistically honors the created causations in continuous creativity.

To that end, in the first section, I reaffirm the significance of the new creation as the basis and goal of creation. In light of the eschatological ontology of creation, I discuss the fundamental contingency of our universe in a broader context of contemporary quantum cosmology in supporting a theological interpretation of the universe and the evolution of life as God's *creatio continua*.

Next, I discuss how the co-suffering and saving presence of God on the cross of Jesus is an essential metaphysical lens for understanding nature as the trinitarian creation. Jesus's cross demonstrates both a moral exemplar and God's soteriological act in creation in the face of the inevitable and contingent power of death and evil. The co-suffering yet redemptive presence of the triune God in *creatio continua*, as revealed in the cross and the resurrection of Jesus, is to be considered seriously in the matrix of the suggested eschatological ontology of creation. I draw upon the theories of contemporary epigenetic and developmental biology and discuss their hypothetic coherence with the suggested idea of kenotic-eschatological immanence of the triune God.

Then, I contend that the triune God's *theopaschitic* co-suffering in creation amidst natural and cosmic evil should be regarded as God's qualified self-limitation. In so doing, I critically re-appropriate the contributions of Peacocke and Keller. Here, in my view, by honoring the contingency of creation, God stands in *co-protesting* solidarity with creatures in the face of natural and cosmic evil through persistently empowering them to fulfill self-transcendence toward the new creation.

Both Pannenberg and Russell celebrate the ecological relationality of the new creation as *creatio ex vetere*. Yet, in my view, Pannenberg and Russell rarely develop a scheme of top-down and whole-part causations in the new creation. Hence, in the following section, I discuss the significance of holistic divine causalities in the new creation. Thereby, I critically engage with those proposals made in developmental biology that present the significant roles of the epigenetic processes of emergent evolution. Considering continuities between the present and the new creation, I maintain that those scientific theories may provide insights into holistic divine action in the new creation. In the last section, based on all these ruminations, I constructively suggest a trinitarian kenotic-eschatological panentheistic vision of creation.

Creatio ex Vetere as the Basis and the Goal of *Creatio ex Nihilo*

In the OT, God mightily brought Israel out of Egypt when they were left with the threat of death without any hope for the future. In the NT, the same God is the One who raised Jesus from the dead and fulfilled the reality of the *basileia* of God in Jesus' resurrection.[1] These saving acts of God are contingent, in that God is not bound to the past, but overcomes the past and fulfills Jesus' triumph over death within creation.

By positing the eternity of God as *temporal infinity*, I reject reductive physicalism but accept the epigenetic processes in the mutations of genes

---

1. Jenson, *Systematic Theology*, 2:13–14.

Envisioning a Kenotic-Eschatological Panentheistic Framework 225

and the variations of species with the increases of complexity through biological evolution. No emergent level is reducible to lower ones, by virtue of the novelty that emerges in the process of evolution through the interplay of chance and regularities. Prigogine writes that "[w]e are becoming more and more conscious of the fact that on all levels, from elementary particles to cosmology, randomness and irreversibility play an ever-increasing role" (i.e., a systems-theory perspective).[2]

Ultimately, God's redemptive future constitutes the ontological ground of creatures' self-transcendence toward the embodiment of the new creation. Therefore, creatures' self-transcendence becomes genuinely contingent and open to novelty in the creative field of the eschatological Spirit. In the same vein, Ted Peters conceives God's eternity as the temporal infinity that "envelops time" through the process of the trinitarian creation. Creatures are granted freedom and purpose from the eschatological perspective of the new creation as the goal of creation. In that way, the eternity of God means temporal infinity.[3]

Since such a belief can be a well-motivated belief in the light of the credible hope for *creatio ex vetere*, the theological vision of reality has to have something with credibility to offer for natural sciences, while the former is to continue to be reshaped in interaction with the latter. For Pannenberg, as discussed in chapter 4, the temporality of flowing time has priority over its spatiality, as the latter is the relation of events taking place in flowing time, as Leibniz understands space as relations. Likewise, there are different frames of reference according to SR. However, Pannenberg does not count seriously the differences that bear ontological values while all of them are in flowing time with the arrow of time.

In contrast, Russell respects the ontological status of the multiple perspectives that exist in the observations made due to relative motions. The multiple perspectives are not merely cognitive but objectively dependent on their motions relative to the speed of light.[4] The multiple

---

2. Prigogine and Stenger, *Order Out of Chaos*, xxviii.

3. Peters, *God as Trinity*, 174–75.

4. Russell maintains the inextricable unity of space and time. In so doing, Russell refutes the spatialization of time found in the idea of the block universe while avoiding temporalizing space like Pannenberg. Furthermore, Russell also does not agree with the neo-Lorentzian positions suggested by Michael Tooley, according to whom the diverse perspectives become only epistemologically relativized. Citing Tooley, *Time, Tense, and Causation*, 342–73.

perspectival frames of reference contribute to the hermeneutical richness of our understanding of reality.

Yet he does not deny that there are objective commonalities shared by the frames of reference.[5] In that sense, Russell stresses the *multidimensionality* of spacetime. However, plurality does not end up in relativism as Russell regards the differentiated tenses of flowing time and the multiple perspectives as *relational* in the matrix of the trinitarian creation. The multidimensional and relational flowing time is in the eschatological lure of the Spirit. Thus, flowing time is *inhomogeneous*. That is, the future has a temporal priority since a sequence of events is open to novelty and only there it finds meaning.

I think Russell's relation of space and time, as well as eternity and omnipresence, make better sense in theology-science dialogue. For Russell, the trinitarian relations create unity-in-distinction among different frames of reference. Pannenberg stresses the unity of the different *tenses* in the trinitarian matrix of creation by temporalizing space. Both Keller and Peacocke also understand the loss of the global present due to SR. They both avoid relativism since they hold on to the existence of persistent emergence of regularities.[6] Nonetheless, unlike Pannenberg and Russell, Peacocke and Keller do not develop an eschatological ontology of time.

Reaffirming the Fundamental Contingency of the Universe as the Nest of Life

The significance of the fundamental contingency of our life-bearing universe is imperative so that we can affirm God's purposeful creation of life and consciousness through biological evolution. As discussed above, in the eschatological ontology of creation, the genuine contingency of *creatio ex nihilo* is not dissolved in the perspective of the eschaton.

In my understanding, the fundamental contingency of creation is not logically falsified by other quantum cosmologies, different from the Hartle-Hawking standard model: namely, by the multiverse theories as well as the oscillating universe theories. First of all, with regard to the theories of multiverse (i.e., Everett-Wheeler many-worlds theory), the

---

5. Russell, *Time in Eternity*, 307–9.

6. Peacocke, *Theology for a Scientific Age*, 33–35; Keller, *Cloud of the Impossible*, 155–57.

existence of other universes with their own unique sets of constants[7] is neither empirically observable nor testable.[8] The countless duplication of a universe at a split second cannot be tested at all. In that sense, Paul Davies writes, considering the absolute lack of empirical evidence, "[w]henever a measurement is performed to determine, for example, whether the cat is alive or dead, the universe divides into two, one containing a live cat, the other a dead one. Both worlds are equally real, and both contain human observers . . . Countless times each second, the universe is replicated."[9]

In that sense, the theory loses its persuasive force because the absolute lack of empirical evidence violates the principle of Occam's razor. This principle, presented by William of Occam in early thirteenth century, is critical in the natural sciences. Natural scientists employ the principle, according to which "the simplest explanation is to be preferred over the complex one unless there is a [reliable and justifiable] reason for the latter . . . [based on] cosmological observations."[10]

Furthermore, as discussed in chapters 3 and 4, even if the multiverses could exist, the contingency of their existence remains because our universe is a *particular* person-making type without our ability to expound why the multiverses exist and how our universe is specifically fine-tuned. Hence, it seems that the multiverse hypothesis defies its misguided use by atheists anxious to undermine the theological significance of the fine-tuning universe.[11] Rather, as McGrath notices, it seems that "substantially the same arguments can be brought to bear for the existence of God in the case of a multiverse as in the case of a universe, with the multiverse hypothesis being consistent with, not the intellectual defeater of a theistic understanding of God."[12] Even with the supposition

---

7. According to string theory, multiverses may be composed of as many as 10500 sets of constants. McGrath, *Fine-Tuned Universe*, 123–24.

8. See Murphy and Ellis, *On the Moral Nature of the Universe*, 56–57.

9. Davies, *God and the New Physics*, 116.

10. Kärkkäinen, *Creation and Humanity*, 114. Citing Spitzer, *New Proofs for the Existence of God*, 68.

11. For example, see Leslie, *Universes*, 198: "My argument has been that the fine-tuning is evidence, genuine evidence, of the following fact: that God is real and/or there are many and varied universes." Here, Leslie sees that the existence of the multiverse does not make the particularity of our universe necessary.

12. McGrath, *Fine-Tuned Universe*, 124.

that every possible form of the universe actually occurs in the multiverse, there still remains "the problem of what determines what is possible."[13]

Also, I think that the question of God the Creator is not disposed of even in the various types of the "bouncing or oscillating models." Primarily, contemporary scientists are skeptical regarding the models of the universe that continue to undergo the infinite cycles of the big bang and the big crunch.[14] This is mainly because of the recent finding that the universe is "accelerating" in its expansion rather than slowing down.

In addition, there are three other reasons why the hypotheses are not plausible. First, as Penzias and Wilson discovered, while 99 percent of light in the universe pertains to the electromagnetic radiation or the cosmic background radiation (CBR) that stems from the Big Bang, only about 1 percent of light is emitted by various light sources, primarily stars. In each cycle between a big bang and a big crunch, stars are formed and emit light.[15] If there were a great number of the expanding cycles of universes, all the scattered starlight from the precedent cycles would be absorbed into the background radiation. If that had been the case, the ratio of starlight to the background radiation would have been much less than 1 percent, the current ratio in our universe.

Second, the hypothesis of many expanding cycles goes against the second law of thermodynamics.[16] Considering the increase of the entropy from the burning stars, throughout the expansion after the Big Bang, our universe should have a much higher level of entropy than it actually does, given that our universe was not the first cycle. Not only that, the entropy at the moment of the Big Bang should have been much more than contemporary astrophysicists currently estimate.

The last reason for renouncing the oscillating universe scenario is the increase in cyclic expansion. Based on Richard Tolman's discovery of the cumulative effects of radiation on cyclic expansion, each expanding cycle should be longer than the previous one, and logically, we would get to the shortest one, the beginning. For these several reasons, the oscillating universe hypothesis seems to be marginalized in the current scientific community.

---

13. Murphy and Ellis, *On the Moral Nature of the Universe*, 57.

14. See Worthing, "Christian Theism and the Idea of an Oscillating Universe," 281–301.

15. Spitzer, *New Proofs for the Existence of God*, 28–29.

16. Spitzer, *New Proofs for the Existence of God*, 29–30.

All in all, I affirm that even though the universe cannot directly prove the existence of God the Creator, it is well motivated to theologically regard the universe with the unnecessary and finite beginning as the contingent creative work of God. This finds coherence with what the Christian faith affirms in *creatio ex nihilo*. I affirm that theology is to continue to take a mutually interactive and creative approach to scientific cosmologies in pursuit of the commonly shared understanding of the world. In so doing, the doctrine should not be reduced merely to t=0 as a scientific theory on the beginning of the universe keeps changing.

Based on the musings above, unlike Peacocke who tends to reduce *creatio ex nihilo* as a doctrine of the ontological dependence of the world on God, I agree with Peters who contends that "[t]o reduce *creation ex nihilo* to a vague commitment about the dependence of the world upon God—though accurate—does not help much."[17] I think as Russell explains, the creative agency of God, on which even the initial quantum tunneling according to quantum cosmologies was dependent, will continue to be actively immanent through general and special ordering of the world in *creatio continua*. This is because transitional changes taking place in the physical and biological levels can be seen as temporally finite and fundamentally contingent by use of the broadened notions of contingency.

The Epigenetic Nature of Evolution as God's Holistic Way to Create Life and Consciousness

For Pannenberg, the Spirit as the life-giving field is eschatological. The Spirit lures creatures to ecstatic self-transcendence through the epigenetic emergence of higher complexity in evolution. In this process, the Son serves as the creative principle of self-differentiation. Therefore, the Son is the ontological ground of creaturely contingency in bottom-up, top-down, and whole-part causations. At the same time, in redemptive action, the trinitarian life of God lures creatures toward the embodiment of the new creation from the eschatological horizons. This eschatological consummation constitutes the ontological ground of general and special providence through "the primacy of future for the understanding of time."[18]

Russell gleans the trinitarian perspective of creation from Pannenberg and affirms it since "both creation and New Creation are part of a

---

17. Peters, "On Creating the Cosmos," 288.
18. Pannenberg, *Metaphysics and the Idea of God*, 77.

single divine act of creation *ex nihilo*" by the triune God.[19] For Russell, the concept of the priority of the future makes possible the strong emergence of genuine novelty in the course of evolution. The eschatological ontology of creation finds coherence with the indeterministic interpretation of the sub-atomic events in physics. That metaphysical choice is also scientifically supported by the empirical evidence. This is because both theological and scientific investigations of reality are performed through *a posteriori* observations and communal discernment of them.

While endorsing Peacocke's whole-part approach to divine causation, I maintain that the divine whole-part information does not preclude the direct and particular presence of God in special divine action considering the genuine contingency of the subatomic level. Here, in my critical engagement with Keller's understanding of divine action in creation, I think if God is the infinite *eros*, God can be seen as luring creatures at particular slices of the created spacetime.

In my view, this suggested holistic *creatio continua* finds theological coherence with the epigenetic theories of contemporary biology. Emergent evolution is not confined to the deterministic central masterplan of the DNA, based on the biological schemes of epigenesis, self-organization, and systems theory. Rather, the history of biological evolution continues to be reshaped by the dynamic interaction between organisms and their environments.

Self-organization may be broadly defined broadly in the matrix of "development as the spontaneous emergence of spatial order." Even in an embryonic cells' development, self-organization is "pervasive . . . from symmetry breaking in the early embryo to tissue patterning and morphogenesis" through intercellular interactions that are mediated by diffusing ligands and mechanical forces. The development of these complex systems is spontaneous and is not fully predictable as they self-organize by the interplay of chance and law.[20] Furthermore, according to systems theory in developmental biology, the developmental cycle of an organism is ecologically embedded and unfolds through the dynamic interaction

---

19. Russell, *Time in Eternity*, 320.

20. Schweisguth and Corson, "Self-Organization in Pattern Formation," 659–77 [659]. Self-organization is also essential in understanding the emergence of novel attributes in the macrolevel, such as the emergence of human quadropedalism. That is, natural selection does not fully explain the contingency of its emergence. Karaca et al., "Humans Walking on All Four Extremities with Mental Retardation and Dysarthric or No Speech," 91.

among distinct developmental systems, rather than being predetermined by the masterplan of the DNA. For example, Susan Oyama contends that "the genome represents only a part of the entire developmental ensemble."[21] The phenotype of a reproduced organism does not result solely from its inherited genes but depends on its environment. Not only ontogeny (an individual's development) but also phylogeny (evolutionary development) relies on "ecologically embedded developmental systems."[22] For this reason, a genotype is phenotypically expressed in diverse, indeterminate, and dynamic manners. If evolution is the process of the emergence of irreducible novelty, theologically, we can think of a metaphor of God's general and special creative lure in the process while not violating the God-established order of nature.[23]

In biological evolution as an epigenetic process, living organisms with certain degrees of complexity are not merely influenced by their environment. Rather, they dynamically interact with their environment, thereby becoming the centers of action that make changes in evolutionary history. The restrictions of their environment do not determine their lives, but they actively change their environment as one can see in the cases of niche construction.[24]

Furthermore, in this creative process, not only the information from the environment is "transmitted to the genes through natural selection," but organisms can contribute to the evolution of their genes by transforming their environment through niche construction. That is, evolutionary history is not necessarily genetically determined. Instead, a

---

21. Oyama, *Ontogeny of Information*, 23–27 [23].

22. Oyama, *Ontogeny of Information*, 182. For similar accounts of the developmental contingency of an organism's life cycle, refer to Moss, "From Representational Preformationism to the Epigenesis of Openness to the Word?," 219–30.

23. Moritz, "Contingency, Convergence, Constraints, and the Challenge from Theodicy in Creation's Evolution," 309–10.

24. Niche construction means "a process where an organism modifies its environment through its behaviors and decisions in such a way that such changes impact the way both its evolution and that of its descendants move forward." Moritz, "Contingency, Convergence, Constraints, and the Challenge from Theodicy in Creation's Evolution," 316. For example, the beaver's construction of dams that leads to the change in the environmental pressure for their evolution, resulting in different sorts of adaptation. Deacon, "Multilevel Selection and Language Evolution," 93–95. For another example, males of some species of the bow bird "build small huts to attract females, bringing fruits, seeds, and fungi to decorate them." This contingent behavior of changing the environment is reinforced by their descendants as the behaviors ensure the long-term supply of food and decorations. Oyama et al., *Cycles of Contingency*, 113.

new niche allows the emergence of a new set of genes that may contribute to survival, while animals' behaviors affect the paths of their descendants' evolution.[25] That is, natural selection serves to constrain and perpetuate the diversification of species. Yet organisms can also affect that process by affecting their environment. In the same vein, natural selection retains, removes, and spreads variants, but, it does not itself bring into any new variants into existence.[26]

Furthermore, there can be many different phenotypic expressions of their genes, depending upon the environment where an organism develops. Its development is not dictated by the information according to the DNA in a bottom-up fashion only. The dynamic interaction between the organism and the environment may affect the future development of the genes of their descendants and their phenotypic expressions.[27] For example, in the regeneration of mammalian animals, the epigenetic tags are developed through their dietary patterns and imprinted in the genes of their parent pairs. They are likely to be passed down to their offspring, even affecting their DNA and their genetic mutations.[28]

As discussed, biological evolution is contingently open to genuine novelty via the *two-directional* input of information between creatures and their environment. The genes are not governed solely by the principle of the survival of the fittest. Rather, there is room for organisms' going beyond the constraints of their environment by creating their environment and changing it through their interaction with the environment. Even in this scheme, creation is never free from eating and being eaten in contingent predation throughout biological evolution. Nonetheless, animals

---

25. Barbour, *When Science Meets Religion*, 92–93, 105–8.

26. Arthur, "Concept of Developmental Reprogramming," 49–57. Similarly, from his process thought, Charles Birch understands biological evolution as a dynamic process of self-organizing rather than understanding natural selection as a determinant driving factor of biological evolution. Birch, "Neo-Darwinism, Self-Organization, and Divine Action," 225–48.

27. Wcislo, "Behavioral Environments and Evolutionary Change," 137–69.

28. Wanjek, "Your Diet Affects Your Grandchildren's DNA, Scientists Say." Citing the recent research of the group led by Randy Jirtle at Duke University as well as the recent research led in part by Ram B. Singh of the TsimTsoum Institute in Krakow, Poland. The former demonstrated how a mother mouse' diet can affect the chronic diseases that develop in her offspring. The latter examined nutrients that affect the chromatin comparable to the chemical soup in which DNA operates.

and their behaviors "become much more than 'the utility functions' of their environment" as is affirmed by neo-Darwinian sociobiologists.[29]

In order for a genuine free will to emerge, there needs to be genuine indeterminacy along with regularities inherent in nature, because without either indeterminacy or regularities, there cannot be development of a subject with an ability to freely make choices. Therefore, not only top-down agency but also the regularities of cosmological constants constrain the individual creatures' life patterns and reproduction.[30] The influence of the environment through whole-part constraints works together with bottom-up and top-down causations in this creative process of the interplay of chance and regularities. In this holistic approach to the contingent evolutionary process, I contend that, theologically, God, the Infinite, can be seen as particularly present in soteriological ways to the extent that the consistency of the universe and biological evolution is preserved but in openness to new possibilities.

The Sufferer-Redeeming Solidarity of the Triune Creator

Considering the inevitable and contingent presence of natural evil across our *thermodynamic-biopic* universe, one needs to think of God's kenotic-eschatological immanence in creation in the light of the cross and the resurrection of Jesus. I appreciate Pannenberg's trinitarian understanding of God's honoring the genuine contingency of creatures in the self-differentiation of the Son from the Father on the cross. Yet, as discussed in chapter 4, I believe that Russell rightly appreciates the *theopaschitic* meaning of the cross as the locus of the trinitarian suffering for redeeming creation from the power of death, evil, and sin. Peacocke and Keller both stress the inevitable and contingent presence of pain and suffering in the natural world and God's participation in creatures' suffering.

As discussed in chapter 3, Peacocke understands the meaning of the cross as God's co-suffering with creatures in terms of God's emptying Godself of divine omniscience and omnipotence. Keller understands the

---

29. Moritz, "Evolutionary Evil and Darwin's Black Box," 182.

30. Moritz, "Contingency, Convergence, Constraints, and the Challenge," 307–9. For Russell, the regularities of the created order represent God's faithfulness and rational intelligibility. Russell, "Divine Action and Quantum Mechanics," 361. Likewise, Pannenberg regards the duration of creatures and the regularities of nature as representing God's faithfulness to creation as well as the rationality of the Creator in abstract forms. Pannenberg, *Toward a Theology of Nature*, 16–18.

meaning of the cross as God's *necessary* co-bearing of the pain and suffering of creatures because both God and creation are "metaphysically" faced with the infinite waves of dissolution and resolution.

Both Keller and Peacocke believe that God brings good out of evil but do not conceive of God's renewal of each creature sacrificed in the Darwinian evolution. Considering God's faithfulness to each creature, I agree with Pannenberg and Russell's call for God's continuing redemptive presence in objectively particular occasions in biological evolution through both general and special providence and in the eschatological consummation of creation. In the following subsections, I discuss the kenotic-redemptive implications of Jesus Christ's cross for biological evolution and the fate of our life-bearing universe in the light of his bodily resurrection. Later, drawing upon the notion of qualified divine self-limitation, I will discuss how Peacocke and Keller contribute to Pannenberg and Russell by further *nuancing* the kenotic meaning of the cross.

The Cross as Christ's Atonement: God's Self-Sacrificial and Saving Presence in the Eschatological Ontology of Creation

In the NT traditions, after the resurrection of Jesus, the Jewish notion of God's theodical involvement radically changed from vengeance on evildoers to conquering evil through self-giving love.[31] The resurrection became the locus where God vindicated the peaceable *basileia* of God that Jesus proclaimed in his life, teaching, and the cross. In reverse, without the cross as self-giving love, there is no resurrection as participating in the *basileia* of God. In that vein, for Stephen Finlan, in the Pauline theology of atonement in the NT, there is not only a "combined judicial-scapegoat idea," but also "a combined cultic-sacrificial-moral idea."[32]

In the NT, the atonement of Jesus Christ informs the Christian ethics of mutual service in self-sacrificing humbleness and love as well as the reconciliation with the rest of creation.[33] That is, self-giving or kenotic love is a way through which the peaceable *basileia* of God is fulfilled through embodying the love of God manifested on the cross of Jesus Christ. Participating in that kenotic love is regarded as a way of God's

---

31. Holmén, *Theodicy and the Cross of Christ*, 85–89, 96–108, 151–56, 162–65.
32. Finlan, *Options on Atonement in Christian Thought*, 2–4.
33. For example, see Rom 8:18–22.

Envisioning a Kenotic-Eschatological Panentheistic Framework 235

redeeming of creation. One may glean this insight from classical liberalism's idea of Christ as a moral exemplar.[34]

Yet I maintain that one should not downplay the significance of the cross as an objectively reconciliatory event while stressing the subjective response of the believers. In light of the resurrection, the cross becomes the soteriological event in which God assumes the power of sin and evil to give the promise of the future of the ultimate triumph over it. Jesus' crucifixion may not be a divinely predetermined event since it represents a result of "a contingent and radical rejection of divine love."[35] However, it can still be part of special providence. That is, the Son purposefully becomes incarnate in the world that is not ready to receive him as its Creator (John 1:9–11).

Thus, when the Son bears the cross that represents contingent evil and sin of the world, the death of the Son is inevitable. In the suffering of the Son, the Father and the Spirit co-suffer in solidarity with creation suffering from sin and evil. Yet in the light of the resurrection of the Son, the cross shows us eternity's participation in time by giving and fulfilling the promise of the ultimate triumph over the power of death and evil. Denis Edwards says that the cross as our murderous response to this divine love "not only does thwart love's purposes, but becomes its most life-giving expression."[36] Yet the promise of the new creation is "worked out in ways that cannot be predicted as the Wisdom of God, the divine Art, responds to creation with new possibilities, and the Spirit of Love breathes life into these new possibilities."[37]

God inevitably permits contingent evils through making creatures independent. Hence, "it is difficult to deny the importance of the need for atonement in terms of divine intervention and overcoming of the severe effects of the Fall,"[38] as written in Romans 5:17–19 and Hebrews 9:12. In the same vein, Moltmann also points out, on the one hand, the cross of Jesus Christ means God's solidarity with our suffering. On the other hand, the first traditional formula, "Christ died for us" (Rom 5:8), speaks of "for us" as "for our sins."[39] In other words, in the light of the resurrection of

---

34. Taylor, *After God*, 188–89.
35. Edwards, *Jesus the Wisdom of God*, 128.
36. Edwards, *Jesus the Wisdom of God*, 128.
37. Edwards, *Jesus the Wisdom of God*, 128.
38. Kärkkäinen, *Christ and Reconciliation*, 331.
39. Moltmann, *The Way of Jesus Christ*, 178–87.

Jesus, God is the subject of reconciling with us by delivering us from evil and sin (2 Cor 5:18–20). The redemptive presence of God continues to be universalized through the Spirit who continues to illumine us to revert us from the powers of sin and evil. Ultimately, in the light of the resurrection of Christ, creation as a whole is granted an eschatological hope that the Shalom of God will be all in all across creation.

All in all, as C. F. D. Moule contends, the substitutionary model advocates should not ignore that that God "puts the wicked right" by exercising God's "sovereign creative power by suffering, not by causing to suffer."[40] In that sense, I affirm that God participates in the suffering of creation in solidarity. The passion of Christ shows that God is "with us and for us."[41] In the *birth pang* for the new creation, the Spirit suffers with the Father and the Son.[42]

As Colossians 1:20 and Ephesians 1:10 say, the blood of Jesus Christ on the cross bears redemptive significance for "the whole of creation" through "redeeming" it from the power of death, violence, and cruelty. Thus, as we look at these biblical accounts, the atoning self-sacrifice of Jesus Christ is essential not only for the reconciliation of humans with God but also for the redemption of the whole of creation, considering the cosmic dimension of the ministry of Christ. The Messiah's suffering and death is a *particular* divine action for the vanquishing of the powers of evil that alienate creation from their participation in the goodness of God.

Divine Co-Suffering as Redemptive Solidarity in Emergent Evolution

I find helpful the kenotic account of creation advanced by George Ellis and Nancey Murphy. For these scholars, answering the metaphysical questions about reality goes beyond their role and ability of natural sciences. From the perspective of epistemological holism, Ellis and Murphy contend that the natural sciences need theology and philosophy in order to more fully understand reality. In the same vein, the cross and the resurrection of Jesus gives natural evil a teleological meaning in view of the Creator's purposeful act of creation. To be specific, Murphy and Ellis contend that while theology constitutes the highest level of the epistemic

---

40. Moule, "Theology of Forgiveness," 260.
41. Moltmann, *The Way of Jesus Christ*, 175.
42. Moltmann, *The Way of Jesus Christ*, 177–79.

hierarchy of disciplines, a kenotic theology of the cross should be consistent with the findings of the natural sciences while transcending them as a meaning-making discipline.

That is, in the light of the cross of Jesus, the holistic perspective of the universe as an emergent hierarchy helps them regard the universe as God's purposeful and good creation where life thrives in diversity through the *self-giving* of creatures for the flourishing of others. We see the universe "as the locus where the self-giving love of Christ is at work in *creatio continua*, as the universe bears life and fulfills the greater good out of pain, suffering, and death."[43] The Spirit of Christ invites every emergent level of creation into the embodiment of Christ's kenotic love for others through participation in the *basileia* of God.[44] For Ellis and Murphy, "all living things must participate not only in taking of life in order to live, but also in the painful *giving* of their lives that others might live."[45] Likewise, they write, "suffering and disorder are necessary byproducts of a *non-coercive* creative process that aims at the development of free and intelligent beings."[46]

Ellis and Murphy profoundly present how the self-organizing universe can be seen as the emergent whole, while not materialistically reduced down to merely a closed web of natural causes. The universe is open to the continuously enlivening and vibrating breath of the Spirit of God toward the interpersonal fellowship with God within the divine providence that embraces all the creatures in non-violent love. I think this scheme coheres with Moltmann's metaphor of the universe as a dissipative system that is open to the life-giving Spirit.[47] In the Spirit, the birth and death of a creature mark their finitude, and their death cannot stop the creative work of God. Rather, in God's creativeness, death becomes fertile soil for life and consciousness to arise. Ultimately, creation is intended for the emergence of those who are able to have interpersonal fellowship with their Creator. In this vein, Ruse writes that "if God was to

---

43. Shin, "Non-Anthropocentric Understanding of the Trinitarian Creatorship," 17.

44. For the significance of the kenotic love of God in Jesus Christ for the different levels of the emergent hierarchy, see Murphy and Ellis, *On The Moral Nature of the Universe*, 1, 64–73.

45. Murphy and Ellis, *On The Moral Nature of the Universe*, 213.

46. Murphy and Ellis, *On The Moral Nature of the Universe*, 247. Emphasis mine.

47. Moltmann, "Reflection on Chaos and God's Interaction with the World," 205–10.

create through law, then it had to be through Darwinian law. There was no other choice."[48]

However, at the same time, for Murphy and Ellis, the evolutionary history of life on our planet is a *gradual* process through which the Creator has lured creaturely beings into the embodiment of mutually loving communion manifested in the life, the teaching and the cross of Jesus: the emergence of the *imago Dei* in communion with God, mutual respect for each other and for non-human living creatures. By appropriating John Yoder's kenotic ethics, Murphy and Ellis maintain that the cross of Jesus shows the loving God's once-and-for-all efficacious self-sacrifice to put an end to all other violence. In that vein, the inevitable existence of pain, suffering, and death in the history of evolution is not only teleological but also involves God's co-suffering and soteriological presence. God's creative immanence consists in both general and special providence. It can be seen as redemptive in that God brings life out of death and diversity and beauty at the sacrifice of God-created "selving" lives.[49]

However, just as the cross of Jesus reveals the sting of violent death caused by the contingent moral evil, so too natural evil not only bears *teleological* significance, but also can be *dysteleological*. There are many individuals that are *unnecessarily* killed *prematurely* without fulfilling their divinely granted potentials or *logoi*. Furthermore, this is not only the case with individual creatures but also with myriad species. It is currently known that approximately 98 percent of the species went extinct in the history of evolution.[50]

If this is the case, the theodical problem of God's goodness would become even more intense if God chose to use the Darwinian evolutionary mechanism for creating the diversity and beauty of life without any particular providential care for the victims of the biological evolution. If the process is the interplay of chance and law-like regularities, one is to conceive of particular and focused mode of divine creative presence in that process.

As Joshua Moritz contends, based on the biological schemes of epigenesis and self-organization, emergent evolution is not limited to the bottom-up deterministic action according to the central masterplan of

---

48. Ruse, "Darwinism and Christianity," 98. However, I critique Ruse's claim that God had no choice other than creating the world as it is. Based on *creatio ex nihilo*, God freely chose to create our universe.

49. I discussed the meaning of this term in chapter 2.

50. Peters and Hewlett, *Evolution from Creation to New Creation*, 23, 118.

the DNA. Instead, biological evolution is subject to the dynamic interaction between an organism and its environment. Thus, a genotype has many different phenotypic expressions in creatures' dynamic interactions with their environments, altering their environmental pressures.[51] If biological evolution is a process of dynamic interactions among creatures and the two-way information between creatures and the environment, I think that one can envision God as involved in that process through the mediation of diverse causalities of nature.

If we posit creation as genuinely open to chance events from the quantum level, as Russell contends, the fundamental level of reality can be theologically interpreted as the locus where God concretely actualizes divine responsive or special lure. In so doing, God does not violate the God-established order of nature that brings about the diversity and beauty of life. God works as a responsive lure in a top-down and whole-part manner while actualizing the potentialities for the future through the mediation of the order of nature in the interplay of chance and regularities. As discussed in chapters 3 and 4, this divine agency is actualized in a bottom-up manner from the fundamental level of physics.

When creatures with autonomy in differing degrees *refuse* the divine lure to life and growth into a loving community, especially when they commit excessive violence, God suffers the creatures' violation of their finitude against other creatures and God. Furthermore, the suffering of a victimized creature is "received by the Son through the brooding immanence of the Spirit, and uttered in that Spirit as a song of lament to the Father."[52]

As discussed above, the dynamic interaction between God and creatures take place in the mode of co-suffering and redemptive solidarity of God with suffering creatures. From the next subsection, based on the genuine contingency of creation, I propose a more nuanced scheme of the pathetic-eschatological immanence of God in *creatio continua*. In so doing, I appropriate from Keller and Peacocke the theological metaphors that are helpful to envision the holistic divine causalities in *creatio continua* and *nova*.

---

51. Moritz, "Evolutionary Evil and Dawkins' Black Box," 143–88.
52. Southgate, "Creation as 'Very Good' and 'Groaning in Travail,'" 68–69.

The Notion of Creaturely Contingency Enriched by Peacocke's and Keller's Metaphors

Russell uses the notion of "the causality of the future"[53] in his understanding of God's eschatological presence in *creatio continua*. Here, I notice that Russell honors the genuine contingency of creatures by adopting the indeterminate interpretation of quantum mechanics. In his eschatological ontology of creation, the emergent novelty in *creatio continua* is the result of God's free act of creating contingent and free-willed agents that are demanded by God's fulfilling the loving communion of creatures.

In his idea of God's non-zero-sum relationship with creatures, the relative freedom and contingency of creation is ontologically grounded in the diversified unity of the intra-trinitarian life. Thus, the former serves God's fulfilling of the latter rather than being exclusive to each other. In that vein, Russell's eschatological ontology of creation is not deterministic. While gleaning from Pannenberg the idea of the eschatological ontology of the trinitarian creation, Russell defines the power of the eschatological future as the causal efficacy of the future of God. The eschatological power of the future constitutes the ontological ground of creatures' contingent being and becoming.[54] They are genuinely independent within the trinitarian field of creation that unfolds through the interplay of chance and law-like regularities.

Accordingly, I think that the notion of an eschatological whole-part constraint could be fit with his overall eschatological ontology of creation.[55] If creation is fundamentally contingent, the self-actualization of the trinitarian life of God can be open-ended as Keller conceptualizes it in her dipolar metaphysics of creation. However, as discussed in chapter 3, the plurality of creation does not have to be placed in the metaphysically

---

53. Russell, *Time in Eternity*, 117–22. Russell denies the Platonic idea of *entelechy* that is regarded as "a germ that already exists in the present and out of which the goal unfolds." *Time in Eternity*, 119.

54. Likewise, Pannenberg denies Aristotle's Platonic idea of the inner teleology deterministically inherent in the present unfolding of history. Pannenberg, *Theology and the Kingdom of God*, 139.

55. For Polkinghorne, the *quasi-localized* divine action is the way that a whole-part constraint is carried out in response to the actions of the free processes of nature. Polkinghorne, *Scientists as* Theologians, 39. However, unlike Russell, Polkinghorne adopts chaos theory and suggests the modification of its classical equations by incorporating the genuine indeterminacy of nature.

Envisioning a Kenotic-Eschatological Panentheistic Framework 241

pan-experiential framework of creation that *dualizes* the perennial existence and agency of creation and God's creative being and becoming.

In her relational metaphysics, Keller presents a non-binary relationship between God and creation. Without the infinite God or the provider of all potentialities, creation cannot develop novelty and order. However, in Keller's scheme of *creatio ex profundis*, God cannot be responsible to creation by ultimately overcoming natural and cosmic evil since the pan-experientialist metaphysics introduces "a dualistic conception of creation."[56]

That said, as discussed in chapter 2, considering the Trinity as *the analogy of relations*, rather than the analogy of being, one can speak of the genuine freedom and contingency of creatures within the infinitely creative field of the Spirit. Here, creaturely independence is not dissolved into the identity with the Spirit. The Father, through the mediation of the Son and the Spirit, fulfills the eschatological purpose of creating the unity of creatures without trumping the plurality of creation.

Then, as Russell contends, God is at creative work continuously through both general and special providence by use of the established order of nature that is open to novelty. Created agents are respected in God's fulfilling the eschatological power of the eschaton in the present creation. Likewise, when Pannenberg understands the priority of the future, God does not determine every occasion of creation. God rather works through the mediation of the created causes.

Here, God can still work in special manners while not violating the created order of nature. In that sense, the Trinity constitutes the ground of creation's contingency when the former is not a static Being but an active and dynamic relational unity. God is powerful enough to fulfill the eschatological *telos* faithfully. The telos does not mean a static or immutable Being but the ontological ground of the contingent becoming of creatures in plurality.[57]

In that vein, I contend that Keller and Peacocke can contribute to the trinitarian framework of creation proposed by Pannenberg and Russell. In so doing, Peacocke and Keller further *nuance* the co-suffering immanence of the triune Creator according to the natural and cosmic theodicy, rather than correcting their basic intuitions as to the God-creation relationship. To be more specific, Keller can enrich the trinitarian framework of creation by providing kenotic metaphors for divine

56. Kärkkäinen, *Creation and Humanity*, 70.
57. Pannenberg, *Theology and the Kingdom of God*, 139.

action. Drawing upon Gershom Scholem's interpretation of the Genesis creation accounts, Keller affirms that "[w]ith the Beginning, [blank] created Elohim."[58] Elohim here signifies that God is a singular subject that embraces plurality. God is the wellspring of all potentials, but not a single source of actualization of those possibilities. With the beginning of the cosmos, the history of the cosmos *conditioned* the history of God who continues to form the world as the Creator as a responsive desire for life.

In the same vein, Keller gleans from Nicholas of Cusa and Gregory of Nyssa the insight of divine infinity as the impossible that endlessly becomes possible yet also remains an endlessly receding horizon of the impossible.[59] Keller learns the same insight from Pseudo-Dionysius the idea of a series of negations or the negation of a negation in apophatic hierarchy.[60] Thereby, Keller speaks of the interplay of light and darkness or the dark infinity.[61] Engaging all these theological alternatives to the classical ontology of substance, Keller rightly champions the relationality inherent among creatures and God's responsive provision of new possibilities for creatures' contingent agency in *creatio continua*.

I affirm that these resources find coherence with the trinitarian framework of creation as discussed earlier. In that scheme, divine action in creation *ex nihilo* continues through the mediation of the contingent agency of creatures. For Peacocke, the eternal Being of God is not exclusive to becoming, in that God participates in the becoming of creation's processes after creating *ex nihilo* the embedded propensities that creatures can freely actualize. God creates all that is *ex nihilo*, yet God does not determine everything that takes place in it. God is the ground of the being and becoming of creatures, but God is not controlling every process of it. In this affirmation, Peacocke puts forth creation as a whole-part constraint.

However, unlike Pannenberg and Russell, Peacocke understands the trinitarian creation in a modalistic sense in which God expresses Godself in general providence. There is no room for special divine action in Peacocke's ENP scheme. In contrast, I think that the holistic approach to divine action does not have to preclude special divine action if natural and cosmic evils are contingent but inevitable within a creation that is

---

58. Keller, *Face of the Deep*, 150. Citing Scholem, *Zohar*, 50.

59. Keller, *Cloud of the Impossible*, 54–64, 112–17. Citing, for example, Gregory of Nyssa, *Contra Eunomium* II, 74, 83; Gregory of Nyssa, *Life of Moses*, 50.

60. Keller, *Cloud of the Impossible*, 71–73. Citing, for example, Pseudo-Dionysius, *Divine Names*, 56; Pseudo-Dionysius, *Mystical Theology*, 139, 141.

61. Keller, *Cloud of the Impossible*, 56–66.

genuinely open to novelty. Furthermore, in my view, it is metaphysically plausible to speak of radical discontinuities in the new creation. If the new creation is not the replacement of the current creation but its fulfillment, God, who created them *ex nihilo*, can faithfully fulfill the divinely granted purpose of each creature.[62]

Theopaschitic Co-Suffering as the Infinite Creator's Embrace of the Potentialities of Creation

If the God of love, manifested in the Incarnation, is infinite, there should be no limitation to God's ability to co-suffer with creatures. Abraham Heschel writes that "[t]he Shekinah shows the participating side of God and his ability to suffer."[63] One could consult the various texts in the OT and the NT that speak of God's co-suffering (i.e., Isa 42:14, Ezek 26:17–18, and Rom 8:26). In light of these biblical sources, Terence Fretheim writes that, in both the OT and the NT, "[t]he human cry becomes God's cry. God takes up the human cry and makes it [God's] own."[64] Considering the multi-layered unity of God's creation, I affirm that God's compassion embraces not only the suffering humans but also the sub-human victims of Darwinian evolution. In the unfolding of history through the mediation of the creaturely agency granted by the Godself, God should be present amidst the suffering creatures in deeply compassionate solidarity. Otherwise, God cannot be truly infinite, since it means God's incapacity to feel the deepest agony of God's beloved creation.[65]

That said, Pannenberg regards God as redeeming creation from death, suffering, and evil in the trinitarian redemptive project of creation. God takes the responsibility for God's creatures throughout *creatio continua*. As discussed in chapter 4, however, Pannenberg rejects the *theopaschitic* significance of Christ's suffering on the cross for keeping the distinction between the human and divine natures of Christ. In my sympathetic

---

62. For a similar argument, see Clayton and Knapp, "Divine Action and the 'Argument from Neglect,'" 194.

63. Moltmann, *Sun of Righteousness, Arise!*, 105.

64. Fretheim, *The Suffering of God*, 108.

65. Pannenberg argue that "[t]he Infinite that is merely a negation of the finite is not yet truly seen as Infinite . . . , for it is defined by delimitation from the finite . . . The Infinite is truly infinite only when it transcends its own antithesis to the finite." Pannenberg, *Systematic Theology*, 1:400. However, ironically, in his Christology and pneumatology, God's co-suffering with creation in a *theopaschitic* sense is eclipsed.

critique, I contended that through *communicatio idiomatum* the suffering of Christ means not only the Father's *sym-pathy* with the Son but also God's *theopaschitic* participation in the cross of the Son. Furthermore, on the cross as the locus of the trinitarian co-suffering, the Spirit is not only a creative force-field but also the co-suffering Redeemer in solidarity with creatures suffering from the power of death, suffering, and evil.

Eberhard Jüngel provides a profound christological scheme of God's redemptive co-suffering in creation. Like Pannenberg, Jüngel also finds the self-distinction of the Son from the Father in the cross of Jesus. Yet, Jüngel contends that God takes place as an event on the cross of Jesus. Here, God *theopaschitically* identifies Godself with the death of Jesus on the cross while finding the differentiation of Jesus the Son from the Father in his resurrection.[66] The Father raises the Son Jesus from the dead in the power of the Spirit who unites them in love. Yet the Father can differentiate from the Son only because God can identify with the death of Jesus the Son in the bond of the Spirit.[67] This understanding of the Son's differentiation from the Father implies God's embracing the finitude of creation in Godself. Based on the self-communication of God in the event of the cross and the resurrection of Jesus, one may see *nothingness* taken up into the history of the Godself. In so doing, nothingness has a new creative function in the God of the resurrection.[68]

Importantly, for Jüngel, on the cross of Jesus the Son, the *potentialities* in creation no longer are an antithesis to God's *pure actuality*. In God's Being, creatures' *transient becoming* matters. God participates in them and elevates them into the Godself by fulfilling their God-granted purpose. In this journey with creatures, God's Being is in becoming while there is nothing that creation can add to the life of God, the infinite ground of creaturely being and becoming. God's actualities are not exclusive to creaturely possibilities. Rather, God non-coercively works with

---

66. Jüngel, *God as the Mystery of the World*, 363–64.

67. Likewise, Moltmann maintains that on the cross, like the Son suffers from Fatherless-ness, the Father suffers from Sonless-ness, and thus, the cross means "the death of the Fatherhood in the death of the Son." Moltmann, *Crucified God*, 243.

68. Jüngel, *God as the Mystery of the World*, 219. For Jüngel, the *opera ad intra* of the Trinity is not exclusive to the contingent creaturely processes of becoming, as the *opera ad extra* of the Trinity shows God's creating of space in God's Being for other beings. Jüngel, *God as the Mystery of the World*, 224. For a similar account of God's self-limitation, see his "Vom Tod des lebendigen Gottes: Ein Plakat," 116–20.

Envisioning a Kenotic-Eschatological Panentheistic Framework

and through them creatively as shown in God's self-identification in the perishability of the Crucified.⁶⁹

I find coherence between Jüngel's understanding of the cross and P. T. Forsyth's notion of divine self-limitation in a qualified sense. For P. T. Forsyth, God voluntarily provides potentialities to creatures by "retracting" omnipotence, omnipresence, and omniscience "from the actual to the potential."⁷⁰ According to this scheme of divine self-limitation in a qualified sense, the created causes and the divine causes do not compete with each other.

As I discussed in chapter 3, I do not agree with Peacocke and Keller that the genuine *contingency* of creation is pitted against divine omniscience and omnipotence. The contingency of creation is demanded by the emergence of the creatures who can interact with God and other creatures freely in love and mutual respect. Yet the freedom of creatures *ontologically* depends on the absolute freedom of God who creates *ex nihilo*. Accordingly, in the suffering of creatures from contingent yet inevitable evil, as discussed above, the loving and faithful Creator is to be seen as compassionately immanent in the history of creation. However, God's co-suffering here does not mean God's self-limitation of omniscience and omnipotence, like Peacocke argues. Rather, in granting and knowing all creaturely possibilities, God limits Godself only by retracting divine actualities to potentialities for creatures to actualize them.

---

69. Jüngel, "World as Possibility and Actuality," 95–123. As the pure act is set against potentiality, atemporal eternity is set against temporal change according to the traditional doctrine of God.

70. Bloesch, *Jesus Christ*, 61. According to Donald Bloesch, it is deemed to be heretical that in Christ God retracted the divine nature, but it still can be regarded as orthodox that God retracted divine power voluntarily for the sake of fulfilling the divine purpose of creation. Bloesch, *Jesus Christ*, 61. After retracting divine consciousness, Christ regains it in the gradual process of the incarnation. Not only P. T. Forsyth, but also A. M. Fairbairn, Bishop Gore, and H. R. Mackintosh share this idea of *kenosis*. In my view, recently, Kathryn Tanner shares this idea of the incarnation as the gradual hypostatic union between the divine and the human. Yet she reduces the significance of the cross as Christ's atonement and does not subscribe to the eschatological resurrection of the body. Tanner, *Christ the Key*, 260–61.

God's Self-Limiting in a Re-Defined Sense as Co-Protesting against Evil

On the contrary to Pannenberg, Russell affirms the trinitarian *theopaschitic* interpretation of the cross as well as its implications for God's *compassionate* yet *redemptive* presence in creation. Yet I propose that Russell's *non-zero-sum* notion of the God-creation relationship can be also compatible with the idea of God who *co-protests* against evil by embracing divine self-limitation in a qualified sense.

Divine self-limitation in a qualified sense, as suggested above, does not necessarily downplay the freedom of God who creates *ex nihilo* and fulfills the new creation in a purposeful project of creation. Rather than using evils for a good purpose, in the light of his resurrection, Jesus' cross means God's *protest* against the inevitable and contingent power of evil and death. In the promised hope for eschatological triumph, the Spirit of Christ is the pledge of the new creation by being "present in history, but above all as *contradiction* and overcoming of present reality."[71] To be specific, in *creatio continua*, God freely chooses to be creative as a co-agent among creatures by granting creation contingency and freedom. Thereby, God stands in solidarity with creatures through co-resisting evil in *creatio continua*. Here, God co-suffers with creatures in empowering creatures to resist evil in the promised hope of the new creation.[72]

By celebrating the freedom and contingency of creatures, Russell also writes about God's voluntary self-limiting of directly determining the outcomes of quantum events. He also contends that his approach here is "compatible with a neo-orthodox or process view of self-limitation."[73] However, in his "both-and" approach to divine and created causalities, Russell rarely uses the doctrine of *creatio continua* as God's *co-resisting* against evil. In his opposition to the Manichaean dualism, Russell tends to avoid the theme of divine resistance to evil. For Russell, the *cross* of Jesus is God's co-suffering participation in creation for eschatologically overcoming the inevitable but contingent evil in creation.[74] Yet I think that the notion of divine self-limitation in a qualified sense may further nuance Russell's understanding of God's compassionate immanence in the suffering of creation by adding the notion of a God who co-protests against evil.

71. Sobrino, *Jesus the Liberator*, 117. Emphasis mine.
72. Migliore, *Faith Seeking Understanding*, 133–34.
73. Russell, "Divine Action and Quantum Mechanics," 386–87.
74. Russell, *Cosmology, Evolution, and Resurrection Hope*, 95–98.

To be more concrete, Russell defines natural evil as the privation of good (*privatio boni*) since the inevitable and contingent increase of entropy is *parasitic* on God's fulfillment of a good creation through cosmological and biological evolution.[75] Like Pannenberg, Russell finds the perfection of creation only in the eschaton as the fulfillment of *creatio continua*. However, Mark Hocknull points out that when natural evil is regarded as the privation of God's good creation rather than a contingent yet inevitable cost of life, there is a risk that the ontological actuality of creatures' death, pain, and suffering is eclipsed.[76]

I notice that Russell acknowledges that *creatio continua* should be a *temporal* process that develops through the mediation of created causes toward the new creation. Here natural and cosmic evil is a contingent yet inevitable cost of life. The ontological status of evil in the process becomes null only when it is placed in light of the eschaton.[77] However, in contrast with the discussed basic intuitions in Russell's theodicy, when Russell posits natural evil as the privation of good in God's perfect creation, the ontological actuality of creatures' suffering and God's co-suffering has a risk of being compromised.

Rather, natural evil is placed in the actual process of being eradicated. God limits God's *direct* causal power by permitting creatures to be co-agents in actualizing the potentially real states of the future. Thereby, God permits the contingent but inevitable existence of evil in creation while not willing it nor taking pleasure in it. If so, I think that on the cross God redeems the suffering creatures not only in compassionate condescension, but also, *beyond* that, in "God's passionate protest against the evil powers that resist the will of God." [78]

As Dietrich Bonhoeffer says, only through powerlessness and suffering can God save creatures.[79] In solidarity with powerless creatures, God resists evil and saves the creatures. God redeems creatures from

---

75. Russell, "Entropy and Evil," 458.

76. Hocknull, *Pannenberg on Evil, Love and God*, 60–62.

77. In the same vein, Russell avoids the Manichaean dualism. On the basis of the eschatological hope of *creatio ex vetere*, I agree with him that such a heretical idea must be avoided. Yet, as Conradie contends, in *creatio continua*, we are placed in between the Manichaean pessimism and the Pelagian optimism in protesting against the powers of death, evil, and sin. The protest has a hope for eschatological victory, but actually takes place in the spacetime of creation contingently. Conradie, "Eat and/or Be Eaten," 20.

78. Migliore, *Faith Seeking Understanding*, 137.

79. Migliore, *Faith Seeking Understanding*, 136. Citing Dietrich Bonhoeffer, *Letters and Papers from Prison*, 361.

death, sin, and evil in the eschatological resurrection hope. Considering the eschatological Redeemership of the triune Creator, evil is under the sovereignty of the triune God. Yet the eradication of evil is in progress. In that vein, evil is regarded as the privation of good only from the perspective of the eschaton.

God is "vulnerable yet unconquerable"[80] in solidarity with suffering creatures as God revealed Godself on the cross and the resurrection of the Son as a trinitarian event. In the garden of Gethsemane, the Son's experience of the fear and dejection is communicated to the Father through the bond of the Spirit (Matt 26:36–46; Mark 14:32–42; Luke 22:40–46). Yet the Spirit co-experiences his sorrow but participates in that event from the perspective of the eschaton. As Moltmann says, in the light of the bodily resurrection of Jesus, the cross of Jesus reveals a protesting God in the face of the power of death, sin, and evil. This divine solidarity liberates creation from all the powers of sin, death, violence, and evil.[81]

That said, Keller's understanding of God as the persistently renewing responsive lure can enrich the kenotic-eschatological idea of God advanced by Pannenberg and Russell. That is, in God's infinite love, God never cease to lure creatures into the loving communion with God and other creatures. This responsive lure can be seen as God's resistance against evil. Yet, as discussed throughout this work, and like Polkinghorne says, "the God who creates us by divine love" also "redeems us in power."[82] Since all created possibilities are knowable to God, God is omniscient. Furthermore, God is omnipotent not as a coercive tyrant, but as the loving womb of creation that gives existence to creatures and faithfully fulfills the genuine freedom of creatures in the eschatological Redeemership.

The Cosmic New Creation as the Continuously Ecological Universe in Holistic Divine Action

I affirm that the faithful Creatorship in the present creation is not only fulfilled in the new creation but also continues therein. The ecstatic vibrancy of the trinitarian creation does not end in the new creation but is fulfilled in the new creation. Both Pannenberg and Russell regard

---

80. Migliore, *Faith Seeking Understanding*, 88

81. Moltmann, *Crucified God*, 226; Moltmann, *Way of Jesus Christ*, 203–4, 206–7. Also, see Highfield, *Faithful Creator*, 355.

82. Polkinghorne, "Kenotic Creation and Divine Action," 90.

the new creation as the goal of God's *creatio continua* of independent creatures living in peaceable interdependence without death, pain, and suffering. Considering the discontinuity between the present and the new creation, the new creation cannot be entirely explained by the phenomena of emergence. The new creation does not involve the increase of entropy that is inevitable in creatures reaching the higher levels of complexity in the emergent hierarchy. However, considering their continuity, the new creation is not a second *creatio ex nihilo* but the fulfillment of the emergent whole created *ex nihilo*. In that vein, if the new creation is the consummation or fulfillment of the present creation, vibrant life in independence-in-unity is to continue in the new creation.

In the new creation, the spontaneous lure of God will not have to be a saving action as it is in *creatio continua*. Nonetheless, God's *creative* lure can be at work in the continuous ecstatic self-transcendence of creatures through whole-part constraints and top-down causalities. In *creatio continua*, there is a diversity of causalities at work in creation.[83] In continuity with the present creation, in the new creation, the continuous actualization of the whole-part constraints may involves specific bottom-up divine action. I believe that not only cosmological, but also ecological, biological and physical levels are to be involved in the interactive *meshwork* of the new creation. The new creation should not be static, if the trinitarian life of God is spontaneously interactive *in se*.

Russell champions the continuously dynamic communion of creatures in the new creation that is *multidimensional, relational*, and *ecological* by updating Pannenberg's engagement with physical theories while appropriating his profound trinitarian scheme of creation. Both Pannenberg and Russell affirm the holistic nature of divine and creaturely agency in the new creation by respecting the contingency of the redeemed creatures.

Yet they rarely present concrete suggestions of the possible continuities in terms of emergent evolution after the fulfillment of the new creation.[84] If not only the physical level but also the higher levels of the

83. There are diverse types of causalities at creative work in creation: "From classical Newtonian causalities, to gravity, to influence of quantum fields, to the 'holistic constraints' or integrated systems—and on to the pervasive role of mental cause in human life." Clayton, "Impossible Possibility," 254–55.

84. Because of the limitations in the available resources, creatures experience death, pain, and suffering in natural selection. Yet natural selection is not a primary driving force in the diversification of life in biological evolution, where there can be *selection-neutral* mutations in biological evolution. Schloss and Liang, "Evolution and the Sting of Death."

emergent whole constitute the new creation, I think that a *more concrete picture* of the top-down and whole-part causation should be envisioned through the mutual dialogue between theology and natural sciences.

In that vein, Peacocke and Keller offer conducive insights for the conceptualization of the new creation as creatures' continuous participation in the trinitarian life. God's continuously creative work *ex profundis* can be compatible with *creatio ex vetere*. In the new creation, creatures continue to exert their top-down agency in the ongoing formation of their environment. Here, I think that the appropriation of God's self-limitation in a qualified sense helps to conceptualize the ecologically dynamic life in the new creation.

Polkinghorne argues that the new creation is *creatio ex vetere*; therefore, it is not a *magical* event but the creative processes of this universe are to be meaningful therein as well.[85] Polkinghorne regards the new creation as continuously generative in dynamic relationships among creatures while he conceptualizes the radical transformation of the cosmos as a whole. The life in the new creation will be the eschatological and panentheistic indwelling of God in creation. In the new creation, not only matter but also all creaturely relations will be redeemed. Creatures will continue "the unceasing exploration of the riches of divine nature."[86]

Likewise, Hans Weder explores continuity and discontinuity between the present and the new creation by positing a metaphorical relationship between theological statements and scientific theories.[87] That is, natural sciences are interested in explaining how things take place in nature. Theology offers a *metaphysical* framework of interpretation to natural scientists by proposing a triune Creator's *transcendent immanence* in the creative processes of nature. This relationship applies to the understanding of the new creation, too.

According to 1 Corinthians 15:44, Paul regards the body as a whole person's contextualized life that involves all the relations with the world. A spiritual body means his or her peaceful relation to God "no longer impeded either by the limitations of earthly life or by the powerful transgressions of sin."[88] In that way, Weder finds continuity between this world and the new creation in terms of continuous vitality and diversity. Weder

---

85. Polkinghorne, "Eschatology," 41–42.
86. Polkinghorne, "Eschatology," 40.
87. Weder, "Hope and Creation," 189.
88. Weder, "Hope and Creation," 195.

draws upon the parable about a farmer who sows and reaps without any obstructions to his harvest. Growth and the generation of new life in this world involve the increase of entropy, the building up of an organism to higher complexity, and its self-organization. In contrast, the new creation is noble in that the growth and diversification of creatures do not involve the increases of entropy, death, and suffering. There is no limitation in their relationships with others and God.

In the new creation, the unpredictability in the self-organization of a creature will also be continued if growth continues in *creatio ex vetere*.[89] God's providence and creaturely contingency and freedom will not conflict with each other. As D. A. Carson maintains, compatibilism is woven into the very fabric of Scripture without dissolving the contingency and freedom of creatures.[90] Likewise, Gunton draws upon John Ireland's notion of divine foreknowledge, according to which the eschaton means the fulfillment of God's *telos* of creation while it is *not* fully deterministic.[91]

That is, God has the purview of the possible choices of creatures. Creatures are constrained by their environments and the divinely established sets of potentials. Therefore, they are not free in an unlimited way like God who creates the world *ex nihilo* and knows every potential actuality in creation.[92] Then, I think that the new creation, the fulfillment of creation, should not be a deterministic reality but a continuously creative and flourishing communion of creatures.

Keller calls for a *counter-apocalyptic* eschatology that does not suffocate the continuous creativity of *creatio continua*. Keller points out that a traditional reading of the book of Revelation led to an understanding of creation's time as a linear flow toward the divinely pre-determined end of creation out of chaos.[93] On the contrary, critically engaging the contemporary world-wide feminist movement, Keller suggests the counter-apocalyptic idea of the continuing convivence of creatures. She approves both an apocalypse and an anti-apocalypse in "an endless flow of connectedness" of creation.[94] Keller affirms that the apocalyptic message of

---

89. Weder, "Hope and Creation," 201.

90. Carson, *Divine Sovereignty and Human Responsibility*; Carson, *How Long, O Lord?*, 199–219.

91. Gunton, *Triune Creator*, 182–83.

92. Broadie, *History of Scottish Philosophy*, 40–43.

93. Keller, *Apocalypse Now and Then*, 151–53.

94. Keller, *Apocalypse Now and Then*, 136.

the Revelation is not monolithic but *manifold* in its prophetic voice.[95] That is, the history of creation does not lineally lead to the eschaton where a single voice is favored over others, unlike the Christian traditions of the West have believed and applied to their political actions.

The book of Revelation calls for our continued prophetic actions in society against the socio-political-economic injustice of our times. A dominant voice, in its finitude, cannot be absolutized but open to the rise of opposing voices that challenges its dominance and the undue silencing of others. Mutual respect among diverse world views, thus, is necessitated in her process metaphysics. Likewise, Keller celebrates continuous dissolution and resolution of lives in the intertwined unity of the biosphere in its larger ecological environment in her counter-apocalyptic view of creation.[96]

I agree with Keller that the new creation should not be a static and atemporal reality, considering the *dynamic interrelations* among creatures in the biosphere. However, I do not think that the eschaton necessarily reflects the monolithic and atemporal eternity. The trinitarian framework of creation can be a generative process that is mediated by *entangled relationships* among creaturely causes. In the ecological unity, creatures can affect each other's self-transcendence. The new creation can be conceptualized as *creatio ex profundis*, yet without the power of death, violence, pain, and suffering.

As Peters argues against Keller, her denial of the endless cycle of dissolution and resolution in our ecosystem does not make sense according to contemporary theories of physics that predict the irreversible increase of entropy and the demise of our universe.[97] Thus, without *creatio ex vetere*, one cannot affirm God's faithfulness to creation. In this vein, Pannenberg and Russell propose the dynamic and ecological reality of the new creation through the notion of co-presence in differentiated unity. However, they rarely discuss the causal efficacy of diverse causalities of creation in a concrete manner.

Accordingly, Peacocke's *panentheistic* insights are helpful in conceptualizing a God who works through the cosmological and ecological *meshwork* of the new creation. I think that since the new creation is *creatio ex vetere*, God will sustain the contingency of creation by granting freedom

---

95. Keller, *Apocalypse Now and Then*, 36–83, 273–310.
96. Keller, *Apocalypse Now and Then*, 279–80.
97. See Peters, "Apocalypse Now and Then," 245–46.

Envisioning a Kenotic-Eschatological Panentheistic Framework

to flourish while continuously working in transcendent immanence in a *bottom-up-in-top-down* manner. In the new creation, not only the physical level but also the living creatures of higher complexity are brought to life along with human beings, based on God's faithfulness to creation.

A Kenotic-Eschatological Panentheistic Vision of the Trinitarian Creation

In Keller's pan-experiential and dipolar panentheism, God is spontaneously responsive to creatures' contingent choices. However, in the *endless* creaturely becoming, there is no freedom for God to fulfill an eschatological *creatio ex vetere*. For Peacocke, by granting creaturely co-creatorship through self-limitation, God spontaneously experiences the joys and suffering of creatures as God continues to be actively creative in creation. However, God does not influence the world in particularly new ways, but rather passively depends on the creatures' embodiment of the inherent propensities embedded in the universe at its beginning. Therefore, God is personal in that God fulfills God's intentions of creating the world. Yet, Peacocke's panentheistic idea lacks in the soteriological power of the faithful trinitarian Creator. Peacocke's understanding of God conflicts with the temporal infinity of God in dynamic interaction with creation as portrayed in Scripture.[98] I believe that God's panentheistic presence in creation should be both kenotic and eschatological in the process of the trinitarian creation.

Pannenberg and Russell advance eschatological panentheism. They both believe that God will be all in all within and beyond creation through the eschatological consummation. *Creatio continua* is ridden with natural, moral, and cosmic evil. Thus, it does not fully reflect the perfectly goodness of God. In that sense, for Pannenberg, the all-embracing field of the Spirit is not physicalized and divine transcendence is not dissolved in creation.[99] The Spirit of God is not conditioned by the spatiotemporal processes of creation, but rather the former always transcends the latter

---

98. Kärkkäinen, *Trinity and Revelation*, 244–45. "[T]he biblical narrative pushes constructive theology to envision God in personal, dynamic, elusive, and emerging terms." Kärkkäinen, *Trinity and Revelation*, 244.

99. Refer to my critical analysis of his "force-field" analogy of the Spirit's immanence in creation in chapter 4.

while the Son and the Spirit cooperates in "arousing the ecstatic response of life" in *creatio continua*.[100]

Considering the otherness of God, Panneberg does not identify his understanding of the Spirit as panentheistic.[101] However, John Cooper maintains that Pannenberg's claim of the immanent Trinity's dependence on the success of the Son's and the Spirit's mission in the trinitarian self-actualization makes his doctrine of creation *implicitly* panentheistic.[102] Cooper is concerned that Pannenberg regards the fate of the immanent Trinity as conditioned by the success of the mission of the economic Trinity.[103] Similarly, Cooper holds that, by identifying the cosmic field with the Spirit of God, Pannenberg "undermine[s] or breach[es] the God-world difference at a basic level."[104]

However, while endorsing the claim that Pannenberg's trinitarian framework of creation is implicitly panentheistic, I disagree with Cooper that his panentheism necessarily dissolves God's transcendence. That is, I believe that Pannenberg's trinitarian framework of creation is panentheistic while not giving up on divine transcendence. As Kärkkäinen contends, divine transcendence does not have to be "associated with hierarchical distance."[105] This sort of transcendence is problematic because it "indicates God's aloofness, separation, independence, and immateriality."[106] Another way of conceiving the transcendence-immanence distinction is to understand divine transcendence as "touching its own limits in the untouchables" in creation.[107] Here, the relational and inclusive notion of God's transcendence does not eliminate the *otherness* of God. Rather, the Infinity of God grounds the finitude of creation and gives it meaning.[108]

In that sense, Pannenberg's trinitarian doctrine of creation is panentheistic, and yet, in his scheme, divine transcendence is not dissolved in

---

100. Pannenberg, *Introduction to Systematic Theology*, 45.

101. Pannenberg, *Introduction to Systematic Theology*, 45–46.

102. Cooper, *Panentheism*, 259–60.

103. Cooper, *Panentheism*, 266–67.

104. Cooper, *Panentheism*, 281. Polkinghorne also opposes panentheism based on his understanding that panentheism has a risk of ontologically fusing God's uncreated existence into creation. Polkinghorne, *Science and the Trinity*, 94–98.

105. Kärkkäinen, *Trinity and Revelation*, 242.

106. Kärkkäinen, *Trinity and Revelation*, 242. Citing Rivera, *Touch of Transcendence*, ix.

107. Kärkkäinen, *Trinity and Revelation*, 243.

108. Kärkkäinen, *Trinity and Revelation*, 244.

Envisioning a Kenotic-Eschatological Panentheistic Framework 255

creation. The cooperation of the Son and the Spirit in *creatio continua* is mediated by the created causes. Yet the Creatorship of the triune Creator is not dissolved in creation but continues to lure them toward self-transcendence and ultimately fulfill the *telos* of creation in the *basileia* of the triune Creator.

Likewise, for Russell, it is the causal efficacy of the eschaton that gives existence to the ontological openness to novelty in nature. *Creatio continua* is the mediated work of the Son and the Spirit from the perspective of the eschaton like Pannenberg affirms. Yet Russell distinguishes the absolute infinity of God from the transfinite of creation both in *creatio continua* and *nova*. Accordingly, I think that Pannenberg's and Russell's understandings of the God-world relationship are categorized as *soteriological panentheism*,[109] as they both champion the *transcendent immanence* of God.

As I maintained in this chapter, in God's self-limitation in a qualified sense, the triune God co-suffers with creatures amidst contingent evil. From the perspective of the eschaton, God's co-suffering means God's solidarity with creatures in resisting the power of death and evil. Thus, soteriological panentheism is to be a kenotic-eschatological vision of creation. Since *creatio continua* involves the universally contingent but inevitable increases of entropy, the cross of Christ becomes meaningful for creation as the locus of the trinitarian co-suffering with creatures in the face of natural and cosmic evil. Yet God's co-suffering becomes God's co-protesting against the power of death and evil in the hope of the resurrection as a cosmic *creatio ex vetere*.

---

109. For my detailed discussion of this category of panentheism, please refer to the subsection on this theme in chapter 2.

6

Conclusion

Summary of the Main Arguments

IN THIS BOOK, I argued that through the trinitarian vision of *creatio ex nihilo*, the cosmological and biological evolution can be seen as a way of God's purposeful and good creation of the universe, life, and consciousness in a kenotic-eschatological mode. Here I posited the eschatological new creation as the *basis* and the *goal* of *creatio continua* in which, hypothetically, the emergence of novelty and higher complexity is ontologically contingent. This implies that the scientific description of the natural regularities is not necessary but contingent.

The present creation reflects the goodness and love of the triune Creator in light of the cross and the bodily resurrection of Jesus. Yet *creatio continua* is on the journey to the fulfillment of the good purpose of God in an eschatological hope. In *creatio continua* the trinitarian Creator *compassionately* participates in the suffering of creatures in the mode of transcendent immanence. As Pannenberg and Russell affirm, this eschatological hope is *hypothetical* as it will be confirmed only in the new creation.

In the hope for the eschatological *basileia* of God, the triune Creator continuously creates through the interplay of chance and law-like regularities by the mediation of nature's genuine openness to the future. Thereby, God embraces the potentialities of both good and evil. Amidst the contingent, universal, and inevitable existence of death, pain, and suffering of creatures, God is present in the processes of nature in co-suffering solidarity as a faithful Creator.

Not only is God *in, with, and under* creation, God's kenotic presence invites creatures to participate in the self-giving love of God as revealed in the self-emptying of the Son on the cross of Jesus Christ. Yet this redemptive presence of God in creation is to be regarded as the trinitarian *co-protesting* against the power of death, sin, and evil, considering the eschatological hope for the ultimate fulfillment of the fundamental freedom and contingency divinely granted in *creatio ex nihilo*.

If this freedom and contingency is grounded in the intra-trinitarian mutual love, the analogy between creation and the Creator is the analogy of relations. The contingency of creatures is essential to the trinitarian Creator's fulfilling the intra-trinitarian mutual love within creation. If so, rather than de-ontologizing the death, pain, and suffering of creation in the Augustinian theodicy, God takes the inevitable existence of nothingness in creating our life-birthing universe into the intra-trinitarian life and brings good out of evil through co-suffering and co-protesting solidarity with creation.

The eschatological hope for *creatio ex vetere* is credible based on the historical hypothesis of the bodily resurrection of Jesus rather than being provable. Until the faithfulness of the Creator is confirmed across the entire creation, the present creation is ridden by the contingent, universal, and inevitable problem of evil in Darwinian evolution and the thermodynamic development of the universe. In the proposed kenotic-eschatological panentheistic vision of creation, one can regard God as co-protesting evil beyond co-suffering in a *theopaschitic* sense. In so doing, the triune Creator, who creates the world *ex nihilo*, gives freedom and contingency to creatures. Thus, God continues to responsively work in, through the mediation of, and beyond the created causes including bottom-up, top-down, and whole-part causations in the creative and redemptive eschatological lure of the Spirit.

Like Peacocke argues, one may regard God as limiting Godself in actualizing the future potentials for creation while providing all the potentials *ab initio* or constituting the ontological ground of the creativity of our universe and living creatures through whole-part and top-down causations. God co-suffers with creatures throughout the contingent-yet-inevitable divinely permitted existence of natural and cosmic evil.

Yet, I affirm that, as Keller argues, the infinity of the faithful Creator means God's continuous participation in creation by persistent and particular (or special lure) of creatures to genuine freedom and flourishing life. However, as Pannenberg and Russell point out, the contingency of creation is hypothetically posited universal from the fundamental level of physics, since without the contingency of the smallest parts there cannot be that of the whole. Along the same lines, I supported Russell's notion of God's mediated action in both direct and indirect modes in the quantum level in the matrix of *creatio ex nihilo*. In so doing, I sympathetically critiqued Keller's *creatio ex profundis* and her fundamentally dipolar metaphysics of the God-world relationship. The ontological dipolarization of God in relating to the world does not sit well with the biblical portrayal of the triune Creator.

The notion of divine action in *creatio originalis*, *continua*, and *ex vetere* is to be open to an open-ended interaction among science, philosophy, and theology in seeking the coherence of the ultimate openness of creation to novelty. If so, scientific cosmologies and the possible diversity of their philosophical interpretations do not preclude the theological belief in *creatio ex nihilo*. That said, based on the trinitarian economy of salvation revealed in history and the hiddenness of its fulfillment, *creatio continua* is God's co-protest against natural and cosmic evil.

The co-protesting immanence of God should not dissolve the *beyond-ness* of the transcendent God. This beyond-ness of God in creation does not stand exclusively against the order of nature but rather fulfills its *telos* eschatologically. God neither violates nor nullifies the established order of nature. Rather, the triune God transcends the order of nature.

The eschatological fulfillment of creation may involve a radical process of transformation in *creatio ex vetere*. The elements of the radical discontinuities in the transformative process become necessary considering the cosmic demise of our life-nesting universe according to contemporary big bang cosmology and the second law of thermodynamics. Neither scientific cosmology nor the eschatological hope according to the Christian faith should be falsified by the other in critical mutual interaction.

For Peacocke, the eschatological hope becomes disembodied without the hope of the new creation as *creatio ex vetere*. For Keller, the resurrection of Jesus and its eschatological hope mean the openness of the dipolar reality of the world and God to the incessant emergence of novelty in the matrix of chaos. For Keller, the eschatological whole of creation is reduced to the objective immortality of creatures in the mind of God and becomes transcendentalized without the embodied transformative event of *creatio ex vetere*.

In my view, these transcendentalized eschatological views find consonance with the Bultmannian "two-language" perspectives of the consummation of creation.[1] That is, while the new creation makes the purpose of *creatio continua* fulfilled, the new creation does not involve God's radical transformation of the present cosmos. In contrast with these views, as discussed throughout this work, we are to seek *hypothetical coherence* between the book of nature and the book of Scripture. The scientific investigation of the world becomes significant, since the God who saves in the economy of salvation is the same God who creates the entire cosmos while acknowledging the difference of the logic and methodology of research that theology and natural sciences employ.

The responsive love of God is the power of God that never gives up on fulfilling the eschatological *telos* in the mind of God when the finely-tuned biopic cosmos was brought into existence *ex nihilo*. In that vein, as David Wilkinson contends, scientific cosmology cannot ultimately falsify the eschatological hope since the latter also involves radical discontinuities that go beyond what sciences can anticipate.[2] However, if the new creation is not exclusive to the present creation but constitutes its fulfillment, the scientifically predicted end of the cosmos, the demise of our universe itself, is to be taken seriously in the concretizing the eschatological hope for *creatio ex vetere*.

As John Haught maintains, just like any scientific theory is open to revision, contemporary big-bang cosmology may be subject to revision down the road. Nonetheless, in conceptualizing a Christian eschatology, theologians are to continuously engage with scientific theories in an open-ended dialogue.[3] As discussed throughout this work, mutual interaction between natural sciences and theology is demanded if they

---

1. In a different manner, neo-orthodox theologians rarely put their energy in engaging in critical mutual interaction between theology and science by subordinating creation under reconciliation. For instance, in his understanding of "Creation as Justification" over which the Triune God rejoices, Barth affirms that creation and salvation are not separate as the work of same the Triune God. Barth, *CD* III/1:366–414. Yet, there is ambiguity about non-human creatures' own value here when Barth seems to subjugate creation to the salvation of humanity by affirming that "creation is the external basis of the covenant and the covenant is the internal basis of creation." Barth, *CD* III/1:231.

2. Wilkinson, *Christian Eschatology and the Physical Universe*, 187.

3. Haught, *Science and Religion*, 174–75.

commonly seek the truths of God who *indirectly* continues to reveal Godself in the history of the universe. Here, the theological language of creation interpretive of physical and biological levels of reality should not be confused with the research programs of physics and biology.[4] In mutual respect, the open-ended interaction between natural sciences and theology has to continue between natural sciences and theology.

I also contended that such a critical mutual interaction is applicable in our conceptualization of the continuity between the present creation and the new creation. I gleaned from Keller and Peacocke the theological metaphors that help to enrich the concept of God's continuing whole-part conditioning of creation and spontaneously interactive relationship between God and living creatures in the new creation. Even in the radical discontinuities, the eschatological reality is to involves the natural processes of *creatio continua* since God is faithful to the present creation.

Both Pannenberg and Russell consider the continuity between the present and the new creation to be essential in their ideas of creation as a trinitarian project. Yet they rarely present a concrete engagement with the essential roles of top-down and whole-part divine action in the new creation. For both, the biological level cannot be reduced to the physical in both the present creation and the new creation. Yet when it comes to the continuities between the present creation and the new creation, they rarely discuss in depth the importance of the genetic mutations, the environmental influences on the genetic processes, and the subjective agencies of sentient and conscious animals, as Schloss, Weder, and Polkinghorne suggest.

Suggestions: From Anticipation to Participation

The eschatological interpretation of the cosmological development of the universe and emergent evolution of life is to be open to consistent dialogue between theology and science while the metaphysical framework

---

4. For example, Peters and Hewlett point out that scientific creationism confuses scientific and theological research programs and results in a misguided interaction between theology and science. Accordingly, the intellectual consistency in God's Creatorship tends to be put at risk. While acknowledging the estimated age of the Earth (4.5 billion years) based on geological data, young-Earth creationists' argument that God made the Earth only "appear" to be ancient threatens the integrity of God's intelligence and faithfulness. Peters and Hewlett, *Evolution from Creation to New Creation*, 89–92. Citing Miller, *Finding Darwin's God*, 61, 76.

of the trinitarian creation is to be hermeneutically open to enrichment in different cultural and political contexts. As Kevin Vanhoozer profoundly contends, theology is not only *scientia* but also *sapientia*. Theology is to seek the prophetic wisdom of the Spirit in diverse contexts with the aim to "form [people] who rightly participate in [the trinitarian drama of creation] precisely by being witnesses to the resurrection."[5] In diverse contexts, the Spirit as the pledge of the new creation calls us to participate in the creative and redemptive *creatio continua* as God's "created cocreators"[6] as Philip Hefner and Ted Peters affirm. Beyond defining the *imago Dei* as the created co-creators, Southgate proposes the notion of the created co-redeemers considering our call to participate in the trinitarian redemptive ministry in *creatio continua*.

As the *imago Dei*, we are called to serve the divine purpose of fulfilling God's good creation in a free yet responsible way. We are to use our sacred freedom with ecological sensibilities that are faithful to the gospel of the triune Creator. This prophetic life becomes possible as our Christocentric reasoning continues to be nurtured by the ecclesial community in accordance with the gospel through the eschatological power of the Spirit.[7] The ecclesial communities are composed of a diversity of cultural backgrounds. The gospel of Christ needs to be incarnate in those diverse root metaphors when the ecological sensibilities are pursued in concrete manners through the use of diverse cultural contexts.

The new experiences may shed novel interpretive lights on our understandings of the world as God's creation. In that vein, I appreciate Pannenberg's vision of the universal truth in his linking theological discourse not only to other secular disciplines but also to cultural/religious traditions in mutual dialogue.[8] As Psalm 104:29–30, Genesis 2:7, and Job 33:4 say, the Spirit of God is to be seen as an all-embracing *ruach/ pneuma*, as the Apostle Paul understands the universal presence of the Spirit of God in the world.

If the whole of the world is in the all-unifying field of the Spirit, God's self-revelation in nature and its history are to be open to the public eye in different cultural contexts since they are creatures of the same Spirit. They may also find diverse expressions in other faith traditions. Hence,

---

5. Vanhoozer, *Drama of Doctrine*, 357–59 [357].
6. Peters, *Playing God?*, 16.
7. Vanhoozer and Treier, *Theology and the Mirror of Scripture*, 177–91.
8. Pannenberg, *Systematic Theology*, 1:107–10.

a Christian theology of nature is placed in open-minded dialogue with other faith traditions while believing in and hoping for the fulfillment of the ultimate telos for creation that is revealed in the historical experiences of Israel, Jesus Christ, the early church, and our diverse contexts.[9] Accordingly, I would like to develop my arguments and present a concrete proposal of ecclesial practice of the suggested ecological sensibilities by expanding this study to ecumenical and interreligious dialogue.

---

9. Kärkkäinen, *Creation and Humanity*, 207–13.

Bibliography

Alcock, John. *The Triumph of Sociobiology*. Oxford: Oxford University Press, 2001.
Ambrose. *On the Holy Spirit*. Translated by H. De Romestin. In *The Nicene and Post-Nicene Fathers*, edited by Philip Schaff, 10:91–158. Peabody, MA: Hendrickson, 1994.
Aquinas, Thomas. *Summa Theologicae*. Translated by Fathers of the English Dominican Province. New York: Benziger, 1947. https://ccel.org/ccel/Aquinas/summa/summa.i.html.
Arthur, Wallace. "The Concept of Developmental Reprogramming." *Evolution andd Development* 2 (2000) 49–57.
Atkinson, James. *Martin Luther: Prophet to the Church Catholic*. Eugene, OR: Wipf & Stock, 2004.
Augustine. *The City of God*. Translated by Marcus Dodds. In *The Nicene and Post-Nicene Fathers*, edited by Philip Schaff, 1:226–44. Peabody, MA: Hendrickson, 1994.
———. *On the Trinity*. Translated by A. W. Hadden. In *The Nicene and Post-Nicene Fathers* 1, edited by Philip Schaff, 3:1–378. Grand Rapids: Eerdmans, 1956.
Axelrod, Robert. *The Evolution of Cooperation*. New York: Basic, 1984.
Badham, Paul. "Do Animals Have Immortal Souls?" In *Animals on the Agenda*, edited by Andrew Linzey and Dorothy Yamamoto, 181–89. Chicago: University of Illinois Press, 1998.
Bailly, Francis, and Giuseppe Longo. "Causes and Symmetries in Natural Sciences." In *New Trends in Geometry: Their Role in the Natural and Life Sciences*, edited by Claudio Bartocci et al., 173–210. London: Imperial College Press, 2011.
Banzhaf, Wolfgang. "Self-Organizing Systems." 1–16. Approachable at http://www.cs.mun.ca/~banzhaf/papers/article3.pdf
Barbour, Ian. "Five Models of God and Evolution." In *Evolutionary and Molecular Biology: Scientific Perspectives on Divine Action*, edited by Robert Russell et al., 3:419–30. Vatican City: VO/CTNS, 1998.
———. *Myths, Models, and Paradigms: A Comparative Study in Science and Religion*. New York: Harper & Row, 1974.

———. "Remembering Arthur Peacocke: A Personal Reflection." *Zygon* 43 (2008) 89–102.

———. *When Science Meets Religion*. New York: HarperSanFrancisco, 2000.

Barrow, J. D., and F. J. Tipler. *The Anthropic Principle*. Oxford: Oxford University Press, 1986.

Barth, Karl. *Church Dogmatics: The Doctrine of Creation*: III/1. Edited by G.W. Bromiley and T. F. Torrance. Translated by J. W. Edwards et al. London: T. & T. Clark, 2007.

Bayer, Oswald. *Martin Luther's Theology: A Contemporary Interpretation*. Translated by Thomas Trapp. Grand Rapids: Eerdmans, 2007.

———. *Schöpfung als Anrede*. Tübingen: Mohr Siebeck, 1990.

Birch, Charles. "Neo-Darwinism, Self-Organization, and Divine Action." In *Evolutionary and Molecular Biology: Scientific Perspectives on Divine Action*, eds. Robert Russel et al., 225–48. Vatican City: VO/CTNS, 1998.

Bloesch, Donald. *Jesus Christ: Savior and Lord*. Downers Grove, IL: InterVarsity, 1997.

Boersma, Hans. *Heavenly Participation: The Weaving of a Sacramental Tapestry*. Grand Rapids: Eerdmans, 2011.

Bohr, Niels. "Causality and Complementarity." In *Philosophical Writings: Causality and Complementarity*, edited by Jan Faye and Henry Folse, 4:289–98. Woodbridge: Ox Bow, 1998.

Bonhoeffer, Dietrich. *Letters and Papers from Prison*. Edited by Eberhard Bethge. New York: Macmillan, 1972.

Bowles, Samuel, and Herbert Gintis. *A Cooperative Species: Human Reciprocity and Its Evolution*. Princeton: Princeton University Press, 2011.

Boyd, Gregory. *Satan and the Problem of Evil: Constructing a Trinitarian Warfare Theodicy*. Downers Grove, IL: InterVarsity, 2001.

Bradshaw, Timothy. *Pannenberg: A Guide for the Perplexed*. London: T. & T. Clark, 2009.

Brett, Paul. "Compassion or Justice?" In *Animals on the Agenda*, edited by Andrew Linzey and Dorothy Yamamoto, 181–89. Chicago: University of Illinois Press, 1998.

Broadie, Alexander. *A History of Scottish Philosophy*. Edinburgh: Edinburgh University Press, 2009.

Brown, R. E. *The Virginal Conception and Bodily Resurrection of Jesus*. New York: Paulist, 1973.

Brueggermann, Walter. "The Loss and Recovery of Creation in the Old Testament Theology." *Theology Today* 53 (1996) 177–90.

Buller, Cornelius. *The Unity of Nature and History in Pannenberg's Theology*. London: Rowman & Littlefield, 1996.

Buxton, Graham. *The Trinity, Creation and Pastoral Ministry: Imaging the Perichoretic God*. Eugene, OR: Wipf & Stock, 2005.

Calvin, John. *Institutes of the Christian Religion*, edited by John McNeil. Translated by Ford Lewis Battles. Louisville, KY: Westminster John Knox, 2006.

Carson, D. A. *Divine Sovereignty and Human Responsibility* and *How Long, O Lord? Reflections on Suffering and Evil*. Grand Rapids: Baker Academics, 2006.

Case, Jonathan. "The Death of Jesus and the Truth of the Triune God in Wolfhart Pannenberg and Eberhard Jüngel." *Journal of Christian Theological Research* 9 (2004) 1–13.

Clayton, Philip. "Conceptual Foundations of Emergence Theory." In *The Re-Emergence of Emergence*, edited by Philip Clayton and Paul Davies. Oxford: Oxford University Press, 2006.

———. "Impossible Possibility: Divine Causes in the World of Nature." In *God, Life, and the Cosmos*, edited by Ted Peters et al., 249–80. Aldershot, UK: Ashgate, 2002.

———. *Mind and Emergence: From Quantum to Consciousness*. New York: Oxford University Press, 2004.

———. *Mind and Emergence: From Quantum to Consciousness*. Oxford: Oxford University Press, 2006.

———. "Panentheism in Metaphysical and Scientific Perspective." In *In Whom We Live and Move and Have Our Being*, edited by Philip Clayton and Arthur Peacocke, 73–91. Grand Rapids: Eerdmans, 2004.

———. *The Predicament of Belief: Science, Philosophy, and Faith*. New York: Oxford University Press, 2011.

———. "Tracing the Lines: Constraint and Freedom in the Movement from Quantum Physics to Theology." In *Philosophy, Science, and Divine Action*, edited by F. LeRon Shults et al., 1:191–226. Leiden: Brill, 2009.

Clayton, Philip, and Steven Knapp. *Adventures in the Spirit*. Minneapolis: Fortress, 2008.

———. "Divine Action and the 'Argument from Neglect.'" In *Physics and Cosmology*, edited by Nancey Murphy et al., 179–94. Vatican City: Vatican Observatory, 2007.

Clifford, R. J. "The Hebrew Scriptures and the Theology of Creation." *Theological Studies* 46 (1985) 507–23.

Cobb, John. "All Things in Christ?" In *Animals on the Agenda*, edited by Andrew Linzey and Dorothy Yamamoto, 173–80. Chicago: University of Illinois Press, 1998.

Cobb, John, and David Griffin. *Process Theology: An Introductory Exposition*. Philadelphia: The Westminster, 1978.

Collins, O'Gerald. *Jesus Risen*. London: Darton, Longman and Todd, 1987.

Comblin, José. *The Holy Spirit and Liberation*. Translated by Paul Burn. Maryknoll, NY: Orbis, 1989.

Cone, James. *Black Theology of Liberation*. Maryknoll, NY: Orbis, 2010.

Conradie, Ernst. "Eat and/or Be Eaten: the Evolutionary Roots of Violence." *Scriptura* 114 (2015). http://www.scielo.org.za/scielo.php?script=sci_arttext&pid=S2305-445X2015000100027.

———. "What is the Place of the Earth in God's Economy? Doing Justice to Creation, Salvation, and Consummation." In *Christian Faith and the Earth: Current Paths and Emerging Horizons in Ecotheology*, edited by Ernst Conradie et al., 65–96. New York: Bloomsbury, 2014.

Cooper, John. *Panentheism: The Other God of the Philosophers*. Grand Rapids: Baker Academic, 2006.

Craig, William. *Time and Eternity: Exploring God's Relationship to Time*. Wheaton: Crossway, 2001.

Crisp, Oliver. *Revisioning Christology: Theology in the Reformed Tradition*. Farnham, Surrey, UK: Ashgate, 2011.

Crüsemann, Frank. "Scripture and Resurrection." Translated by Clarke Seha. In *Resurrection: Theological and Scientific Assessments*, edited by Ted Peters et al., 89–102. Grand Rapids: Eerdmans, 2002.

Davies, Paul. *The Edge of Infinity*. London: Penguin, 1994.

———. *God and the New Physics*. New York: Simon & Schuster, 1983.

———. "The Physics of Downward Causation." In *The Re-Emergence of Emergence: The Emergentist Hypothesis from Science to Religion*, edited by Philip Clayton and Paul Davies, 35–52. Oxford: Oxford University Press, 2006.

———. "Teleology without Teleology." In *Evolution and Molecular Biology*, edited by Robert Russell et al., 151–62. Vatican: Vatican Observatory, 1998.

Dawkins, Richard. *The Selfish Gene*. New York: Oxford University Press, 1989.

De Vries, Paul. "Naturalism in the Natural Sciences." *Christian Scholar's Review* 15 (1986) 388–96.

Deacon, Terrence. "Multilevel Selection and Language Evolution." In *Evolution and Learning*, edited by Bruce Weber and David Depew, 81–105. Boston: The MIT Press, 2003.

Deleuze, Gilles. *Difference and Repetition*. Translated by Paul Patton. London: Continuum, 2004.

———. *The Fold: Leibniz and the Baroque*. Translated by Tom Conley. London: Continuum, 2006.

Denis, Edwards. *Breath of Life: A Theology of the Creator Spirit*. Maryknoll, NY: Orbis, 2004.

Derrida, Jacques. *Specters of Marx*. New York: Routledge, 1994.

Downey, Edward, Jr. *The Knowledge of God in Calvin's Theology*. New York: Columbia University Press, 1952.

Dukatin, Lee A. *Cheating Monkeys and Citizen Bees: The Nature of Cooperation in Animals and Humans*. Cambridge, MA: Harvard University Press, 1999.

Dyson, Freeman. *Disturbing the Universe*. New York: Basic, 1981.

Edwards, Bruce. *C. S. Lewis: Apologist, Philosopher, and Theologian*. London: Greenwood, 2007.

Edwards, Denis. "Discovery of Chaos and the Retrieval of the Trinity." In *Chaos and Complexity: Scientific Perspectives on Divine Action*, edited by Robert Russell et al., 157–75. Vatican City: Vatican Observatory; Berkeley: CTNS, 1995.

———. *Jesus the Wisdom of God: An Ecological Theology*. Eugene, OR: Wipf & Stock, 2005.

Eldridge, Niles, and Stephen Jay Gould. "Punctuated Equilibria: An Alternative to Phyletic Gradualism." In *Models in Paleobiology*, edited by Thomas Schopf, 82–115. San Francisco: Freeman, Cooper & Co., 1972.

Ellis, George, and William Stoeger. "Intimations of Transcendence: Relations of the Mind and God." In *Neuroscience and the Person*, edited by Robert Russell et al., 449–74. Vatican City: Vatican Observatory, 1999.

———. "Introduction to General Relativity and Cosmology." In *Quantum Cosmology and the Laws of Nature: Scientific Perspectives on Divine Action*, edited by Robert Russell et al., 33–48. Vatican City: Vatican Observatory, 1993.

Finlan, Stephen. *Options on Atonement in Christian Thought*. Collegeville, MN: Liturgical, 2007.

Flanagan, Owen. "Varieties of Naturalism." In *The Oxford Handbook of Religion and Science*, edited by Philip Clayton and Zachary Simpson, 430–52. New York: Oxford University Press, 2006.

Fretheim, Terence. *God and World in the Old Testament: A Relational Theology of Creation*. Nashville: Abingdon, 2005.

———. *The Suffering of God: An Old Testament Perspective: Overtures to Biblical Theology*.Philadelphia: Fortress, 1984.

Gilkey, Langdon. "Pannenberg's *Basic Questions in Theology*: A Review Article." *Perspective* 14 (1973) 34–56.

Goodenough, Ursula. *Sacred Depths of Nature*. New York: Oxford University Press, 1998.

Gooding, David, and John Lennox. *Suffering Life's Pain: Facing the Problems of Moral and Natural Evil*, 2018.
Gould, Stephen. *Punctuated Equilibrium*. London: Belknap, 2007.
———. *Wonderful Life*. New York: W.W. Norton, 2007.
Green, Joel. "Bodies—That Is, Human Lives." In *Whatever Happened to the Soul?: Scientific and Theological Portrait of Human Nature*, edited by Warren Brown et al., 149–54. Minneapolis: Fortress, 1998.
Gregersen, Niels. "Emergence: What is at Stake for Religious Reflection?" In *The Re-Emergence of Emergence: The Emergentist Hypothesis from Science to Religion*, edited by Philip Clayton and Paul Davies, 19–35. Oxford: Oxford University Press, 2006.
———. "Three Varieties of Panentheism." In *In Whom We Live and Move and Have Our Being*, edited by Philip Clayton and Arthur Peacocke, 19–35. Grand Rapids: Eerdmans, 2004.
Gregory of Nazianzus. *Epistle 101*. Translated by Charles Brown and James Swallows. In *The Nicene and Post-Nicene Fathers* 2, edited by Philip Schaff and Henry Wace, 7:439–43. Peabody, MA: Hendrickson, 1999.
Gregory of Nyssa. *Contra Eunomium II*. Edited by Lenka Karfíková et al. Leiden: Brill, 2007.
Grantham, E. G. "Frontal Lobotomy for the Relief of Intractable Pain." *The Southern Surgeon* 16 (1950) 181–90.
Gregersen, Neils. "Deep Incarnation: Why Evolutionary Continuity Matters in Christology." *Toronto Journal of Theology* 26 (2010) 173–88.
Grenz, Stanley. *Reason for Hope: The Systematic Theology of Wolfhart Pannenberg*. Grand Rapids: Eerdmans, 2005.
———. *The Social God and Relational Self: A Trinitarian Theology of the Imago Dei*. Louisville, KY: Westminster John Knox, 2001.
———. "Wolfhart Pannenberg: Reason, Hope, and Transcendence." *The Asbury Theological Journal* 46 (1991) 73–90.
Griffin, David. "Panentheism: A Postmodern Revelation." In *In Whom We Live and Move and Have Our Being*, edited by Philip Clayton and Arthur Peacocke, 36–47. Grand Rapids: Eerdmans, 2004.
———. *Process Christology*. Philadelphia: Westminster, 1973.
Groening, Julia, et al. "In Search of Evidence for the Experience of Pain in Honeybees: A Self-Administration Study." *Science Report* 7 (2017). https://www.nature.com/articles/srep45825.
Gunton, Colin. "Introduction." In *Doctrine of Creation: Essays in Dogmatics, History and Philosophy*, edited by Colin Gunton, 1–16. London: T. & T. Clark 1997.
———. *The Triune Creator: A Historical and Systematic Study*. Edinburgh: Edinburgh University Press, 1998.
———. *The Triune Creator*. Grand Rapids: Eerdmans, 1998.
Gutenson, Charles. *Reconsidering the Doctrine of God*. London: T. & T. Clark, 2005.
Gutierrez, Gustavo. *A Theology of Liberation: History, Politics, and Salvation*. Translated by Caridad Inda and John Eagleson. Maryknoll, NY: Orbis, 1988.
Haag, James. "Nature and Nurture: The Irony of Sociobiology Debate." In *The Evolution of Evil*, edited by Gaymon Bennett et al., 99–119. Göttingen: Vandenhoeck & Ruprecht, 2008.
Hamilton, William D. "The Genetical Evolution of Social Behavior I." *Journal of Theoretical Biology* 7 (1968) 1–16.

Hardy, J. D. "The Pain Threshold and the Nature of Pain Sensation." In *The Assessment of Pain in Man and Animals*, edited by C. A. Keele and R. Smith, 170–212. London: Livingstone, 1962.

Haught, John. *Is Nature Enough?: Meaning and Truth in the Age of Science*. Cambridge: Cambridge University Press, 2006.

———. *Science and Religion: From Conflict to Conversation*. New York: Paulist, 1995.

Hawking, Stephen, and J. Hartle. "The Wave Function of the Universe." In *Physical Review* D 28 (1983) 2960–75.

Hawking, Stephen, and L. Mlodinow. *A Brief History of Time*. New York: Bantam, 2005.

Hegel, Georg. *Hegel's Philosophy of Nature: Part II of the Encyclopedia of the Philosophical Sciences (1830)*. Translated by A. V. Miller. Oxford: Clarendon, 2004.

Hick, John. *Evil and the God of Love*. San Francisco: Harper San Francisco, 1977.

Highfield, Ron. *The Faithful Creator: Affirming Creation and Providence in the Age of Anxiety*. Downers Grove, IL: InterVarsity, 2015.

Hocknull, Mark. *Pannenberg on Evil, Love and God: The Realization of Divine Love*. London: Routledge, 2016.

Holmén, Tom. *Theodicy and the Cross of Christ*. Edinburgh: T. & T. Clark, 2019.

Ingold, Timothy. *Being Alive: Essays on Movement, Knowledge, and Description*. London: Routledge, 2011.

Irenaeus. *Against Heresies*. In *The Ante-Nicene Fathers*, edited by Alexander Roberts and James Donaldson, 1:463–525. Peabody, MA: Hendrickson, 1996.

Isham, C. J., and John Polkinghorne. "The Debate over the Block Universe." In *Quantum Cosmology and the Laws of Nature: Scientific Perspectives on Divine Action*, edited by Robert Russell et al., 135–44. Vatican City: Vatican Observatory, 1993.

———. "Quantum Gravity." In *GR11: General Relativity and Gravitation*, edited by M. A. MacCallum, 99–129. Cambridge: Cambridge University Press, 1987.

Jack-McCollough, Ralph T., and James C. Nieh. "Honeybees Tune Excitatory and Inhibitory Recruitment Signaling to Resource Value and Predation Risk." *Animal Behaviour* 110 (2015) 9–17.

Jenson, Robert. *Systematic Theology: Volume 2: The Work of God*. New York: Oxford University Press, 1999.

———. *The Triune Identity: God According to the Gospel*. Eugene, OR: Wipf & Stock, 2002.

Jeon, Kwang W. "Amoeba and x-Bacteria: Symbiont Acquisition and Possible Species Change." In *Symbiogenesis as a Source of Evolutionary Innovation*, edited by Lynn Margulis and Renè Fester, 118–31. Cambridge, MA: MIT Press, 1991.

John of Damascus, "Exposition of the Orthodox Faith." Translated by S. D. F. Salmond. In *The Nicene and Post-Nicene Fathers* 2, edited by Philip Schaff and Henry Wace, 9:1–101. Peabody, MA: Hendrickson, 1994.

Johnson, Elizabeth. *She Who Is: The Mystery of God in Feminist Theological Discourse*. New York: Cross, 2017.

Jüngel, Eberhard. *God as the Mystery of the World: On the Foundation of the Theology of the Crucified One in the Dispute between Theism and Atheism*. Translated by Darrell Guder. Grand Rapids: Eerdmans, 1983.

———. "Nihil Divinitatis, Ubi Non Fides." *Zeitschrift für Theologie und Kirche* 86 (1989) 204–35.

———. "Vom Tod des lebendigen Gottes: Ein Plakat." In *Unterwegs zur Sache*, 105–25. Munich: Chr. Kaiser, 1972.

———. "The World as Possibility and Actuality: The Ontology of the Doctrine of Justification." In Eberhard Jüngel, *Theological Essays*, 95–123. Translated by J. B. Webster. Edinburgh: T. & T. Clark, 1989.

Karaca, Sibel, et al. "Humans Walking on All Four Extremities with Mental Retardation and Dysarthric or No Speech." In *Developmental Disabilities: Molecules Involved, Diagnosis, and Clinical Care*, edited by Ahmad Salehi, 81–105. Rijeka, Croatia: InTech, 2013.

Kärkkäinen, Veli-Matti. *Christ and Reconciliation: A Constructive Christian Theology for the Pluralistic World*, vol. 1. Grand Rapids: Eerdmans, 2013.

———. *Creation and Humanity*, vol. 3, *A Constructive Christian Theology for the Pluralistic World*. Grand Rapids: Eerdmans, 2015.

———. "How to Speak of the Spirit among Religions." *International Bulletin of Missionary Research* 30 (2006) 121–27.

———. *Trinity and Revelation: A Constructive Christian Theology for the Pluralistic World*, vol. 2. Grand Rapids, Eerdmans, 2014.

Kastner, R. E. "'Einselection' of Pointer Observables." *Studies in History and Philosophy of Modern Physics* 48 (2014) 56–58.

Keller, Catherine. *Apocalypse Now and Then: A Feminist Guide to the End of the World*. Minneapolis: Fortress, 2005.

———. *Cloud of the Impossible: Negative Theology and Planetary Entanglement*. New York: Columbia University Press, 2016.

———. *The Face of the Deep: The Theology of Becoming*. Abingdon: Routledge, 2003.

———. *On the Mystery: Discerning Divinity in Process*. Minneapolis: Fortress, 2008.

———. "Tingles of Matter, Tangles of Theology." In *Entangled Worlds: Religion, Science, and New Materialisms*, edited by Catherine Keller and Mary-Jane, 111–35. Rubenstein. New York: Fordham University, 2017.

Kelsey, David. *Eccentric Existence: A Theological Anthropology*, vol. 1. Louisville: Westminster John Knox, 2009.

Khuong, Thang M., et al. "Nerve Injury Drives a Heightened State of Vigilance and Neuropathic Sensitization in Drosophila." *Science Advances* 5:7 (2019). https://www.science.org/doi/10.1126/sciadv.aaw4099.

Kim, Jaegwon. "The Non-Reductivist's Troubles with Mental Causation." In *Mental Causation*, edited by John Heil and Alfred Mele, 189–210. Oxford: Oxford University Press, 1995.

———. *Physicalism, or Something Near Enough*. Princeton: Princeton University Press, 2006.

Kingsley, Charles. *The Water Babies*. London: Hodder and Stoughton, 1930.

Knight, Christopher. "Theistic Naturalism and the World Made Flesh: Complementary Approaches to the Debate on Panentheism." In *In Whom We Live and Move and Have Our Being*, edited by Philip Clayton and Arthur Peacocke, 48–61. Grand Rapids: Eerdmans, 2004.

Koperski, Jeffrey. "God, Chaos, and the Quantum Dice." *Zygon* 35 (2000) 545–60.

Kropf, Richard W. *Evil and Evolution: A Theodicy*. Cranbury: Associated University Press, 1984.

Kryst, Slias. *Quest Profundus*. London: Balboa, 2012.

Küng, Hans. *The Beginning of All Things: Science and Religion*. Translated by John Bowden. Grand Rapids: Eerdmans, 2007.

Lakatos, Imre. "Falsification and the Methodology of Scientific Research Programmes." In *Criticism and Growth of Knowledge*, edited by I. Lakatos and A. Musgrave, 91–196. Cambridge: Cambridge University Press, 1970.

Learn, Joshua R. "Killer Whales are Bullies, and Humpback Whales are Bouncers." *Hakai Megazine: Coastal Science and Societies* (08/03/2016). https://hakaimagazine.com/news/killer-whales-are-bullies-and-humpbacks-are-bouncers/.

Leslie, John. *Universes*. London: Routledge, 1989.

Linzey, Andrew. *Christianity and the Rights of Animals*. London: SPCK, 1987.

Lossy, Vladimir. *Mystical Theology of the Eastern Church*. Cambridge: James Clarke & Co., 1991.

Louth, Andrew. "The Cosmic Vision of Saint Maximus the Confessor." In *In Whom We Live and Move and Have Our Being*, edited by Philip Clayton and Arthur Peacocke, 184–96. Grand Rapids: Eerdmans, 2007.

Luther, Martin. *Luther's Works*, vol. 1. Edited by Jaroslav Pelikan. Philadelphia: Fortress, 1958.

———. "On the Councils and the Church" (1539). In *Luther's Works*, edited by Jaroslav Pelikan and Helmut Lehmann, 41:9–178. Philadelphia: Fortress, 1966.

———. *Weimarer Ausgabe*. Vol. 10. Weimar: Hermann Böhlau, 1889.

MacIntyre, Alasdair. *In Whose Justice? Which Rationality?* Notre Dame: The University of Notre Dame Press, 1988.

Margulis, Lynn, and Sagan, Dorion. *Acquiring Genomes: A Theory of the Origin of Species*. New York: Basic, 2006.

McDaniel, Jay. "Can Animal Suffering be Reconciled with Belief in an All-Loving God?" In *Animals on the Agenda*, edited by Andrew Linzey and Dorothy Yamamoto, 161–72. Chicago: University of Illinois Press, 1998.

McFague, Sallie. *Body of God: An Ecological Theology*. Minneapolis: Fortress, 1993.

———. *Metaphorical Theology: Models of God in Religious Language*. Philadelphia: Fortress, 1982.

McFarland, Ian A. *Creation and Humanity: The Sources of Christian Theology*. Kentucky: WJK, 2009.

McGrath, Alister. *Christian Theology: An Introduction*. Hoboken: Wiley-Blackwell, 2011.

———. *A Fine-Tuned Universe: The Quest for God in Science and Theology*. Louisville, KY: Westminster John Knox, 2009.

———. *A Scientific Theology*, vol. 1, *Nature*. Grand Rapids: T. & T. Clark, 2001.

———. *A Scientific Theology*, vol. 2, *Reality*. Grand Rapids: Eerdmans, 2003.

———. *A Scientific Theology*, vol. 3, *Theory*. Grand Rapids: Eerdmans, 2003.

Migliore, Daniel. *Faith Seeking Understanding: An Introduction to Christian Theology*. Grand Rapids: Eerdmans, 2014.

Miller, Kenneth R. *Finding Darwin's God*. New York: Cliff Street, 1991.

Moltmann, Jürgen. *The Crucified God: The Cross of Christ as the Foundation and Criticism of Christian Theology*. Translated by Margaret Kohl. Minneapolis: Fortress, 1993.

———. *God in Creation: A New Theology of Creation and the Spirit*. Translated by Margaret Kohl. Minneapolis: Fortress, 1993.

———. "Reflection on Chaos and God's Interaction with the World from a Trinitarian Perspective." In *Chaos and Complexity: Scientific Perspectives on Divine Action*, edited by Robert Russell et al., 205–10. Vatican City: Vatican Observatory, 1995.

———. *The Spirit of Life: A Universal Affirmation*. Translated by Margaret Kohl. Minneapolis: Fortress, 1992.

———. *Sun of Righteousness, Arise!* Translated by Margaret Kohl. Minneapolis: Fortress, 2010.

———. *The Way of Jesus Christ: Christology in Messianic Dimensions*. Translated by Margaret Kohl. Minneapolis: Fortress, 1993.

Monod, Jacques. *Chance and Necessity*. London: Penguin, 1997.

Moritz, Joshua. "Contingency, Convergence, Constraints, and the Challenge from Theodicy in Creation's Evolution." In *God's Providence and Randomness in Nature: Theological and Scientific Perspectives*, edited by Robert Russell and Joshua Moritz, 293–332. West Conshohocken: Templeton, 2019.

———. "Evolutionary Evil and Darwin's Black Box." In *The Evolution of Evil*, edited by Gaymon Bennett et al., 143–88. Göttingen: Vandenhoeck and Ruprecht, 2008.

———. "Evolutionary Evil and Dawkins' Black Box." In *The Evolution of Evil*, edited by Gaymon Bennett et al., 143–88. Göttingen: Vandenhoeck & Ruprecht, 2008.

Morowitz, Harold. *The Emergence of Everything*. New York: Oxford University Press, 2002.

Morris, Henry. "Biblical Eschatology and Modern Science." *Bibliotheca Sacra* 125 (1968) 291–99.

Moss, Lenny. "From Representational Preformationism to the Epigenesis of Openness to the Word?" *Annals of the New York Academy of Sciences* 981 (2002) 219–30.

Mostert, Christiaan. *God and the Future: Wolfhart Pannenberg's Eschatological Doctrine of God*. New York: T. & T. Clark, 2002.

Moule, C. F. D. *The Holy Spirit*. Eugene, OR: Wipf & Stock, 1997.

———. "The Theology of Forgiveness." In *Essays in New Testament Interpretation*, 250–60. Cambridge: Cambridge University Press, 1982.

Muller, Richard. *Post-Reformation Reformed Dogmatics: The Divine Essence and Attributes*, vol. 3. Grand Rapids: Baker, 2003.

Murphy, Nancey. *Bodies and Souls, or Spirited Bodies?* Cambridge: Cambridge University Press, 2006.

———. "Divine Action and Natural Order: Buridan's Ass and Schrödinger's Cat." In *Chaos and Complexity: Scientific Perspectives on Divine Action*, edited by Robert Russell et al., 289–324. Vatican City: Vatican Observatory, 1995.

———. "Emergence, Downward Causation and Divine Action." In *Scientific Perspectives on Divine Action: Twenty Years of Challenge and Progress*, edited by Robert Russell et al., 111–32. Vatican City: Vatican Observatory, 2008.

———. "Evidence of Design in the Fine-Tuning of the Universe." In *Quantum Cosmology and the Laws of Nature*, edited by Robert Russell et al., 407–36. Vatican City: Vatican Observatory, 1993.

Murphy, Nancey, and George Ellis. *On the Moral Nature of the Universe*. Minneapolis: Fortress, 1996.

Murphy, Nancey, and Warren Brown. *Did My Neurons Make Me Do It?: Philosophical and Neurobiological Perspectives on Moral Responsibility and Free Will*. New York: Oxford University Press, 2007.

Murray, Michael. *Nature Red in Tooth and Claw: Theism and the Problem of Animal Suffering*. New York: Oxford University Press, 2008.

Nagel, Thomas. *Mind and Cosmos: Why the Materialist Neo-Darwinian Conception of Nature is Almost Certainly False*. New York: Oxford University Press, 2012.

Newbigin, Lesslie. *The Gospel in a Pluralist Society.* Grand Rapids: Eerdmans, 1994.
Ngien, Dennis. *Luther's Theology of the Cross.* Eugene, OR: Cascade, 2018.
Nicholas of Cusa. "De Visione Dei." In *Nicholas of Cusa: Selected Spiritual Writings,* edited and translated by H. Lawrence Bond. New York: Paulist, 1997.
———. "On the Summit of Contemplation." In *Nicholas of Cusa: Selected Spiritual Writings,* edited and translated by H. Lawrence Bond. New York: Paulist, 1997.
Numbers, Ronald. "Science without God: Natural Laws and Christian Beliefs." In *When Science and Christianity Meet,* edited by David Lindberg and Ronald Numbers, 265–86. Chicago: The University of Chicago, 2003.
O'Collins, Gerald. *Jesus Risen.* London: Darton, Longman and Todd, 1987.
Olsen, Roger. "Wolfhart Pannenberg's Doctrine of the Trinity." *SJT* 32 (1990) 175–206.
Oord, Thomas Jay. *The Uncontrolling Love of God.* Downers Grove, IL: InterVarsity, 2015.
Oyama, Susan. *The Ontogeny of Information: Developmental Systems and Evolution.* Durham: Duke University, 2000.
Oyama, Susan, et al. *Cycles of Contingency: Developmental Systems and Evolution.* Cambridge, MA: The MIT Press, 2001.
Page, Ruth. *God and the Web of Creation.* London: SCM, 1996.
Pannenberg, Wolfhart. "The Concept of Miracle." *Zygon* 37 (2002) 759–62.
———. "Den Glauben an Ihm Selbs Fassen und Verstehen: Eine Antwort." *Zeitschrift für Theologie und Kirche* 86 (1989) 355–70.
———. "Divine Economy and Eternal Trinity." In *Theology of John Zizioulas,* edited by Douglas Knight, 79–86. Aldershot, UK: Ashgate, 2007.
———. "The Doctrine of Creation and Modern Science." *Zygon* 23 (1988) 3–21.
———. *The Historicity of Nature: Essays on Science and Theology.* Edited by Niels Gregersen. Philadelphia: Templeton Foundation, 2007.
———. *An Introduction to Systematic Theology.* Grand Rapids: Eerdmans, 1991.
———. *Metaphysics and the Idea of God.* Translated by Philip Clayton. Grand Rapids: Eerdmans, 1990.
———. *Revelation as History.* Translated by David Granskow. New York: MacMillan, 1969.
———. "Speaking about God in the Face of Atheistic Criticism." In *The Idea of God and Human Freedom.* Translated by R. A. Wilson. London: SCM, 1973.
———. *Systematic Theology,* vol. 1. Translated by Geoffrey Bromiley. Grand Rapids: Eerdmans, 1992.
———. *Systematic Theology,* vol. 2. Translated by Geoffrey Bromiley. Grand Rapids: Eerdmans, 1991.
———. *Systematic Theology,* vol. 3. Translated by Geoffrey Bromiley. Grand Rapids: Eerdmans, 1998.
———. "Theological Appropriation of Scientific Understandings: Response to Hefner, Wicken, Eaves, and Tipler." *Zygon* 24 (1989) 255–71.
———. "Theological Appropriation of Scientific Understandings." In *Beginning with the End,* edited by Carol Albright and Joel Haugen, 427–44. Chicago: Open Court, 1997.
———. "Theological Questions to Scientists." In *Beginning with the End: God, Science, and Wolfhart Pannenberg,* edited by Carol Rausch Albright and Joel Haugen, 37–50. Chicago: Open Court, 1997.

———. *Theology and the Kingdom of God*. Edited by Richard John Neuhaus. Louisville, KY: Westminster John Knox, 1969.

———. *Theology and the Philosophy of Science*. Translated by Francis McDonaugh. Philadelphia: Westminster, 1976.

———. "Theology and Science." *Princeton Seminary Bulletin* 13 (1992) 299–310.

———. *Toward a Theology of Nature: Essays on Science and Faith*. Edited by Ted Peters. Louisville: Westminster/John Knox, 1993.

———. "The Working of the Spirit in the Creation and in the People of God." In *Spirit, Faith, and Church*, edited by Wolfhart Pannenberg, et al., 13–31. Philadelphia: Westminster, 1970.

Peacocke, Arthur. "Biological Evolution: A Positive Theological Appraisal." In *Evolutionary and Molecular Biology: Scientific Perspectives on Divine Action*, edited by Robert Russell et al., 357–76. Vatican City: VO/CTNS, 1998.

———. "Biology and a Theology of Evolution." *Zygon* 34 (1999) 695–712.

———. "Chance and Law in Irreversible Thermodynamics, Theoretical Biology, and Theology." In *Chaos and Complexity: Scientific Perspectives on Divine Action*, edited by Robert Russell et al., 124–43. Vatican: Vatican Observatory, 2000.

———. "The Cost of New Life." In *The Work of Love*, edited by John Polkinghorne, 21–42. Grand Rapids: Eerdmans, 2001.

———. *Creation and the World of Science: The Reshaping of Belief*. Oxford: Oxford University Press, 2004.

———. "Emergence, Mind, and Divine Action." In *The Re-Emergence of Emergence: The Emergentist Hypothesis from Science to Religion*, edited by Philip Clayton and Paul Davies, 257–78. Oxford: Oxford University Press, 2006.

———. "God's Interaction with the World." In *Chaos and Complexity: Scientific Perspectives on Divine Action*, edited by Robert Russell et al., 263–88. Vatican City: Vatican Observatory, 1995.

———. "A Naturalistic Christian Faith for the Twenty-First Century: An Essay in Interpretation." In *All That Is: A Naturalistic Faith for the Twenty-First Century*, edited by Philip Clayton, 3–56. Minneapolis: Fortress, 2007.

———. *The Palace of Glory: God's World and Science*. Adelaide: ATF, 2005.

———. *Paths from Science Towards God: The End of All Our Exploring*. New York: One World, 2001.

———. *Theology for a Scientific Age: Being and Becoming—Natural, Divine, and Human*. Minneapolis: Fortress, 1993.

Penrose, Roger. *The Emperor's New Mind: Connecting Computers, Minds, and the Laws of Physics*. Oxford: Oxford University Press, 2016.

———. "Quantum Physics and Conscious Thought." In *Quantum Implications*, edited by B. J. Hiley and F. David Peat, 105–20. London: Routledge, 1987.

Peters, Karl. *Dancing with the Sacred: Evolution, Ecology, and God*. Harrisburg: Trinity Press International, 2002.

Peters, Ted. "Apocalypse Now and Then: A Feminist Approach to the End of the World." *Theology Today* 54 (1997) 243–46.

———. "Evolution, Evil, and the Theology of the Cross." *Svensk Teologisk Kvartalskrift* 83 (2007) 98–120.

———. "The Evolution of Evil." In *The Evolution of Evil*, edited by Gaymon Bennett et al., 19–52. Göttingen: Vandenhoeck and Ruprecht, 2008.

———. *God as Trinity: Relationality and Temporality in Divine Life*. Louisville, KY: Westminster John Knox, 1993.

———. *God—The World's Future: Systematic Theology for a New Era*. Augsburg: Fortress, 2002.

———. "On Creating the Cosmos." In *Physics, Philosophy, and Theology*, edited by Robert Russell et al., 273–96. Vatican Observatory, 1988.

———. *Playing God?* NY: Routledge, 2003.

———. "Resurrection: The Conceptual Challenge." In *Resurrection: Theological and Scientific Assessments*, edited by Ted Peters et al., 297–321. Grand Rapids: Eerdmans, 2002.

———. A Review of Keller's *Apocalypse Now and Then*, *Theology. Today* 54 (July 1997) 243–46.

———, ed. *Science and Theology: New Consonance*. Boulder, CO: Westview, 1998.

———. "Science and Theology: Toward Consonance." In *Science and Theology: New Consonance*, edited by Ted Peters, 13–21. Boulder, CO: Westview, 1998.

Peters, Ted, and Martinez Hewlett. *Evolution from Creation to New Creation*. Nashville: Abingdon, 2003.

Peterson, Gregory. "Whither Panentheism?" *Zygon* 36 (2001) 395–405.

Pinnock, Clark. *Flame of Love: A Theology of the Holy Spirit*. Downers Grove, IL: InterVarsity, 1996.

Polkinghorne, John. "Eschatological Credibility: Emergent and Teleological Processes." In *Resurrection: Theological and Scientific Assessments*, edited by Ted Peters et al., 43–55. Grand Rapids: Eerdmans, 2002.

———. "Eschatology: Some Questions and Some Insights from Science." In *The End of the World and the Ends of God: Science and Theology on Eschatology*, edited by John Polkinghorne and Michael Welker, 29–41. Grand Rapids: Eerdmans, 2002.

———. *Faith, Science and Understanding*. London: SPCK, 2000.

———. "Fields and Theology: A Response to Wolfhart Pannenberg." *Zygon* 36 (2001) 795–97.

———. *The God of Hope and the End of the World*. New Haven, CT: Yale University Press, 2002.

———. "Kenotic Creation and Divine Action." In *The Work of Love: Creation as Kenosis*, edited by John Polkinghorne, 90–106. Grand Rapids: Eerdmans, 2001.

———. *The Quantum World*. Princeton, NJ: Princeton University Press, 1984.

———. *Science and Religion in Quest of Truth*. London: SPCK, 2011.

———. *Scientists as Theologians: A Comparison of The Writings of Ian Barbour, Arthur Peacocke, and John Polkinghorne*. London: SPCK, 1996.

———. *Science and Theology: An Introduction*. London: SPCK, 1998.

Prigogine, Ilya, and Isabelle Stenger. *Order Out of Chaos: Man's New Dialogue with Nature*. 2nd ed. London: Verso, 2017.

Pseudo-Dionysius. "The Divine Names." In *Pseudo-Dionysius: The Complete Works*. Translated by Colm Luibhéid and Paul Rorem. New York: Paulist, 1983.

———. *The Mystical Theology*. Translated by Colm Luibhéid and Paul Rorem. New York: Paulist, 1987.

Rahner, Karl. "A Fragmentary Aspect of a Theological Evaluation of the Concept of the Future." In Karl Rahner, *Theological Investigations*, 10:235–41. New York: Crossroad, 1973.

———. *The Trinity*. Translated by Joseph Donceel. New York: Crossroad, 1996.

Ritchie, Sarah. *Divine Action and the Human Mind*. Cambridge: Cambridge University Press, 2019.

Rittgers, Ronald. *The Reformation of Suffering: Pastoral Theology and Lay Piety in Late Medieval and Early Modern Germany*. Oxford: Oxford University Press, 2012.

Rivera, Mayra. *The Touch of Transcendence: A Postcolonial Theology of God*. Louisville, KY: Westminster John Knox, 2007.

Rolston, Holmes, III. *Science and Religion: A Critical Survey*. New York: Random House, 1987.

Rothschild, Lynn. "The Role of Emergence in Biology." In *The Re-Emergence of Emergence: The Emergentist Hypothesis from Science to Religion*, edited by Philip Clayton and Paul Davies, 151–65. Oxford: Oxford University Press, 2006.

Ruse, Michael. "Darwinism and Christianity: Does Evil Spoil a Beautiful Friendship?" In *The Evolution of Evil*, edited by Gaymon Bennett et al., 86–98. Göttingen: Vandenhoeck and Ruprecht, 2008.

Russell, Robert. "Arthur Peacocke on Method in Theology and Science and His Model of the Divine/World Interaction: An Appreciative Assessment." In *All That Is*, edited by Philip Clayton, 140–51. Minneapolis: Fortress, 2007.

———. "Contingency in Physics and Cosmology: A Critique of the Theology of Wolfhart Pannenberg." *Zygon* 23 (1988) 23–43.

———. *Cosmology, Evolution, and Resurrection Hope: Theology and Science in Creative Mutual Interaction*. Edited by Carl Helrich. Ontario: Pandora, 2001.

———. "Divine Action and Quantum Mechanics." In *Philosophy, Science, and Divine Action*, edited by F. LeRon Schultz, et al., 1:351–404. Leiden: Brill, 2009.

———. "Entropy and Evil." *Zygon* 19 (1984) 449–69.

———. "Eschatology and Physical Cosmology: A Preliminary Reflection." In *The Far-Future Universe*, edited by George Ellis, 266–315. Vatican City: Vatican Observatory, 2002.

———. "Eschatology and Scientific Cosmology." In *What God Knows: Eternity and Divine Knowledge*, edited by Harry Poe and Stanley Mattson, 95–120. Waco, TX: Baylor University Press, 2005.

———. "The Groaning of Creation: Does God Suffer with All Life?" In *The Evolution of Evil*, edited by Gaymon Bennett et al., 120–42. Göttingen: Vandenhoeck & Ruprecht, 2008.

———. "Physics, Cosmology, and the Challenge to Consequentialist Natural Theodicy." In *Physics and Cosmology, Scientific Perspectives on the Problem of Natural Evil*, edited by Nancey Murphy, et al., 1:109–30. Vatican: Vatican Observatory; Berkeley: CTNS, 2007.

———. "The Physics of David Bohm and Its Relevance to Philosophy and Theology." *Zygon* 20 (1985) 135–58.

———. "Time and Eternity: Special Relativity & Eschatology." *Dialog: A Journal of Theology* 39 (2000) 46–55.

———. *Time in Eternity: Pannenberg, Physics, and Eschatology in Creative Mutual Interaction*. Notre Dame: University of Notre Dame Press, 2012.

———. "What We've Learned from Quantum Mechanics." In *God's Providence and Randomness in Nature: Theological and Scientific Perspectives*, edited by Robert Russell and Joshua Moritz, 136–69. West Conshohocken: Templeton, 2019.

Santimire, Paul. *The Travail of Nature: The Ambiguous Ecological Promise of Christian Theology*. Minneapolis: Fortress, 1985.

Schloss, Jeffrey. "From Evolution to Eschatology." In *Resurrection: Theological and Scientific Assessments*, edited by Ted Peters, et al., 65–85. Grand Rapids: Eerdmans, 2002.

Schloss, Jeffrey, and John D. Liang. "Evolution and Death." https://biologos.org/series/southern-baptist-voices/articles/southern-baptist-voices-evolution-and-death.

Scholem, Gershom. *Zohar: The Book of Enlightenment*. Mahwah, NJ: Paulist, 1983.

Schwarz, Hans. *Eschatology*. Grand Rapids: Eerdmans, 2001.

Schweisguth, Frančois and Francis Corson. "Self-Organization in Pattern Formation." *Developmental Cell* 3 (2019) 659–77.

Shin, Jongseock. "The Church as a Messianic Fellowship in Jürgen Moltmann's and Wolfhart Pannenberg's Public Ecclesiology." *The Evangelical Review of Theology and Politics* 7 (2019) 23–37.

———. "The Cosmic Spirit's Creatorship and Redeemership in the Context of Natural Theodicy." In *T. & T. Clark Handbook of Suffering and Evil*, edited by Matthias Grebe and Johannes Groessl. Edinburgh: T. & T. Clark, forthcoming.

———. "Non-Anthropocentric Understanding of the Trinitarian Creatorship and Redeemership in an Age of Science." *Neue Zeitschrift für Systematische Theologie und Religionsphilosophie* 64 (2022) 1–23.

———. "The Spirit's Pathetic and Redemptive Presence in Global Capitalism." *Pneuma* 42 (2020) 24–49.

Shults, F. LeRon. *Reforming the Doctrine of God*. Grand Rapids: Eerdmans, 2005.

Sobrino, Jon. *Jesus the Liberator: A Historical Theological Reading of Jesus of Nazareth*. Translated by Paul Burns and Francis McDonagh. London: Burns and Oates, 1994.

Sollereder, Bethany. *God, Evolution, and Animal Suffering: Theodicy without a Fall*. New York: Routledge, 2018.

Southgate, Christopher. "God and Evolutionary Evil: Theodicy in the Light of Darwinism." *Zygon* 37 (2002) 803–24.

———. *The Groaning of Creation: God, Evolution, and the Problem of Evil*. Louisville, KY: Westminster John Knox, 2008.

———. "Varieties of Theodicy." In *Physics and Cosmology, Scientific Perspectives on the Problem of Natural Evil*, edited by Nancey Murphy, et al., 1:67–92. Vatican: Vatican Observatory, 2007.

Southgate, Christopher, and Robinson, Andrew. "Creation as 'Very Good' and 'Groaning in Travail': An Exploration in Evolutionary Theology." In *The Evolution of Evil*, edited by Gaymon Bennett et al., 53–85. Göttingen: Vandenhoeck & Ruprecht, 2008.

Spitzer, Robert. *New Proofs for the Existence of God*. Grand Rapids: Eerdmans, 2010.

Stoeger, William. "The Immanent Directionality of the Evolutionary Process, and Its Relationship to Teleology." In *Evolutionary and Molecular Biology: Scientific Perspectives on Divine Action*, edited by Robert Russell et al., 163–90. Vatican City: VO/CTNS, 1998.

———. "Scientific Accounts of Ultimate Catastrophes in Our Life-Bearing Universe." In *The End of the World and the Ends of God: Science and Theology on Eschatology*, edited by John Polkinghorne and Michael Welker, 19–28. Philadelphia: Trinity Press International, 2000.

Tanner, Kathryn. *Christ the Key*. New York: Cambridge University Press, 2010.

Taylor, Iain. *Pannenberg on the Triune God*. London: T. & T. Clark, 2007.

Taylor, Mark. *After God*. Chicago: The University of Chicago Press, 2007.

Terrence, Deacon. "Multilevel Selection in a Complex Adaptive System." In *Evolution and Learning: The Baldwin Effect Reconsidered*, edited by Bruce Weber and David Depew, 81–106. Cambridge, MA: MIT Press, 2003.

Theophilus of Antioch. *To Autoclycus*. In *The Ante-Nicene Fathers*, edited by Alexander Roberts and James Donaldson, 2:87–122. Peabody, MA: Hendrickson, 1996.

Tillich, Paul. *Systematic Theology*, vol. 1. Chicago: The University of Chicago Press, 1973.

Tooley, Michael. *Time, Tense, and Causation*. Oxford: Clarendon, 1997.

Torrance, T. F. *Divine and Contingent Order*. Edinburgh: T. & T. Clark, 1998.

Trivers, Robert L. "The Evolution of Reciprocal Altruism." *The Quarterly Review of Biology* 46 (1971) 35–57.

Troeltsch, Ernst. "On the Historical and Dogmatic Methods in Theology [1898]." Translated by Jack Forstman. In *Gesammelte Schriften*, 2:728–53. Tubingen: J.C.B. Mohr, 1913.

Vanhoozer, Kevin. *The Drama of Doctrine*. Louisville, KY: Westminster John Knox, 2005.

Vanhoozer, Kevin, and Daniel Treier. *Theology and the Mirror of Scripture*. Downers Grove, IL: InterVarsity, 2015.

Van Til, Howard. "The Creation: Intelligently Designed or Optimally Equipped?" *Theology Today* 55 (1998) 344–64.

Wanjek, Christopher. "Your Diet Affects Your Grandchildren's DNA, Scientists Say." *Live Science*, July 27, 2012. https://www.livescience.com/21902- diet-epigenetics-grandchildren.html.

Ward, Keith. *God, Chance and Necessity*. Oxford: One World, 1996.

———. "Personhood, Spirit, and the Supernatural." In *All That Is*, edited by Philip Clayton, 152–62. Minneapolis: Fortress, 2007.

———. *Rational Theology and the Creativity of God*. New York: Pilgrim, 1982.

———. *Religion and Revelation: A Theology of Revelation in the World's Religions*. New York: Oxford University Press, 1994.

Ware, Kallistos. "God Immanent yet Transcendent: The Divine Energies according to Saint Gregory Palamas." In *In Whom We Live and Move and Have Our Being*, edited by Arthur Peacocke and Philip Clayton, 157–68. Grand Rapids: Eerdmans, 2004.

Wcislo, W. T. "Behavioral Environments and Evolutionary Change." *Annual Review of Ecology and Systematics* 20 (1989) 137–69.

Weder, Hans. "Hope and Creation." In *The End of the World and the Ends of God: Science and Theology on Eschatology*, edited by John Polkinghorne and Michael Welker, 184–202. Philadelphia: Trinity Press International, 2000.

Wegter-McNelly, Kirk. "Atoms May Be Small, But They're Everywhere." In *God's Action in Nature's World: Essays in Honour of Robert John Russell*, edited by Ted Peters and Nathan Hallanger, 93–112. New York: Routledge, 2016.

Wenz, Gunther. *Introduction to Wolfhart Pannenberg's Systematic Theology*. Göttingen: Vandenhoeck & Ruprecht, 2013.

Wesley Wildman. "Use and Meaning of the Word 'Suffering' in Relation to Nature." In *Physics and Cosmology: Scientific Perspectives on the Problem of Natural Evil*, edited by Nancey Murphy et al., 1:53–66. Vatican City: Vatican Observatory, 2008.

Westermann, Claus. *Creation*. Translated by John Scullion. Philadelphia: Fortress, 1974.

Whitehead, Alfred. *Religion in the Making*. New York: The World, 1960.

Whitfield, J. B. "Phylogeny and Evolution of Host-Parasitoid Interactions in Hymenoptera." *Annual Review of Entomology* 43 (1998) 129–51.

Wicken, Jeffrey. "Theology and Science in the Evolving Cosmos." *Zygon* 23 (1988) 45–55.

Whitehead, Alfred. *Religion in the Making.* New York: The World, 1960.

Wilkinson, David. *Christian Eschatology and the Physical Universe.* New York: Continuum, 2010.

Worthing, Mark. "Christian Theism and the Idea of an Oscillating Universe." In *God, Life, and the Cosmos,* edited by Ted Peters et al., 281–301. Aldershot, UK: Ashgate, 2002.

Wright, Christopher. *The Mission of God: Unlocking the Bible's Grand Narrative.* Downers Grove, IL: InterVarsity, 2006.

Wright, N. T. "Jesus' Resurrection and Christian Origins." *Gregorianum* 83 (2002) 615–35.

———. *The Resurrection of the Son of God.* London: SPCK, 2003.

Wright, N. T., and John Dominic Crossan. "The Resurrection: Historical Event or Theological Explanation?: A Dialogue." In *The Resurrection of Jesus: John Dominic Crossan and N.T. Wright in Dialogue,* edited by Robert B. Stewart, 16–47. Augsburg: Fortress, 2006.

Wright, Terry. *Providence Made Flesh: Divine Presence as a Framework for a Theology of Providence.* Eugene, OR: Wipf & Stock, 2009.

Zeil, Jochen, et al. "Looking and Homing: How Displaced Ants Decide Where To Go." *Philosophical Transactions of the Royal Society B* 369 (2014) 1–13.

Zizioulas, John. "Preserving God's Creation." *KTR* 12 (1989) 1–5.

Index

adaptation, 62, 231
altruism, 62, 123–24, 159, 200, 208–10
Anthropic Principle, 80, 100, 144, 164, 170, 173, 179, 195
Aristotle, Aristotelian 54, 70, 240
arrow of time, 225, 143–47, 160, 225
assimilation, 22, 109
atheism, 24, 65, 78
Augustine, 35, 59, 145, 179, 193

Barbour, Ian, 9, 20, 22, 62, 104, 107, 110, 167, 191, 202, 203, 204, 232
Barth, Karl, 259
Bell's Theorem, 176,203
Bloesch, Donald, 245
big-bang cosmologies, 115, 117, 141, 142, 164, 170, 173, 181, 194, 197, 228, 259
biology, 1, 4, 8, 32, 45, 47, 52, 68, 79, 111, 137, 148, 149, 210, 224, 230, 260
Brett, Paul 8
Bultmannian "two-language" perspectives, 127, 259

Calvin, John, 36, 43, 65, 94
causation
    bottom-up, 3, 5, 22, 75, 82–83, 89, 117–21, 123, 159, 175, 201–6
    lateral, 178

    Top-down, 178, 206–10
    whole-part, 11, 13, 81–83, 240, 242, 243, 257
chance and law-like regularities, 4, 24, 45–48, 56–57, 62, 65, 69, 77, 83, 85, 95, 97, 108, 115, 153, 162, 175, 223, 238, 256
Christology, cosmic, 7, 16, 27, 35, 36, 38, 39, 41, 43, 60, 67, 131
chromosome, 200
complexity, 9, 10, 11, 21, 33, 45, 46, 76, 80, 81, 85, 87, 91, 95, 110, 159, 178, 199, 206, 208, 216, 218, 220, 225, 229, 231, 249
concursus, 158, 163
contingency, 3, 7, 12, 18, 23, 27, 30, 39, 50, 54–57, 63, 66, 73, 76, 83, 101, 112, 116, 121, 123, 132–34, 143, 146, 148, 152–54, 159, 170 74, 195, 206, 208, 222–24, 226–29, 240–43, 246, 251
cosmology, 116, 137, 142, 160, 170, 174, 176, 181, 183, 194, 195, 258
creatio continua, 2–5, 26–27, 43, 48, 56–57, 71, 76, 79–86, 98–101, 126, 132–34, 136–38, 143–47, 153–57, 169, 174–78, 181, 184, 194–202, 240–43, 246–48

Index

creatio ex nihilo, 1–5, 12–13, 15, 30, 38–44, 53, 58, 75, 78–81, 108, 112–16, 125–26, 133–34, 141–43, 160, 170–74, 224–26
creatio ex profundis, 13, 98–101, 250, 258
creatio ex vetere, 13, 27, 75, 92, 133, 160, 169, 181, 196, 224–26
creationism, 4, 260
critical mutual interaction (CMI), 137, 164, 184, 193, 258, 259, 260
cross, the theology of, 26–27, 39, 43, 61–63, 71, 91, 102, 108, 131, 180, 211, 217, 233

Darwin, Charles, 47
(neo-) Darwinian, 47, 51, 56, 61, 125, 198, 210, 238, 257
Davies, Paul, 120, 227
death and decay, 6, 29, 31, 58, 72, 101, 153, 216
deism, 11, 24, 65, 72, 74, 85, 107, 175
determinism, 119, 159, 176, 204, 205
divine action, 5, 11, 12, 15, 18, 52, 62, 64, 75, 78, 86, 109, 117, 119, 121, 124, 133, 135–36, 157, 164, 174–78, 198, 201, 206, 216, 221
divine providence, 2, 24, 36, 38, 109, 202, 237
dualism(s), 35, 38, 171, 215, 246

Eastern orthodox, 2, 35, 36, 63, 66
ecological, 81, 162, 177, 200, 201, 215, 248
economy of salvation, 8, 35, 131, 258
Edwards, Denis, 69, 235
Eldridge, Niles, 47
Ellis, George, 20, 61, 205, 236–38
embodiment, 36, 56, 86, 93, 105, 129, 160, 189, 210, 215, 216,
emergence of consciousness, 85, 87, 108, 124, 210
emergence, strong, 52, 120, 230
emergence, weak, 52, 82
energies, divine, 66, 70
Enlightenment, 38
entropy, 31, 45, 57–58, 87, 101, 115, 153–55, 180, 197–98, 228, 247
environment, 68, 230, 239, 251,

epigenesis, 61, 148, 199, 230–232, 238
epistemological holism, 11, 236
eschatological ontology, 5, 13, 28, 62, 137, 164, 168, 190, 223, 226, 230, 234–36, 240
evolution, theistic, 50, 170, 175, 180
evil, natural and cosmic, 5–7, 34–35, 75, 101, 162, 179, 190
evolutionary biology, 1, 8, 47, 56, 68, 137
evolutionary/developmental biology, 148
extinction, 9, 33, 58, 61, 180, 198

faith, 160, 167, 190, 229, 258, 262
fall, 18, 35, 235
field theory, 149, 150, 202, 207
flowing time, 54, 183–90, 201, 218, 223, 225, 226
foreknowledge, divine, 65, 251
free will, 186, 206, 233
freedom of God, 66, 160, 196, 245, 246
free-will and free-process defense, 58
fundamentalism, 4

general theory of relativity, 57, 121, 146, 171, 181
genetic mutations, 15, 200, 206, 210, 232, 260
genome, 231
Gilkey, Langdon, 4, 146
Gnosticism, 42, 112
good-and-harm analysis, 58, 60, 88, 102, 163, 197
Goodenough, Ursula, 51
goodness of creation, 1, 9, 18, 58, 67, 73, 92, 102, 122, 133, 143, 154, 168, 182, 190, 198, 237, 247
Gould, Stephen Jay, 47, 51
governance, divine, 2–3, 201, 208
gradualism, 47
Gunton, Colin, 8, 25, 26, 43, 54, 65, 223, 251

habitat, 33, 68
Hartle-Hawking model, 80, 170–74, 194–95, 206, 226
Haught, John, 51, 259
Hefner, Philip, 261

Index

Heisenberg unpredictability principle, 80, 117, 176
Hoknull, Mark, 247
Homo erectus, 45
Homo sapiens, 45, 48, 58, 80, 84, 108, 124
Hume, David, 18, 127
hylomorphism, 55
hypostatic union, 68, 245

idealism, 24, 203
imago Dei, 35–36, 44, 56, 61, 157, 238, 261
immanence, divine, 5, 26, 28, 60, 63, 72, 86, 92, 103, 112, 118, 138, 233, 246
immanent Trinity, 155, 187, 254
immanent transcendence, 132, 147
immutability, 156, 241, 245
Incarnation, 179, 212, 223, 243, 245
indeterminacy, 20, 76, 83, 96, 117, 118, 143, 154, 176, 191, 196, 202, 207, 223, 233
inerrancy, biblical, 4
infinity, divine, 94, 147, 152, 184, 187, 197, 220, 223
initial conditions, 48–49, 96, 204
intelligence, 36, 174, 260
irreducible emergence, 4, 46, 52, 80, 82, 120, 218, 231
irreducible physical monism, 52

Kärkkäinen, Veli-Matti, 7, 23, 34, 63, 70, 126, 128, 129, 136, 254
Keller, Catherine, 10, 93–112, 240–43
kenosis, 13, 27, 42, 223, 245
Kingdom of God, 42, 69, 125, 142, 161, 163, 187, 211
knowledge, participatory, 139–40

Lakatos, Imre, 165,
law of thermodynamics, the second, 4, 45, 57, 62, 115, 143–44, 153, 179, 185, 197, 200, 228, 258
liberalism, classical, 38
life, emergence of, 44, 49, 174, 181, 200
Logos Christology, 36, 37, 41, 132, 211

love, divine, 22, 63, 108, 125, 234, 237, 257
Luther, Martin, 55, 212, 213

MacIntyre, Alastair, 192
macromolecular systems, 46
Manichaean dualism, 246, 247
many worlds, 204, 226
McFague, Sallie, 15, 104, 198
McGrath, Alister, 17, 20, 21, 39, 227
metaphors, 22, 86, 94, 98, 105, 147, 180, 186, 188, 201, 214, 231,
microscopic physical levels, 46, 96, 98, 175
Moltmann, Jürgen, 2, 8, 15, 39, 41, 43, 67, 71, 91, 114, 124, 132, 213, 216, 221
Monism, emergent, 4, 52, 79, 81, 83, 86, 122, 218
Moritz, Joshua, 10, 62, 124, 198, 216, 231, 238
multiverse, 173, 226, 227, 228
Murphy, Nancey, 52, 61, 121, 123, 165, 207, 236–38

natural and cosmic theodicy, 5–7, 9, 16, 62, 88, 117, 182, 197
natural laws, 27, 76, 143, 148, 150, 173
natural selection, 5, 9, 15, 33, 47, 56, 61, 81, 87, 159, 230, 231, 232, 249
naturalism(s), 4, 5, 35, 50–51, 77–79, 86, 109, 178
Neo-Orthodoxy, 4, 246, 259
niche construction, 231, 232
non-interventionist objective divine action (NIODA), 5, 164, 175
nonlocality, 176, 203, 312

ontological indeterminism, 169, 176, 203, 205
ontological pluralism, 4
Oord, Thomas, 124, 209
original creation, 2, 4, 43, 142, 174
Otherness of God, 66, 254
otherness-in-unity, 3, 114

panentheism(s), 12, 16, 24–27, 63–73, 253–55

Pannenberg, Wolfhart, 10, 11, 13, 14, 22, 25, 28, 44, 62, 135–64, 197–221
pantheism, 66, 72, 171
Peacocke, Arthur, 74–93, 106–26, 129, 131, 196, 219, 223, 226, 229, 233, 234, 241, 242, 250, 253, 257, 260
Pelagianism, 247
Penrose, Roger, 176, 204
perichoresis, 17, 133, 216
Peters, Ted, 6, 9, 23, 42, 109, 133, 169, 198, 199, 210, 217, 225
physical closure, 52
physicalism(s), 52, 80, 120, 224
Platonism, 17, 37, 55, 150, 240
plenitude, 59
pneumatology, cosmic, 39, 41, 43
positivism, 139, 140
punctuated equilibrium, 47

quantum decoherence, 202, 203, 204
quantum theory, 201–6, 220

Rahner, Karl, 79, 169, 220
reconciliation, 72, 234, 236, 259
redemption, cosmic, 2, 7, 10, 12, 40, 62, 73, 88, 93, 104, 137, 154, 185, 193, 202, 216, 236
resurrection and creation, 42, 126–32, 233–39
Russell, Robert, 6, 10, 164–90, 190–221

scientism, 3, 4
self-organization, 24, 45, 52, 94, 95, 96, 98, 99, 114, 115, 148, 174, 237
solidarity, divine, 15, 28, 71, 132, 210, 214–15, 222, 224, 233–39
soteriological panentheism, 24, 255, 25, 28, 65–68, 70

Southgate, Christopher, 261, 10, 57, 60, 69
special theory of relativity, 23, 185, 189, 201
Spirit Christology, 37, 41, 42, 132, 211
string theories, 189, 227
superposition, 97, 98, 118, 176, 177, 195, 203, 223
supervenience, 82, 83, 121
Stoicism, 150
symbiogenesis, 61, 209
symbiosis, 8, 209

Tanner, Kathryn, 245
telenomy, 47
teleology for creation, 58, 59, 108, 110, 135, 207, 236, 238
theistic evolution, 50–54, 170, 175, 180
theology and science, 3, 4, 17, 22, 23, 53, 73, 220–21
transcendent immanence, 14, 24, 63, 70, 73, 74, 79, 86, 132, 158, 250
transformability, 169, 218
Trinitarian panentheism, 1, 23, 30, 63, 67, 72

Universe, fine-tuning of, 8, 48–50, 80, 116, 144, 173, 175, 227

wave function, 118, 175, 176, 203, 204, 205
wave/particle duality, 98, 176

young earth theory, 215, 260

Zizioulas, John, 8

www.ingramcontent.com/pod-product-compliance
Lightning Source LLC
Chambersburg PA
CBHW071240230426
43668CB00011B/1522